ANDREKOS VARNAVA

Andrekos Varnava is Lecturer in Modern History at Flinders University, Australia. He was born and raised in Melbourne and completed his PhD in the Department of History at the University of Melbourne. His areas of expertise are Cyprus and the Eastern Mediterranean and British history, especially the history of the British Empire. His academic research focuses on issues ranging from imperialism, strategy and warfare to questions about cultural history, oral history, minority studies and identity formation. Andrekos Varnava's articles have been published in a wide range of publications, including *Byzantine and Modern Greek Studies*, *The Cyprus Review*, the *Annual Review* of the Cyprus Research Centre and in the book *Britain in Cyprus: Colonialism and Post-Colonialism 1878–2006*. He is the author of *British Imperialism in Cyprus, 1878–1915: The Inconsequential Possession* and he is also co-editor (with Nicholas Coureas and Marina Elia) of *The Minorities of Cyprus: Development Patterns and the Identity of the Internal-Exclusion*.

HUBERT FAUSTMANN

Hubert Faustmann is Associate Professor in International Relations at the University of Nicosia, Cyprus. He is the editor of the academic journal *The Cyprus Review* and president of the Cyprus Academic Forum (CAF). He has published extensively on the history and politics of modern Cyprus. Among his recent publications are 'History in the Making? A New Drive for a Solution of the Cyprus Problem' in *Mediterranean Politics* and 'The Political Culture of the Republic of Cyprus' in *The Government and Politics of Cyprus*. He is also the editor (with Nicos Peristianis) of *Britain in Cyprus: Colonialism and Post-Colonialism 1878–2006*; (with James Ker-Lindsay) of *The Government and Politics of the Republic of Cyprus* and (with James Ker-Lindsay and Fiona Mullen) *An Island in Europe: The EU and the Transformation of Cyprus* (I.B.Tauris).

REUNIFYING
CYPRUS

THE ANNAN PLAN AND BEYOND

Edited by
Andrekos Varnava and **Hubert Faustmann**

New paperback edition published in 2011 by I.B.Tauris & Co Ltd
6 Salem Road, London W2 4BU
175 Fifth Avenue, New York NY 10010
www.ibtauris.com

First published in hardback in 2009 by I.B.Tauris & Co Ltd

Copyright selection and editorial matter © 2009, 2011
Andrekos Varnava & Hubert Faustmann

Copyright individual chapters © 2009, 2011 Tozun Bahcheli, Costa Carras, Achilles C. Emilianides, Hubert Faustmann, Erol Kaymak, James Ker-Lindsay, Klearchos A. Kyriakides, Neophytos G. Loizides, Alexandros Lordos, Dinos Lordos, Sid Noel, Stavroula Philippou, Zenon Pophaides, Tim Potier, Robert I. Rotberg, Panicos Stavrinides, Yiouli Taki, Nicos Trimikliniotis, Andrekos Varnava, Christalla Yakinthou.

The right of Andrekos Varnava & Hubert Faustmann to be identified as the editors of this work has been asserted by the editors in accordance with the Copyright, Designs and Patent Act 1988.

All rights reserved. Except for brief quotations in a review, this book, or any part thereof, may not be reproduced, stored in or introduced into a retrieval system, or transmitted, in any form or by any means, electronic, mechanical, photocopying, recording or otherwise, without the prior written permission of the publisher.

ISBN: 978 1 84885 959 3

A full CIP record for this book is available from the British Library
A full CIP record is available from the Library of Congress

Library of Congress Catalog Card Number: available

I dedicate this book to all those who believe in a reunified Cyprus, which embraces pluralism and meritocracy and is free of ethnic nationalism, inter-communal conflict and prejudice.

Andrekos Varnava

Meinen Eltern

Hubert Faustmann

Contents

	Contributors	ix
	Introduction	1
Part I	**The History**	
Chapter 1	A History of Cyprus Peace Proposals *James Ker-Lindsay*	11
Part II	**The Plan**	
Chapter 2	Consociational Democracy and Cyprus: The House that Annan Built? *Christalla Yakinthou*	25
Chapter 3	A Comparative Analysis of the Five Versions of the Annan Plan *Tim Potier*	40
Chapter 4	The International Relations Aspect of the Annan Plan *Costa Carras*	55
Chapter 5	Contra: The Political Workability of the Annan Plan *Klearchos A. Kyriakides*	68
Chapter 6	Pro: An Appraisal of the Functionality of Annan Plan V *Neophytos G. Loizides*	82
Chapter 7	Contra: Constitutional Structure of the Annan Plan *Achilles C. Emilianides*	95
Chapter 8	Pro: Rethinking the Un-viability of the Constitutional Arrangement *Nicos Trimikliniotis*	107
Chapter 9	Contra: The Economic Aspects of Annan V – Recipe for Growth or Destabilisation? *Dinos Lordos*	122
Chapter 10	Pro: Economic Viability of Annan Plan V *Zenon Pophaides*	133
Chapter 11	The Turkish Cypriot Views on Annan V *Erol Kaymak*	145
Part III	**The Referendums**	
Chapter 12	From Secret Diplomacy to Public Diplomacy: How the Annan Plan Referendum Failure Earned the Cypriot Public a Seat at the Negotiating Table *Alexandros Lordos*	163
Chapter 13	The Plan, Public Discourse and the Role of the Mass Media in Getting to 'No' *Yiouli Taki*	180
Chapter 14	Constructions of Solution(s) to the Cyprus Problem: Exploring Formal Curricula in Greek Cypriot State Schools *Stavroula Philippou & Andrekos Varnava*	194
Chapter 15	A Psychological Analysis of the Greek Cypriot 'No' *Panicos Stavrinides*	213
Chapter 16	The Role of Security: Perceptions of Advantage and Disadvantage *Hubert Faustmann*	224
Chapter 17	The Rise of the AK Party and Ankara's Changing Role: Paving the Way for the 'Yes' *Tozun Bahcheli & Sid Noel*	236
Part IV	**The Aftermath**	
Chapter 18	Reunifying Cyprus: Essential Challenges *Robert I. Rotberg*	251
	Selected Bibliography	265
	Index	273

Contributors

Contributors (in alphabetical order of surname)

TOZUN BAHCHELI
Tozun Bahcheli is a Professor of political science at King's University College at the University of Western Ontario, London, Canada. He has written widely on Turkish foreign policy issues, Greek-Turkish relations and Cypriot politics. During 1995 and 1996, he was senior fellow at the United States Institute of Peace in Washington, D.C. He is the author of *Greek-Turkish Relations Since 1955* (Westview Press, 1990) and co-editor of *De Facto States: The Quest for Sovereignty* (Routledge, 2004).

COSTA CARRAS
Costa Carras has followed the Cyprus problem since he was a schoolboy in Britain in the 1950s. He founded the London-based organisation 'Friends of Cyprus' in 1974 and has written articles for most of the issues of its Report ever since. Since 1999, now based in Athens, he has been Greek coordinator of the 'Greek Turkish Forum', in which capacity he gave a talk at Tufts University in March 2002 predicting the likely outcome of the Annan Plan and its quite possible rejection by the Greek Cypriots.

ACHILLES C. EMILIANIDES
Achilles C. Emilianides is an advocate and a partner of the firm Achilles & Emile C. Emilianides. He holds a PhD in Law and an LLM in History, Philosophy and Sociology of Law from the Aristotelion University of Thessaloniki and an LLM in European Law and Integration from Leicester University. He is the editor of the *'Cyprus and European Law Review'*, co-editor of the 'Cyprus Yearbook of International Relations', the Director of the 'Cyprus Institute of State and Church Relations', the Vice – President of 'Citizenship Association', the Secretary - General of 'Human Rights Cyprus' and a member of the Board of the 'Cyprus Institute of Mediterranean, European and International Research'. Major recent publications include: *Parliamentary History of Cyprus 1964 – 1976* (2007 in Greek), *Beyond the Cyprus Constitution* (2006 in Greek) and *Bibliography of Cyprus Law* (2005).

EROL KAYMAK
Erol Kaymak is Chair of the Department of International Relations at Eastern Mediterranean University, in Famagusta, Cyprus. He has published on the Cyprus problem and other issues of problematic political integration in journals including *Nationalism and Ethnic Politics* and *Mediterranean Politics*. He authored the northern Cyprus section of the CIVICUS Civil Society Index report for Cyprus that provides a comprehensive analysis of civil society's structure, environment, values and impact. Erol Kaymak participated at the technical level negotiations of the 'Annan Plan' for a comprehensive settlement to the Cyprus problem. He is a founding member of the Cyprus Academic Forum (CAF), which is actively working to enhance dialogue among academics on both sides of Cyprus. He also serves on the executive board of the Political Science Association (of northern Cyprus).

JAMES KER-LINDSAY
James Ker-Lindsay is IAA Senior Research Fellow at the Hellenic Observatory, London School of Economics (2008-2009) and a Senior Fellow at Kingston University, London. A frequent commentator on regional affairs, he has also covered Greek and Cypriot politics for the Economist Intelligence Unit. He has also written and edited a number of sig-

nificant studies on Cyprus. He is the co-editor (with Oliver Richmond) of, *The Work of the UN in Cyprus: Promoting Peace and Development*, published by Palgrave Macmillan in 2001 and the author of, *Britain and the Cyprus Crisis*, 1963-64, by Bibliopolis in 2004 and, EU Accession and UN Peacemaking in Cyprus, published by Palgrave Macmillan in 2005. He is also the editor (with Hubert Faustmann) of the forthcoming book titled The Government and Politics of the Republic of Cyprus, to be published by Peter Lang.

KLEARCHOS A. KYRIAKIDES

Klearchos A. Kyriakides is a practising solicitor as well as a lecturer in the School of Law of the University of Hertfordshire. He holds an LLB (Hons.) in Law and a Politics Degree from the University of Birmingham together with M.Phil. and PhD Degrees in International Relations from the University of Cambridge. He is the co-editor (with Professor Robert Holland) of the British Documents on the End of Empire Project Volume on Cyprus, to be published by the Stationery Office and the Institute of Commonwealth Studies of the University of London. He is also the author of a number of articles, chapters and pamphlets on various aspects of history, law and international relations. These include (with Van Coufoudakis) *The Case Against the Annan Plan* (Lobby for Cyprus, London, 2004). His doctoral dissertation, which was completed in 1996, is entitled *British Cold War Strategy and the Struggle to Maintain Military Bases in Cyprus, 1951-60*.

NEOPHYTOS G. LOIZIDES

Neophytos Loizides received his PhD in Political Science from the University of Toronto in 2005. He is currently a Lecturer in International Politics and Ethnic Conflict at Queen's University, Belfast. He has previously been a research fellow at the Belfer Center at the Kennedy School of Government, Harvard University, and he taught at the Politics Department of Princeton University. He is interested in negotiations and conflict resolution in deeply divided societies and he is currently working on a British Academy funded project titled 'Doves against hawks in the framing of peace policies and nationalist mobilization'. He has published in *Security Dialogue, International Studies Perspectives, Southeast European Politics, Weltpolitik* and *Etudes Helleniques/ Hellenic Studies*.

ALEXANDROS LORDOS

Alexandros Lordos is the director of the Cyprus Institute for Policy Analysis, an independent research organization, which utilises mathematical and statistical tools in the context of policy research. In the years since the 2004 referendum, he has undertaken a number of inter-communal polls in Cyprus with the aim of discovering consensus-based grass roots solutions to the various issues that are still blocking a comprehensive settlement of the Cyprus problem. His surveys, including 'Options for Peace: Mapping the Possibilities for a Comprehensive Settlement in Cyprus' (May 2005) and 'Building Trust: An Inter-communal analysis of Public Opinion in Cyprus' (April 2006) are available online from the author's website at www.CyprusPolls.org. Alexandros Lordos has also served as consultant to the UN Force in Cyprus (UNFICYP) in the first-ever inter-communal survey of public opinion that the UN conducted in Cyprus, during the spring of 2007. The results of the UN survey are available online at www.unficyp.org

DINOS LORDOS

Dinos Lordos is the Chairman and CEO of the Lordos Organisation for over 37 years, a diversified holding group involved in many activities including property and property development, construction, hotels, holiday resorts and travel, manufacturing and food. The group's activities extend to Greece and the UK. He graduated in Architecture and continued his studies in Economics, Accounting, Politics and Law. He has served in various public positions ranging from Chairman of the Cyprus Employers and Industrialists Federation (1974-1976) to Member of Parliament (1981-1991), as well as numerous other posts in the Public Sector. Queen Elizabeth honoured him with an OBE in 1992. In recent years, in addition to his business activities, he is also very involved in creating bicommunal contacts between the Greek Cypriot and Turkish Cypriot communities of Cyprus contributing to intercommunal understanding and reconciliation. He has published numerous articles and studies on socio-economic and political issues, the natural and man-made environment, international affairs and the Cyprus Problem.

Sid Noel
Sid Noel is a Senior Fellow at King's University College at The University of Western Ontario. He is internationally known for his writing on the politics of deeply divided societies and particularly for his work on ethnic conflict and the theory and practice of consociational power sharing. He is general editor of *Studies in Nationalism and Ethnic Conflict*, McGill Queen's University Press. Among his publications as editor are *From Power Sharing to Democracy: Post-Conflict Institutions in Ethnically Divided Societies*, McGill Queen's University Press, 2005.

Stavroula Philippou
Stavroula Philippou is currently an Assistant Professor in the School of Arts and Education at the European University Cyprus. Her postgraduate studies include an M.Ed. in Curriculum Studies (University of Sydney, Australia, 1999) and a PhD in Education (University of Cambridge, UK, 2004). Her doctoral dissertation explored how the concept of "Europe" could shift ethnocentric discourses in history and geography curricula as well as in children's constructions of identity and citizenship. Her research interests include Curriculum and Textbook Development and Design, Teaching Methodology, European Union and Council of Europe Educational Policies, Curriculum Studies, Children's National and European identities, Citizenship Education. She has participated in a number of conferences and published work drawn from her thesis and recent research. Her most recent publication is 'On the Borders of Europe: Citizenship Education and Identity in Cyprus', which appeared in *Journal of Social Science Education*, VI, 1, in June 2007.

Zenon Pophaides
Zenon Pophaides was born in Nicosia, Cyprus. He was educated at the Pancyprian Gymnasium in Nicosia and read economics at the London School of Economics and Political Science at the University College of the University of London. After the 1974 events he worked for the Planning Bureau of the Republic of Cyprus, the government, institution responsible for formulating developmental policies. He is now in the private sector running his own business. He has written extensively on the Cyprus problem and current political and financial affairs in the local newspapers and journals.

Tim Potier
Tim Potier is Associate Professor of International Law and Human Rights, Department of Law, University of Nicosia, and Visiting Fellow (Hughes Hall), Centre of International Studies, University of Cambridge (UK). His most recent publication is *A Functional Cyprus Settlement: The Constitutional Dimension*, published in 2007.

Robert I. Rotberg
Robert I. Rotberg is President of the World Peace Foundation and the Director of the WPF Program on Intrastate Conflict, Conflict Prevention, and Conflict Resolution in the Kennedy School of Government, Harvard University. He was Professor of Political Science and History, MIT; Academic Vice President, Tufts University; and President, Lafayette College. He was a presidential appointee to the Council of the National Endowment for the Humanities and is a Trustee of Oberlin College. He is the author and editor of numerous books and articles on US. foreign policy on Africa, Asia, and the Caribbean.

Panicos Stavrinides
Panicos Stavrinides is member of the research and teaching staff at the Department of Psychology, University of Cyprus. He undertook his undergraduate studies in Psychology at St. Francis College, New York (1997), and received his MSc in Psychological Research Methods from the University of Reading, UK in 1999. In 2005, he completed his PhD in Developmental Psychology at the University of Cyprus. He is now a post-doctoral fellow at the Graduate School of Education (HGSE), Harvard University. His research interests include the area of child development.

Yiouli Taki
Yiouli Taki is Senior Researcher and Project Manager for *INDEX: Research and Dialogue*, and a visiting professor at the University of Nicosia. Between 2001 and 2004, she was the Greek Cypriot representative of the *International Peace Research Institute, Oslo* (PRIO). During that period, she coordinated an information campaign on the Annan Plan and co-authored a series of booklets on its various versions. She was subsequently the senior researcher on the '*Study of the Information Environment of the Referendum in Cyprus & an Outline of International Referendum Standards*' (2005). Recent work has focused on the politics of urban development in Nicosia, the relationship between state and civil society in Cyprus as well as an assessment of initiatives to combat human trafficking in Cyprus.

Nicos Trimikliniotis
Nicos Trimikliniotis is adjunct Assistant Professor of Law and Sociology at the University of Nicosia; he directs the Cyprus National Focal Point for RAXEN; and has researched on ethnic conflict and resolution, constitutional and state theory, migration, and discrimination. He is a qualified barrister, holds an MA in Gender and Ethnic Studies and a PhD (sociology), titled *The Role of State Processes in the Production and Resolution of 'Ethnic' and 'National' Conflict: The Case of Cyprus* from the University of Greenwich. He has published several articles in books and journals. His book, currently in print, is titled *The Nation-State Dialectic: The Euro-Cypriot Conjucture and the National Question in the Post-Annan Era*.

Christalla Yakinthou
Christalla Yakinthou completed her PhD in the Department of Political Science and International Relations at the University of Western Australia in 2008. Her thesis examines the application of consociational approaches to governance in Cyprus and develops an under-explored aspect of the theory, namely that certain factors or pre-conditions are critical to the successful adoption and operation of consociational institutions. Her fields of interest include constitutional engineering in divided societies, power-sharing theories of institutional design and the role of historical memory in peace-making and constitutional engineering.

INTRODUCTION
Reunifying Cyprus:
The Annan Plan and Beyond

This book is about the failure to reunify Cyprus after over forty years of political and physical division since the constitution of the Republic of Cyprus collapsed in 1963 (slightly over three years after independence) and after the new state of affairs resulting from the Turkish invasion and *de facto* partitioning of the island in 1974. The focus will be on the recent efforts of the United Nations (UN), the European Union (EU), the United States (US), the Guarantor Powers of the Republic of Cyprus (the United Kingdom (UK), Greece and Turkey) and the Cypriots to reunify the island in time for Cyprus's accession to the EU in 2004. The initiative, which began in January 2002, produced five versions of the 'Comprehensive Solution to the Cyprus Problem', popularly known as the Annan Plan.[1] But, the end result was failure. In two simultaneous referendums on the fifth version held on 24 April 2004, the Turkish Cypriots approved the plan (64.9 per cent said 'yes' with an 87 per cent turnout) and the Greek Cypriots rejected it (75.8 per cent said 'no' with an 88 per cent turnout). This book attempts to bring into academic focus the provisions of the Plan, the debate surrounding and to provide explanations for the results of the referendums.

From an academic perspective, the literature on the Annan Plan and the referendums has been primarily restricted to a few book chapters and numerous articles in academic journals, with the exception of a few specialised monographs and accounts from players in the drama.

The first academic book on the subject appeared in October 2004 by Andreas Theophanous and was titled *The Cyprus Question and the EU: The Challenge and the Promise*. It is argued in this monograph that the British and American governments, and the UN Secretariat, knew that the plan they devised had weaknesses, but still pushed for its acceptance. The key to a 'just and viable' solution, the author claims, is the Turkish government abandoning its expansionist designs on Cyprus and the EU playing a greater role in achieving a solution based on EU norms.

Then appeared Natalie Tocci's study titled *EU Accession Dynamics and Conflict Resolution: Catalysing Peace or Consolidating Partition in Cyprus?* The book explores the interrelationship between the evolution of the conflict and the development of EU-Cyprus relations within the accession process. It explains the factors driving EU policies towards the conflict and it demonstrates that the EU framework could have added important incentives for a resolution of the conflict by providing an alternative context within which to address the basic needs of the principal parties. The study, therefore, focuses on the involvement of the EU and does not attempt a comprehensive analysis of the 2002-2004 reunification initiative from the perspective of the blueprints themselves or the ultimate result.

In August 2005, James Ker-Lindsay's *EU Accession and UN Peacekeeping in Cyprus* appeared as a very timely account of the UN effort to reunify Cyprus prior to EU accession. The book pays particular attention to the ways in which the positions of

Turkey, the Turkish Cypriots and the Greek Cypriots changed during the two and a half years of negotiations and analyses how the chance to solve the Cyprus issue failed.

Two further books appeared in 2005, this time by actors involved in the events. *Cyprus: The Search for a Solution*, published by I.B. Taurus and written by David Hannay (Lord Hannay) the British special representative to Cyprus from 1996-2003, is valued as a primary source. Hannay takes into account the positions of both sides and understands them well. He also recognises the British responsibility for the 'Cyprus Problem' and feels guilt for past British policies.[2] In *An International Relations Debacle – The UN Secretary-General's Mission of Good Offices in Cyprus 1999-2004*, published by Hart Publishing in May 2005, Claire Palley, the Constitutional Consultant to successive Presidents of Cyprus from 1980 to 2004, offers a very detailed account of the negotiations and also compares all the five versions of the Annan Plan. The book supports the positions of the Papadopoulos government.

In 2006, Frank Hoffmeister, a member of the European Commission Legal Service who participated in the Annan Plan negotiations, published *Legal Aspects of the Cyprus Problem: Annan Plan and EU Accession*. Within his analysis of the Cyprus Problem since 1960, he focuses on its legal dimensions. A considerable part of the book is dedicated to the Annan Plan and the final phases of the EU accession negotiations of the Republic of Cyprus. He focuses on situating the legal controversies surrounding the Annan Plan within the normative framework of the EU, claiming that it was within the common EU standards.

In 2006 and 2007, the Athenian publisher Papazisis Press published two books by disgruntled party members of the Social Democrats – EDEK – who had voted 'no' in the referendum. The first by Takis Hadjidemetriou titled *Το Δημοψήφισμα της 24ης Απριλίου 2004 και η Λύση του Κυπριακού* (*The Referendum of 24 April 2004 and the Solution to the Cyprus Problem*) was a damning enditement on the handling of the efforts to reunify Cyprus by the Papadopoulos government and a strong case for accepting the Annan Plan as a basis for reunification. The second book by Chrysostomos Pericleous titled *Το Δημοψήφισμα του 2004, το Περιφερειακό και Διεθνές Περιβάλλον, η Πρόσληψη της Λύσης και η Συγκυρία* (*The Referendum of 2004, the Regional and International Environment, the Reception of the Solution and the Determining Factor*) was a much more detailed critique of the handling of the Cyprus Problem, ethno-nationalism and the recent efforts to reunify the island. Pericleous argues that the Annan Plan was better than previous plans, that the Papadopoulos government believed that Denktas would reject the plan, but when the Turkish Cypriot leadership changed, becoming pro-reunification, it preferred to join the EU without the reunification of the island.

Also in 2007, Tim Potier published *A Functional Cyprus Settlement: The Constitutional Dimension*. The book, as Potier explains in his foreword, arose from the need to 'heavily revise' the plan that he claims was 'deeply flawed' and proposes detailed changes to the document.

Reunifying Cyprus seeks to explore questions such as whether Annan V was flawed and whether it can be revised to the satisfaction of both communities, but also to go beyond such issues and present a wide-ranging analysis of the Annan Plans, especially Annan V, from various perspectives. Explanations to account for the results of the referendums will be offered that cut across academic disciplines and approaches. There are two diametrically opposed views about the recent initiative that inflames the passions of both sides and from within each side, but at the same time the views are not monolithic. Whilst most books offer one 'yes or no' argument, this book takes a unique approach: the arguments of supporters and opponents of the Annan Plans will be presented in a unique format, with controversial themes thoroughly explored. It explores through parallel chapters the pros and cons of the constitutional, political and economic provisions of Annan V, with a focus on the Greek Cypriot perspective because of the controversy over and criticism of their rejection of the plan. The debate within the Turkish Cypriot community over specific provisions of the plan is covered in one concise but comprehensive chapter. The idea is to provide the reader with a complete picture of the various arguments used by supporters and opponents of the plan, including those who were unsure, from equally qualified experts. This will allow readers to make up their own mind about the most controversial aspects of the Annan Plan. Additionally, the book presents analyses of media, psychology, education and security to account for the rejection by Greek Cypriots and its acceptance by the Turkish Cypriots plans. Insights from various scholars on how to move forward from the current stalemate are also provided.

The book is divided into four parts. The first section offers a historical overview of the various efforts and proposals to solve the Cyprus problem across periods. James Ker-Lindsay, an authority on this subject,[3] explores this theme from the 1960s-90s. He analyses and compares the various initiatives on their fairness and viability, within their historical contexts, as well as the approaches, policies and decision-making processes of the various leaderships. The Annan Plans are discussed in their relation to their position within this wider historical framework.

The second part or the book analyses different aspects of the Plan and presents the arguments of its supporters and opponents from both communities. The second chapter explores why, in the light of previous failure, consociationalism was again chosen as the means of governance in the Annan Plan. Consociational democracy is a type of political engineering centred on the idea of keeping disputing groups within a 'pillared' system, with each community's elites in the social, political and economic fields forming a kind of roof over the pillars while jointly governing a country. Christalla Yakinthou[4] examines why the particular institutions of the Annan Plan were chosen and the factors which influenced these choices. Her objective is to ascertain the extent to which consociational theory has influenced institutional engineering in Cyprus and to examine the interaction between political reality and consociational theory. Yakinthou argues that the elites and the engineers selected a consociational system and that consociational principles were manipulated into a form satisfactory to the interlocutors. The design was dictated by elements such as historical memory and fear (historical legacy and the first constitution); the strategic interests of domestic and regional powers; and the strategic non-participation in negotiations by the elites.

Chapter three analyses and compares the five versions of the Annan Plan. Tim Potier, who has written a monograph on this subject,[5] assesses whether changes made were favourable or adverse to either side and whether the changes altered the plan's basic philosophy. Special focus is on Annan I, II and III. The debates surrounding the changes, whom they favoured and disfavoured, is also explored.

The next chapter, by the founder of the London based Friends of Cyprus and coordinator of the Greek-Turkish Forum, Costas Carras,[6] explores the shifting international balance during the Annan Plan period. The second and connected theme examined concerns the effect the Plan had on European institutions, the regional balance of power and the relations between the international players.

The book then moves into the pro and contra chapters on the themes of constitution, politics and economics. Political viability is the first block of these chapters, with Klearchos A. Kyriakides[7] writing the 'no' and Neophytos G. Loizides[8] the 'yes' chapter. For Kyriakides, the Annan Plan was 'conceptually flawed, substantively defective and intentionally dysfunctional'. In his view, the Annan Plan 'ostensibly sought to promote the 'independence' of the proposed United Cyprus Republic (UCR); but in reality it would have curbed this independence by *inter alia* entrenching, enhancing and legitimising the controversial rights reserved by the 'guaranteeing Powers' namely Greece, Turkey and the UK. Any future solution attempts should 'proceed on a fundamentally different basis'. Loizides evaluates three main arguments made by opponents of the plan: the analogy drawn between the Annan Plan and the Zurich-London Agreements of 1959; the criticism of federalism and consociationalism as unfair and dysfunctional; and, finally, Turkey's role and reliability in implementing the agreement, especially if it were denied EU membership. The author questions and criticizes the arguments and assumptions of the anti-Annan camp but is not in complete disagreement with Kyriakides' recognising limitations and gaps in the Plan as well.

The next chapters examine the thorny constitutional issues. Achilles C. Emilianides[9] writes the 'no' and Nicos Trimikliniotis[10] the 'yes' chapter. Emilianides argues that the method of establishing the new state of affairs was deeply undemocratic and it satisfied Turkey's aim for the partition of the island. He also deals with the two main principles of the constitutional structure of the new state of affairs, namely the principle of increased and political equality. The issue of the Turkish settlers is also covered. He suggests that the constitutional structure was based upon division and discrimination and not upon democracy or the protection of fundamental rights. Emilianides then focuses on the constitutional character of the new state of affairs, including the executive, the legislative and the judiciary, as well as the position of the UCR as a member of the EU. He argues that the intended UCR would be unviable and it would not have sufficient constitutional guarantees in order to function properly. The fourth and final part of the chapter argues that the UCR envisaged in the Annan Plan would have resulted in Cyprus becoming a servant state – a protectorate. The author of the 'yes' chapter, Nicos Trimikliniotis, argues that 'despite the post-colonial Zurich legacy and the flaws contained' in Annan V, it 'provided the basis for a viable, workable and…fair constitutional arrangement for both Greek Cypriots and Turkish Cypriots'. Trimikliniotis proposes that the interested parties go *beyond* the Annan Plan not only because it was rejected by the Greek Cypriots but also because there is scope for significant improvement to meet the post-Annan and post-EU accession era without abandoning the Plan as the basis for negotiations.

Lastly, the economic viability of Annan V is covered favourably by Zenon Pophaides, who worked on the report assessing the economic provisions of the plan[11] commissioned by the former president, George Vassiliou, and negatively by the activist and businessman Dinos Lordos[12]. Lordos points particularly at the consequences of the Annan Plan on the property prices in Cyprus and the repercussions this would have had on the economy in general, and therefore, on the viability of the entire settlement. Pophaides shares some of Lordos' concerns on the property settlement, but considers that these concerns are exaggerated. Conceding that a number of amendments would improve the proposed settlement, the Plan conforms to generally accepted principles of fiscal federalism and can provide the basis for sustainable growth for both constituent states. Both authors focus on the considerable cost of reconstruction, agreeing that it is unlikely that the economy of Cyprus could manage this alone, although they disagree on the degree of problems the economy would face and on whether or not foreign aid would be forthcoming.

Chapter 11, by Erol Kaymak[13], deals with the Annan Plan from a Turkish Cypriot point of view. Kaymak assesses the various discourses on the five versions of the plan emanating from political parties, pressure groups and the media. The chapter first introduces the political context prevalent during the period and the significance of the Annan Plan; then it assesses the plan in some detail; and, finally, it summarizes the referendum process.

The book's third section moves away from the making and analysis of the Plan to the referendum results and processes. The first chapter, by Alexandros Lordos, is a survey based evaluation of the motives of voters before, during and after the referendums. The voting patterns are thoroughly explored across ages, genders, occupations and voting in elections.

Chapter 13, by Yiouli Taki,[14] a researcher at the Norwegian non-governmental organisation PRIO during the Annan Plan period, covers the issue of alleged media manipulation by those in the political establishment supporting a 'no' or 'yes' in the referendum. It analyses media coverage, namely television and print media, to determine if there was an effort by those in the 'no' and 'yes' camps to influence the vote. The use of language and its presentation are examined as well. Finally, there is an analysis of how the media were used by the leading politicians.

The next chapter, jointly written by Stavroula Philippou,[15] a Curriculum Studies expert, and Andrekos Varnava,[16] a historian of modern Cyprus, is an analysis of the role of education in framing national expectations in the solution to the Cyprus Problem. It analyses primary and secondary state school formal curricula in the Social Studies subjects of History, Geography and Citizenship Education and discusses how solutions to the Cyprus problem are discursively constructed in text. The chapter serves as a case-study of how a curriculum operates as a political text in the context of a prolonged and intractable conflict such as the 'Cyprus problem' and how it shapes a particular vision of the future by constructing a national identity which draws upon a particular vision of the past.

Chapter 15 argues that the Greek Cypriot rejection of the Annan Plan also had a psychological expression. It was the manifestation of fear against something that was perceived as a threat. This conclusion is based upon the 2006 empirical study conducted by Panicos Stavrinides' research group at the University of Cyprus, which examined the intensity and the quality of fears for coexistence in the two Cypriot communities from a psychological perspective.

The next chapter explores the role of security in the Greek Cypriot 'no'. Hubert Faustmann[17] argues that the Greek Cypriots felt that their security needs were not adequately addressed in the fifth version of the Annan Plan. This chapter will assess if this perception was justified. By way of contrast, the overwhelming majority of the Turkish Cypriots voted in favour of the agreement. Given that their security concerns were as grave as those of the Greek Cypriots, it is fair to assume that the Turkish Cypriots considered the security arrangements of Annan V sufficient, an assumption which will be also tested. The strategic considerations and the security concerns of Greece and Turkey will be assessed as well.

Chapter 17 examines the changes that produced the Turkish Cypriot 'yes'. It will discuss Ankara's role and debate the reasons for its altered position on working to change the *status quo* and agree to a settlement. The rise of the AKP and CTP (along with other Turkish Cypriot 'yes' parties) will be investigated. Tozun Bahcheli and Sid Noel[18] argue that the decision of the newly elected AKP government in Ankara to pursue Turkish accession to the EU as its highest priority illustrates how a policy decision taken externally, for reasons unrelated to Cyprus, fundamentally affected the path of future political events on the island.

The book ends in its fourth section with a contribution on the way forward by Robert I. Rotberg[19]. He argues that the biggest obstacle to a negotiated settlement – to the acceptance of a reconfigured Annan Plan or something different – is that the status quo works and has long worked. Rotberg provides some essential advice and suggestions on how to move forward.

This is a timely ending to the book given the developments since the presidential elections in Cyprus, in February 2008. The two candidates who survived the first round of the elections strongly supported immediate meetings with Turkish Cypriot leaders and the resumption of negotiations. The victor, the AKEL leader Demetris Christofias, instantly embarked on establishing good relations with the Turkish Cypriot leader, Mehmet Ali Talat, and they quickly agreed on a way forward. Technical and working committees were formed and started work on preparing the ground for direct talks between the two leaders in April 2008. During the first weeks of the Christofias' presidency, Ledra Street, which goes through the heart of divided Nicosia and has been closed since the intercommunal violence of 1963-4, was reopened. This was a symbol of hope for the reunification of the entire island. Progress on a committee level seems to have been not as far reaching as hoped in particular on the most controversial themes like security, property, territory and the question of settlers from Turkey. But, expectations are still high for the direct talks between the two leaders which started in September 2008. The internal political situation in Turkey could cast a giant shadow over the reunification process in Cyprus. The chances for solving the Cyprus problem are currently better then ever, but that does not mean that they are good. This book, whose manuscript was made available to the technical and working committees of both sides, aims to assist those working towards the reunification of the island. Regardless of the end result, this book will aid in understanding how and why the island was reunified or how and why it was not.

Reunifying Cyprus is the first book to provide a comprehensive academic analysis of Annan V and the reasons that underpinned its rejection by Greek Cypriots and acceptance by Turkish Cypriots. How did the Cypriots receive the latest initiative – the Annan Plans and specifically Annan V – compared to other efforts to reunify the island? Were the Annan Plans missed opportunities? What were the real or imagined flaws? How did the initiative differ from other efforts to reunify the island? How are the Cyprus Problem and the latest failure seen today by the states and players involved, the international community, the diplomatic and academic communities and commentators in general? What place does the fundamental spirit of the Annan Plan have in future blueprints to reunify the island?

Scholars of divided societies, ethnic conflict, constitution/state building, conflict resolution and direct democracy will find this volume of interest. It is vital for anybody interested in learning about this effort to reunify Cyprus and why it failed. Ways to move forward are suggested. We hope that those involved in future attempts to reunify the island will use this book as an essential source of information.

Nicosia, Cyprus, July 2008

The editors would like to thank Nicoletta Livera for her tireless efforts in proof reading and editing this volume.

ENDNOTES

1. For Annan V, www.unficyp.org/media/Other%20official%20documents/annanplan.pdf
2. Andrekos Varnava, Review of William Mallinson, *Cyprus: A Modern History*, London, 2005 and David Hannay, *Cyprus: The Search for a Solution*, London, 2005, *University of Melbourne Repository*, 21 July 2006, (Greek) *Περιπέτειες Ιδεών*, 28 January 2007, 26-8.
3. James Ker-Lindsay, *EU Accession and UN Peacemaking in Cyprus*, London, 2005.
4. Christalla Yakinthou, *Between Scylla and Charybdis: Cyprus and the Problem of Engineering Solutions for Divided Societies*, unpublished PhD, Uni. Western Australia, 2008 (forthcoming, Palgrave).
5. Tim Potier, *A Functional Cyprus Settlement: The Constitutional Dimension*, Mainz and Ruhpolding, 2007.
6. Costa Carras 'Greek-Turkish Forum – First Public Event, March 2002 – Cyprus: Year of Decision', *The Cyprus Review*, XIV, 1, 2002, 87-100.
7. Van Coufoudakis and Klearchos Kyriakides, *The Case Against the Annan Plan*, London, 2004.

8. Neophytos Loizides and Eser Keskiner, 'The Aftermath of the Annan Plan Referendums: Cross-Voting Moderation for Cyprus?', *Southeast European Politics*, V, 2-3, 2004, 158-171.
9. Achilles Emilianides, *Οι Συνταγματικές Πτυχές του Σχεδίου Ανάν, Το Σχέδιο Ανάν: Πέντε Κείμενα Κριτικής*, Athens, 2003.
10. Nicos Trimikliniotis, 'A Communist's Post-Modern Power Dilemma: One Step Back, Two Steps Forward, 'Soft No' and Hard Choices', *The Cyprus Review*, XVIII, 1, 2006, 37-86.
11. George Vassiliou, *The Economics of the Solution Based on the Annan Plan*, 2003. http://www.kema.com.cy/Annan%20Plan%20En.pdf
12. Dinos Lordos, 'No Voter Vindicated?', *Report of the Friends of Cyprus*, XLVII, 2004, 28.
13. Hannes Lacher and Erol Kaymak, 'Transforming Identities, Beyond the Policies of a Non-Settlement in North Cyprus', *Mediterranean Politics*, X, 2, 2005, 147-166.
14. Alexis Alexiou, Ayla Gurel, Mete Hatay, Yiouli Taki, *The Annan Plan for Cyprus: A Citizens' Guide*, and *The Property Regime in the Annan Plan: A Citizens' Guide*, both Oslo, 2003; *Το Σχέδιο Ανάν: Όσα σας Ενδιαφέρουν*, (The Annan Plan: Issues of Interest to You), Oslo, 2004; Yiouli Taki and Erol Kaymak, *A Study of the Information Environment & an Outline of International Referendum Standards*, Politics, Index, 2005.
15. Stavroula Philippou, 'European Citizenship/Identity and Curriculum in Cyprus', Proceedings CDRom of Conference 'Citizenship, Multiculturalism, Cosmopolitanism', University of Cyprus, Nicosia, 2007.
16. Andrekos Varnava, 'Cyprus: A Rendezvous with History?', *Neos Kosmos English Edition*, Monday 18 August 2003; 'No Turning Back on Future of Cyprus', *Neos Kosmos English Edition*, Monday 8 December 2003; 'Still Waiting for a Balanced History of Cyprus', *Cyprus Mail*, 4 September 2005; 'Moving Forward after the Presidential Elections', *Cyprus Mail*, 2 March 2008, 17; and Review of, (ed.) Murat Metin Hakki, *The Cyprus Issue: A Documentary History, 1878-2007*, I. B. Tauris, London, 2007, *The Cyprus Review*, XX, 1, 2008, 135-9.
17. Hubert Faustmann 'The Cyprus Question Still Unresolved: Security Concerns and the Failure of the Annan Plan', *Südosteuropa-Mitteilungen*, 2004, 44-68 and 'The Role of Security Concerns in the Failure of the Annan Plan and in the Post-Annan Plan Period', *The International Spectator*, XLI, 2, 2006, 7-18.
18. Tozun Bahcheli, 'Searching for a Cyprus Settlement: Considering Options for Creating a Federation, a Confederation, or Two Independent States', *Publius*, XXX, 1-2, 2000, 203-216 and 'Saying Yes to EU Accession: Explaining the Turkish Cypriot Referendum and its Aftermath', *The Cyprus Review*, XVI, 2, 2004, 55-66; Tozun Bahcheli and Sid Noel 'Power-Sharing for Cyprus (again)? EU Accession and the Prospects for Reunification Under a Belgian Model of Multi-level Governance', in Sid Noel (ed.), *From Power Sharing to Democracy: Post-Conflict Institutions in Ethnically Divided Societies*, London, 2005.
19. Robert I. Rotberg, 'Cyprus After Annan: Next Steps Towards a Solution', *World Peace Foundation Reports*, 37, 2003 and 'The Cyprus Crucible: the Importance of Good Timing', *Leadership*, XXV, 3, 2003.

PART I

THE HISTORY

CHAPTER 1

A HISTORY OF CYPRUS PEACE PROPOSALS

James Ker-Lindsay

Introduction

As the campaign over the Annan Plan entered its final few weeks in April 2004, arguments raged within the Greek Cypriot community as to whether it should be accepted or rejected. In some cases, debate focused on the economics of the settlement. At other times, the key issues were the viability of the constitutional arrangements, or the justice of property provisions. Many were concerned about the degree of security the proposals offered, while others argued that the plan was a hasty effort to deprive the Greek Cypriots of their rights under the European Union – an argument supporters refuted, arguing that it had received a clean bill of health from the European Commission and that all of the member states, including Greece, supported it. However, one of the more controversial arguments presented in favour of the plan was that, in as much as the Annan Plan conformed to the Greek Cypriot demand for a bi-zonal and bi-communal federation, history had shown that when a settlement was rejected the next one offered had invariably been worse.

This chapter examines the history of peace plans in Cyprus with this in mind. It starts by examining the historical background of the conflict and shows that from the nineteenth century onwards, the basic Greek Cypriot demand was for Cyprus to be united with Greece – an aspiration known as *enosis*. Eventually, a military campaign against British colonial rule developed, which led to the polarisation of the communities and the direct involvement of the Greek and Turkish governments. In the end, the involved parties opted for a compromise none had desired: independence. The second part of the piece examines the period from 1960-1974. Specifically, it looks at the outbreak of intercommunal violence on the island in 1963 and looks at the Acheson Plan, which envisaged *enosis* with some concessions to Turkey, in 1964, but was rejected by the Greek Cypriots. The following year, Galo Plaza, the UN appointed mediator, presented a report that called for *enosis* to be put into temporary abeyance, which was rejected by Turkey. Following a further bout of intercommunal fighting in 1967, *enosis* ceased to be a practical option. Instead, attention focused on creating a new place for the Turkish Cypriots within a unitary, but independent, state. The third and final part of the piece investigates the period since the island was divided in 1974. Following the Turkish invasion, the basic parameter of a settlement became the creation of a bi-zonal, bi-communal federation. This model formed the basis of subsequent peace plans and formulas presented to the two sides in the decades that followed. The article concludes by looking at the Annan Plan, which again conformed to the model of a bi-zonal, bi-communal federation, but was regarded by many as verging on a confederal political model. In this sense, and looked at against the various plans that have come before, it is indeed possible to say that each successive effort to resolve the political differences on the island has resulted in a plan that is worse, when viewed against the prevailing aims and aspirations of the day, for the Greek Cypriot community.

Historical Background

It has long been said that Cyprus lies on the geo-strategic crossroad between Europe, the Middle East and Africa. In this sense, it has long been regarded as vital strategic territory for many empires and civilisations. Following the arrival of the first Greek settlers, who arrived on Cyprus three and a half thousand years ago, the island subsequently came under the rule of the Assyrians, Phoenicians, Egyptians, Romans, Arabs, Byzantines, Lusignans and Venetians. In 1571, it was captured by the Ottoman Empire, who brought in large numbers of settlers from across the Empire. As a result, a Turkish Muslim population emerged which forms the basis of today's Turkish Cypriot population.

In 1878, Britain took administrative control of the island in return for supporting the Ottoman Empire against Russian threats to Turkey's eastern provinces. By the end of the century, some of the Greek Cypriot elite began to ask that the island be united with the Kingdom of Greece, which had become an independent state fifty years earlier. However, viewing no reason to relinquish the territory, and arguing that Cyprus was still formally a part of the Ottoman Empire, Britain refused to consider the request. A reason to relinquish Cyprus arose in December 1912 and it was pursued until the island, which had been annexed upon the Ottoman Empire's entry into World War I on the side of the Central Powers, was offered to Greece in October 1915.[1] However, the Greek King rejected the offer. Five years after the end of the War, in 1923, the Treaty of Lausanne saw the new Turkish Republic abandon any claim to the island. Two years later, in 1925, Britain formally declared sovereignty over the island, which became a crown colony. Greek Cypriot elite increased calls for the island to be united with Greece. In 1931, there were violent riots against the British authorities, which were in large part driven by pro-*enosis* Greek nationalism. This led to the introduction of new laws preventing further political agitation. But this did not end hopes for union. Instead, the movement went underground.

At the end of the Second World War, during which the calls for *enosis* were put on hold, the Greek Cypriots once again became politically active. In 1948, Britain responded with the Winster Proposals. This envisaged a new constitution for Cyprus based on Greek Cypriot majority rule, but self-determination was ruled out. Under these circumstances, the Greek Cypriots rejected it.[2] In 1950, the Greek Orthodox Church organised a referendum on union with Greece, which showed that an overwhelming majority of Greek Cypriots were still in favour of joining Greece. However, the British refused to give up control of the island, a policy that continued even after Greece attempted to internationalise the issue at the United Nations. Therefore, starting on 1 April 1955, an armed uprising – the EOKA campaign – was launched to end British colonial rule over Cyprus. Within months, many Greek Cypriots had left their jobs in the government and police. In response, the colonial authorities were forced to rely more and more on the Turkish Cypriot community. This contributed to accusations that Britain was following its usual 'divide and rule' policy on the island.[3] Regardless of whether this was true or not, tensions between the Greek and Turkish communities nevertheless grew. In December 1956, another set of proposals – the Radcliffe Plan – was presented to the Greek Cypriots. This granted full internal self-rule to Cyprus, under the authority of a locally elected legislature. It also acknowledged a right of self-determination, "when the international and strategic situation permits and provided that self-government is working satisfactorily." However,

Britain would keep control of foreign and defence policy and internal security. The proposals were once again rejected by Greek Cypriots.

At this point, the Turkish Cypriot community moved beyond their traditional desire to see continued British rule over the island, or see Cyprus placed under Turkish rule, and instead started to call for partition between Greece and Turkey. Importantly, this idea, the Macmillan Plan, along with the Tricondominium Plan for joint British, Greek and Turkish rule over Cyprus, came to be seen in an increasingly favourable light by London, which was still determined to exclude majority self-determination.[4] However, increasingly violent clashes between the two communities were leading to growing tensions between Greece and Turkey, the 'motherlands'. This, in turn, raised the possibility of a war in the Eastern Mediterranean between two NATO allies. In December 1958, Greece and Turkey therefore decided that the best course of action would be to give Cyprus independence. The British government and Cypriot leaders accepted this in early 1959 with agreements signed in Zurich and London.[5] On 16 August 1960, the British rule over the island ended. Cyprus became an independent sovereign state.

The constitutional system that was put in place attempted to create a balance between the two communities. In most areas of government – such as the Council of Ministers, the civil service and the 50-seat parliament – power was split between the two communities 70:30 in favour of the majority Greek Cypriot community, which represented 78 per cent of the population, and the Turkish Cypriots, who represented 18 per cent. (The remaining 4 per cent was composed of the three religious communities: the Maronites, the Latins and the Armenians.) However, in the security forces, the balance was 60:40. As for the political structure of the new state, a presidential system was instead chosen instead of a parliamentary form of governance. Under this model, the president would always be a Greek Cypriot, whereas the vice-president would be Turkish Cypriot. Both had a right of veto over vital legislation. At the same time, Britain, Greece and Turkey were given constitutional responsibility for ensuring that the sovereignty and independence of the island remained intact. In order to further this, Greece was allowed to station 950 troops on the island. Turkey was allowed 650. Meanwhile, Britain was permanently granted approximately 99 square miles of territory as sovereign territory for use as military bases.[6] All things considered, for most of the parties the agreement was acceptable. Britain kept a military presence in the region, Greece and Turkey avoided confrontation and the Turkish Cypriots avoided coming under direct Greek rule and were given a strong say in the government. For the Greek Cypriots, on the other hand, independence was a severe disappointment – especially as the constitution banned any future efforts to unite with Greece.[7] Moreover, many felt that the powers given to the Turkish Cypriots were excessive. At the same time, while many Turkish Cypriots found the settlement broadly acceptable, rather than desirable,[8] many still wanted to partition the island.

Constitutional Proposals, 1964-1974

Just a couple of years after independence, tensions between the two communities started to grow over a number of issues, such as taxation and the administration of city councils. As a result, in November 1963, the Greek Cypriot president, Archbishop Makarios, proposed a number of constitutional amendments that, he argued, would ease the running of the state. In reality, the proposals would have reduced the Turkish Cypriots to minority status. Thus, Turkey quickly rejected them. In late-December 1963, fighting broke out between the two communities in several of the island's towns. This, in turn, led to the end of the Turkish Cypriot participation in the government.[9] In response, a peace keeping force was established by Britain, which managed to keep serious conflict on hold until a formal United Nations peace keeping force – the United Nations Force in Cyprus, UNFICYP – was established in March 1964.[10] At the same time, the Security Council authorised the Secretary-General, U Thant, to appoint a mediator to try to resolve the political differences between the two communities. Soon afterwards, the position was given to Sakari Tuomioja, a Finnish diplomat, who quickly made it clear that he viewed the problem as essentially international in nature. While he saw *enosis* as the most logical course for a settlement, he rejected union on the grounds that it would be inappropriate for a UN official to propose a solution that would lead to the dissolution of a UN member state.[11]

Acheson Plans, 1964

Despite the appointment of a UN mediator, the United States made the first major effort to break the deadlock. In early June, following a Turkish threat to intervene militarily in Cyprus, Washington launched an independent initiative under Dean Acheson, a former Secretary of State under Truman. In July, he presented a plan to unite Cyprus with Greece. In return for accepting this, Turkey would receive a sovereign military base – most probably on the northern Karpas Peninsula – and the Turkish Cypriots would also be given minority rights, which a resident international commissioner would oversee. Makarios rejected the proposal. He argued that a sovereign Turkish base on the island was a limitation to full *enosis* and would give Ankara too strong a say in the island's affairs.[12] Soon afterwards, a second version of the plan was presented. This offered Turkey a 50-year lease on a base, rather than full sovereignty. This time, both the Greek Cypriots and Ankara rejected the offer. After several further attempts to reach an agreement, the United States was eventually forced to give up its effort.

Galo Plaza Report, 1965

In August 1964, just months after being appointed mediator, Tuomioja died suddenly. In his place, U Thant appointed Galo Plaza Lasso. Rather than approach Cyprus as an international problem, Plaza instead saw it in communal terms. In March 1965, he presented a sixty-six page report that criticised both sides for not having shown enough commitment to reaching a settlement.[13] While he understood the Greek Cypriot aspiration of *enosis*, he believed that it should be held in voluntary abeyance. He also argued that the Turkish Cypriots should refrain from demanding a federal solution to the problem. Controversially, he also agreed that the abrogation of the core constitutional treaties by the Greek Cypriots should be recognised. Although the Greek Cypriots eventually accepted the report, in spite of its opposition to immediate *enosis*, Turkey and the Turkish Cypriots rejected the plan and called on Plaza to resign on the grounds that he had exceeded his mandate by submitting formal proposals rather than acting as mediator. But, the Greek Cypriots made it clear that if Galo Plaza resigned they would refuse to accept a replacement. With this, the UN mediation process now fell into abeyance.[14]

Intercommunal Talks, 1968-1974

In March 1966, a more modest attempt at peacemaking was initiated by U Thant. Instead of trying to develop formal proposals for the parties to bargain over, he aimed to encourage the two sides to agree to a settlement through direct dialogue. As a result of political upheaval in Greece, which eventually led to the formation of a military government in April 1967, this process failed to make any headway for the next eighteen months. In September 1967, the Greek and Turkish foreign ministers met for two meetings on either side of their border in Thrace. Turkey flatly rejected the Greek proposal for *enosis*.[15] Greece was now forced to abandon the idea for the foreseeable future.[16] Just two months later, there was another severe bout of intercommunal fighting in Cyprus. Turkey again threatened to invade and Greece was forced to reduce its forces on the island to the limit of 950 set under the 1960 constitution. Capitalising on the situation, the Turkish Cypriots proclaimed their own provisional administration. Although Makarios condemned the move, he nevertheless realised that the Turkish Cypriots would have to have some degree of political autonomy and that *enosis* was not feasible under the prevailing local and regional conditions.[17]

This recognition of the need to accept greater Turkish Cypriot self-rule paved the way for intercommunal talks between the two sides under the auspices of the Good Offices of the UN Secretary-General. During the first round, which lasted from May until August 1968, the Turkish Cypriots were prepared to make concessions on the constitutional questions in return for significant autonomy. Makarios refused to accept this. The second round of talks, which focused on local government, was equally unsuccessful, even though the Greek military junta lobbied hard for a settlement. In December 1969, a third round of discussion started focussing on constitutional issues. Yet again there was little progress. When they ended, in September 1970, the Secretary-General blamed both sides for the lack of movement.[18] A fourth and final round of intercommunal talks, which also focused on constitutional issues, again failed to make tangible headway before they were forced to a halt by events in July 1974.

Reunification Plans, 1974-

Meanwhile, tensions had been growing within the Greek Cypriot community as well as between the Greek Cypriot leadership and Greece, which was under military rule. Although Makarios had effectively abandoned the pursuit of *enosis* in favour of an acceptance of independence, many others continued to believe that the only legitimate political aspirations for Greek Cypriots was *enosis*.[19] In the early 1970s, an armed movement – EOKA B – emerged, that sought to unite Cyprus and Greece. Fearing that this organisation was being supported by the military government then in power in Athens, Archbishop Makarios requested that all Greek troops leave the island. In response, the Greek government ordered the overthrow of Makarios. In his place, they appointed Nicos Sampson, a former EOKA gunman who supported *enosis*. Believing that this would lead to the union of the island with Greece, Turkey invaded Cyprus on 20 July 1974. Within days, the Greek military government collapsed and democracy was restored. This led to peace talks in Switzerland. During the second round of these talks, Turkey offered a federal settlement based on a number of cantons. This was seen as a significant concession given that Rauf

Denktash, the Turkish Cypriot leader, was calling for the creation of a bi-zonal federation. However, Ankara demanded a quick answer and refused to consider a Greek Cypriot request for more time to consider the offer. As a result, on 14 August, the Turkey resumed its military campaign.[20] By the middle of August, the Turkish army had occupied 37 per cent of the island. This meant that 160,000 Greek Cypriots, a quarter of the Greek Cypriot population had become refugees. Similarly, over forty thousand Turkish Cypriots left their homes in the southern part of the island, either seeking sanctuary in the British Bases or making their way north. The island was now completely divided, both geographically and politically.

1977 High Level Agreement

In April 1975, Kurt Waldheim, the UN Secretary-General, launched a new mission of good offices. Over the course of the following ten months, discussions were held over a range of humanitarian issues. However, no progress was made on the substantive political issues, such as territory and the nature of the central government, and the talks fell apart in February 1976. In January 1977, the UN managed to organise a meeting in Nicosia between the two sides and, on 12 February, the two leaders, Makarios and Rauf Denktash, signed a four point agreement confirming that a future Cyprus settlement would be based on a federation made up of two states (bi-zonal) and two communities (bi-communal). Economic viability and land ownership would determine the size of the states. The central government would be given powers to ensure the unity of the state. Various other issues, such as freedom of movement and freedom of settlement, would be settled through discussion.

The agreement marked a monumental change of direction for the Greek Cypriots. They had been forced to accept that Cyprus would be reunited as a federation with the Turkish Cypriots controlling their own zone and that *enosis* was officially dead. Meanwhile, the Turkish Cypriots affirmed their commitment to a united island and put aside hopes of partition. However, despite the apparent agreement between the two sides on the general nature of a settlement, new talks quickly showed that the two sides were an ocean apart on the specifics. The Greek Cypriots presented proposals on territorial issues that took little notice of the principle of bi-zonality. Meanwhile, the Turkish Cypriot presented ideas on the role and functions of the central government that were more confederal, rather than federal, in nature. The discussions soon came to an end.

Twelve Point Proposal

In November 1978, the United States, Britain and Canada drafted a twelve-point proposal that the Secretary-General presented to the two sides.[21] In line with the 1977 agreement, the proposal envisaged a federation of two states. One would be predominantly Greek Cypriot and the other mainly Turkish Cypriot. The central government would deal with foreign affairs, external defence, currency and central banking, inter-regional and foreign trade, communications, federal finance, customs, immigration and civil aviation. Any issue not specifically covered by the central government would be the responsibility of the states. A bicameral parliament would be established. The upper chamber would be composed of equal numbers of representatives from the two communities. The lower chamber would be proportional to the size of the two populations. The system of a Greek Cypriot president and a Turkish Cypriot vice-president would be maintained. Importantly, the number of Greek and Turkish troops on the island would be reduced to 1960 levels – 950 and 650, respectively. Moreover, Greek Cypriots would re-settle Varosha. Despite the fact that the initiative was broadly in line with the 1977 agreement, the Greek Cypriots rejected it. They objected to the fact that the agreement did not enshrine the three basic freedoms that they insisted must be part of any 'just and viable' settlement: the freedom of movement, the freedom of settlement and the right to own property.[22]

1979 High Level Agreement and Interim Agreement

The UN remained undeterred. In May 1979, Waldheim visited Cyprus and secured a further ten-point set of proposals from the two sides. These not only reaffirmed the 1977 agreement, but also included a number of new provisions, such as demilitarisation and a commitment to refrain from destabilising activities and actions. It was also agreed that the question of Varosha would also be addressed as a matter of priority and that the two sides would deal with all territorial and constitutional aspects of the problem. Shortly afterwards, a new round of discussions began in Nicosia. Again, they were short lived. For a start, the Turkish Cypriots did not want to discuss Varosha, which was a key issue for the Greek Cypriots. Secondly, the two sides failed to agree on the concept of 'bi-communality'. Rather than call a complete halt to the talks, the UN decided to put the negotiations on hold.[23]

The following summer, Waldheim tried to resurrect the process by putting forward a proposal for an interim agreement. This included measures to promote a more positive atmosphere on the island, such as the return of Varosha to civilian control and the lifting of the economic embargoes placed on the Turkish Cypriots. It also called for the opening of Nicosia International Airport, which had in fact been agreed by the two sides during the first round of the Vienna Talks. On 9 August, new negotiations opened under Hugo Gobbi, the Secretary-General's Special Representative. They focused on four areas: improving levels of goodwill between the two sides, the return and resettlement of displaced Greek Cypriots in Varosha, constitutional matters and territorial issues. But, this time the talks ran into difficulties over the term 'bi-zonality'. The Turkish Cypriots interpreted this in terms of a confederation, arguing that the two states should have their own sovereignty. The Greek Cypriots insisted sovereignty must rest with the central state, in line with more generally accepted notions of a federal political system.

Five Point Proposals

Despite having accepted to reunite in a federation, in 1983, the Turkish Cypriots unilaterally declared independence and formed the 'Turkish Republic of Northern Cyprus' (TRNC). The UN Security Council condemned the move, called on states not to recognise the new entity and declared that the move represented a setback to efforts to reach a settlement.[24] As a result, the only country to recognise the Turkish Cypriot state was Turkey. Naturally, even though the illegal declaration of independence certainly harmed the negotiation process, the UN continued its efforts to find a solution. However, these initiatives failed to produce any results.

In early 1984, steps were taken to resume the peace process. In March, Javier Perez de Cuellar, Waldheim's successor, presented the two sides with a five-point suggestion for confidence building measures. New talks began in September. After three rounds of discussions, a blueprint was reached. Cyprus would become a bi-zonal, bi-communal, non-aligned federation. The Turkish Cypriots would retain 29 per cent for their federal state and all foreign troops would leave the island. In January 1985, the two leaders met for their first face-to-face talks since the 1979 agreement. While the general belief was that the meeting was being held to agree to a final settlement, Kyprianou insisted that it was a chance for further negotiations. The talks collapsed.[25] Kyprianou was heavily criticised, both at home and abroad. Denktash won a public relations victory and a reprieve. More importantly, he made it clear that he was unlikely to make so many concessions again.[26]

Draft Framework Agreement

Despite the setback, De Cuellar continued his attempts to broker an agreement. In March 1986, he presented the two sides with a 'Draft Framework Agreement'. Again, the plan envisaged the creation of an independent, non-aligned, bi-communal, bi-zonal state in Cyprus. However, the Greek Cypriots were unhappy with the proposals. They argued that the questions of removing Turkish forces from Cyprus was not addressed, nor was the repatriation of the increasing number of Turkish settlers on the island. Moreover, there were no guarantees that the full three freedoms would be respected. Finally, they saw the proposed state structure as being confederal in nature.[27] Further efforts to produce an agreement failed as the two sides remained steadfastly attached to their positions. Meanwhile, increased Greek-Turkish tension in the Aegean reduced hopes for a solution. However, a thaw in relations between Greece and Turkey, in early 1988, opened the way for de Cuellar to initiate a new effort in August that year. At a series of meetings in Geneva, the two leaders agreed to abandon the March 1986 Draft Framework Agreement and return to the 1977 and 1979 High Level Agreements.[28]

Set of Ideas

Negotiations resumed in August 1988, following the victory of a moderate political novice, George Vassiliou, in presidential elections earlier that year. At the time, the hope was that an agreement would be secured by the following summer. In June 1989, the UN presented a new document to the two communities – the 'Set of Ideas'. Denktash quickly rejected it, disagreeing with the substance of the proposals but also argued that the Secretary-General had no right to present formal plans to the two sides; a complaint reminiscent of the Galo Plaza Report in 1965. Following a failed attempt to open direct talks with the Greek Cypriots, free from UN involvement, the two sides met again in New York in February 1990. Again, the talks proved fruitless as Denktash demanded that the Greek Cypriots recognise the existence of two people in Cyprus and their basic right to self-determination. Matters were further complicated in July 1990, when Cyprus formally applied to join the European Community (EC). Furious at the move, Denktash called off all talks with UN officials. Undeterred, de Cuellar tried unsuccessfully to restart the process. In his last report to the Security Council, he noted that progress on his proposals could go no further largely due to Denktash's demand that the two communities should have equal sovereignty and a right to secession.[29]

In January 1992, Boutros Boutros-Ghali took over as UN Secretary-General. He continued to work on the Set of Ideas and, in April 1992, he presented the Security Council with the outline plan for the creation of a bi-zonal, bi-communal federation that would prohibit any form of partition, secession or union with another state.[30] While the Greek Cypriots accepted this as a basis for negotiation, Denktash refused to engage in substantive discussions on the plan and again criticised the Secretary-General for exceeding his authority. In response, the Turkish Cypriot leader again called for direct talks with the Greek Cypriots, free from UN involvement. The offer was rejected. When he did eventually return to the table, the Turkish Cypriot leader complained that the proposals failed to recognise his community. In November, Ghali called a halt to the process. Although the Turkish Cypriot side had accepted 91 of 100 of the proposals, Denktash's unwillingness to engage in substantive talks on the remaining nine areas of difference meant that further progress was unachievable.[31] After this, the plan fell by the wayside, as the new Greek Cypriot government, formed under Glafcos Clerides in 1993, also sought to move away from the Set of Ideas.

The Annan Plan

Despite this wish to abandon the Set of Ideas, the Greek Cypriots remained outwardly committed to the creation of a bi-zonal, bi-communal federation. The same could not be said for Rauf Denktash, the Turkish Cypriot leader, who became more and more hard line in the years that followed. By the middle of the 1990s, he had decided that he would no longer accept a federation as the model for a settlement. Instead, he now insisted that any settlement must be based on a loose confederation in which the two states would each be fully sovereign. However, the parameters of the Cyprus issue now started to change. In 1998, formal accession negotiation started between the European Union and Cyprus. At first, the Turkish Government believed that there was no chance that the European Union would risk provoking a crisis with Turkey, a major state of 60 million people, in favour of Cyprus, with just 700,000 inhabitants. Just to be sure, Turkey threatened to annexe northern Cyprus if the Republic of Cyprus was admitted as an EU member.

However, by 2001, it was clear that the European Union was serious about accepting Cyprus as a member. In December 2001, the Turkish Cypriots leader therefore proposed new talks. These started in January 2002. However, initial optimism that a breakthrough could now take place soon faded as it quickly became clear that it was simply meant to be a delaying tactic aimed at trying to stop the EU from admitting Cyprus. This was a miscalculation. The EU repeatedly made it clear that it would prefer to see a united Cyprus join, but if that were not possible a divided island would still become a member. This policy might have led to a crisis had it not been for a change in Turkish government in November 2002. The hard line government in Turkey, which supported Denktash, was replaced by an administration formed by the Justice and Development Party, which saw EU membership as the country's national priority. It rejected the notion put forward by other Turkish administrations that Cyprus had been 'solved' in 1974 and accepted that the island needed to be reunified. Just two weeks after the elections in Turkey, the United Nations presented a comprehensive peace plan for the island. Almost immediately, it simply became known by the name of the UN Secretary-General who presented it. The Annan Plan was now on the table.

Conclusion

Although it is still unclear whether the decision to reject the Annan Plan in April 2004 will see the Greek Cypriots obtain a 'better' set of proposals in the future, it is certainly possible to say that, in retrospect, each incarnation of settlement proposals have indeed been progressively worse for the Greek Cypriots than those that came before – either in terms of the general political framework envisaged or in terms of specific provisions. Over the decades, there has been a steady dilution of the Greek Cypriot position. Indeed, as has been shown, this was seen even before independence. Determined to achieve immediate *enosis*, or at least a clear British commitment to the idea as an end result, the Greek Cypriots rejected several options for self-rule that almost certainly would have led to self-determination.[32] In any case, Cyprus was eventually forced to accept independence and a unitary state in which the Turkish Cypriots had significant constitutional powers. At the time of independence, Cyprus truly was, as one historian of the Cyprus issue famously put it, a 'reluctant republic'.[33] The new state did not command the loyalty of the vast majority of Greek Cypriots, who saw the Republic of Cyprus as a mark of their failure to achieve *enosis*. As a result, the main aim of the Greek Cypriot leadership was to find a way to bring about union with Greece. Nevertheless, an opportunity for *enosis* did arise following the first bout of intercommunal fighting in 1963. But, Makarios rejected this on the grounds that giving Turkey sovereign bases on the island would amount to an unacceptable limitation. Only full and complete union would suffice. Further attempts to refine the plan failed. Little did the Greek Cypriots realise that this was their one and only chance to gain *enosis* after independence – assuming, of course, that Turkey would have actually agreed to the proposal if it had been accepted by the Greek Cypriots.

The next major plan to address the Cyprus issue, which was proposed by Galo Plaza the following year, set aside *enosis*. It called for a continuation of the Republic of Cyprus with greater autonomy for the Turkish Cypriots, who were asked to forego a federal settlement. This time Turkey rejected the proposals, refusing to accept any limitation on their constitutional right to intervene in Cyprus. A further attempt to promote *enosis* in 1967 failed miserably when Greece and Turkey met for high level talks. Shortly afterwards, renewed fighting forced Greece and the Greek Cypriots into a humiliating climb down. The Turkish Cypriots seized the opportunity to declare their own autonomous structures of governance. Makarios, while condemning the move, nevertheless was forced to come to terms with the fact that the pursuit of *enosis* was effectively over. Moreover, he now had to accept that the Turkish Cypriots would have to be given greater autonomy. Despite this, he could not bring himself to grant even limited self-government.

The Turkish invasion of the island ended any prospect that might have existed of maintaining a unitary state under majority Greek Cypriot control. The Turkish Cypriots now demanded a federal settlement. Devastated by war and at risk of losing international sympathy, the Greek Cypriots had no choice but to agree. The search for a federal settlement based on the twin principles of bi-zonality and bi-communality has formed the basis of the Cyprus solution since then. In this regard, settlement attempts have not become progressively worse in terms of the overarching political system on offer. Instead, proposals have been worse for the Greek Cypriots in terms of the degree to which they have had to recognise the changing facts on the ground. The most obvious example of this relates to the Turkish settlers. After thirty years, many of the first settlers are now parents to children born on the island. Few believe that they can be sent home. In this sense, time has played against the Greek Cypriots. At the same time, the consolidation of the structures of the Turkish Cypriot state has also required successive plans to increase the autonomy given to the Turkish Cypriot community within a federal model of governance. Few people now believe that a strong federation is an acceptable or viable model for a solution. Most instead view a loose federation as the only viable option. Indeed, such a system may now have to be so loose as to blur the differences between a federation and confederation.

Importantly, it must be stressed that the progressive deterioration of plans has not been due to Greek Cypriot rejection of agreements. From the mid-1980s until the election of Tassos Papadopoulos, the burden of responsibility for the deadlock lay with Rauf Denktash, who has been heavily criticised by successive UN Secretaries-General and by other prominent diplomats involved with Cyprus, such as Richard Holbrooke and David Hannay.[34] Nevertheless, Denktash's rejection of various initiatives has meant that successive plans have had to consider the changing realities on the island. The longer the division has remained in place the stronger the Turkish and Turkish Cypriot bargaining position has become. In view of this, was the Greek Cypriot rejection of the Annan Plan a grave miscalculation? By rejecting the deal and entering the EU divided, have the Greek Cypriots managed to alter the balance in the relationship with Turkey in a manner that will eventually reverse the losses over the years? Or, have they made the search for a settlement even more difficult by ensuring that it is so closely tied up with Turkey's EU accession process? Twenty years from now, assuming that the status quo has been broken, it seems hard to envisage Cyprus united as a strong federation, let alone a unitary state. Going on past experience, one would have to take a more pessimistic view. Future negotiations could well be focused on a confederal settlement, or perhaps even a formal division.

ENDNOTES

1. Andrekos Varnava, 'Cyprus is of No Use to Anybody: The Pawn, 1878-1915', Hubert Faustmann & Nicos Peristianis (eds.), *Britain in Cyprus: Colonialism and Post-Colonialism 1878-2004*, Mannheim and Moehnesee, 2006, 35-60.
2. George H. Kelling, 'British Policy in Cyprus 1945-1955: The Pigeons Come Home to Roost', Ibid., 187-189.
3. For a detailed account of the EOKA campaign and the period leading to independence see Robert Holland, *Britain and the Revolt in Cyprus, 1954-59*, Oxford, 1997.
4. Evanthis Hadzivassiliou, 'British Stretregic Priorities and the Cyprus Question, 1954-1958', Faustmann and Peristianis (eds.), *Britain in Cyprus*, 206.
5. Colonial Office, *Conference on Cyprus: Documents Signed and Initialled at Lancaster House on*

February 19, 1959, Command 679, London, HMSO, 1959.
6. The texts of the documents can be found in Nicholas Macris (ed), *The 1960 Treaties on Cyprus and Selected Subsequent Acts*, Mannheim and Moehnesee, 2003.
7. Kyriacos C. Markides, *The Rise and Fall of the Cyprus Republic*, London, 1977, 88.
8. Clement Dodd (ed), *The Political, Social and Economic Development of Northern Cyprus*, Huntingdon, 1993, 6.
9. The events are heavily disputed. Greek Cypriots argue that the Turkish Cypriots deliberately withdrew from the government. The Turkish Cypriots argue that they were forced out. In reality, both views are correct. While there were cases where Greek Cypriot prevented Turkish Cypriots from returning to work, there are also instances where Turkish Cypriot authorities ordered them to leave their posts.
10. For a full analysis of the period see James Ker-Lindsay, *Britain and the Cyprus Crisis, 1963-64*, Mannheim and Moehnesee, 2004.
11. Claude Nicolet, *United States Policy Towards Cyprus, 1954-1974: Removing the Greek-Turkish Bone of Contention*, Mannheim and Moehnesee, 2001, 247.
12. In April, Makarios had visited Athens and had agreed with Papandreou that any future efforts to deal with Cyprus would be based on four principles: a) the resolution of the problem would be achieved only through the UN b) that the ultimate target would be enosis c) every effort would be made not to provoke Turkey and d) that Greece would come to the assistance of the Greek Cypriots if Turkey attacked. Andreas Papandreou, *Democracy at Gun Point*, London, 1970, 100.
13. *United Nations Security Council Document*, S/6253, 26 March 1965.
14. Oliver Richmond, *Mediating in Cyprus*, London, 1998, 106.
15. Nicolet, *United States Policy Towards Cyprus*, 370.
16. Christopher M. Woodhouse, *Modern Greece*, London, 1991, 293.
17. Richmond, *Mediating in Cyprus*, 109.
18. *United Nations Security Council Document*, S/10199, 20 May 1971.
19. Stavros Panteli, *The Making of Modern Cyprus: From Obscurity to Statehood*, London, 1990, 224.
20. The most comprehensive account of the talks in Switzerland and Turkey's actions over July and August 1974 can be found in Mehmet Ali Birand, *Thirty Hot Days*, Nicosia, 1985.
21. Edward Newman, 'The Most Impossible Job in the World: The Secretary-General and Cyprus', in Richmond and Ker-Lindsay, *The Work of the UN in Cyprus: Promoting Peace and Development*, Basingstoke, 2001, 136.
22. Farid Mirbagheri, *Cyprus and International Peacemaking*, London, 1998, 96-97.
23. Richmond, *Mediating in Cyprus*, 154.
24. *UN Security Council Resolution 541*, 18 November 1983.
25. Newman, 'The Secretary-General and Cyprus', 139.
26. Rauf R Denktash, *The Cyprus Triangle*, London, Allen & Unwin, 1988, 142.
27. *UN Security Council Document*, S/18102/Add.1, 11 June 1986.
28. Richmond, *Mediating in Cyprus*, 193.
29. *UN Security Council Document*, S/23121, 8 October 1991.
30. *UN Security Council Document*, S/23780, paras.17-25 & 27, 2 April 1992. The Council endorsed the plan soon afterwards, see *UN Security Council Resolution 750*, 12 April 1992.
31. *UN Security Council Document*, S/24472, 24 August 1992.
32. For instance, Malta, the nearest comparable example, became independent in 1964.
33. Stephen Xydis, *Cyprus: Reluctant Republic*, The Hague, 1973.
34. David Hannay, *Cyprus: The Search for a Solution*, London, 2005, 17-21; Richard Holbrooke, 'The United States and Turkey: Mending Fences?', presentation to the Washington Institute for Near East Policy, 3 November 2003.

PART II

THE PLAN

CHAPTER 2

CONSOCIATIONAL DEMOCRACY AND CYPRUS: THE HOUSE THAT ANNAN BUILT?

Christalla Yakinthou

This chapter examines the most significant attempt to craft a comprehensive political solution to the Cyprus conflict since the breakdown of the constitutional order in 1963. It argues that the Annan plan was carefully and methodically constructed to create a state which addressed both groups' primary concerns and fears, as well as their most important demands. The experiences of the failed 1960 state shaped much of the Annan Plan. Thus, the constitutional engineers were keen not to replicate the flaws of the 1960 constitution. At the same time, domestic elites have internalised communal history and memories, which have become friction points in peace negotiations. Therefore, many of the plan's provisions were designed to overcome particular communal fears caused by the 1960 state's breakdown. This chapter analyses the plan's development.

The 2004 Annan Plan

Consociationalism is a form of institutional engineering which maintains that ethnic or inter-group tension can be resolved democratically by the creation of a permanent multi-group coalition government. It emphasises conflict resolution by elite co-operation rather than societal cohesion. The theory predicts that if, in a fractured society, a system of governance is created which shares governmental decision making between political representatives of the disputant groups, then the conflict can be contained and the groups are able to contribute to a form of democratic governance. Consociational theorists outline a number of mechanisms by which to encourage elite co-operation and regulate conflict. The theory's primary concept is 'pillarisation'; the idea of separating disputant groups, and engineering a series of institutional levers which require each group's political elites to co-operate in order to govern the country. Its aim is therefore to encourage inter-group trust by instilling a culture of co-operation which originates with political elites and 'trickles down' to the community level.

The United Cyprus Republic (UCR), as the proposed new state of Cyprus was to be titled, was to comprise a set of institutions inspired by consociational models drawn from European states. Throughout the crafting of the Annan Plan, the engineers took great pains to explain their institutional choices. The UN Secretary-General's Reports on Cyprus[1] extensively discuss the choice of institutions in the context of each side's interests and in the context of lessons from the 1960 Republic of Cyprus. The decision to use consociational institutions was effectively made for the UN by the fact that little else would have been acceptable to both sides, and the solution's broad outline had been long established. Both the Swiss and Belgian models of governance were suggested by Turkish Cypriot interlocutors, and in the Secretary-

General's 2003 Report on Cyprus,[2] Annan suggests that the model of Switzerland provides an acceptable and functional compromise in relation to the motivations and needs of both sides.[3]

In mid-2000, the UN Special Representative on Cyprus, Alvaro de Soto, began constructing a team of experts to resume work on the stalemated negotiations, with an eye to resolving the conflict before Cyprus' likely entry into the EU.[4] It quickly became clear to the UN team that, if left to the interlocutors, the talks would remain indefinitely at the pre-negotiation stage. To progress the situation towards tangible negotiations, the UN began to work on the outline of a comprehensive solution to the Cyprus conflict. The first of the UN's documents was submitted on 12 July 2000. Called 'Preliminary Thoughts', it was a bland document, designed to 'sound out' the groups. A second document followed on 8 November 2000, suggesting that a single negotiating text should be the basis of further negotiations. Soon after, Denktash terminated the negotiations for a year on the basis that the issue of Turkish Cypriot sovereignty had been insufficiently addressed. The first Annan Plan (Annan I) called the 'Comprehensive Settlement of the Cyprus Problem', was submitted to the Greek and Turkish Cypriot communities in November 2002. The second revised plan (Annan II) was submitted one month later, on 10 December. Annan III was submitted in February 2003. In the same month, presidential elections in south Cyprus brought into power the conservative party DIKO in a ruling alliance with communist party AKEL, lending increased caution to the negotiating atmosphere. The president-elect was DIKO leader Tassos Papadopoulos, who, before the submission of Annan IV in March 2004, had replaced outgoing president Glafkos Clerides as chief negotiator for the Greek Cypriot community. By this time, parliamentary elections in north Cyprus also saw Mehmet Ali Talat's CTP become the largest party and Talat chief negotiator of his community. As the first left-wing leader of the Turkish Cypriots, his election was a significant break from the past, reflecting Turkish Cypriot pro-settlement and anti-status quo public sentiment which had been building for some time. The election also marked a tangible changing point in Turkish Cypriot negotiating dynamics, replacing Denktash' combativeness and intransigence with a negotiating party which co-operated with the UN team, providing a clear list of negotiating goals and compromises.[5] This changed dynamic was carried through to Annan V.

The UCR was designed as a federal, consociational state. The new state of affairs would result in an indissoluble partnership between the federal government and two equal constituent states, called the Greek Cypriot Constituent State and the Turkish Cypriot Constituent State. Following consociational principles, the constitution specified the powers and functions vested in the federal government, devolving the bulk of powers (including the day-to-day functioning of the states) to the constituent states. Each constituent state was to exercise powers related to the administration of justice at the state level; law and order; criminal, company and family law; public safety; industry and commerce; social security and labour; environmental protection; tourism; fisheries and agriculture; zoning and planning; sports; education; and health. Each constituent state would have also had corresponding executive, legislative and judicial offices to that outlined for the federal level.

Consociationalism and the Annan Plan

Consociational models are designed to absorb and diffuse societal tensions within a country. They generally revolve around four basic institutional devices and principles: proportionality; grand coalitions; cultural autonomy; and minority veto. In crafting the UCR, the constitutional engineers utilised each of these devices.

Proportional representation was used in the construction of the Presidential Council, the Chamber of Deputies, the federal administration, and the federal police. The election and function of the Presidential Council encouraged compromise and the building of inter-group coalitions. The Presidential Council's election on a common list meant that the candidates must build alliances with parties from the other community to create that common list. Moderate political behaviour amongst potential candidates would also have been encouraged by the need for bi-communal endorsement of the list in parliament. Cultural autonomy is a central tenet of the Plan and underlies the construction of the UCR. It is most obviously represented in the autonomy of the constituent states vis-à-vis each other and the federal state; constituent state power over educational, cultural, and religious matters, as well as holding residual powers; the depoliticisation of issues at the federal level by devolving powers over most matters likely to be controversial to the constituent states, or to the EU; voting for federal senators on the basis of mother-tongue, and voting generally according to internal constituent state status; the allocation of citizenship according to mother-tongue; and limitations on the right of primary residence within the 'other' constituent state.

The principle of minority veto was subtly integrated into the institutional structure. In the plan, it was allied with the principle of co-operation, and was somewhat diffused by being embedded within the federal structure: so that 'the companion concepts that no decision could be taken by persons from one constituent state alone and that no single person could veto decisions or block the running of the state run like a golden thread throughout the plan'.[6] A form of veto was intrinsic to the plan; but the veto was institutionalised in the senate level and a series of complex deadlock-breaking mechanisms meant that the veto would not reach the executive, therefore quelling Greek Cypriot fear that minority veto will again cause the paralysis of the state.

Consociational theorists subscribe to the maxim that the ends justify the means: high levels of autonomy and firm separation of disputant groups at the popular level (segmental isolation) encourages compromise and negotiation at the elite level of decision-making. It should therefore facilitate a culture of co-operation, through a 'trickling down' of toleration from elite to mass society, eventually rendering consociational institutions obsolete. The Plan attempted to ensure that issues likely to cause friction were encased within the legislative jurisdiction of each constituent state. The two societies' reunification was intended to be gradual, facilitated by a sanitised political agenda at the federal level. The Presidential Council's election on a single ticket and the requirement that they obtain at least 40 percent of votes from senators representing each constituent state would necessitate compromise and negotiation within the executive. Additionally, the condition of special majority voting for the passing of certain types of legislation[7] was designed to develop a culture of exchange and negotiation, as one group should be encouraged to support the other with an eye to its own future legislative requirements.

In line with consociational theory, which primarily utilises multi-person, or collegial executives, the UCR executive was a multi-person council chosen on a proportional basis, linked to the population of each constituent state. In addition, the EU would have contributed another consociational principle to the executive's functioning by removing much decision-making responsibility from the executive. EU membership would have left the UCR Presidential Council a largely ceremonial machine whose importance lay primarily in the symbol it presents of communal representation and inter-communal co-operation at the head of government.

Unable, or unwilling, to undertake the monumental task of reconstructing the psyches of Greek and Turkish Cypriot society, the negotiators – working in concord with Turkish and Greek Cypriot elites – opted for a constitutional construct which allowed both sides to retain many of their respective visions of statehood and selfhood, whilst providing for the political reunification of the country. The underpinning philosophy, in line with consociational theory, was that through appropriate institutions, a reshaping of consciousness would follow.

The Annan Plan's Development

The Plan was built from information gleaned from previous years of negotiations, rather than as a document negotiated from scratch between the Cypriot interlocutors. There were two reasons for this: the first was that over the course of the plan's four-year development there were considerable periods where one or both sides were not providing the UN with various negotiating positions required for the construction of a compromise solution. As a result, 'the UN team under de Soto was driven *faute de mieux* to draw up the first Annan Plan based on drafts and concepts that had been in circulation for years and in some instances for decades'.[8] A core member of the UN negotiating team maintained that there was 'very little engagement in [the] negotiations' by either side, and that the interlocutors were 'more willing to discuss options' in one-on-one shuttle talks than they were during face-to-face negotiations.[9] This is reflected in the high number of proximity and shuttle talks as measured against face-to-face discussions. During the Annan negotiations, there were only 72 face-to-face meetings between the leaders, as compared to 150 bilateral meetings between de Soto and each leader separately and 54 meetings in the proximity phase.

Second, almost forty years of negotiations, policy papers and high-level agreements had established a set of guidelines that were accepted by and acceptable to both groups. 'What we came up with was something which built on past plans. It was not a creation out of nothing, but a consideration of previous negotiation processes, ideas, maps, and plans'.[10] Michael Klosson, then US Ambassador to Cyprus, reinforced this, emphasising that the plan:

> includes ideas that have been supported by leaders of one or *both* communities at various times. For example, under the Annan Plan, the Turkish Cypriot State would control slightly more than 29 percent of the island's ter-

ritory. This number was not pulled out of a hat. It was discussed extensively as far back as 1985, when the Turkish Cypriot side accepted it at a UN summit. At the talks in 1992, the Turkish Cypriot side agreed to the eventual demilitarisation of Cyprus, the desirability of a single sovereignty and single citizenship, and the importance of freedom of movement and settlement. All of these are reflected in the Annan Plan.[11]

Cypriot political leaders have themselves suggested various power-sharing models and the institutional structure of the UCR was dictated by the ideological positions of the interlocutors. These ideologies were closely intertwined with (and often stemmed from) the fears and concerns each group had for its survival and its position in a reunified Cyprus. A complicating factor over the years was each side's use of international norms and laws about conflict within (or between, depending on the perspective) states. Both communities have made much use of their differing interpretations of concepts such as sovereignty, freedom, democracy, and group rights. They have both brought with them into negotiations their definitions of these terms, around which are folded their visions of both the spirit and the practicalities of a 'viable' solution.

The UN engineers identified the groups' opposing conceptualisations of the conflict and its solution as a major obstacle. In constructing the Annan Plan, the UN team sought to 'allow each side to maintain its position on how the new state of affairs would come into being'.[12] In his 2003 report on the situation in Cyprus, Annan articulated that he was driven by the 'need to find a form of government which (a) reflected and guaranteed the political equality of Greek Cypriots and Turkish Cypriots but also reflected in a democratic manner the significantly larger numbers of Greek Cypriot citizens; and (b) carried cast-iron guarantees against domination while ensuring that the government would function effectively'.[13] In other words, his intention was to balance power between the communities in a way which both guaranteed the existence of each and reflected population differences between them.

The Influence of the 1960 Constitution: Institutional Learning

The 2004 system's design was consciously affected by certain elements of the 1960 constitution considered positive or negative by either the interlocutors or the engineers, and both sides' experiences of the 1960 Republic.

At several points, the authors of the Annan Plan sought to address deficiencies of the 1960 constitution that were identified by the interlocutors or the engineers. When asked in interviews to identify weak or 'dangerous' elements of the 1960 constitution, UN negotiators singled out a number of perceived institutional flaws. They identified a danger in creating separate electorates for the election of president and vice-president 'because both were playing to antagonistic audiences, and likely to run on nationalist platforms'.[14] They highlighted that without institutional encouragement of pre-election elite co-operation, candidates would be most likely to run on populist, nationalist platforms. Another danger was of creating a dual presidency effect such as in the 1960 system, which established a significant need for consensus between the president and vice-president without a correspondingly strong incentive for their co-operation. In addition, it was frequently emphasised that the 1960 constitution was a compromise that 'no-one really wanted'.[15] The engineers attempted to apply these 'lessons' to the 2004 plan.

Negotiators from both communities also often used the 1960 constitution as an example to highlight both satisfactory and unsatisfactory proposals for the Plan under negotiation. 'Each side would use the 1960 constitution as an example to highlight certain points, positive or negative: [they would say] "we want X, like the 1960 constitution, but it's obvious that Y didn't work well in 1960, so it shouldn't be included"'.[16]

Greek Cypriot negotiators had a significant desire to avoid repeating what they perceived as being the destructive misperceptions caused by the contested and delayed implementation of the 1960 constitution's laws.[17] Alecos Markides, the then head of the Greek Cypriot delegation to the Committee on Laws and Attorney-General of the Republic, emphasised this: 'Having the experience of Zurich in 1960, we suggested in October 2002, in New York…that all the laws needed by the federation should be operational on the very first day of the new arrangement'.[18] Their concern was that there should be no obvious gaps or uncertainties which might lead both communities to feel that the other would seize an advantage, as was the case in the 1960 Republic. The UN engineers clearly agreed with this hypothesis: 'we were convinced that ambiguity was very much the seed for the next conflict, and for failure'.[19]

The UN was thus asked to create a detailed blueprint of institutional and political reunification which would leave no unanswered questions. Its goal was to address all contentious issues, and 'propose a crystal-clear solution'.[20] The complexity and importance of this task was compounded by the situation's fragility: the architects of the Annan Plan had to reconstruct reality for mutually suspicious communities that had lived entirely separate – refusing to acknowledge even the existence of the other as a political entity – for a generation. To avoid clashing interpretations of its provisions, the Annan Plan was remarkably thorough in its detail. This point was highlighted by UN Special Representative to Cyprus, Alvaro de Soto: 'if you look around in the last few years, at the different peace agreements that have been signed, a lot of them are very jerry-built essentially and have raised enormous questions that create for somewhat chaotic situations. Whereas here it is all spelled out…'.[21] Thus, a significant cause of conflict in 1960s Cyprus was removed in the 2004 Annan Plan.

Every element of the federal state had to be fully fleshed out. By Annan V, there were some 140 draft laws, set to be in operation from the first day of the UCR's establishment. There was also a provision that 'if by reason of the complexity of the system you fail to amend a particular law, it continues as it is, unless amended'.[22] This vast task involved 300 Cypriots and some 50 UN experts working in 14 technical committees. One UN engineer labelled it an almost 'super-human' effort by those involved.[23] The resulting plan in its entirety ran to some 9,000 pages.

The UCR Presidential Council may be used as an example of the engineers' efforts to address Greek and Turkish Cypriot fears caused by the 1960 state's breakdown. Turkish Cypriot concerns about preventing Greek Cypriot domination of government stemmed primarily from the 1960s legislative struggles between the Greek Cypriot-dominated Council of Ministers and the Turkish Cypriot Communal Chambers. The 1961 taxation battle was stressed, where communal disagreement on a new tax law after the expiry of the provisional colonial taxation laws left the Republic without the authority to collect taxes. Each community's attempts to implement new taxation laws were opposed by the other. Makarios' subsequent attempts to modify the 1960 constitution against Turkish Cypriot wishes were also emphasised.[24] The Presidential Council was therefore designed to meet the Turkish Cypriot desire to 'underline political equality and prevent any domination',[25] while also addressing Greek Cypriot worries about executive functionality. The Secretary-General also recognised these Greek Cypriot concerns in his 2003 Report on Cyprus, noting that '[t]he Greek Cypriot side, concerned with the workability of the government, wished to eliminate the veto (which it considered to be a major ingredient in the deadlocks and conflict that arose in the early years of the Republic's existence) and separate electorates (which it thought tended to affect workability and promoted division)'.[26]

In the context of EU membership and significant constituent state powers, the Presidential Council's main function was to 'guarantee the harmony of Cyprus, and not really to have decisive government action…it was going to guarantee proper representation'.[27] The engineers canvassed the three primary models. Options were the French semi-presidential dual executive, election of the president and vice president by an electoral college on a single ticket, and the Swiss system of an executive council with rotation of the head of state around the executive council over its fixed term. Turkish Cypriot resistance to mixed electorates meant that the main options explored were power-sharing with a rotational head of state.[28]

In the end, the UCR Presidential Council was modelled upon the seven-person Swiss Federal Council, with some adjustments. Unlike the Swiss system, the legislature would elect the Cypriot Presidential Council from a single, closed list. Election of the Presidential Council required separate majorities of Turkish and Greek Cypriot members of parliament.[29] This would 'ensure that those elected would have clear support from their own constituent state (a Turkish Cypriot concern) and from both constituent states (a Greek Cypriot concern)'.[30] This provided an institutional encouragement for moderation: if one wanted to play a role in national politics, s/he would have to be at least marginally acceptable to the other side. 'The system presupposed politicians from the Greek Cypriot and Turkish Cypriot side to come together and to have a common programme of government, and be elected by parliament to govern'.[31]

The rotating presidency was designed to reinforce political equality and replaced the 1960 condition that only a Greek Cypriot could hold the position of president and a Turkish Cypriot only hold the position of vice-president. Rotation was highlighted as positive by several sources on both sides and even, in some cases, by the plan's detractors. Prominent Turkish Cypriot journalist and political activist, Sener Levent, was vociferously opposed to the Annan Plan, desiring the reinstating of the 1960 constitution, but supported rotational presidency.[32]

Both the 1960 Cypriot constitution and subsequent UN proposals employed what was in many ways a dual head of state, with a Greek Cypriot president and Turkish Cypriot vice president, each elected by their particular community and each enjoying veto rights over certain issues. According to the 2004 Annan Plan's main architect, the substitution of a rotating presidency was a significant improvement on the 1960 system, and an incentive for moderation.[33] In order to combat the Greek Cypriot fear of executive paralysis brought on by veto, a layered mechanism was designed where Council decisions were to be taken in the first instance by consensus, and then by simple majority if consensus proved impossible (so long as the majority included one member from each constituent state).[34]

Removal of the 1960 constitution's executive veto highlights the determination of the interlocutors and the UN engineers to ensure that significant weaknesses of the 1960 design would not be copied into the Annan plan. By minimising federal executive powers, and maximising both communities' decision-making autonomy, the engineers consciously controlled the risk of causing deadlock in a critical area of government. The difference in impact between the 1960 vice-presidential veto and the UCR's requirement for majority support in the executive was highlighted by Markides as significant because '[in the 1960s] the veto paralysed the particular function of the whole state. Whereas the lack of one vote from a Turkish member of government would only paralyse the particular function of the federal government, which however, has very minimal powers. This was not a haphazard choice'.[35] Didier Pfirter, legal advisor to the Secretary-General's Special Advisor, confirms this: 'the government envisaged in the Plan is designed to be lean and efficient, with only a small number of members. Unlike the 1960 constitution, this plan also does not allow any single person to veto any decision, and no separate majorities are required for any decision'.[36] As this statement makes equally clear, the UN engineers were cognisant of the need to show tangible improvements upon the 1960 constitution and to stress to the Cypriot public that their plan would not contain the weaknesses of 1960.

The construction of the legislature also reflects the engineers' efforts to address both groups' concerns about the 1960 state's weaknesses. A bicameral parliament was proposed in order to address the concerns of each side. The 50-50 composition of the Senate was designed to reflect the Turkish Cypriot emphasis upon the political equality of each constituent state, while the construction of the Chamber of Deputies met the Greek Cypriot desire for representation by population ratio. The Secretary-General emphasised this balance in his 2003 Report: 'The decision-making procedures of the Senate are designed to ensure that decisions enjoy substantial support from both constituent states'.[37]

Great attention was paid in the Annan Plan to the effective design of conflict-breaking mechanisms. This was a direct consequence of the 1960 Supreme Constitutional Court's failure to moderate conflict. Repeated reference was made during the negotiations to the Supreme Constitutional Court's contribution in 1963 to the breakdown of the Republic. This is supported by consociational theory, which recommends the implementation of a strong system of conflict mediation, generally encompassing the juridical and political realms. As a result of the legal equality of federal and constituent state laws, the Supreme Court in the Annan Plan was designed to be a final deadlock-breaking mechanism. It was quickly agreed that an equal number of judges from each constituent state should preside over the Supreme Court. Yet, the engineers saw the most effective conflict breaking mechanism as being the inclusion of non-Cypriot judges in cases where the court's decision was divided along ethnic lines and disagreement would cause paralysis in the function of the state.

Annan's team drew on the experience of the 1960 state's breakdown in deciding to 'allow for the sharing of the burden of possible regular exercise of the casting vote…[by including] three such [neutral] judges'.[38] This provision, suggested by the advisory team from Greece,[39] was ill-received by both sides, and was only "reluctantly" agreed upon in January 2003. As a result, provision was made for the federal parliament to remove from the constitution (by qualified parliamentary majority) the need for neutral judges when trust was sufficiently high between the groups. The unorthodox concept of using the Supreme Court as an emergency device to overcome deadlock in institutional or legislative arenas was considered an incentive for compromise. That the Supreme Court could break the deadlock should have become motivation for compromise by the parties to the conflict, because their intransigence would run the risk of returning a Supreme Court decision which may have been less favourable than a compromise solution worked out by the parties themselves.

The Influence of post-1963 Cypriot History

The events which resulted in the 1960 state's breakdown created a past whose memory must be overcome if Cyprus is to be reunified. The Annan Plan's engineers were clearly aware that history had raised a number of design issues, which they needed to defeat. The most significant of these was the issue of sovereignty. The 'Turkish Federated State of North Cyprus' was declared in 1975 very soon after the Turkish intervention. In 1983, the 'Turkish Republic of Northern Cyprus' (TRNC) was unilaterally declared, against Greek Cypriot and international opposition.[40] Since then, a cold war over recognition has been fought between the communities, where the Turkish Cypriot side has made significant efforts to garner international support for its breakaway status, and the Greek Cypriot side has made equally significant efforts to block that recognition.

The issue has frequently become a deal-breaker during negotiations for peace. Ex-TRNC President Rauf Denktash has habitually insisted that resolution of the conflict be based upon the idea of two sovereign states (the TRNC and the Greek Cypriot 'administration', or Republic of Cyprus) coming together to form a loosely confederal state. He has frequently stalled negotiations by insisting that Greek Cypriot negotiators recognise the TRNC's sovereignty – an abhorrent idea for the Greek Cypriot community. Since the 1977 High Level Agreement, when Makarios agreed to a federal solution along bicommunal lines, Greek Cypriot negotiators have grudgingly accepted a federal arrangement – a compromise linked in the Greek Cypriot mind with the surrender of a degree of sovereignty to the Turkish Cypriot community.[41] But the issue of sovereignty has remained highly contentious.

British Special Representative to Cyprus, Lord David Hannay, has commented extensively on the UN's concern that Denktash' sovereignty pre-occupation would hamper the negotiations. He noted that this 'began to worry de Soto, who was concerned that it might bring the whole negotiation to a halt'.[42] De Soto's concern was justified: the Annan negotiations were halted for a year between November 2000 and 2001 by Denktash' refusal to proceed without recognition of the TRNC's existence. Following a meeting with the Turkish government, Denktash stated publicly that 'co-existence of two states, two peoples, two sovereignties and two democracies'[43] was the only acceptable foundation of any resolution, and that proximity talks were 'a waste of time as long as our parameters are not accepted. They are being run on the basis that the Greek Cypriots are the sole legitimate government on the island'.[44]

Denktash' fixation on the sovereignty issue stems directly from two stages in modern Cypriot history. The first is the post-1963 environment, when the Greek Cypriots unilaterally amended the 1960 constitution[45] after the Turkish Cypriot representatives walked out of government in protest when their veto of the proposed budget was overruled. The Turkish Cypriot representatives found themselves unable to return to government unless they approved the constitution's amendments,[46] which removed a number of provisions they considered communal safeguards against Greek Cypriot domination, but whose removal the Greek Cypriot representatives considered necessary to ensure the smooth operation of government.

The Turkish Cypriots subsequently lobbied the international community to refuse recognition to the Republic of Cyprus government without Turkish Cypriot representation. The international community responded that Cyprus was a *sovereign* country and any interference in its internal affairs was outside the international community's jurisdiction. This response catalysed the Turkish Cypriot fixation on sovereignty.

This assumption was compounded in the post-1974 environment, when the Greek Cypriots were able to use the Republic of Cyprus as a vehicle to legitimise their protests against the Turkish occupation. The Republic of Cyprus, which was originally a *bi*-communal state, became an exclusively Greek Cypriot ticket into international forums. From this vantage point, the Greek Cypriots gained the international community's tacit support: a significant advantage in the diplomatic war. Equally, because the Turkish Cypriots lacked international standing, they were denied a voice in international forums to articulate their own version of a just solution to the conflict.

There are two primary consequences of that situation for efforts to create peace in Cyprus. Firstly, until very recently, the only forum in which Turkish Cypriots have had international standing, enabling their perspective on the conflict to be legitimated, is at the negotiating table. As a result, there has been every incentive at the elite level to continue the negotiations indefinitely. Second, insistence on the recognition of Turkish Cypriot sovereignty has both stalled negotiations and influenced the shape of the 2004 resolution. It has been recognised as a key factor for both communities by the engineers, publicly in the Secretary-General's reports[47] and in private interviews.

The text of the Annan Plan itself is a delicate attempt to appease both communities' demands about sovereignty. During interviews, particular members of the UN core team showed a nuanced (and realist) understanding of the Greek Cypriot emphasis on protecting their own sovereignty and legitimacy:

> The Turkish Cypriots had the arms on the ground and the Turkish soldiers on the ground and the Greek Cypriots had international legality on their side. So that's why the Greek Cypriots are excessively touchy about anything that could imply even a scratch on this thing that *they* are the government of Cyprus and the others are a nothing. One cannot have any contact with them or anything that could imply a little bit of recognition of the Turkish Cypriots; it had to be fought against strongly because it could diminish what was the main asset that the Greek Cypriots had.[48]

Evidently, Greek Cypriots were equally sensitive over the sovereignty issue. Legally, the Greek Cypriot argument against even unofficial acknowledgement of the TRNC centres on the capacity of non-state actors implicitly to bestow recognition upon an invalid state.[49] International law maintains that only *states,* represented by *governments,* can give or withdraw recognition of other states or governments. However, a second strand, the 'law of implied recognition' asserts that unofficial contacts by non-state or state actors may imply recognition of the other state, *even when* state authorities have explicitly rejected claims of statehood; this is known as recognition through the 'backdoor'.[50] But, strong international legal precedents have affirmed that if the other side *formally* and *clearly* denies (or withdraws) recognition, then there is no possibility for the piecemeal application of the law of implied recognition by any number of individual contacts. Therefore, recognition of the TRNC is not within the legal capacity of non-state actors.

The constitutional engineers acknowledged the close relationship between each side's concerns on this matter and its negotiating ideals:

> A breakdown of the new state of affairs followed by secession of a sovereign Turkish Cypriot state and the consequent partition of Cyprus could be described as the Greek Cypriot nightmare…a breakdown of the new state of affairs followed by the larger Greek Cypriot population alone exercising the sovereignty of the state could be described as the Turkish Cypriot nightmare.[51]

Unable to find a middle ground, the engineers for a time worked around the issue of sovereignty by carefully withholding use of the term. However, the Secretary-General ultimately decided that remaining silent on the issue would 'leave unanswered questions and not put the nightmares to rest'.[52]

The Belgian model was useful in solving this problem. In order to satisfy Greek Cypriot concerns, the Plan states that the UCR 'has a single international legal personality and sovereignty, and partition or secession are expressly prohibited'.[53] To meet Turkish Cypriot concerns, the Plan 'provides that the constituent states sovereignly exercise all powers not vested in the federal government, organising themselves freely under their own constitutions consistent with the overall agreement, as well as providing (as in Belgium) for no hierarchy between federal and constituent state laws'.[54]

Recent history has also played a role in the way the UCR has structured electoral participation and citizenship. Consociationalism is criticised for freezing ethnic relations as they stand at the period of highest tension. It is argued that the system builds political structures around a particular set of demographic and social conditions and, because of its rigidity, cannot reflect any changes over time in domestic dynamics. Considerable controversy surrounded particular elements of the Annan Plan which linked citizenship, electoral participation, and right of residence to one's ethnicity. All federal political rights but one were to be exercised on the basis of internal constituent state citizenship status. However, a provision was inserted into Annan V that voting for federal senators would be determined by mother-tongue, rather than internal citizenship status.[55] This was designed to meet Turkish Cypriot concerns of 'being undermined in the long term by Greek Cypriots establishing residency in the north and seeking Turkish Cypriot internal constituent state citizenship status'.[56] The Turkish Cypriots feared that the more populous Greek Cypriots might come with time to dominate both constituent states. If voting and citizenship rights were not tied to ethnicity, then what would stop Greek Cypriots becoming citizens of the Turkish Cypriot state, and electing Greek Cypriot representatives, leaving the Turkish Cypriot community voiceless again? This fear has clear roots in the 1960 constitution's perceived failure to protect Turkish Cypriot communal rights and the ease with which Greek Cypriots became the dominant voice in government after 1963.

The Annan Plan and Future Political Development

Opponents of the Annan Plan argued that the provisions which linked ethnicity to electoral participation, citizenship, and right of residence immortalised the ethnic divide between Greek and Turkish Cypriots by tying ethnicity to a number of important aspects of a citizen's life. They argued that to make ethnicity the common vehicle of electoral and legislative participation at both the federal and constituent state level would guarantee that rigid segmental isolation on the basis of ethnicity would continue indefinitely.

The distribution of powers between the constituent and federal states also touched deep fears in both communities. Greek Cypriots feared that the constituent states would be so powerful as to render the federal state meaningless, creating a *de facto* partition of Cyprus. The opposing Turkish Cypriot concern was that the federal government would be imbued with powers that would strip the Turkish Cypriot constituent state of its ability to make major decisions concerning the welfare of its population. This raised the Turkish Cypriot fear of being dominated again by the Greek Cypriots. Consequently, powers in the Plan were distributed along consociational lines: the federal government was given a certain number of important functions, but none which were likely to cause inter-ethnic tension; and the constituent states were largely left to govern themselves. The engineers displayed awareness and significant concern about the idea that the Annan Plan's structure might leave the communities saddled in a calmer future with unnecessary provisions. To overcome what they saw as the structure's necessary rigidity, they implemented a relatively low threshold for constitutional change. 'We tried to make it easy for the Cypriots to eventually shape [the constitution] in the way that they want it, but to provide them with something that works and it works forever if they cannot agree to change it'.[57] To change any article in the constitution,[58] a simple majority of one quarter of senators present and voting from each constituent state is required.[59] The change must then be approved by the people of both constituent states by referendum.[60]

Critics argued that with this kind of structure, it would be impossible to overcome ethnic separation. Therefore, path dependency would ensure the perpetuation of an ethnically divided society. Consociational theorists (and perhaps the engineers) might counter that the very reason that such rigid institutions would be implemented in a situation like Cyprus was because ethnic identity was so deeply entrenched at the time of engineering. Therefore, it was the most appropriate basis upon which to restructure a state in internal conflict.

Conclusion

This chapter has argued that the constitutional engineers' careful construction of the Annan Plan showed a nuanced understanding of the way history and memory must be addressed when crafting the political structures which will underpin a post-conflict state. The engineers' painstaking approach created a Plan which would minimise inter-communal conflict, avoid deadlock, and meet both communities' primary needs. The central government's structure and minimal responsibility, and the high degree of group autonomy are examples of ways the engineers sought to reduce the chances of conflict. The Supreme Court had the power to break executive deadlocks, and, because of the complexity of the system, if particular laws were the subject of disagreement, they would continue to function until such time as an amendment could be agreed upon. The Turkish Cypriot fear of being dominated by the Greek Cypriot community was assuaged by the high level of group autonomy mentioned above, proportional representation in the public service, and the rotating presidency. The Greek Cypriot need for validation of their majority status was reinforced by their greater representation in the Chamber of Deputies, and in the Presidential Council.

In creating such structures, the constitutional engineers seemed to have succeeded in overcoming the 1960 constitution's most significant weaknesses and other institutional problems, which have been identified in the chapter. To the extent that the Plan had weaknesses, these were also guided by the engineers' need to incorporate into the solution a number of protections against strong inter-communal fears. Also, the engineers showed awareness of the plan's weaknesses and tried to incorporate provisions which could create a more dynamic constitution, as elite co-operation and inter-group trust grew.

ENDNOTES

1. Kofi Annan, 'Report of Kofi Annan on Good Offices in Cyprus', *United Nations Document*, 1 April, 2003 UN doc S/2003/398; Kofi Annan, 'Report of the Secretary-General on Cyprus',

United Nations Document, 16 April, 2004 UN doc S/2004/302; Kofi Annan, 'Report of the Secretary-General on his Mission of Good Offices in Cyprus', United Nations Document, 28 May, 2004 UN doc S/2004/437.
2. Annan, 'Report on Good Offices in Cyprus', 1 April, 2003 paragraph 77.
3. Ibid.
4. Information for this section was drawn from interviews with members of the UN negotiating team and from David Hannay, *Cyprus, the Search for a Solution,* London, 2005.
5. However, in the face of Denktash' reluctance to engage with the UN engineers, Talat became unofficially involved in the plan's development from after the submission of Annan I. This is based on interviews with members of the UN negotiating team in 2005 and 2006.
6. Annan, 'Report on Good Offices in Cyprus' (S/2003/398), paragraph 85.
7. Including international agreements which fall within the legislative competence of the constituent states; ratification of treaties and adoption of laws regulating airspace, continental shelf, and territorial waters; adoption of laws and regulations regarding citizenship, immigration, taxation, and water resources; election of the Presidential Council; approval of the federal budget. Constitution of the United Cyprus Republic, Article 25 (2).
8. Keith Kyle, 'A British View of the Annan Plan', *Cyprus Review,* XVI, 1, 2004, 17.
9. Member of UN negotiating team in Cyprus, confidential interview with author. Reiterated by Alecos Markides in interview with author, 2 July 2004.
10. Ibid.
11. US Ambassador Michael Klosson comments, Turkish Cypriot Nicosia Bar Association, 30 September 2003.
12. Annan, 'Report of the Secretary-General on his Mission of Good Offices in Cyprus', 28 May 2004, 17. Also reiterated to the author by a member of the UN negotiating team.
13. Annan, 'Report on Good Offices in Cyprus', 1 April 2003 paragraph 82.
14. Interview with Didier Pfirter, Legal Advisor to Annan's Special Assistant, 6 October 2006.
15. A number of these points were reiterated separately by different members of the UN's negotiating team in Cyprus in interviews with the author.
16. Member of UN core negotiating team, interview with author.
17. Alecos Markides, interview with author, 2 July 2004.
18. Ibid.
19. Didier Pfirter, interview with author, 6 October 2006.
20. Ibid.
21. Opening Statement and Press Conference by Secretary-General's then Special Advisor on Cyprus, Alvaro de Soto, Ledra Palace, Nicosia, 20 April 2004.
22. Alecos Markides, interview with author, 2 July 2004.
23. Member of UN core negotiating team in Cyprus, confidential interview with author.
24. Kyriakides cites three examples given by Vice President Küçük of Turkish Cypriot experiences of executive domination. The first was the taxation crisis, the second concerned the composition of the Cyprus Army units, and the third was the municipality issue. Stanley Kyriakides, *Cyprus: Constitutionalism and Crisis Government,* Philadelphia, 1968, 108-109, fn.10.
25. Annan, 'Report on Good Offices in Cyprus', 1 April 2003, paragraph 81.
26. Ibid., italics added.
27. Didier Pfirter, interview with author, 6 October 2006.
28. Denktash had a significant aversion to any form of cross-voting, because, to his mind, it would inhibit the election of 'pure Turks'. The implication was that any Turkish Cypriot

voted into power because s/he was acceptable to the Greek Cypriot community was a sort of quisling. This was a significant disappointment to some of the UN engineering team, who would have liked to implemented mixed electorates for executive elections.

29. Constitution of United Cyprus Republic, Article 26 (2).
30. Annan, 'Report on Good Offices in Cyprus', 1 April 2003, paragraph 84.
31. Alecos Markides, interview with author, 2 July 2004.
32. ener Levent, editor Afrika Newspaper, interview with author, 17 June 2004.
33. Didier Pfirter, interview with author, 6 October 2006.
34. Constitution of the United Cyprus Republic, Article 5 (2) (b).
35. Alecos Markides, interview with author, 2 July 2004.
36. Didier Pfirter. Television interview on Mega TV, 29 February 2004.
37. Annan, 'Report of Kofi Annan on Good Offices in Cyprus', 1 April, 2003, paragraph 86.
38. Ibid, paragraph 93.
39. Alecos Markides, interview with author, 2 July 2004.
40. UN Resolution 541 (1983) (S/RES/541 (1983)), and subsequent resolutions.
41. Fromer President Glafkos Clerides was the first Greek Cypriot politician to support a federal solution in a 1975 speech at Agro Gallery in Lefkosia. Being the first time such a solution was proposed, he received much criticism from the Greek Cypriot community.
42. Hannay, *Cyprus, the Search for a Solution,* 128.
43. Ibid., 143.
44. Ibid., 142.
45. For details of the constitutional changes made, see Kyriakides, *Cyprus,* 114-119.
46. For support see Ibid., 115.
47. Annan, 'Report on Good Offices in Cyprus', 1 April 2003, paragraphs 73-77 and 'Report of the Secretary General on his Mission of Good Offices in Cyprus', 28 May 2004.
48. Member of the UN core negotiating team, confidential interview with author.
49. Costas M. Constantinou and Yiannis Papadakis, 'The Cypriot State(s) *in situ:* Cross-ethnic Contact and the Discourse of Recognition', *Global Society,* XV, 2, 2001, 141.
50. Ian Brownlie, *Principles of Public International Law,* Oxford, 1990, 88; Thomas D. Grant, *The Recognition of States: Law and Practice in Debate and Evolution,* Westport, 1999; Colin Warbrick, 'Recognition of States', *International and Comparative Law Quarterly,* XLI, 1992, 473-482.
51. Annan, 'Report on Good Offices in Cyprus', 1 April 2003, paragraphs 74 and 75.
52. Ibid., paragraph 76.
53. Ibid.
54. Ibid.
55. Constitution of United Cyprus Republic, Article 22 (3).
56. Annan, 'Report of the Secretary-General on his Mission of Good Offices in Cyprus', 28 May 2004, paragraph 52.
57. Didier Pfirter, interview with author, 6 October 2006.
58. Excluding articles 1 & 2 (Constitution of United Cyprus Republic, Part VI, Article 37 (2)).
59. Constitution of United Cyprus Republic, Article 25 (1).
60. Ibid., Article 37 (3).

CHAPTER 3

A COMPARATIVE ANALYSIS OF THE FIVE VERSIONS OF THE ANNAN PLAN

Tim Potier

'The Comprehensive Settlement of the Cyprus Problem', or Annan Plan, had reached its fifth and final draft ('Annan V') by the time UN Secretary-General Kofi Annan presented it, at Bürgenstock, on 31 March 2004. The first version had been presented to the sides on 11 November 2002. Subsequent revisions were made on 10 December 2002 ('Annan II'), 26 February 2003 ('Annan III') and 29 March 2004 ('Annan IV'). Naturally, since April 2004, debate and scholarship has focussed on the finally submitted text (Annan V). The earlier drafts have been generally forgotten. They *must* not.

In this chapter all five versions of the Plan are reviewed. The number of changes made, over the course of the eighteen months, run into the hundreds. It would require a book to do justice to them. What, therefore, follows are the highlights, the most telling changes, divided into fourteen headings.

Troops

Annan III permitted up to 6,000 (all ranks) Greek and Turkish contingents to be stationed in the respective constituent state under the Treaty of Alliance[1]. However, crucially, and without prejudice to the Treaty and its Additional Protocols, it added that: upon accession of Turkey to the European Union, all Greek and Turkish troops shall be withdrawn from Cyprus unless otherwise agreed between Cyprus, Greece and Turkey[2].

Annan IV removed the full withdrawal, Article 3(1-3) of the Additional Protocol to the Treaty of Alliance and Article 8(1)(b)(iii) of the Main Articles providing, instead:

Article 3(1-2)

The Greek and Turkish contingents shall be permitted to be stationed under the Treaty of Alliance in the Greek Cypriot State and the Turkish Cypriot State respectively.

Without prejudice to the relevant provisions in Additional Protocol I to the Treaty of Alliance[3], the Greek and Turkish contingents shall, for a transitional period, not exceed 6,000 all ranks until 1 January 2011, and 3000 all ranks thereafter until 1 January 2018 or Turkey's accession to the European Union, whichever is sooner.

Article 8(1)(b)(iii), 'continuing':

(iii) the Greek contingent not to exceed 950 all ranks and the Turkish contingent not to exceed 650 all ranks thereafter, subject to five-yearly review with the objective of total withdrawal[4].

Article 3(3) of the Additional Protocol 'concluding':

Thereafter [following 1 January 2018 or Turkey's accession to the

European Union], Cyprus, Greece and Turkey shall review troop levels every five years[5] with the objective of total withdrawal. This will in no way undermine the provisions of the Treaty of Alliance and its Additional Protocols, and the rights and responsibilities conferred thereby.

The 'return' of the Treaty of Alliance (troop) numbers in Annan IV, only very slightly compensated by a five-yearly review (with the objective of total withdrawal), had, without question, a negative impact on the Greek Cypriot community. It may have meant that a key demand of Ankara's was realised, but it strengthened the argument of those Greek Cypriots who maintained that the Plan could not be accepted. The latter have come to associate withdrawal of Turkish troops with complete withdrawal, cancelling, therefore, the value of the 1960 constitutional arrangement. The psychological impact of the period since 1974 on the Greek Cypriots, has rendered it unlikely that any long-term and constitutionalised Turkish military presence could be accepted. If Ankara was sincere in its desire for reunification in 2004, this move (in IV) proved to be one of its major undoings. If there can be any 'silver lining' on this matter, the fact that complete withdrawal has been evidenced as possible means that there is an opportunity that it can be negotiated over next time.

International Military Operations

The placing of Cyprus' territory at the disposal of international military operations was turned 'somewhat on its head' between Annans I to III. Under Annan I, this could not be done other than with the consent of Greece and Turkey[6]. In Annan II, this was changed to (Article 6(2) of the UCR Constitution, at Part II):

(2) Cyprus shall not put its territory at the disposal of international military operations other than with the consent of Greece and Turkey or the consent of the governments of both <component states>[7].

By Annan III this was changed again to (Article 8(4), Main Articles):

(4) Cyprus shall not put its territory at the disposal of international military operations other than with the consent of both constituent states; until the accession of Turkey to the European Union, the consent of Greece and Turkey shall also be required.[8]

This gradual weakening of the long-term 'influence' of Greece and Turkey in respect of international military operations, and the parallel bolstering of the 'independence' of the constituent state governments (away from 'their' guarantor power) is significant. In II, provided the consent of both 'constituent states' had been obtained, the consent of Greece and Turkey was obviated. This was 'corrected' somewhat, in III, with the necessity of Greek and Turkish consent until Turkey's accession to the European Union.

With Cyprus a member of the European Union, it would be very unlikely that Cyprus' territory would be used for any international military operation without it forming a part of any wider *EU-led* operation. Cognisant of this, Ankara would have appreciated that it could have affected any such possibility (from another quarter) upon its accession. The more Cyprus is removed from being a potential (even EU-led) launchpad, the better. Any means of control (even and indirectly) from Ankara should be regarded positively. Inevitably, though, (as a non-headline issue) it had little impact.

Sovereign Base Areas (SBAs)

The two SBAs in Cyprus (Akrotiri and Dhekelia) were 'established' (along with the Republic of Cyprus) under Article 1 of the Treaty of Establishment. They cover 98.1 square miles of the island. Had the Plan been accepted, the British government would have relinquished 49.7 square miles from both SBAs.[9] This decision was reflected in Annan III by the insertion, in Appendix C (Appendix II), of an Additional Protocol to the Treaty of Establishment. The areas relinquished described in a Codicil to the Protocol. Under the new Article 3 of Appendix C,[10] the Protocol was to enter into force '…on the day following that on which the United Kingdom' notified '…the other parties of the completion of its constitutional requirements for…' its implementation.[11]

The Protocol would have altered (/ narrowed), on account of the international status of the SBAs, the areas between which Cyprus could not claim a territorial sea. Article 5 of the Protocol, therefore, provided (in Annan III):
Section 3 of Annex A to the Treaty of Establishment[12] shall be replaced by the following:

> Section 3 Cyprus shall not claim, as part of its territorial sea, waters lying between the lines described in the report referred to in the Additional Protocol to this Treaty.

The lines referred to in Section 3, as amended, of the Treaty of Establishment, which delimit the territorial seas between Cyprus and the Sovereign Base Areas, shall be set out in a report to be prepared by a duly qualified person to be designated by the Government of the United Kingdom. S/he shall begin the work not later than one month after the entry into force of this Protocol and complete it as soon as possible and in any event within a period of nine months. The designated person may appoint technical advisers to assist him/her. S/he shall report to the appropriate authorities of the United Kingdom and Cyprus upon completion of the work.

In Annan IV, paragraph (2) (of, by now, Article 6 of the Protocol) was amended with the report being prepared by two persons designated (this time) 'by the Governments of the United Cyprus Republic and of the United Kingdom'. The second person and the involvement of the government of the UCR was removed in Annan V. Thus, here, reverting to the position outlined in Annan III.

Compare this with the progression of Article 2 of the Codicil (in Annans III to V). In Annan III, this provided:

> The land boundaries of the Akrotiri Sovereign Base Area and of the Dhekelia Sovereign Base Area shall be marked clearly and effectively on the ground by a duly qualified person to be designated by the Government of the United Kingdom[13]. S/he shall begin the work not later than one month after the entry into force of this Protocol and complete it as soon as possible and in any event within a period of nine months. The designated per-

son may appoint technical advisers to assist him/her. S/he shall report to the relevant authorities in the United Kingdom and Cyprus upon completion of the work.

In Annan IV, the designated person 'may be accompanied by a Cypriot observer'. However, this was removed in V, Article 2 providing (instead) for the appointment of two persons (à la Annan IV, regarding the delimitation of the territorial seas) designated (again) 'by the Governments of the United Cyprus Republic and the United Kingdom'.

The British government's offer was substantial. Almost certainly, it was an attempt to 'sugar the pill' for the Greek Cypriot side who, by the publication of Annan III, had already strongly suggested a more long-term opposition to the settlement Plan. With hindsight, it was an error for it not to have been made from the outset; thus tendering an air of panic (/ desperation) about the move. London must, in this respect, learn to be more vigilant in the future. All the same, as ought to have been expected, it did not receive any thanks. Objection to the SBAs, for the overwhelming majority of (Greek /) Cypriots, is not over a 'few fields', but Britain's continued presence altogether. This will not alter. Rather and in actual fact, London would probably have achieved more by doing nothing.

Territorial Adjustment

The role of the United Nations in territorial adjustment was enhanced under Annan IV. Article 4(1) (of Annex VI[14]) of Annan I had provided, from the outset, that:

> Areas within the agreed territorial boundaries of a <component state> which are subject to territorial adjustment, while legally part of that <component state> upon entry into force of the Foundation Agreement, shall be administered during an interim period no longer than three years by the other <component state>, by which time, administration shall have been completely transferred.

By Annan IV, this territorial adjustment was to have been undertaken in six phases (the last of these after three years and six months from the entry into force of the Foundation Agreement). However, Article 3(3) of Annex VI 'added':[15]

> During the last months of phases three to six,[16] when supervision by the United Nations of the activities relating to the transfer of areas subject to territorial adjustment shall be enhanced in the relevant areas, administration shall be shared between the entrusted authorities[17] and the United Nations. The United Nations shall assume territorial responsibility for those areas, without prejudice to the administration of the daily lives of the local population by the entrusted authorities. The United Nations may issue directives to local officials, and, should it be necessary, preclude a local official from duty in the area; United Nations police shall have full powers in the area and the right to give operational instructions to local police.

Many Greek Cypriots were not convinced that Ankara would withdraw its troops or relinquish territory when the time came for it. This refrain continues to this day. The enhanced role of the UN, from IV, was an attempt to alleviate these concerns, with the introduction of a more guided adjustment. In truth, its value should have been seen from the outset, (hopefully) guaranteeing (or at the least minimising) any late obstruction or stand-off, whether orchestrated from afar or not. By the time it *was* introduced, most Greek Cypriots had (no doubt) already made up their minds (requiring little prompting from President Papadopoulos); uppermost in their minds being the 'absence' of security provided by the Plan. Such may have had a positive impact, helping to ease those basic concerns of the Greek Cypriots, if it had been included from Annan I. However, by the publication of Annan IV, too many had stopped listening. The extent of Greek Cypriot insecurity needs to be at the forefront of outside actors' minds next time.

Residence for Cypriots

Besides Cypriot citizenship, Cypriots were to hold the internal citizenship of one of the constituent states. Restrictions on residence, in a constituent state, by persons holding the other internal citizenship status were increased for an interim period / (eventually) 'lifted' thereafter between Annans I to IV. The relevant part of Article 3(2) of the Main Articles to Annan I[18] provided:

> …A <component state> may… limit the establishment of residence for persons not holding… [its internal <component state> citizenship status] Such limitations shall be permissible if the number of residents hailing from the other <component state> has reached 1 per cent of the population in the first year and 20 per cent in the twentieth year, rising by 3 per cent every three years in the intervening period. Thereafter, any limitations shall be permissible only if one third of the population hails from the other <component state>.

Article 3(4) of the Main Articles to Annan II provided:

> During the first four years after entry into force of this Agreement, a <component state> may establish a moratorium on the establishment of residence for persons not holding the internal <component state> citizenship status of the relevant <component state>. Thereafter, pursuant to Constitutional Law, a <component state> may limit the establishment of residence for persons not holding its internal <component state> citizenship status, if the number of residents hailing from the other <component state> has reached 8 per cent of the population of a village or municipality between the 5th and 9th years and 18 per cent between the 10th and 15th years. Thereafter, any limitations shall be permissible only if 28 per cent of the population of the relevant <component state> hails from the other <component state>. No later than 25 years after entry into force of this Agreement, the <common state> and the <component states> shall review the relevant Constitutional Law in light of experience.

However, by Annan III, such limitations could only subsist '[u]ntil Turkey's accession to the European Union'. This was 'adjusted' in Annan IV (in what was now Article 3(7)) to 'for a transitional period… until the 19th year or Turkey's accession to the European Union, whichever is earlier…' On the other hand, restrictions during the interim period were tightened: (i) the moratorium on the establishment of residence was increased (under Annan III) 'until the end of the sixth year', reduced (back) 'until the end of the fifth year' (in Annan IV); and, (ii) 'thereafter' reduced to 7 per cent, then 6 per cent 'between the 7th and 10th years' and 'the 6th and 9th years' (in Annans III and IV respectively), 14 per cent to 12 per cent 'between the 11th and 15th years' and 'the 10th and 14th years' (again respectively), and finally, 21 per cent to 18 per cent 'thereafter' (III and IV). From Annan III the following new final sentence was added to the paragraph:

> … After the second year, no such limitations shall apply to former inhabitants over the age of 65 accompanied by a spouse or sibling, nor to former inhabitants of specified villages.[19]

The 'lifting' of restrictions on residence for persons holding the other internal citizenship status, from Annan III, was somewhat qualified in IV with the addition of a 'new' paragraph ((2)) to new Article 2 of Appendix D. This provided:

> (2) Notwithstanding the above, either constituent state may, with a view to protecting its identity, take safeguard measures to ensure that no less than two-thirds of its Cypriot permanent residents speak its official language as their mother tongue.[20]

The federalisation of Cyprus is well-established. It has been long understood (if not, from every quarter, appreciated) that the island, upon reunification, would be 'divided' into two 'constituent states' and, therefore, for the Greek Cypriots, that certain towns and villages in the far north of the island would not come under 'Greek Cypriot' administration. Beyond the territorial adjustment (see above), this is the place of these provisions. However, it must be said that it is very doubtful that the persons coming to reside in the constituent state other than the one from which they hail would have got close to the percentages provided.

For many Greek Cypriots, even those who are not 'refugees', what matters is not any actual return, but whether they have the right to return at any time of their choosing. The placing of any restrictions on that return, therefore, was bound to provoke a reaction. In light of the realities, they could not have been more unnecessary. More to the point, the percentages are an administrative absurdity; in fact, they are rather childish. The only reasonable explanation that can be given for their inclusion must be that they were intended to kill off any prospect of significant return. Instead, all they helped to achieve was an overwhelming 'no' from the Greek Cypriots.

If the intention on the part of the international community is (truly) to reunify the island, such kind of limitations are a very grave mistake. Europe does not need a neo-apartheid state in the early 21st century which, on account of its disjunction, would eventually fail.

Reinstatement of Property

Dispossessed owners, in areas not subject to territorial adjustment, were not (necessarily) entitled to reinstatement (even) in those circumstances where they had elected not to seek compensation via the Property Board[21]. Article 10(3)(d) and (e) of the Main Articles (in Annan V) provided:

> (d) Current users, being persons who have possession of properties of dis-

possessed owners as a result of an administrative decision, may apply for and shall receive title, if they agree in exchange to renounce their title to a property, of similar value and in the other constituent state, of which they were dispossessed;

(e) Persons who own significant improvements to properties may apply for and shall receive title to such properties provided they pay for the value of the property in its original state[.]

Minus these obstacles, a dispossessed owner could seek reinstatement.

In Annan III the level of reinstatement was not personal, but subject to a limit based on total land area and the number of residences at both constituent state and municipality or village level (10 per cent and 20 per cent respectively[22])[23]. Eligible claimants would be awarded reinstatement based on priority in descending order of age, 'until the agreed levels are reached'[24]. In Annan IV reinstatement was personalised. A new definition (titled: 'Reinstatement entitlement') was added to Attachment 1 of Annex VII, providing:

> 12. *Reinstatement entitlement* – The reinstatement entitlement is one third of the land area and one third of the *current value* of the land (whichever applies) of the aggregated *affected property* of a dispossessed owner, who is not an *institution*[25].

(The philosophy of) Article 16((1-6)) of Annex VII was, thus, amended (in Annan IV), accordingly, to (additions in Annan V being underlined):

> Any *dispossessed owner* (other than an *institution*) is entitled to *reinstatement* of his/her *affected property* within the limits of his/her *reinstatement entitlement*. To this effect, s/he may elect any of his/her *affected property* which is eligible for *reinstatement*.
>
> [paragraph (3), in V]
>
> If the dispossessed owner elects to be reinstated to a dwelling which s/he has not built and in which s/he did not live for a period of at least 10 years and which has been used by the same *current user* for the last 10 years, the Property Board shall use its discretion, taking into account all relevant factors, in deciding whether to grant reinstatement. Should the Property Board not grant reinstatement of such a dwelling, the *dispossessed owner* shall choose another of his/her affected properties eligible for reinstatement. In the absence of such eligible property, the following paragraph shall apply.
>
> [paragraph (4), in V]
>
> If the *reinstatement entitlement* is larger than the area or the value of a *dispossessed owner's affected property* which is eligible for reinstatement, <u>or if the *dispossessed owner* who would be eligible for reinstatement under paragraphs 1, 2 or 3 of this Article voluntarily defers to the current user,</u> such owner may:
>
> sell his/her *reinstatement entitlement* to another dispossessed owner from the same municipality or village;
>
> exchange his/her *reinstatement entitlement* for a property in the same village or municipality of his/her choosing from among the holdings of the Property Board, or if no equivalent land is available, in a neighbouring village or municipality; or
>
> receive compensation and buy property of equivalent size and value in the same village or municipality; provided s/he was displaced after his/her 10th birthday.
>
> (4) [paragraph (2), in V]
>
> If the *reinstatement entitlement* is not sufficient to permit the dispossessed owner to be reinstated in a dwelling which s/he owned when it was built or

in which s/he lived for at least ten years, the *dispossessed owner* will be entitled to reinstatement of the dwelling and up to one *donum* of the adjacent land area of which s/he was dispossessed. If the *affected property* of a *dispossessed owner* has been distributed or sub-divided since dispossession, this special rule only applies to the aggregated *reinstatement entitlements* of all the successors in title as though a single claim was being made by the original *dispossessed owner*. <u>Should such *dispossessed owner* voluntarily defer to a current user, s/he shall be entitled to the options under paragraph 4 for the same size and value of *property* to which s/he could have been reinstated under this paragraph.</u>

(5) Agricultural land shall not be reinstated if this warrants a sub-division into plots of less than five *donums*, or less than two *donums* for irrigable land. <u>The Property Board shall regulate and decide the minimum size for reinstatement of other plots of land</u>[26].

(6) If the *reinstatement entitlement* does not allow the reinstatement of a dwelling or the minimum size of agricultural plots, the dispossessed owner may sell his/her *reinstatement entitlement* to another dispossessed owner from the same municipality or village or may elect to receive compensation for it. Purchased *reinstatement entitlements* can be aggregated with other *reinstatement entitlements* from the same municipality or village and used to obtain property in that municipality or village.

The determination of a current user should not supersede that of a dispossessed owner. Any dispossessed owner should not be frustrated reinstatement on account of any exchange by a current user or as a result of significant improvements made. The philosophy, reflected in Article 10(3) of the Main Articles, renders reinstatement (to a significant degree) into some form of lottery, and dependent on the will / earlier activity of the current user. Such provisions will not alleviate conflict, after any settlement, but only (in many instances) engender it. Thus, the opinion of the dispossessed owner should be given 'first shout'. Interestingly, the personalisation of reinstatement (of property), in IV, reflected this. It not only (beneficially) equalised the ('potential') right of reinstatement for all dispossessed owners, it also (beneficially) removed the limits of the reinstatement (by constituent state and municipality or village) in general. This was, without question, a positive development for the Greek Cypriot community. However, it needs to be rendered more complete next time.

Basic Articles

The first two Articles of the Constitution of the United Cyprus Republic are titled (Article 1) 'The United Cyprus Republic' and (Article 2) 'The Constituent States'. These 'Basic Articles', constituting Part I of the Constitution, cannot be amended. Interestingly, it was not until Annan II that such a condition was introduced.[27] By contrast, the 1960 Constitution contains 48 'Basic Articles' listed in Annex III.[28]

The 1960 (Republic of Cyprus) Constitution has many more entrenched articles. Still, it could not save the constitutional arrangement. At least, from Annan II, the Basic Articles were very limited: 'guaranteeing' (*inter alia*) the existence of a single international legal personality, two constituent states (including their equal status), the country's integrity and bizonality. These are necessary and minimum conditions. However, as the 1960 Constitution demonstrated, whilst such type of provision may help settle some hearts, nothing can be kept permanent if there is sufficient will to defeat it.

Presidential Council

The Presidential Council is the executive organ of the United Cyprus Republic. Non-voting members were introduced in Annan IV (retained in V). 'Prior to that', the Presidential Council was composed (only) of six members, at least two hailing from each constituent state[29]. In Annan IV this was adjusted to[30]:

> The Office of Head of State is vested in a Presidential Council, which shall exercise the executive power. The Council shall have six voting members. Parliament may elect additional, non-voting members. Unless it decides otherwise by special majority, it shall elect three non-voting members.
>
> All members of the Presidential Council shall be elected by Parliament for a fixed five-year term on a single list by special majority. The list shall specify the voting members…
>
> (6) The composition of the Presidential Council shall be proportional to the numbers of persons holding the internal constituent state citizenship status of each constituent state, though at least one third of voting and one third of non-voting members must hail from each constituent state…
>
> (8) Notwithstanding voting rights, the members of the Presidential Council shall be equal…[31]

The introduction of non-voting members in the Presidential Council (from IV) was impractical and advantaged neither community. It may have added one further Turkish Cypriot and further expanded the wider membership of the Presidential Council, but it did not alter the Council's basic and innate composition. The concept should, thus, be swiftly discarded next time.

Representation of Cyprus in the EU

The European Council is a twice-yearly gathering, in June and December, of the Heads of State and/or Government of the member countries of the European Union. This was broadly reflected in Annan I and II by the President of the Council representing Cyprus at meetings of heads of government[32]. However, this was 'reversed' in Annan III with the insertion of the following new paragraph:

> The member of the Presidential Council responsible for European Union affairs shall represent the Presidential Council (in its function as Head of Government) at meetings of the European Council, and shall be assisted on such occasions by the member of the Presidential Council responsible for external relations, unless the Presidential Council, deciding with separate majorities of members from each constituent state, decides otherwise[33].

In Annan IV this was corrected ('back') to:

> (4) The President of the Council, when representing Cyprus at meetings of the European Council, shall be accompanied by the Vice-President[34].

Having Cyprus represented, in III, at European Council meetings by the Ministers of European Union Affairs and External Relations is incomprehensible. Little wonder that it was swiftly discarded.

Presidency of the Federal Parliament

The federal Parliament of the United Cyprus Republic was to be made up of two chambers: the Senate and Chamber of Deputies. Each chamber of the federal parliament was to be served by a president and two vice-presidents. The presidents of the two chambers would not hail from the same constituent state. Until Annan IV, the presidents and vice-presidents would serve for a period of one year[35]. This was increased, in Annan IV, to five years (the duration of a parliament). Also in Annan IV (in the same paragraph), it was provided that 'two consecutive Presidents of either Chamber' should not come from the same constituent state[36].

The introduction of rotation (by constituent state) of the Presidents of the two chambers of the federal Parliament, in IV, was at least partly (but only partly) compensated by extending the term to a full parliament. Political equality does not have to entail literal equality on every item. However, what it does aim to secure is an equal right of participation. The 'pre-IV' position, as concerns 'consecutive Presidents', need not defeat this, but the proviso would, at least, guarantee certainty and (for the Turkish Cypriots) a sense of (constitutional) security *and* participation.

Public Service

Annan IV brought job security for ('Greek and Turkish') Cypriot public servants, by providing:

> (1) Any person holding any public office whatsoever in any authority in Cyprus immediately prior to the coming into being of the new state of affairs is a member of the public service of the United Cyprus Republic.[37]

The concerns of public servants over (possibly) losing their jobs ought to have been quelled by IV. They were not. Doubts still remained on referendum day. Indeed, they had drawn a reaction from Alvaro de Soto, the UN Secretary-General's Special Advisor on Cyprus, during a press conference held in the Ledra Palace on 20 April 2004, saying:… there are intensive discussions regarding the personnel who would be involved in the federal structure. And incidentally in that regard, I should mention in passing that we have seen very disturbing reports about something that would amount almost to scare-mongering amongst civil servants, that they would lose their jobs or their rights or their benefits or their pensions. We are very, very disturbed about that and we have raised this in the appropriate quarters.[38]

Human Rights

A Catalogue of Human Rights and Fundamental Freedoms (being an attachment to the UCR Constitution[39]), (and) consonant with the European Convention for the Protection of Human Rights and Fundamental Freedoms and its Additional Protocols, was included from Annan IV. Article 11(1) of the Constitution, in Annan V, (being adjusted to read /) providing:

> (1) In accordance with Article 4(3) of this Constitution[40], the human rights

and fundamental freedoms enshrined in the European Convention for the Protection of Human Rights and Fundamental Freedoms and its Additional Protocols which are in force for the United Cyprus Republic shall be an integral part of this Constitution (catalogue attached). The United Nations Covenant on Civil and Political Rights shall also be an integral part of this Constitution.[41]

The Catalogue was an attempt to lock-in European Convention rights. The fact that Cyprus continued to be a party to the Convention and its Protocols, under Annex V (of the Plan)[42], rendered the Catalogue completely unnecessary.

Entry into Force

Under Annans I to III, the Foundation Agreement was to enter into force '... at 00:00 hours on the day following confirmed approval by each side at separate simultaneous referenda...'[43] However, under Annans IV and V, this was moved to a (later) date following approval (by each side) at the separate simultaneous referenda '... and the signature by Greece, Turkey and the United Kingdom no later than [Y] April of the attached Treaty on matters related to the new state of affairs in Cyprus...'[44]

Consequently, in light of this adjustment, a new paragraph (2) to Article 1 of Annex IX[45] was inserted, that:

Should the Foundation Agreement not be approved at the separate simultaneous referenda, or any guarantor fail to sign the Treaty on matters related to the new state of affairs in Cyprus by [Y] April 2004, it shall be null and void, and have no legal effect.

In Annan V, '[Y] April' was changed to '29 April'.

The Foundation Agreement was to be considered an integral part of the Treaty[46]. A 'yes' vote from both communities would constitute approval. This was, at least, an improvement on the situation in August 1960 when the Cypriot people were not consulted[47]. Greece, Turkey and the United Kingdom were co-founders, by way of the Treaty of Establishment, of the Republic of Cyprus in 1960. This can explain their required additional signature. What, however, was absent (until Annan IV) was provision for the holding of a signing ceremony, where the signature of Greece, Turkey and the United Kingdom would be effected[48]. This does not mean that Annans I to III suggested that such signatures could not be secured (including at a signing ceremony) by midnight 'on the day following', only that the 'moment' of such signature was not indicated.

It is inconceivable that any one of the guarantors would fail to sign the Treaty (even by '29 April'), but any such failure was provided for.

Roma

Of course, not everything in the Plan directly affected the Greek or Turkish Cypriots. Pity the Roma. Added for the first time besides the Maronites, Latin and Armenians, as one of the minorities (of Cyprus), in Annan IV, by Annan V they were ('once more') erased from view, and, consequently, denied of existence, rights, self-government (in certain areas)[49] and representation in the federal Parliament[50].

Turkey has proved resistant to the division of Turkish nationals into various communities. It is a country proud of its multinational heritage, but anxious about the outcome of any separation into what would, in effect, be rendered minority communities. This has been evidenced by the country's failure to (sign or) ratify the Council of Europe's Framework Convention for the Protection of National Minorities[51]. Hardly surprising, therefore, that the Roma should be swiftly air-brushed out of the final draft of the Annan Plan.

Conclusion

Although it could not have been anticipated, perhaps one of the weaknesses of the Annan Plan was the fact that it had five incarnations. In this way, however fairly or accurately, each side could select those changes that suited their argument and (particularly for the 'naysayers') expand an argument around those taking a deleterious turn. Next time, it would be better if there were no 'agreement' (text) until there is agreement.

Despite attempts to portray it otherwise, there were no real winners. The Greek Cypriot community, generally, regarded the Annan Plan with hostility from the outset. The United Nations (throughout) was conscious of (and tried to address) the positions of both sides. Its mistake was, very swiftly, to assume ownership of the text and, by the end and most likely because of exhaustion, to be dismissive of considering more significant changes. The (international) timetable (and intention) was for reunification by 1 May 2004 (Cyprus' accession to the European Union) 'at all costs'. Sadly, even the most tightly-controlled plans are liable to fail.

All this being equal, the Annan Plan did not fail because of the changes (made to it) or any individual event, but because Cyprus' people were not ready and the Greek Cypriots certainly not yet ready to make the necessary compromises. Next time the latter may be, or may feel that because there may be no further next time then such compromise may be the least of all possible evils. Time will tell.

ENDNOTES

1. A 'Reference' to Article 8(1)(b) of the Main Articles provided that the number of 6,000 '…may be changed if the Additional Protocol to the Treaty of Alliance is revised by agreement between Cyprus, Greece and Turkey'. The same sub-paragraph, in Annan II, had indicated a figure of '…between 2,500 and 7,500…' to be determined '…prior to the signature of the Comprehensive Settlement…' Annan I had provided no indication, other than a 'request' that a '4-digit figure' be inserted.
2. Main Articles, Article 8(1)(b); and Appendix C, Appendix IV (Additional Protocol to the Treaty of Alliance), Article 3.
3. Paragraph (I) of the first Additional Protocol to the Treaty of Alliance provides: 'The Greek and Turkish contingents…shall comprise respectively 950 Greek officers, non-commissioned officers and men, and 650 Turkish officers, non-commissioned officers and men'. A Tripartite Headquarters is established under Article 3 of the Treaty of Alliance.
4. A 'Reference' to this sub-paragraph (and also identically to the number 6,000 in Article

8(1)(b) of Annan III) states: 'This number may be changed if the Additional Protocol to the Treaty of Alliance is revised by agreement between Cyprus, Greece and Turkey'.
5. Reduced to every three years under Annan V.
6. Main Articles, Article 8(4); Annex I (UCR Constitution), Part I, Article 6(2).
7. Article 8(4) of the Main Articles (in II) is the same as Article 6(2) (of the Constitution) except that it does not include 'of the governments'.
8. This was reflected (III) in the UCR Constitution by (an amended) Article 6(2) and a new Article 52 [titled: "International military operations"] (respectively).
9. See Maps A and B of the Appendix to the Additional Protocol to the Treaty of Establishment (Appendix C, Annex II). Under Annans III and IV, 44.4 square miles were to have been relinquished.
10. The Treaty between Cyprus, Greece, Turkey and the United Kingdom on matters related to the new state of affairs in Cyprus.
11. See also Article 9 of the Additional Protocol.
12. See further Section 3 of Annex A to the Treaty of Establishment.
13. No indication is given as to whether this is the same ('designated') person.
14. Titled: 'Territorial Arrangements'.
15. See and compare also Article 9(2) of the Main Articles in Annans III and IV.
16. Attachment 3 to Annex VI (Annan IV) states: 'Phase 3 – Handover to the Greek Cypriot State after 1 year and three months, with enhanced United Nations supervision in the last three months… Phase 4 – Handover to the Greek Cypriot State after 2 years and six months, with enhanced United Nations supervision in the last six months… Phase 5 – Handover to the Greek Cypriot State after 3 years, with enhanced United Nations supervision in the last six months… Phase 6 – Handover to the Greek Cypriot State after 3 years and six months, with enhanced United Nations supervision in the last ten months…'
17. From Annan IV, the Turkish Cypriot State. The first sentence of Article 3(1) of Annex VI providing: '(1) Administration of areas subject to territorial adjustment (other than the United Nations Buffer Zone) is entrusted by the constituent state of which they are legally part ('the entitled constituent state') to the authorities of the other constituent state ('the entrusted authorities') for specified periods from the day of entry into force of the Foundation Agreement…'.
18. In Annan I to III, see Appendix E, Article 1(b). For Annan IV, Appendix D, Article 2.
19. These are under Section 8(4)(b) of the Constitutional Law on Internal Constituent State Citizenship Status and Constituent State Residency Rights (Annex II, Attachment III): '… the Tillyria villages of Amadhies/Gunebakan, Limnitis/Yesilyirmak, Selemani/Suleymaniye, Agios Georgios/Madenlikoy, Kokkina/Erenköy, Agios Georgoudi, Agios Theodoros, Alevga, Mansoura and Selladi tou Appi, and the Masaoria [sic.] villages of Pyla/Pile, Skylloura/Yilmazkoy and Agios Vasilios/Turkeli, and the Karpas villages of Rizokarpaso/Dipkarpaz, Agialousa/Yeni Erenkoy, Agia Trias/Sipahi and Melanarga/Adacay'. A 'Clarification' to Section 8(4) (generally) states: 'Residents who fall within the description in section 8(4) [that is, including also 'former inhabitants over the age of 65'] may be counted for the purpose of calculating the number of residents not holding the internal constituent state citizenship status of a constituent state under section 8(2)'. Section 8(2) outlines the permissible limitations.
20. In Annan V, '[n]otwithstanding the above' was changed to '[t]hereafter'.
21. Established under Article 1 of Attachment 2 (titled: 'The Cyprus Property Board and Compensation Arrangements') of Annex VII.

22. In Annan II, these percentages were lower: 9 per cent and 14 per cent respectively.
23. The second sentence of Article 16(1) (at Part II) of Annex VII (in III) providing: 'to this effect, the Property Board shall first decide any claims for reinstatement of residences and thereafter, claims for land within any given municipality or village'. An 'Observation' to the word 'land' indicating: 'the land on which a residence is built shall also be counted towards the total'.
24. Ibid., Article 16(2).
25. In Attachment 1 (titled: 'Definitions') of Annex VII, '*Institutions*' are described as: 'entities other than natural persons, including privately or publicly-owned or controlled bodies, such as public or private trusts, religious institutions; military forces and companies (other than sole corporations)'.
26. An 'Observation' to the inserted sentence, in Annan V, provides: 'Buildings which have a single owner, other than corporations, the shareholders of which hold shares that related to separate and self-contained tenements used for their own purposes, shall not be subdivided for the purposes of reinstatement'.
27. In Annan II, a new paragraph ((2)) to Article 36 (titled: 'Amendments of this Constitution') was added, providing: '(2) The Basic Articles of this Constitution cannot be amended'. Under Annan I, Articles 1-8, including what were to become the 'Basic Articles', constituted Part I, titled 'General Provisions'. From Annan II, 'General Provisions' constituted Part II.
28. Article 182(1) of the 1960 Constitution states: '(1) The Articles or parts of Articles of this Constitution set out in Annex III hereto which have been incorporated from the Zurich Agreement dated 11 February, 1959, are the basic Articles of this Constitution and cannot, in any way, be amended, whether by way of variation, addition or repeal'. Of the 48 'Basic Articles', 16 cannot be amended in their entirety, parts of the remaining 32 being amendable. The 16 are Articles: 1, 5, 61, 78, 86, 108, 123, 129, 130, 131, 132, 170, 178, 181, 182 and 185. The 32 are Articles: 3, 4, 23, 36, 39, 42, 43, 44, 46, 50, 51, 52, 53, 57, 62, 65, 87, 89, 92, 112, 115, 118, 126, 133, 137, 138, 139, 153, 157, 159, 160 and 173.
29. In Annan III, Article 26(6) of the UCR Constitution (at Part V) provides: 'The composition of the Presidential Council shall be proportional to the number of persons holding the internal constituent state citizenship status of each constituent state, though at least two members must hail from each constituent state'.
30. See (and 'compare') also (in Annan IV): Main Articles, Article 5(2)(a) and (c).
31. The third and final sentence of Article 26(7) provides: '(7)… In case of absence, a voting member may delegate his/her voting right to a non-voting member'.
32. Article 28(1) of the UCR Constitution (at Part V, Annan II) establishes the President of the Presidential Council as Head of State. Paragraph (3) adds: '(3) The President of the Council shall represent Cyprus at meetings of heads of government, unless the Presidential Council, deciding with separate majorities of members from each <component state>, designates another member'.
33. Annex I, Part V, Article 29(4). Intriguingly, in Annan III, the relevant sentence of Article 5(2)(d) of the Main Articles still ('merely') provided: '(2)(d)… The President, and in his absence or temporary incapacity, the Vice-President, shall represent the Council as Head of State and Head of Government…'
34. The equivalent new sentence was added to Article 5(2)(d) of the Main Articles: '(2)(d)… The Vice-President shall accompany the President to meetings of the European Council…'
35. (Annan III) Annex I, Part V, Article 23(2).
36. Article 23(2) of Annan IV.

37. Annex I, Part VII, Article 46(1). An 'Observation' to this paragraph adds, in its second sentence: 'The phrase "authority in Cyprus" extends to any foreign posting in service of such authority'. Under the federal / constituent state arrangement, this would work as follows: '(2) Any such person whose name is not included in the list of offices and personnel of the federal government dated 16 April 2004 shall serve in the public service of the relevant constituent state. (3) Any such person whose name is included in the list of offices and personnel of the federal government dated 16 April 2004 shall serve in the public service of the federal government'.
38. Alvaro de Soto was answering a question about a letter allegedly sent by President Papadopoulos requesting certain changes to the Plan. For text of the press conference: www.un.org/Depts/dpko/missions/unficyp/stmt200404.pdf
39. Attachment 5.
40. Article 4(3) (at Part II) provides: '(3) The federal government as well as the constituent state shall respect international law, including all treaties binding upon the United Cyprus Republic, which shall prevail over any federal or constituent state legislation'.
41. At Part III.
42. Titled: 'List of International Treaties and Instruments Binding on the United Cyprus Republic'.
43. (Annan III) Main Articles, Article 13(1). The implication is that the Treaty between Cyprus, Greece, Turkey and the United Kingdom would have been signed into force just prior to '00:00 hours'.
44. (Annan IV) Annex IX, Article 1(1).
45. Annex IX is titled: 'Coming into Being of the New State of Affairs'.
46. Appendix C, Article 1 provides (in IV and V): 'The annexed Foundation Agreement is herewith approved and agreed and shall be considered an integral part of this Treaty'.
47. The following documents (other than the fourteen Exchanges of Notes) were signed by Archbishop Makarios and Dr Fazil Küçük on 15-16 August 1960: (by order of signature) (i) Greek and Turkish texts of the Constitution of the Republic of Cyprus; (ii) Treaty concerning the Establishment of the Republic of Cyprus; (iii) Treaty of Guarantee; (iv) Treaty of Alliance; and (v) Agreement for the Application of the Treaty of Alliance.
48. A new second paragraph to Article 1(1) of Annex IX was inserted in Annan IV, providing: 'and the signature by Greece, Turkey and the United Kingdom no later than [Y] April of the attached Treaty on matters related to the new state of affairs in Cyprus at a signing ceremony in the presence of the Secretary-General of the United Nations (or his representative)'.
49. Article 11(4) (of Annan IV), at Part III, provided: '(4) The rights of religious and other minorities, namely the Maronite, the Latin, the Armenian and the Roma, shall be safeguarded. The federal government and the constituent states shall, within their respective spheres of competence, afford minorities the status and rights foreseen in the European Framework Convention for the Protection of National Minorities, in particular the right to administer their own cultural, religious and educational affairs and to be represented in the legislature'.
50. Article 22(5) (of Annan IV), at Part V, provided: '(5) The Maronite, Latin, Armenian and Roma minorities shall each be represented by no less than one deputy. Members of such minorities shall be entitled to vote for the election of such deputies irrespective of their internal constituent state citizenship status. Such deputies shall be counted against the quota of the constituent state where the majority of the members of the respective minority reside'. Article 4(3) of the Main Articles (in IV) refers to: '… as well as representation in federal Parliament and constituent state legislatures'.
51. See www.coe.int/T/E/Human_Rights/Minorities

CHAPTER 4

THE INTERNATIONAL RELATIONS ASPECT OF THE ANNAN PLAN

Costa Carras

Conflicting Premises

To evaluate the international relations aspect of the Annan Plan the opposing sets of assumptions held by leading actors, all dating to before the Plan itself, must be appreciated. A senior UN diplomat revealed one to me when criticizing as irresponsible the actions of former President George Vassiliou and then President Glafcos Clerides in not preparing Greek Cypriots to accept their defeat. I suggested that defeat was not inevitable: less than a decade earlier no-one would have predicted a genuinely independent Ukraine. His response was that what had happened in the Ukraine would never happen here. The international community had indeed an interest in the preservation of international legality, but apart from this it would be a matter of the vanquished accepting harsh realities.

Glafcos Clerides describes the phenomenon from a different angle. The Greek junta's coup and the Turkish invasion had shocked the world. General Assembly and UN Security Council Resolutions followed in 1974 demanding the withdrawal of military forces and in 1983 condemning UDI. The major international powers were never however prepared to add legal sanction to the moral force of these Resolutions by making them subject to Chapter VII of the UN Charter. Thus the call for a negotiated solution on an equal basis between Greek-Cypriots and Turkish-Cypriots, a uniform element in all relevant Resolutions, was in practice a call for the Greek-Cypriots to negotiate with an occupying Turkish army no permanent Security Council member was seriously prepared to shift.[1]

This 'realist' approach to the Cyprus problem, held both by most international actors and by prominent Greek and Greek Cypriot leaders, although dominant, was not consummated in an agreement.

Furthermore the process from which the Annan Plan later emerged originated not from realism but from creative thinking by pro-Europeans. They, together with such Americans and Britons as honour the tradition of effective moral action in politics, were the audience to which the initiative that began the process was addressed.

The Process Before the Plan

Alvaro de Soto became Kofi Annan's Special Advisor on the Cyprus issue on 1 November 1999 and the late Thomas Weston became the US Special Coordinator at about the same time. The process had however begun much earlier.

Previous UN efforts had culminated in the then UN Secretary-General Butros Ghali's 'Set of Ideas' in August 1992. Although President Vassiliou was welcoming, Glafkos Clerides narrowly won the February 1993 Presidential election after campaigning against some of the provisions. Rauf Denktash, then still very popular among Turkish Cypriots, was straightforwardly negative. Security Council Resolution 774 (26 August 1992) endorsed the Set of Ideas, while Resolution 789 (24 November 1992) under point six called upon Turkish Cypriots:

> to adopt positions that are consistent with the Set of Ideas on those issues identified by the Secretary-General in his report, and for all concerned to be prepared in the next round of talks to make decisions that will bring about a speedy agreement.

The Turkish-Cypriot positions were not consistent with the Set of Ideas on the concept of the federation, displaced persons and territorial adjustments.

Effectively however SC Resolution 789 refocused UN efforts from the Set of Ideas to Confidence Building Measures, themselves ultimately fated to fail. For a long period thereafter substantive efforts to secure a Cyprus settlement ceased. On the one hand, Denktash was unwilling to negotiate within the Secretary-General's parameters. On the other, Resolution 789, which pointed this out, was as ineffective as previous Resolutions since the US and UK, despite the latter being a guarantor power, proved unwilling to make use of Chapter VII provisions against Turkey's military occupation.

The 'Set of Ideas' however established the principle that any settlement would need to be approved in popular referendums. This was a recognition of democracy's triumphs in the early 1990s and an acknowledgement of a historical error. The 1960 constitutional settlement had been imposed by Ankara, Athens and London on the Greek-Cypriots to their evident discontent. It was hard, in the framework of Western democratic principle, to accuse a whole community of lack of respect for the complex constitution that broke down in 1963-64 when they had never been requested to ratify it in the first place. This time around, there should be no question that Greek Cypriots and Turkish Cypriots had freely accepted newly negotiated constitutional arrangements.

During the Greek EU Presidency in 1989 Theodore Pangalos, then Alternate Minister for Foreign (European) Affairs, had suggested Cyprus apply for EU membership. President Vassiliou did so in July, 1990. In June 1993 the European Commission gave a favourable opinion, accepted by the Council of Ministers in October. This application caused waves during the Set of Ideas negotiations. SC Resolution 750/1992 specifically endorsed paragraphs 17-25 and 27 of the Secretary-General's April 1992 Report on his Good Offices mission 'as an appropriate basis for reaching an overall framework agreement', thus excluding paragraph 26 which had recommended membership in the European Communities should 'be submitted for the approval of the two communities in separate referendums'. Even at this early stage therefore Cyprus' EU prospects were not envisaged as subject to a settlement.

The crucial initiative came from Athens after Yiannos Kranidiotis became Secretary-General at the Ministry of Foreign Affairs in late 1993. For some years Greek politicians had become increasingly weary of other Europeans hiding behind

Athens to conceal their own distaste for Ankara. Yiannos Kranidiotis elaborated an indirect bargain. He succeeded in obtaining the support first of Richard Holbrooke, then Assistant Secretary at the State Department, and through him of Alain Juppe, then Foreign Minister of France, holder of the EU Presidency in early 1995, for Cyprus to obtain a firm date for opening EU accession negotiations and for Turkey to obtain a Customs Union with the EU.

With the support of EU Commissioner, Hans van der Broek, these proposals were separately adopted by the EU Council of Ministers in March 1995, unquestionably the most important development between the Set of Ideas and the agreement on Cyprus' EU Accession in December 2002. Ankara now knew that Nicosia was ahead of it on the road to Brussels. It might therefore have seemed logical to negotiate, but the then Turkish Prime Minister, Tansu Ciller, responded instead by threatening to annex Northern Cyprus, thus illustrating the exact degree of the 'TRNC's' 'independence'. London moved with resolute speed, appointing David Hannay in May 1996 as Britain's Special Representative on the Cyprus issue.

Yiannos Kranidiotis' initiative already postulated that a long road towards the EU should be opened for Ankara in the hope Turkish society would evolve favourably and ultimately end the occupation of Cyprus. The EU context, fully upholding human liberties and rights, would permit important Greek Cypriot concessions on the structure of governance – very few then imagined the EU would jettison fundamental principles at London and Washington's behest. The crucial point however is that it was a fervent believer in European unity and not one of the realists, masters of the subsequent negotiations, who initiated the process.

Richard Holbrooke played a crucial role in 1995, but, after his appointment as Presidential Special Representative in June 1997, found himself trapped by contradictory premises. On the one hand was the conviction, held by every US administration in memory, that Turkey was a strategically important partner, an ally of Israel and a secular Muslim state of great economic potential whose future ideological direction was sufficiently uncertain as to require pressure on European Union countries to incorporate it. On the other was the sympathy felt for those who had lost lives, homes and livelihoods in the aggressions of 1974. By May 1998 Holbrooke had concluded that Denktash was setting as preconditions for negotiating the substance of the result he was seeking. And, very logically given the premises under which he operated, he effectively withdrew from the process, confining himself to strong support for Ankara's EU candidacy.

Holbrooke was notably creative in taking Track 2 diplomacy seriously. Occasional meetings of Greek and Turkish businessmen had begun in 1984. He organized four meetings of Greek, Turkish, Greek Cypriot and Turkish Cypriot businessmen, which produced useful ideas and challenged ingrained approaches. In 1997 not only was it almost impossible to cross the Green Line but, incredibly today, even to telephone from one side to the other! Dinos Lordos, a Greek Cypriot active in the cause of rapprochement, proposed and Holbrooke shamefaced Denktash into accepting such a seemingly simple measure. Track 2 diplomacy also mobilized bodies of opinion favourable to a negotiated solution.

Kofi Annan became UN Secretary-General at the beginning of 1997 but the green light given by Tansu Ciller, now Foreign Minister, for a UN initiative turned to red in just two meetings, at Troutbeck and Glion in July and August 1997. At these Denktash insisted on the freezing of Cyprus' EU application. Instead, Cyprus' EU application remained on course while negotiations for a settlement were frozen: the opening of EU accession negotiations was approved in Luxemburg in December 1997 and they commenced in March 1998.

Hannay distinguished himself in 1998, during the British Presidency, in prevailing on President Clerides to offer the Turkish Cypriots participation on Cyprus' EU negotiating team. The EU considered this reasonable. Denktash's rejection meant George Vassiliou was left to negotiate alone on Cyprus' behalf. He did an outstanding job.

The Luxemburg Meeting acknowledged Turkey's eligibility for accession in principle but did not accept its formal candidature. This led to fierce reactions in Turkey and a crackdown on intercommunal meetings in Cyprus. In 1999 events moved in favour of Ankara's application. In February, the capture of Abdullah Ocalan brought Greece and Turkey to the brink of war and George Papandreou to the Foreign Ministry. The air bombardment of Serbia in March, publicly if speciously justified in part both by President Clinton and Prime Minister Blair, on the grounds Greece and Turkey might otherwise become involved, alerted officials to the ease with which their public hostility could be exploited. Hence the first exchange of letters between George Papandreou and Ismail Cem that summer. In August a disastrous earthquake hit Turkey and in September a strong one Athens, creating a reciprocal outpouring of human sympathy. The Greek government could now take Yiannos Kranidiotis' 1994 initiative to its logical conclusion. At Helsinki in December 1999 the EU Council decided to consider favourably Turkey's application for membership once the country conformed with the Copenhagen criteria.

Earlier in 1999, Tom Miller, Richard Holbrooke's assistant, proposed using the G8, theoretically not a legal institution, to redefine the parameters of Cyprus negotiations. It was an intelligent move: neither Greece nor Cyprus could influence discussion at a forum where they were unrepresented and, the parameters once redefined, the UN SC endorsed the decision (Resolution 1250/1999). This requested Annan to call together Greek Cypriots and Turkish Cypriots, on the basis of four principles:

No preconditions.
All issues on the table.
Commitment in good faith to continue to negotiate until a settlement is reached.
Full consideration of relevant UN resolutions and treaties.

Here indeed was a triumph for realism. Good faith commitment to negotiate until a settlement would be a condition as little binding on Rauf Denktash and Ankara as any previous UN Resolutions.

This Resolution represented a setback for the Greek Cypriots, as settlement talks could be spun out long beyond the time required for Cyprus' EU accession nego-

tiations. At Helsinki, influenced by the British Foreign Secretary, Robin Cook, personally sympathetic to Cyprus, the EU gave them the following qualified comfort:
> The European Council underlines that a political settlement will facilitate the accession of Cyprus to the EU. If no settlement has been reached by the completion of the accession negotiations, the Council's decision on accession will be made without the above being a precondition. In this the Council will take account of all relevant factors.[2]

The British and Americans could legitimately feel proud of their work. The Greek Cypriots knew they had always to appear the reasonable party. The Turks knew there was no longer time without limit. But what if keeping the status quo in Cyprus was thought more important? Only the US could move them, which was precisely what in the past it had never seriously attempted to do.

A Plan in Seven Acts

Two strands ran consistently through the drama. One was the close collaboration between the US and UK, whom the UN treated as exclusive partners. The other was the UN's insistence on secrecy which, if often disregarded, gave leaders the opportunity to make concessions without public opinion becoming immediately aware of them.

The first act featured the four rounds of proximity talks in 2000. Glafkos Clerides showed himself amenable to negotiation: Rauf Denktash did not. In July the UN set out its 'Preliminary Thoughts'. In September Alvaro de Soto prepared for Kofi Annan a text which caused turmoil among Greek Cypriots though it went no further than speaking of a 'new partnership' and each party representing only its own side as the political equal of the other, language consistent with earlier agreed statements. In November a statement by Kofi Annan indicated Alvaro de Soto would be working towards a single text as the basis for negotiations, a procedural point of fundamental importance since it meant the UN was now grasping pen and paper from the hands of the two parties. Whether for this reason or because the US election results in November encouraged Ankara to test the new Administration, a meeting between Rauf Denktash and the Turkish President, Prime Minister and Chief of Staff led to breakdown.

The second act, from November 2000 to November 2001, at first appears more like a premature interval. In this period Cyprus' accession negotiations advanced as rapidly as the economy in Turkey and that area of Cyprus it controlled deteriorated. David Hannay [pp.149-151] indicates it was now too, interestingly without any reference to the parties, that the UN team decided most of the elements of the future Plan. These included the Swiss conciliar model of government, a deadlock-breaking Supreme Court with a controlling vote for three foreign judges and the idea of a politically but not legally new state, the product allegedly of a 'virgin birth'. This title was engaging but a misnomer, for its utility proved to lie rather in legalising the incestuous relationship between one of the so-called 'mother countries' and its illegitimate local creature and partner.

Tom Weston had by June 2001 negotiated with Ankara a scenario for reopening negotiations, only to see Rauf Denktash reject it in September. Turkish diplomacy however proved adept at tactical bluff and sudden policy reversal. In November 2001 Denktash unexpectedly wrote to Clerides proposing face-to-face meetings in Cyprus. This was agreed without reference to any of the preconditions Denktash had been demanding, although the UN presence was very briefly demoted to that of 'a fly on the wall'. This 2001 episode witnesses to what might have been if the US had, at any time since 1974, truly given priority to a just resolution of the Cyprus problem.

The third act ran from November 2001 until the presentation of the first Annan Plan in November 2002. It will provide painful material for future Greek Cypriot historians. A gap now opened between what public opinion was prepared to tolerate and what its leadership indicated as acceptable. Glafkos Clerides does not contradict David Hannay's account, which states he accepted US and UK advice to make immediate concessions on security to the Turkish military, and this not just in the form of a continuation of the Treaty of Guarantee but in the asymmetric offer of total Cypriot demilitarization, inclusive of air defences, combined with a continuing Turkish military presence which would enjoy effective air cover that an equivalent Greek detachment would lack.

This move failed tactically after Kofi Annan's visit to Cyprus in May 2002 when the two parties came close to a formal agreement on security issues, one immediately withdrawn by Denktash and Ankara. It failed strategically because the Turkish military consistently supported Denktash's hard-line stance until the 2004 Referendum. It failed diplomatically because the UN/US/UK no longer needed to meet Greek Cypriot concerns over security, the issue on which Greek Cypriots could have anticipated the most sympathy among EU member states. It failed democratically at the 2004 Referendum, when an exit poll showed three-quarters of Greek Cypriots rejected the Plan for security reasons – a finding confirmed in opinion polls thereafter. It failed morally because it surrendered the Republic of Cyprus' highest ground, the unanimous 1974 General Assembly and Security Council Resolutions which, with Turkey, the UK and US concurring:

> Calls upon all states to respect the sovereignty, independence, territorial integrity and non-alignment of the Republic of Cyprus and to refrain from all acts and interventions directed against it.

Urges the speedy withdrawal of all foreign armed forces and foreign military presence and personnel from the Republic of Cyprus and the cessation of all foreign interference in its affairs.

Granted Glafkos Clerides was the Greek Cypriots' supreme realist, even realists do not usually give up their highest moral ground save in return for the substance rather than the mirage of an agreement.[3]

An unproven hypothesis that might explain such a negotiating strategy and also Clerides' emphasis on regaining territory as opposed to maintaining human rights to settlement and property – another serious error since it facilitated EU acceptance of the pernicious precedent of permanent derogations – is that he may have received reports similar to courteous comments made to me by a senior Turkish political figure. Any agreement negotiated would remain under judgement: and if Ankara decided it was not working satisfactorily, partition would follow, whatever the texts might provide. The Greek Cypriots would however retain whatever territory had been returned up to such time. Knowing from experience that the US and UK would not then exert themselves, Clerides might well have been negotiating for the maximum territorial advantage in the minimum possible time, together with immediate EU membership to ensure even a partitioned Cyprus had a home, if or when the worst came to the worst.

However this may be, in the words of 'The Threepenny Opera': 'The answer to a kick in the pants is just another kick in the pants' and this was what the Greek Cypriots were now to endure, their strongest cards having been given up in their name but without their acquiecence, until, in April 2004, they finally kicked back. The next example was the meeting between Kofi Annan and the two leaders on 6 September in Paris, by which time it was clear he would submit his plan after Turkish elections that already looked certain to bring to power a government more amenable than that of Ecevit. In Paris there was probably discussion of the 'virgin birth' concept, since in a corrective letter dated 21 October Clerides accepted he had agreed the word 'sovereignty' should not be used, although it featured in UN Resolutions. He wrote however that the 'Swiss model', in lieu of a President and Vice President elected by cross-voting, had not been accepted by him, a point on which he was simply ignored. David Hannay [p.177] indicates that by this time an informal group was already working on 'the international obligations the new Cyprus would assume from those entered into by the Republic of Cyprus and the 'TRNC', which, if so, would be equivalent to recognizing not just internal legislation but agreements with Turkey entered into by an entity hitherto adjudged illegal internationally.[4]

The October meeting in New York verged on farce. Rauf Denktash agreed to all three working groups the UN demanded, then cancelled his agreement to one of them, and finally, having withdrawn to hospital, insouciantly failed to appoint representatives to the other two for a further two months. Thus the UN began to negotiate with Ankara direct. The talks between Alvaro de Soto and Ugur Ziyal, the undersecretary at the foreign ministry considered close to the military, went well. In some instances, as with the Swiss model, Ankara simply got what it – and the UN – wanted. In others, as with property, Hannay honestly notes [p.180]: 'they continued strongly to prefer a scheme based on compensation alone but seemed to understand that the complexities of the UN ideas were designed to come up with a result that was not too different from that in practice.'

The UN had thus every reason, at the opening of the fourth act, when the Annan Plan was submitted on 11 November, to anticipate success. The same impression prevailed in Washington and in European capitals. The Turkish Chief of General Staff was giving the US reassurance, while a new Turkish government rewrote Ecevit's principle to read 'no solution in Cyprus is no solution'. Instead the West was to learn a lesson on the tenacious power of the 'deep state'. The UN had sought to appease Rauf Denktash, even at serious risk to the Plan's viability, by providing that for a full three years Clerides and Denktash would act as co-Presidents. Nevertheless he first delayed his reply to Annan, and then in a virtuoso display obtained the support of President Sezer and the military, reversed all favourable signals and sent his 'foreign minister' to Copenhagen in December, for the sole purpose of saying 'no'. The rejection was of Annan's second plan, a mildly revised version of the first, whose amendments clearly favoured Ankara, except for a map that would have created a Greek Cypriot canton in the Karpas.

Copenhagen represented a summit of achievement for both the two old colleagues and opponents, the absent Denktash for his mastery of Ankara politics and Clerides for the EU agreement to Cyprus' accession. A decision concerning Ankara was put off until December 2004.

The fifth act saw dramatic changes. Turkish Cypriot public opinion was now demonstrably moving against Denktash, Greek Cypriot opinion, with Presidential elections due in February 2003, against Clerides. No-one reading the above account, even though far less was known at the time, can doubt the reasons.

The new Turkish government, with Abdullah Gul as temporary Prime Minister, appreciated the extent of popular Turkish Cypriot support, but also realized that to obtain Rauf Denktash's agreement there had to be a substantive change of opinion in certain circles in Turkey. As a senior Turkish political figure stated, they intimated their requirements to the UN and these were duly accommodated. Where Karpas was concerned, the US and UK had anyway never much liked the UN's suggestion [Hannay, p.192]. They knew the Turkish army, who consistently preferred boundaries running in straight lines, would object. A Greek Cypriot canton in the Karpas would make a future partition more troublesome. Inevitably the UN backed down.

Thus just as the Greek Cypriots were exchanging a President who was, not only physically, all curves, for a President who was, not only physically, all edges, the US and UK were moving the UN further in the direction of satisfying Ankara. By February 2003 they were on the brink of invading Iraq. Cyprus as an autonomous problem could not but move lower on their agenda.[5] The time limits were asphyxiatingly short. Tassos Papadopoulos was elected on 16 and installed on 28 February. Annan had already submitted his third plan on 26 February and called for a meeting at The Hague on 10 March, where the two leaders would commit themselves to holding the separate Referendums. Rauf Denktash prepared himself as usual by a visit to Ankara where he enjoyed a final triumph with President Sezer and Tayyip Erdogan, now Prime Minister. At The Hague Tassos Papadopoulos stated he did not think the plan was yet ready for a Referendum but that if Rauf Dentash did not reopen negotiations he would not either. Rauf Denktash however retained both his fundamental objections and Ankara's support. For him a final rejection was no tragedy either for the Turkish Cypriots or for Turkey. He thus secured for the Republic of Cyprus, which he had fought so tenaciously, its greatest ever victory, signature of the EU Treaty of Accession on 16 April 2003. The sixth act had by that time already begun with the Secretary-General's Report to the Security Council – on 1 April! – blaming Denktash but carefully avoiding blame of

Ankara, with whom Denktash had consistently acted. The Secretary-General was only prepared to reopen his initiative if the two leaders committed themselves to finalize the plan with UN assistance.

This became possible because of three developments on the Turkish side, assisted by a serious tactical error of the Greek Cypriots. The first was the sudden opening of the Green Line on 23 April. Then on 14 December 2003, the Turkish Cypriot opposition won the narrowest of victories in assembly elections. Almost immediately Tassos Papadopoulos, following a visit by Tom Weston and supported by the Greek Cypriot National Council, wrote to the Secretary-General asking him to reopen negotiations. Given Tassos Papadopoulos' conviction that the Plan required significant changes, this was a clear mistake, one compounded when in January 2004 Erdogan told first the Secretary-General and then President Bush that Ankara was now ready to move. The result was a meeting in New York at which Rauf Denktash, no longer master in his camp, and Tassos Papadopoulos, never fully master in his, were pressured into accepting what in effect turned a mission of 'Good Offices' into UN mediation.

The only issue that remained was how the UN would use its mandate. The reply of a senior UN diplomat in New York in March was as honest as it was painful. The US now dominated the world and the UN with it, the cost of the UN Secretary-General opposing the US was colossal, as had already been proven over Iraq. On Cyprus, the UN would do whatever the US recommended. To my observation this ensured a Greek Cypriot rejection of the Plan, he responded that Turkey would then obtain full EU candidate status in December.

This conversation puts the Burgenstock meeting at the end of March in perspective. Ziyal presented his famous letter with its eleven points, the Fifth Plan incorporated them and Ankara accurately spoke of a signal victory.[6]

The seventh act was high drama. The implications of popular sovereignty now reasserted themselves with a vengeance. As ordinary Greek Cypriots, not least in AKEL, made their anger plain, it became evident that either the Referendum had to be postponed from 24 April until after Cyprus' EU accession on 1 May – which would allegedly, in the revealing words of a senior UN diplomat, 'give the Greek Cypriots an unfair advantage' – or the Plan would fail. Briefly there appeared to be a third alternative: a Security Council Resolution that would give Greek Cypriots reassurance on the issue of security. Here however the UK and US were nothing if not consistent, accepting application of Chapter VII only regarding trade in arms, the sole security issue that concerned Ankara as much as Greek Cypriots! In the Security Council, Russia, purposefully and at Burgenstock insultingly excluded from the process, when the US had taken full part by gift of the UK as guarantor, exercised its veto. The last attempt to persuade, or delude, Greek Cypriots as to their future security thus failed. They sent the Annan Plan down to resounding defeat.

Thus it was in the conceptual world of international relations the process was initiated, through skill in the handling of international relations it came close to success, and from a consistent inconsistency in international relations by which

Washington and London used the UN increasingly to tilt a settlement towards Ankara, that the Plan ultimately failed.

The Plan as Part of a Productive Process

The usual judgement on the Plan as a fine document but a failed process, needs to be challenged. I contend it was part of a productive process that improved the situation in and around Cyprus for all parties, while as a document it was profoundly flawed.

The Republic of Cyprus, a state that has survived the initial distaste of both its communities, aggressions by its two so-called 'motherlands' and step-motherly negligence by its former colonial master, became a full EU member and is now on the point of entering the eurozone itself. The Turkish Cypriots have obtained individual citizenship of the EU, a generous EU financial package, rapid economic development, and improved access to health care. Whereas in 1994 it was nearly impossible for Greek Cypriots and Turkish Cypriots to meet or even to speak on the telephone on the island, communication between them is now open, a fundamental prerequisite for work towards a genuinely federal policy.

Greece and Turkey have also both gained in a rapid growth of cultural and economic collaboration. Greece has enjoyed her only major foreign policy success since it joined in 1981. Turkey succeeded in joining the Customs Union and then becoming an EU candidate country, responding to both challenges with notable success. The economic and political convergence with the EU, particularly since 2002, has been remarkable. That there is, politically at least, a long way still to go, only indicates how wide the gap had been over the previous decades.

Turkey has also gained valuable time. True, the longer Ankara exploits its support for the Annan Plan to avoid substantive progress over Cyprus, the worse for Turkey's EU negotiations. On balance however time is a benefit. As a candidate country it is easier to strengthen democracy, liberties and the rule of law. Similarly, time is required to reach a Cyprus settlement. This would promote the Turkish people's best interests, making Turkish an official EU language, bringing Turkish Cypriots into EU institutions and, via offices in Cyprus, Turkish businesses into the process of EU economic decision-making. There would be a cost, that of confining herself to an equitable and secure settlement for Turkish Cypriots, but a European security formula for Cyprus could bring Turkey even closer to the EU.

The US and Britain have influenced the EU's development through the acceptance of Turkey's candidacy. Russia has gained, reestablishing itself as a power not to be offended and well able to make use of international law. The EU preserved its basic principles intact, and can now consider Turkish accession not as an issue of strategy but of identity – since a developing, though never complete, identity of its member states, rather than federation or merely a common market, is what the EU is about.

The UN has retained both its influence and integrity. It now commissions opinion polls in Cyprus. That of 2007 demonstrated both Greek Cypriots and Turkish Cypriots, though doubting the UN's impartiality, see it as an essential element in the search for a Cyprus settlement. The Third High-Level Agreement, between Tassos Papadopoulos and Mehmet Ali Talat, of 8 July 2006 was achieved under UN auspices. If it moves forward at a snail's pace this is not the UN's fault. For the process, however positive, has not altered three parameters of the Cyprus problem: US and UK unwillingness to effectively apply international law to this particular example of foreign military occupation, Turkish military control of the Turkish Cypriots and the now open crisis between the political and military leaderships in Ankara.[7]

The Plan and International Relations Principles

By contrast, the Annan Plan provisions related to international relations should be recognised as a failure, one largely responsible for the despondency and uncertainty in and around Cyprus today.

The 1977 and 1979 High Level Agreements created the basis for a new partnership between Greek Cypriots and Turkish Cypriots, a single and sovereign state, federal, bicommunal and bizonal, both partition and unification with another state being excluded. This entailed Turkish Cypriots, not Turkey, controlling the Turkish Cypriot region. It did not entail a diminution of the human rights of Greek Cypriots in residing or owning property there, in accordance with the UN General Assembly and Security Council Resolutions of 1974 'that all refugees should return to their homes in safety', which, like all relevant UN Resolutions, was incorporated in the High Level Agreements.

Instead, the Plan would effectively have cancelled the UN Charter's fundamental injunction against aggression, establishing the precedent that occupation by an outside military power against the will of the large majority of a victim country's population could ultimately prevail through a 'rechristening' of the occupation as a guarantor or security force. It would have cancelled by agreement of the victim the fundamental UN Security Council Resolution on Cyprus, of 1974, demanding 'speedy withdrawal of all foreign armed forces'. It would have abused the term 'demilitarization' to mean 'disarmament of Cypriots', with two outside states in military control.

Cyprus' sovereignty would have been dramatically diminished by a statutory inability to defend itself even by means of an international (EU or NATO) security force, while the Guarantor Powers' right to intervene would have been extended from the common to the constituent states. This revised Treaty of Guarantee however effectively operated to the exclusive benefit of Turkey since only Turkish forces would enjoy air cover. One UN diplomat told me an international force, although obviously the correct solution, found 'absolutely no enthusiasm among permanent Security Council members'. The question that needed to be asked however was: Did not such proposals amount to a UN member becoming the protectorate of another state? And, given the evident diminution in their already low level of security, why should the Greek Cypriots accept them?

The Plan would have effectively legitimated demographic change under foreign occupation in contempt of the Fourth Geneva Convention. Furthermore it failed to engage with the demographic elements specific to Cyprus, namely the arguments for preserving traditional population ratios and for differentiating between adult settlers and those of their children both born and permanently resident in Cyprus. In short it neither enforced existing law nor innovated in a creative search for justice.

The Plan would have created the disastrous precedent that a victim country may be forced to assume the burden of compensating its citizens for damages repeatedly established by the European Court of Human Rights as the responsibility of an occupying power.

The Plan proposed permanent derogations from the fundamental EU principles of freedom of residence and property ownership. Greek Cypriots never denied the legitimacy of expropriation for a genuine public interest and the majority would probably accept the maintenance of Turkish Cypriot displaced persons in their new homes as such an interest. They rightly contested the preference given to a British or Israeli purchaser or a Turkish settler over the legitimate Greek Cypriot owner as representing any such public interest of Cyprus.

The Plan adopted elements of foreign constitutions for Cyprus without considering that the Belgian model is under increasing strain, while the Swiss system that works superbly with 26 cantons is not easily adjustable to only two. 'Friends of Cyprus' had over 25 years of discussions with Greek Cypriots and Turkish Cypriots. It developed the concept of cross-voting as a means both to develop a commonality of interest and to permit indisputable Turkish Cypriot control of their region without depriving Greek Cypriots of the right of residence there. This was consistently adopted by the Greek Cypriot leadership, vetoed by Rauf Denktash and finally described as a 'red herring' by a senior international diplomat. Yet if a constitution failed, foreign diplomats and journalists would not blame those who prepared the plan but the locals, despite timely warnings the proposals were inoperable without innovations aimed at developing a commonality of interest. International civil servants who ignore contributions from civil society and those who must live with their conclusions should reflect that a little humility is profitable for those who genuinely seek peace.

Finally the Plan, though declaring partition impermissible, prepared the ground for precisely such a result. The Turkish military would have remained in place in reduced but adequate numbers. It can be assumed that those prepared to intervene unconstitutionally in their own country, as in 2007, would have no scruples about doing so against a government to which they owed no loyalty and in a country they had occupied for 30 years. In any such crisis there would have been no greater obligation on the international community to intervene than in 1974. Washington and London would most likely yet again push the weak to make concessions to the strong. Only this time the legality of partition would be bolstered by the recognition in the Plan of agreements made by the 'TRNC' with Turkey before the settlement.

When Tassos Papadopoulos declared in his broadcast address calling for a 'no' vote on 7 April 2004 that the Plan would effectively dismantle the state, he was speaking the unvarnished truth. It is my belief that in the long run the "unknown Greek Cypriot voter" will be seen to have earned the respect, indeed the gratitude, of the international community. With their vote in 2004, the Greek Cypriots stood up for the principles of justice and international law, thus again opening the way to a genuine and lasting peace for Cyprus.

ENDNOTES

1. Apart from personal recollections, I have used five accounts by major participants in the ongoing process: Glafkos Clerides, *Documents of an Era* (Ντοκουμέντα μιας Εποχής), Lefkosia, 2007; David Hannay, *Cyprus: The Search for a Solution,* London, 2005; Claire Palley, *An International Relations Debacle: the UN Secretary-General's Mission of Good Offices in Cyprus 1999-2004,* Oxford, 2005; Didier Pfirter, 'Cyprus: A UN Peace Effort under Conditions of EHCR Applicability', Liber Amicorum Luzius Wildhaber, *Human Rights, Democracy & The Rule of Law,* 2007, 595 and George Vassiliou, 'Britain and the EU Accession of Cyprus' in Hubert Faustmann and Nicos Peristanis (eds), *Britain in Cyprus: Colonialism and Post-Colonialism 1878-2006* Mannheim, 2006.
2. George Vassiliou emphasizes Robin Cook was consistently helpful. He himself mentioned this drafting contribution to Mary Southcott, the 'Friends of Cyprus' Coordinator.
3. Exit poll conducted by Athens' MEGA TV, under the supervision of psephologist Ilias Nikolakopoulos. 'Can the Cyprus Problem be Solved' by Alexandros Lordos (Cymar Market Research Ltd., Nicosia 2004), based on a survey of 1000 Greek Cypriots in September 2004, and a survey in 2005 by Cymar Market Social Research Ltd., confirm this figure.
4. 57 agreements were concluded by the 'TRNC' with Turkey, listed in Appendix V of the Annan Plan. This would have created a cogent argument for recognition of a Turkish Cypriot state as sovereign were the Annan constitution ever to have broken down.
5. At a briefing of prominent Greek Americans in Washington on 12 June 2003 Daniel Fried, then of the White House Security Council, spoke of two incentives offered to Ankara to allow the passage of US troops through Turkey to Iraq, first monetary and second a Cyprus settlement in the form of the Annan Plan. There were too many witnesses present for one to doubt the accuracy of the report.
6. That victory was certainly fortunate and perhaps necessary for the AKP government. Relevant to any such judgement is the alleged diary of Admiral Ozden Ornek, in 2004 Chief of Naval Staff, as published in 'Nokta' magazine (29 March 2007), which led to its closure. This represents the then Chief of General Staff, General Hilmi Ozkok, as unwilling to mount a coup against the AKP government in 2003-2004 in contrast to others in the high command. Cyprus provided one of their main causes of dissatisfaction.
7. The relevant UNFICYP poll was carried out in early 2007 with a sample of 1000 Greek Cypriots and Turkish Cypriots, whereas in the year preceding the Referendum the UN had turned down suggestions to carry out polling. The UN cannot have been unaware that close collaboration with the US and UK entailed a cost. Alvaro de Soto's May 2007 End of Mission Report as UN Special Coordinator for the Middle East Peace Process [p.117], is relevant to Cyprus and might have been written by Claire Palley herself.

CHAPTER 5

CONTRA: THE POLITICAL WORKABILITY OF THE ANNAN PLAN

Klearchos A. Kyriakides

Introduction

In his majestic work, *The Politics*, Aristotle suggests that the 'task' confronting all those who seek to set up a constitution within a democracy 'is not only, or even mainly, to establish it [i.e. the constitution], but rather to ensure that it is preserved intact.' By way of parenthesis, the great philosopher adds that 'Any constitution can be made to last for a day or two'. Amongst other things, this means that 'The constitution ought, if possible, to command the support of all citizens'.[1] To this end, citizens must be inculcated into the special status of the constitution. Aristotle avers that 'of all the safeguards that we hear spoken of as helping to maintain constitutional stability, the most important, but today universally neglected, is education for the way of living that belongs to the constitution in each case.' Indeed, Aristotle warns that 'It is useless to have the most beneficial laws, fully agreed upon by all who are members of the constitution, if they are not going to be trained and have their habits formed in the spirit of that constitution'.[2]

If one accepts Aristotle's philosophy, then the viability of a constitution is enhanced if it does more than merely constitute a body of principles and rules of governance. A constitution should reflect the ethos and what Aristotle referred to as the ethical standards of those for whom the constitution has been designed to protect. As such, the viability of a constitution may hinge upon whether it is regarded by the citizens as a source of inspiration and a symbol of national unity.

The foregoing principles were seemingly overlooked prior to the establishment of the Republic of Cyprus in 1960 and prior to the 'double referendum' on the proposed Comprehensive Settlement to the Cyprus Problem ('the Annan Plan') which was held on 24 April 2004. This may help explain the post-independence turmoil experienced by the Republic of Cyprus and the fate of the Annan Plan the latter of which is deemed to be 'null and void'[3] having been rejected by an overwhelming majority of Greek Cypriot voters. In the opinion of many of these voters, the Annan Plan was conceptually flawed, substantively defective and intentionally dysfunctional.

The Annan Plan ostensibly sought to promote the 'independence' of the proposed United Cyprus Republic ('UCR'); but in reality it would have curbed this independence by *inter alia* entrenching, enhancing and legitimising the controversial rights reserved by the 'guaranteeing Powers' namely Greece, Turkey and the United Kingdom ('the UK'). The Annan Plan ostensibly sought to promote 'demilitarisation'; but in reality it would have authorised each of the 'guaranteeing Powers' to maintain a permanent military presence in the UCR. The Annan Plan ostensibly sought to facilitate 'reunification'; but in reality it would have legitimised the fragmentation of a small island by establishing a nominally federal republic, the UCR, which would have been broken into two constituent states, governed by three constitutions and attached to two scaled-down UK Sovereign Base Areas ('SBAs'). The Annan Plan ostensibly sought to engender 'democracy'; but in reality it would have negated democracy by blunting the supremacy of the majority and by handing tie-breaking authority to a panel of nine unelected Supreme Court judges, including three non-Cypriots. The Annan Plan also sought to procure a 'new state of affairs'; but in reality it would have renewed the much maligned arrangements dating from the end of British colonial rule.

The Annan Plan in the Context of the Zurich-London Agreements

From the standpoint of international law, the Republic of Cyprus was formally established – while two areas of the island remained under British sovereignty – on 16 August 1960 upon the coming into force of the Treaty of Establishment, the Treaty of Guarantee and the Treaty of Alliance (jointly referred to hereafter as 'the three Treaties').[4] The three Treaties were embedded within the Annan Plan,[5] subject to variations,[6] a simple fact which, in the eyes of many Greek Cypriot voters, rendered the whole of the Annan Plan unacceptable.[7] Accordingly, an understanding of the origins and provisions of the three Treaties is necessary in order to appreciate the substance and fate of the Annan Plan.

The three Treaties sprang from the Zurich-London Agreements of February 1959. These originated with an accord, which was reached by Greek and Turkish ministers in Zurich on 11 February and thereafter approved by British ministers in London. On 17 February 1959, a conference was convened at Lancaster House in London so that Greek Cypriot and Turkish Cypriot leaders could endorse 'the foundation of the final settlement'[8]. This 'foundation' envisaged the establishment of a nominally independent Republic of Cyprus subject to various treaty rights in favour of Greece, Turkey and the UK. Archbishop Makarios initially demurred in the futile hope of extracting concessions at the conference. However, the other parties stood their ground and, eventually, on 19 February 1959, the Archbishop joined them in signing what has become known as the Zurich-London Agreements.[9]

'Actions', Aristotle points out in *Ethics*, 'are commonly regarded as involuntary when they are performed *(a)* under compulsion, [or] *(b)* as the result of ignorance.'[10] If the decision of Makarios to sign was ill-judged, it was taken under diplomatic pressure (if not under compulsion), without adequate time to digest their detailed provisions, in ignorance of their full ramifications and in the absence of any popular mandate. Consequently, the proceedings at Lancaster House provoked a widespread feeling that the people of Cyprus were hostage to external actors rather than masters of their own destiny. Even Lord Hannay of Chiswick, the *bête noire* of many Greek Cypriots due to his controversial efforts as the UK's Special Representative for Cyprus (from 1996 to 2003), acknowledges this:

> Neither the Greek nor the Turkish Cypriots much liked the situation they found themselves in following the [1960] settlement, and neither felt

any sense of ownership of or loyalty towards it. ... It was something imposed on them by Greece and Turkey and by the indifference of Britain.[11]

All of which meant that in August 1960 British colonial rule was replaced with what the last colonial governor, Sir Hugh Foot, depicted as 'Agreement rule'.[12] By virtue of the three Treaties, the political independence of the new Republic of Cyprus was curtailed to an unprecedented extent in the post-1945 history of international relations and its territorial integrity was made subject to foreign military forces from Greece, Turkey and the UK. Indeed, the sovereignty of the new Republic was prevented from extending as far as the two SBAs, over which the UK continued to assert sovereignty. Moreover, under the Treaty of Establishment, the UK reserved various rights within the decolonised areas of the island to enable British forces to use the ports, roads and airspace of the Republic and to retain forty or so sites and installations within the Republic including the summit of Mount Olympus. Perhaps most astonishing of all, the 'guaranteeing Powers' jointly reserved a right of questionable legality under international law, namely the right to 'take action' under the terms of Article IV of the Treaty of Guarantee:

> In the event of a breach of the provisions of the present Treaty, Greece, Turkey and the United Kingdom undertake to consult together with respect to the representations or measures necessary to ensure observance of those provisions.
>
> In so far as common or concerted action may not prove possible, each the three guaranteeing Powers reserves the right to take action with the sole aim of re-establishing the state of affairs created by the present Treaty.

On account of their extraordinary provisions, the three treaties – all of which, to repeat, were embedded in the Annan Plan – have been subject to intense political controversy and legal debate, particularly as regards the rights of Greece and Turkey under the Treaty of Alliance, the rights of the UK under the Treaty of Establishment and the rights of all three 'guaranteeing Powers' under the Treaty of Guarantee. Inevitably, the debate has been coloured by the events of 1974, when one 'guaranteeing Power', Turkey, invaded the Republic of Cyprus following a *coup d'état* in Nicosia which was instigated by the junta governing a second 'guaranteeing Power', Greece; meanwhile, the third 'guaranteeing Power', the UK, failed to take any effective action with a view to 're-establishing the state of affairs' created by the Treaty of Guarantee.

In the opinion of many lawyers including Criton G. Tornaritis QC, the first Attorney-General of the Republic of Cyprus:

> there is no other similar case in which the form of government and the structure of the new state were imposed in every minute detail by the respective treaties and the exercise of the state powers restricted both on the internal and the international plane in such a way that they are in fact subjected to the will of the guaranteeing Powers. ... As any other international treaty or convention, they [the Treaty of Guarantee and the Treaty of Alliance] are liable to termination in any of the ways known to

international law. Both the aforesaid Treaties offend against peremptory rules of customary international law and as far as they so offend cannot be valid and enforceable.[13]

This view is not shared by the Turkish government and numerous Turkish Cypriot lawyers.[14] The position of Ankara was summed up in a letter to the UN, dated 29 March 2001:

> It is a principle of international law that treaties can be changed only by the consent of the interested parties. In fact, respect for pledges and commitments embodied in international treaties is the foundation upon which stability in international relations is achieved. In the case of Cyprus, the 1960 Agreements gave each party certain rights and privileges in return of each of them making certain concessions from their original positions. Thus, Great Britain reserved for itself sovereign bases and relinquished sovereignty over the rest of the island as a British colony; Turkey and the Turkish Cypriots abandoned their demand for partition in consideration of Greece and the Greek Cypriot side abandoning *enosis* and affirming the rights of the Turkish Cypriots as provided in the state of affairs so created. ...[15]

It bears emphasising that the three Treaties lay at the core of the Annan Plan, subject to additional protocols, the effects of which, in relation to two of the treaties, were neatly summarised in October 2003 by the US Ambassador to Nicosia:

> The Treaties of Guarantee and Alliance will continue, not end. The scope of the Treaty of Guarantee, in fact, is enlarged to embrace the territorial integrity, security and constitutional order of the two constituent states. That is an important *enhancement*, not diminution of Turkey's guarantee. [The italics appear in the original text.] ... In addition, a UN force will remain on the island to assist the parties with implementation of the settlement and to prevent any misunderstanding or incidents in the early going. The UN mandate, however, does not in any way diminish the rights and obligations of the guarantor powers.[16]

If implemented, the Annan Plan would have produced an incongruous outcome. On the one hand, the territory of the UCR would have been 'demilitarised' by means of the prohibition of the 'supply of arms to Cyprus' and the dissolution of 'all Greek Cypriot and Turkish Cypriot forces, including reserve units'. On the other hand, in pursuance of the Treaty of Alliance, as varied, Greece and Turkey could have each maintained within the territory of the UCR an armed military contingent of 6,000 until 2011 and of 3,000 until 2018 or the accession of Turkey to the EU, whichever would have been sooner.[17] Be that as it may, Greece and Turkey would have reserved the irreversible right, under the Treaty of Alliance, to station military contingents of 950 and 650 respectively. Notwithstanding a reference in the Annan Plan to a 'three-yearly review with the objective of total withdrawal',[18] the Annan Plan was silent as to how or indeed whether a 'total withdrawal' would - or could - ever arise. This was significant bearing in mind that under the Annan Plan each of these contingents could 'be structured to include…a headquarters element, armour, reconnaissance, infantry, field engineers, artillery, signals, aviation, air defence, logistic, administrative and medical support'; each contingent could be equipped with up to 50 battle tanks (of 'up to 55 tonnes' each), up to 18 air defence missiles (with a 'short range up to 7000m') and various other types of weaponry and equipment; and each of the contingents could be based within 'no more than six delineated military facilities' to be designated by Greece and Turkey.[19] The prospect of a permanent Turkish military presence in the UCR inevitably pleased Turkey,[20] whereas it dismayed many Greek Cypriots.

Under the Annan Plan the UK could have perpetuated its long-standing presence on the island.[21] Although the Annan Plan would have obliged the UK to surrender British sovereignty over 'approximately half'[22] of the 98 square miles retained in 1960, the UK would have retained sovereignty over the remainder encompassing the Headquarters at Episkopi, the RAF base at Akrotiri, the garrison at Dhekelia and the intelligence-gathering communications centre at Ayios Nikolaos. Furthermore, the UK would have retained its extensive rights across the whole island by virtue of the Treaty of Establishment. Besides, the UK would not have been bound by the constraining provisions of the Treaty of Alliance to which the UK has never been a party. Above all, the SBAs would have secured a semblance of electoral legitimacy for the first time and the UK would have secured the exclusive right, not given under the original Treaty of Establishment, to designate a 'duly qualified person' to prepare a report in connection with the delimitation of 'the waters adjacent to the SBAs that the UCR shall not claim as part of its territorial sea'.[23]

All of which helps explain why many Greek Cypriots regarded the Annan Plan as anathema. Many believed the Annan Plan sought, by means of a 'double yes' in the referendum, to sweep away the uncertainty over the conduct of the Lancaster House Conference, to convey a semblance of retrospective electoral legitimacy upon the Zurich-London Agreements and to kill off the debate over the three Treaties, particularly in relation to Article IV of the Treaty of Guarantee. In the words of Professor Alfred de Zayas, a lawyer who is a former secretary of the United Nations Human Rights Committee:

> The Annan Plan … failed to remove the neo-colonial anachronism posed by the intervention rights of the "guarantor powers". This remains an important issue, frequently overlooked, and a situation incompatible with the right of self-determination of the people of Cyprus.[24]

Part of the explanation for the incorporation of the three Treaties into the Annan Plan may lie in an article written by David Wippman, currently Professor of Law at Cornell University, New York (who served as Director of the US National Security Council's Office of Multilateral and Humanitarian Affairs from 1998-9). According to this article, which was published in 1995 against the backdrop of a precursor to the Annan Plan, the so-called 'Set of Ideas' of the then UN Secretary-General, Mr. Boutros Boutros Ghali:

> The circumstances surrounding [the] execution of the 1960 Treaty of Guarantee illustrate the fine line between external coercion and permissible international pressure…From a purely majoritarian perspective, Cyprus did not consent to the 1960 Accords, and it should not be bound by them. But if one accepts the view that Cyprus is composed of two separate and equal political communities, then evaluating the voluntary character of its consent to the 1960 Accords becomes more complicated. … [I]f in the future the two Cypriot communities accept a constitutional framework along the lines envisioned in the 'Set of Ideas' their joint consent should be deemed the voluntary consent of the state of Cyprus. … In such divided states, the values associated with sovereignty may be better protected by striking a balance between the rights of the relevant subnational communities, even if external guarantees are required to maintain that balance, than by rigid application of state system principles premised on the notion of the state as a single political community. From this perspective, even a countermajoritarian political settlement coupled with external enforcement powers is valid and consistent with *jus cogens* norms because the joint assent of the communities that form the state constitutes the consent of the state. Such consent does, as a matter of law, and should, as a matter of policy, validate the use of force, so long as the use of force remains within the limits set by the state's consent.[25]

The demise of the Annan Plan precluded such a grave outcome. Accordingly, it remains possible that any future settlement may provide for the amendment of the three Treaties or the rescission of elements thereof, notably Article IV of the Treaty of Guarantee.

The Constitutional Framework Envisaged by the Annan Plan

The constitutional arrangements in the Annan Plan would have created other forms of external interference in addition to those laid down by the three Treaties. The Annan Plan envisaged the demise of the unitary Republic of Cyprus and the genesis of the UCR as 'an independent state in the form of an indissoluble partnership, with a [single] federal government [situated in 'Greater Nicosia'] and two equal constituent states, the Greek Cypriot State and the Turkish Cypriot State.'[26] The UCR would have been 'organized under its Constitution in accordance with the basic principles of the rule of law, democracy, representative republican government, political equality, bizonality, and the equal status of the constituent states.'[27] The UCR Constitution, 'the supreme law of the land' and 'binding on all federal authorities and the constituent states',[28] would have been complemented by the Greek Cypriot Constituent State ('GCCS') Constitution and the Turkish Cypriot Constituent State ('TCCS') Constitution.

This fragmentary state of affairs would have been in keeping with the Preamble to the proposed Main Articles of the Annan Plan under which Greek Cypriot and Turkish Cypriots would have acknowledged *inter alia* 'that our relationship is not one of majority and minority but of political equality where neither side may claim authority or jurisdiction over the other'.[29] Quite apart from legitimising the demographic consequences of the Turkish invasion, the Annan Plan would have turned democracy on its head, since Greek Cypriots constitute the substantial majority of the population.

Under the Annan Plan, the federal government of the UCR would have been empowered to 'sovereignly' exercise legislative and executive competences in relation to twelve specified matters namely a. 'external relations', b. 'relations with the European Union', c. 'Central Bank functions', d. 'federal finances', e. 'natural resources', f. 'meteorology, aviation, international navigation and the continental shelf and territorial waters of the UCR', g. 'communications', h. 'Cypriot citizenship', i. 'combating terrorism, drug trafficking, money laundering and organized crime'; j. 'pardons and amnesties (other than for crimes concerning only one constituent state)'; k. 'intellectual property and weights and measures'; and l. 'antiquities'.[30] The federal government would have been endowed with these powers so that 'Cyprus can speak and act with one voice internationally and in the European Union, fulfill its obligations as a European Union member state, [and] protect its integrity, borders, resources and ancient heritage.'[31] However, in various material respects, the Annan Plan would have tied the hands of the new federal government. For example, the Annan Plan stipulated that:

> Cyprus shall maintain special ties of friendship with Greece and Turkey, respecting the balance in Cyprus established by the Treaty of Guarantee and the Treaty of Alliance and this Agreement, and as a European Union member state shall support the accession of Turkey to the Union.[32]

By the same token, the Annan Plan also stipulated that:

> Until the accession of Turkey to the European Union, the UCR shall not put its territory at the disposal of international military operations other than with the consent of Greece and Turkey, in addition to the consent of the governments of both constituent states.[33]

Such provisions reinforced the impression that the UCR would not have been truly 'sovereign' in connection with fundamental areas such as foreign policy and defence.

As regards the powers of the two Constituent States, the Annan Plan proposed that: 'Within the limits of the [UCR] Constitution, they sovereignly exercise all powers not vested by the Constitution in the federal government, organizing themselves freely under their Constitutions.'[34] Each Constituent State would have its own distinctive separation of powers and its own approach to governance, to human rights and to other matters. It is emblematic of the dysfunctional nature of the Annan Plan that it would have injected Kemalism, the political ideology of mainland Turkey, into the education system and constitutional fabric of the TCCS. Under the proposed TCCS Constitution, an integral part of the Annan Plan, the TCCS would have been required 'to provide for the educational and training needs of the people…in accordance with the principles and reforms of Atatürk'. Besides, the President of the TCCS and the Deputies in the Assembly of the TCCS would have been obliged to swear an oath of allegiance to 'the principles of Atatürk'.³⁵ This oath would have effectively precluded anybody who frowned upon Kemalism from assuming the Presidency or from occupying a seat in the Assembly of the TCCS. It goes without saying that no corresponding oath would have been required under the GCCS Constitution.³⁶

The Annan Plan was likewise dysfunctional in relation to judicial interpretations of human rights law. On the one hand, under the proposed GCCS Constitution:
> In the interpretation of fundamental rights and liberties and their restrictions due account shall be taken to jurisprudence and other guidance from European and international human rights bodies in accordance with Article 11 of the Constitution of the United Cyprus Republic.³⁷

On the other hand, the corresponding provision in the proposed TCCS Constitution would have included exactly the same wording save for a subtle yet crucial variation: the inclusion of the word 'may' instead of the word 'shall'.³⁸ Thus, judges in the GCCS would have been placed under a constitutional obligation to take 'due account' of the jurisprudence and guidance referred to above, whereas judges in the TCCS would have had a discretion to do so. No explanation has been given as to the reasons for this difference.

Freedom of expression is a fundamental, though qualified, human right which is essential in a free and democratic society. Under the proposed TCCS Constitution:
> Books published within the boundaries of the State may be seized by an order of a judge in cases provided by law for the protection of secularism, public safety, public order and public morals, only if necessary in a democratic society.³⁹

Under this provision, books 'may be seized by an order of a [TCCS] judge' and, in view of the above, such a judge would have been under no constitutional obligation to take 'due account' of international human rights jurisprudence. By contrast, under the proposed GCCS Constitution, the seizure of newspapers or other printed matter would *not* have been allowed in the absence of a two-stage process, the second of which would have obliged a judge of the GCCS to take 'due account' of such jurisprudence.⁴⁰

Furthermore, the proposed TCCS Constitution would have expressly included provisions relating to the declaration of a state of emergency 'in the event of natural disasters, dangerous infectious diseases, serious economic crisis, and widespread acts of violence'. Such a state of emergency could apply 'in one or more areas or in the whole of the [Turkish Cypriot Constituent] State for a period not exceeding three months'. Under the proposed TCCS Constitution: 'In the case of emergency, the exercise of the basic rights and freedoms mentioned below may be suspended wholly or partially as necessary in proportion to the exigencies of the situation'. These rights would have included Articles 20 ['Rights relating to Judicial Trials'], 25 ['Freedom of Communication'], 26 ['Freedom of Movement and Residence'], 27 ['Freedom of Conscience and Religion'], 29 ['Freedom of Science and Art'], 37 ['the Right to Form Associations'], 38 ['Right to Good Administration'], 60 ['the Right to Collective Agreement and to Strike'] and 61 ['Right to social security'].⁴¹

Interestingly, the proposed GCCS Constitution contained no provisions as regards the declaration of a state of emergency or the suspension of fundamental human rights. It is beyond the scope of this chapter to consider the wider ramifications of this discrepancy. It suffices to say that, under the Annan Plan, fundamental human rights would have rested on a weaker constitutional footing in the TCCS than in the GCCS.

Decision-making

In *The Politics*, Aristotle draws attention to the importance of a separation of powers: if 'the three elements in each constitution' are 'well arranged, the constitution is bound to be well arranged'.[42] He adds that the 'most essential' function of a constitution is to provide 'a method of arriving at decisions about matters of expedience and justice as between one person or another.'[43] The Annan Plan purported to facilitate unity and decision-making by means of an unwieldy and extraordinary set of arrangements. The US Ambassador to the Republic of Cyprus summed up the philosophy underpinning these arrangements thus:

> [A]n organizing principle throughout the plan [is that] no decision can be taken by persons from one constituent state alone. ... no decision can be taken in any federal organ without substantial support from both constituent states.[44]

In relation to decision-making in the federal legislature, the Annan Plan stipulated that:

> Unless otherwise specified in the Constitution, decisions of [the federal] Parliament need the approval of both Chambers with simple majority of members present and voting, including one quarter of senators present and voting from each constituent state.[45]

By the same token, the Annan Plan provided that in the Presidential Council at the federal executive level decisions would have been taken 'by simple majority of members present and voting unless otherwise stated in this [UCR] Constitution. Such majority must in all cases comprise at least one member from each constituent state.'[46] The loaded word 'veto' may have been absent from the Annan Plan but its provisions would have ensured that, in the legislative and executive institutions, Greek Cypriots could not take a decision without Turkish Cypriot support and vice versa.

As for the provisions concerning the judiciary at the federal level, there would have been a Supreme Court containing an 'equal number of judges from each constituent state, and three non-Cypriot judges until otherwise provided by law.'[47] Under the Annan Plan 'the Supreme Court shall strive to reach its decisions by consensus and issue joint judgments' but all decisions 'may be taken by simple majority as specified by law'.[48] As regards the ambit of its powers:

> The Supreme Court shall uphold the [UCR] Constitution and ensure its full respect...The Supreme Court shall, inter alia, resolve disputes between the constituent states or between one or both of them and the federal government, and resolve on an interim basis deadlocks within federal institu-

tions if this is indispensable to the proper functioning of the federal government. ...[The Supreme Court shall have] exclusive jurisdiction to determine the validity of any federal or constituent law under this Constitution or any question that may arise from the precedence of Constitutional laws.[49]

Accordingly, the Supreme Court would have been endowed with extraordinary tie-breaking powers. Thus, in contrast to, say, the Appellate Committee of the House of Lords (in England and Wales) but in common with, say, the Supreme Court of the United States, the Supreme Court of the UCR would have had the power to strike down legislation. Furthermore, the Supreme Court could have been used to resolve political deadlock. According to the following provision, the origins of which reportedly emanated from a suggestion of the Greek Government:[50]

If a deadlock arises in one of the federal institutions preventing the taking of a decision without which the federal government or its institutions could not properly function, or the absence of which would result in substantial default on the obligations of the UCR as a member of the European Union, the Supreme Court may, upon application of a member of the Presidential Council, the President or Vice-President of either Chamber of Parliament, or the Attorney-General or the Deputy Attorney-General, take an ad interim decision on the matter, to remain in force until such time as a decision is taken by the institution in question. In so acting, the Supreme Court shall exercise appropriate restraint. The Law on the Central Bank may exempt the Central Bank from this provision.[51]

According to Lord Hannay, a keen advocate of the Annan Plan, the purpose of the provisions relating to the Supreme Court was 'to avoid the possibility of deadlock' and 'to ensure' that the Supreme Court could 'exercise the tie-breaking function allocated to it in the event of the other institutions becoming deadlocked.'[52] Be that as it may, the Annan Plan sought to promote excessive judicial interference in the political arena. It would have produced an ingenious if not improper separation of powers under which three unelected non-Cypriot judges would have wielded ultimate judicial power, ultimate quasi-legislative power and ultimate quasi-executive power. These arrangements would have been most unpalatable, particularly if one accepts the traditional English view that unelected judges should not have the power to trump the will of elected legislators, still less wield the power to intrude into areas normally within the exclusive province of the executive. The potential for constitutional instability would have been enormous. All of which brings to mind the memorable words of Lord Diplock, composed in the context of the 'unwritten' English Constitution: 'It endangers continued public confidence in the political impartiality of the judiciary, which is essential to the continuance of the rule of law, if judges, under the guise of interpretation, provide their own preferred amendments to statutes'. Lord Diplock uttered these words because in England and Wales 'Parliament makes and unmakes the law' whereas the duty of the judges is 'to interpret and to apply the law'.[53]

The Annan Plan would have produced an incongruous outcome. A fundamental if not *the* fundamental feature of democracy is that the will of the majority should normally prevail, subject to the rule of law. Yet, in the UCR, the will of the majority would have been blunted and rule by judges would have prevailed. In some other parts of the world, majorities and minorities have successfully come together without impairing the will of the majority. South Africa provides the prime example from recent times. This has been transformed from an oligarchy characterised by *Apartheid* into a multi-cultural democracy where the people are 'united' in their 'diversity'.[54] However, another example is provided by Northern Ireland, an integral part of the United Kingdom where thousands of Protestants and Catholics were killed during the 'Troubles' from 1969 until the late 1990s. Northern Ireland has been becalmed thanks in large part to the Good Friday Agreement of 1998 and the Northern Ireland Act 1998. Indeed, section 1 of the Act carries particular resonance: 'It is hereby declared that Northern Ireland in its entirety remains part of the United Kingdom and shall not cease to be so without the consent of a majority of the people of Northern Ireland voting in a poll held for the purposes of this section …'.[55]

Conclusions

'At the end of the day,' UN Secretary General Kofi Annan announced upon the conclusion of the negotiations at Bürgenstock on 31 March 2004, 'it does not matter what I think. It is what the people think that counts. They decide – and rightly so'.[56] In his post-referendum report, Mr. Annan reflected that 'The referenda mark a watershed in the history of United Nations efforts in Cyprus. They are the first time that the people have been asked directly for their views on a settlement proposal.'[57] These were laudable sentiments delivered by a diplomat with a generally distinguished record of championing international law and human rights. Even so, these sentiments disguised the historical, legal, political and geo-strategic considerations which underlay the Annan Plan. The sad truth is that the Annan Plan was neither 'fair' nor 'well judged',[58] as Tony Blair asserted at Prime Minister's Question Time in July 2004. For a host of reasons,[59] including those outlined in this chapter, the Annan Plan was widely perceived to be defective, deficient and dysfunctional.

In the conclusion to his book published in 2005, Lord Hannay claims that 'it is difficult to see any solution straying far away from the Annan Plan'.[60] This is wishful thinking. If, in future, international diplomats take any steps to procure a 'solution' to the 'Cyprus Question', they ought to proceed on a fundamentally different basis. The Republic of Cyprus, now an EU member-state, should not be expected to languish in the shadow cast by the Zurich-London Agreements nor should the Republic remain under the perpetual strangle-hold of 'guaranteeing Powers'. Any future settlement must respect the rule of law and it must be consistent with established principles of international law, including those relating to human rights; at the very least, any future settlement must pave the way towards the immediate or eventual rescission of elements of the three Treaties, notably the right reserved by the 'guaranteeing Powers' to 'take action' under Article IV of the Treaty of

Guarantee. Above all, any future settlement must be designed with a view to attracting widespread if not universal popular support so that all citizens, irrespective of their background, can come together to promote the common good. As Aristotle suggests in *The Politics*, 'the task of all the citizens, however different they may be, is the stability [*soteria*] of the association, that is, the constitution.'[61]

ENDNOTES

Crown copyright material appearing in this chapter is reproduced by permission of the Controller of Her Majesty's Stationery Office.

1. Aristotle, *The Politics* (translated by T.A. Sinclair, revised and re-presented by Trevor J. Saunders), London, Revised Edition, 1981, Book VI, 373-4.
2. Ibid, Book V, 331.
3. Written Statement by Jack Straw MP, the Secretary of State for Foreign and Commonwealth Affairs of the UK, Hansard, *Written Statements*, 28 April 2004, 45WS.
4. For the three Treaties, see HMSO Command Paper Cmnd 1093, *Cyprus*, London, 1960.
5. Under Article 1.2 of the proposed Main Articles: 'The treaties listed in this Agreement bind Cyprus…'. The three Treaties are listed as Items 5, 6 and 7 in the proposed List of International Treaties and Instruments Binding on the UCR. The said List contained 1,134 items but, to the chagrin of the government of the Republic of Cyprus, it included various agreements between the 'Turkish Republic of Cyprus' and Turkey on Civil Aviation (Item 1002) and Coastal Security (Item 1035) and it excluded the Montreux Convention of 1936 regarding the Regime of the Straits (Dardanelles and Bosporus). See Ambassador Nicholas Emiliou, 'Treaties, Whose Treaties?', *Report of the Friends of Cyprus*, 47, Autumn 2004, 26.
6. See the proposed Treaty between Cyprus, Greece, Turkey and the UK related to the New State of Affairs in Cyprus and the instruments annexed thereto, namely the proposed Foundation Agreement (Annex 1), the proposed Additional Protocols to the Treaty of Establishment (Annex II), the Treaty of Guarantee (Annex III) and the Treaty of Alliance (Annex IV) and the Transitional Security Arrangements (Annex V).
7. In a letter to Mr Annan, dated 7 June 2004, President Tassos Papadopoulos claimed his 'legitimate concerns refer mainly to (a) the question of Turkish mainland settlers… (b) the permanent stationing of Turkish military forces in Cyprus, even after Turkey's eventual accession to the EU; (c) the expansion of the guarantor powers' rights emanating from the Treaty of Guarantee, through the inclusion of an additional protocol.' See: www.cyprus.gov.cy/moi/pio/pio.nsf/All/E570E4948868A105C2256EAE003CAAE0?OpenDocument
8. Observation of Selwyn Lloyd QC MP, the Secretary of State for Foreign Affairs of the UK, 'Verbatim Report', 18 February 1959, Document FO371/144641, folio RGC1073/35B, UK National Archives, Kew Gardens.
9. HMSO Command Paper Cmnd 679, *Conference on Cyprus: Documents signed and initialled at Lancaster House*, London, 1959.
10. Aristotle, *Ethics* (trans. J.A.K. Thomson) London, 1955, Book Three, 77.
11. Between these two sentences, Lord Hannay asserts in parentheses: '(Indeed throughout the 1960s President Makarios openly described the creation of the state of Cyprus as a step on the road to enosis.)' David Hannay, *Cyprus: The Search for a Solution* London, 2005, 3.

12. Robert Holland and Diana Markides, *The British and the Hellenes*, Oxford, 2006, 240.
13. Criton G. Tornaritis, *Cyprus and its constitutional and other legal problems,* Nicosia, Second Edition, 1980, 57-8. Tornaritis was alluding to Article 53 of the Vienna Convention, under which 'A Treaty is void if, at the time of its conclusion, it conflicts with a peremptory norm of general international law.'
14. See, for example, Zaim M. Necatigil, *The Cyprus Question and the Turkish Position in International Law*, Oxford, Second Edition, 1993.
15. Letter dated 29 March 2001 from Umit Pamir, the Permanent Representative of Turkey to the UN Secretary-General, UN General Assembly Document A/55/866-S/2001/307.
16. Ambassador Michael Klosson, 'The Annan Plan: Securing Cyprus' Future for All', English text, *Kibris* newspaper, 6 October 2003, (archived on the website of the US Embassy in Nicosia at http://cyprus.usembassy.gov/USpolicy/sp-Kibris_oct6_03.htm). A similar view was expressed in the House of Lords by Baroness Symonds of Vernham Dean, the Minister for Trade. Hansard, *House of Lords*, 12 May 2003, Column *WA6*.
17. Article 8.1.b, proposed Main Articles. Also see Article 3 of the proposed Additional Protocol to the Treaty of Alliance.
18. Article 3.3, proposed Additional Protocol to the Treaty of Alliance.
19. Articles 3 and 4, Codicil to the proposed Additional Protocol to the Treaty of Alliance.
20. James Ker-Lindsay, *EU Accession and UN Peacekeeping in Cyprus,* Basingstoke, 2005, 100.
21. See Klearchos Kyriakides, 'The Sovereign Base Areas and British Defence Policy Since 1960', Hubert Faustmann and Nicos Peristianis (eds.), *Britain in Cyprus*, Mannheim and Moehnesee, 2006, 511-534 and 'The Island of Cyprus and the Projection of Sea Power by the Royal Navy Since 1878', Carmel Vassallo and Michela D'Angelo (eds.), *Anglo-Saxons in the Mediterranean: Commerce, Politics and Ideas*, Malta, 2007, 219-236.
22. The land was 'mainly arable'. Written Answer by Denis MacShane, UK Minister of State, Foreign and Commonwealth Office, Hansard, *House of Commons*, 29 June 2004, Col. *236W*.
23. Article 5 of the proposed Additional Protocol to the Treaty of Establishment.
24. Alfred de Zayas, 'The Annan Plan and the implantation of Turkish settlers in the occupied territory of Cyprus'. This is published online at: http://alfreddezayas.com/Articles/cyprussettlers.shtml
25. David Wippman, 'Treaty-Based Intervention: Who Can Say No?,' 62 *University of Chicago Law Review*, 607-687.
26. Article 2.1.a, proposed Main Articles.
27. Ibid.
28. Article 3.1, proposed UCR Constitution.
29. Preamble to the proposed Main Articles.
30. Article 14.1, proposed Constitution of the UCR.
31. Article 2.1.b, proposed Main Articles.
32. Article 1.5, proposed Main Articles. Also see Article 18.1 of proposed UCR Constitution.
33. Article 53, proposed Constitution of the UCR.
34. Article 2.1.c, proposed Main Articles.
35. Articles 65.4, 88 and 105, proposed TCCS Constitution. The full oath to be sworn by TCCS Deputies (Article 88) would have read as follows: 'I do swear upon my honour and dignity that I shall preserve the existence, rights and sovereignly exercised powers of the State within the United Cyprus Republic; that I shall be bound by the principle of the supremacy of law and by the principles of a democratic secular State, social justice and the principles of Atatürk; that I shall work for the welfare and happiness of my people; that I

shall not depart from the ideal that every citizen must benefit from human rights and that I shall remain loyal to the Constitution.'
36. However, any representative in the GCCS House of Representative would have been obliged to make the following affirmation – not an oath – before assuming their seat. 'I do solemnly affirm faith to, and respect for, the Constitution of the Greek Cypriot State and the Constitution of the United Cyprus Republic, [and] the Laws made there under.' Article 72, proposed GCCS Constitution.
37. Article 10.2, proposed GCCS Constitution.
38. Article 12) 4, proposed TCCS Constitution.
39. Article 32) 2 of Chapter II, 'The Right to Publish Books', proposed TCCS Constitution.
40. 'Seizure of newspapers or other printed matter is not allowed without the written permission of the Attorney-General of the Greek Cypriot State, which must be confirmed by the decision of a competent court within a period not exceeding seventy-two hours, failing which the seizure shall be set aside.' Article 34.4, proposed GCCS Constitution, 'Freedom of Expression'. Article 34.4 uses the same wording as Article 19.4 of the 1960 Constitution of the Republic of Cyprus, except that 'the Greek Cypriot State' is substituted for 'the Republic of Cyprus' and 'set aside' is substituted for 'lifted'.
41. Article 128, proposed TCCS Constitution.
42. Aristotle, *The Politics*, Book IV, 277.
43. Ibid., Book VII, 413-414.
44. Klosson, 'The Annan Plan', *Kibris*, 6 October 2003.
45. Article 5.1, proposed Main Articles.
46. Article 26.7, proposed Constitution of the UCR.
47. Article 6.2. proposed Main Articles.
48. Article 36.8, proposed UCR Constitution.
49. Articles 6.1 and 6.3, proposed Main Articles and Article 36.3, proposed UCR Constitution.
50. 'This conferment of executive and legislative power to resolve hotly-disputed political issues was a suggestion emanating from the Greek Government.' Claire Palley, *An International Relations Debacle,* Oxford, 2005, 35, ftn 9.
51. Article 36.6, proposed UCR Constitution.
52. Hannay, *Cyprus*, 183-4.
53. *Duport Steels Ltd v Sirs* [1980] 1 All England Reports Reports 529 at 542 & 551 per Lord Diplock.
54. Preamble to the Constitution of the Republic of South Africa Act, 1996.
55. Northern Ireland Act 1998 (c. 47).
56. UN Press Release, SG/SM/9239, 31 March 2004, archived on the UN website (at http://www.un.org/News/Press/docs/2004/sgsm9239.doc.htm)
57. Report of the UN Secretary-General on his mission of good offices in Cyprus, S/2004/437, 28 May 2004, paragraph 2. Archived on the website of UNFICYP at: http://www.unficyp.org/news/SG%20report%20on%20his%20mission%20of%20Good%20Offices%20in%20Cyprus.htm
58. Hansard, *House of Commons Debates*, 14 July 2004, Column 1408.
59. For an analysis of the errors in the Plan, see Tim Potier, *A Functional Cyprus Settlement*, Mannheim and Moehnesee, 2007.
60. Hannay, *Cyprus*, 246.
61. Aristotle, *The Politics*, Book III, 179.

CHAPTER 6

PRO: AN APPRAISAL OF THE FUNCTIONALITY OF ANNAN V

Neophytos G. Loizides

With the majority of peace agreements facing implementation problems at a global scale[1], it is not surprising that questions about the political viability and workability of Annan Plan V featured prominently in the 2004 referendum campaigns of the two Cypriot communities. Preceding the referendum, one of the two major Greek Cypriot political parties, AKEL, justified its refusal to endorse the plan, citing issues of implementation, while in polls following the referendum the majority of Greek Cypriots (61.9 per cent) stated they would support the plan if concerns on security and implementation were guaranteed.[2] Similar arguments on security and implementation were put forward in the Turkish-Cypriot community, albeit with less success for the 'no' camp. This chapter evaluates three main arguments made by opponents of the plan: a) the analogy drawn between the Annan Plan and the Zurich-London Agreements of 1959; b) the criticism of federalism and consociationalism as unfair and dysfunctional; and, finally, c) Turkey's role and reliability in implementing the agreement, especially if it were denied EU membership. The chapter questions and criticizes the arguments and assumptions of the 'no' camp, while also recognizing important limitations and gaps in the Annan Plan V itself.

The Annan Plan and the Zurich-London Agreements

Critics of the UN proposed settlement in Cyprus (the 'Annan Plan') have drawn parallels between the proposed settlement and the 1959 Zurich-London Agreements which led to the establishment of the Republic of Cyprus.[3] These Agreements, however, and their subsequent failure cannot be compared with the Annan Plan V or any other form of bicommunal bizonal federation proposed for the current political stalemate in Cyprus.[4] The chapter presents the case that the two arrangements, the nature of the Cypriot society then and today, as well as the international environment influencing Cyprus, are not comparable and that such comparisons often imply what theorists of International Relations call a *false historical analogy*.[5] In such instances, actors who look at their immediate neighbourhood or earlier historical experience often misapply 'the correct lessons of that case to a new situation which differs from it in important respects'.[6]

Consociationalism and Federalism

Analyses of the Annan Plan and the Zurich-London Agreements are made without distinguishing two interrelated concepts, that of consociationalism from federalism.[7] Consociationalism (or power-sharing), among other characteristics[8], requires power to be shared between majorities and minorities and it implies formal or informal veto rights for all parties.[9] Federalism refers to situations where authority is divided between the central and provincial governments, with both enjoying constitutionally separate competencies.[10] Federations can be consociations, as in the cases of Belgium, Switzerland or Annan V, but not all federations are consociations as suggested by the cases of United States and Australia or semi-consociations, such as Canada and India.[11] Finally, there are consociational agreements usually with territorially intermingled populations that do not take a federal form, such as post-1960 Cyprus, Lebanon and Northern Ireland after the Good Friday Agreement in 1998.[12]

In Cyprus, a consociational agreement which includes two federal units could be more stable and functional than the 1960s arrangement. Under Annan V, for example, each community will run its own domestic affairs, ranging from road infrastructure to health and social welfare. Thus, there will be less demand for common decision-making in most areas of daily public life, and hence, less chance of acrimony. In fact, in federations, constituent states have multiple options; they can decide to share the costs and benefits of a new infrastructure (i.e. a specialized hospital unit or sewage system in a major urban centre) or they can maintain their own individual programs.

Moreover, in every society there are moderates and hawks, as well as cycles when the former or the latter come to power. The management of daily affairs can take the form of close and cordial cooperation when moderates are in power and more distant cautious interaction when hardliners govern, with the risk of minimizing the benefits of cooperation. A federal system with flexible structures allows adaptation to changing circumstances and is fairly sensitive to shifts in leadership attitudes.

Under Annan, part of the decision-making relevant for a reunited Cyprus will be done at the European level. With the introduction of the Euro, there will be no need to coordinate policies on important monetary issues. Borders will be regulated in accordance with Schengen Agreement which has already abolished systematic border controls between participating members in most EU countries. Moreover, important legislation from fisheries to environmental regulation will be made in Brussels. In fact, the Europeanization of decision-making might be one reason why no federation has collapsed within the European Union, despite problems with emerging nationalisms in Belgium[13], bitter feelings of injustice and victimization in the Basque country and Catalonia[14], or the absence of any clear incentive for England and Scotland to stay together.[15]

This is not to say that the European Union makes the state opaque, quite the contrary. The Annan Plan has proposed the Belgian model concerning decision-making at the European level; it allows Cyprus to have a voice only when the two communities agree on an issue or to abstain in the event of a disagreement.[16] This arrangement provides an incentive for the two sides to work together in areas of common interest. It also presents an opportunity to negotiate concessions at the EU level in return for concessions at the federal one, thereby minimizing conflict on both levels.[17] More importantly, the EU provides a safeguard for functionality at the higher political level because it is against the best interests of its members to maintain a dysfunctional member or a collapsing federation. Partition of a federated Cyprus would imply similar considerations in Spain, the UK and Belgium, with unprecedented and undesirable consequences for the whole continent.

The Evolution of Political Structures since the 1960s

Another major difference in contemporary Cypriot politics compared with earlier decades is the way in which communities have evolved socially and politically. Several commentators, particularly from the 'yes' camp, compare the Tassos Papadopoulos administration with the administrations of the 1960s, when the latter served as a minister in Archbishop Makarios's cabinet. The Papadopoulos administration has certainly been retrospective in many ways, but the analogy with the 1960s is problematic. Fortunately, today's Cyprus is far removed from the era of disappearances, political assassinations and indiscriminate killing of ordinary civilians due to their ethnic background or because of political beliefs particularly in the Left.

On the one hand, the 1959 constitution was preceded by a period of intercommunal violence, the imprisonment of suspected EOKA sympathizers in camps manned primarily by Turkish Cypriot auxiliary forces to the British colonial rulers and forced dislocations of populations among both communities living in mixed areas.[18] On the other hand, the 2004 referendum was preceded by amicable and occasionally emotional encounters between Greek and Turkish Cypriots, especially after the opening of the checkpoints in 2003.[19] More importantly, during this period, Turkish Cypriots gathered in tens of thousands in Nicosia to demonstrate for the reunification of the island, calling for the end of Rauf Denktash's era which started in the 1950s with the mass mobilization of Turkish Cypriots in favour of *taksim* (partition).

Cyprus fulfils several criteria to which scholars point to when they discuss factors influencing the success of federalism and consociationalism. An important criterion is how deeply divided a society is in terms of its ethnicity. Cyprus today is a moderately divided society compared to the deeply divided society of 1959 or other deeply divided societies around the world which experience regular violence. Brendan O'Leary argues that consociations may only be practical in moderately rather than deeply divided societies.[20] Like other solutions, federalism and consociationalism are difficult to operate in deeply divided societies, especially as many choose these conflict management mechanisms when it is too late, after too much bad blood has been shed and central authority has been weakened to the extent that secession is possible. But when federalism and consociationalism precede deep division chances of success are great.

Cyprus meets other often-cited criteria. Federations are unlikely to fail in economically developed societies.[21] In fact, there has been no example of a federation falling apart among the economically advanced countries. Evidently, the economy can play a moderating role as it brings together several overlapping interests and creates a strong incentive for everyone to maintain peace. It offers opportunities to exchange political concessions for financial redistribution and administer resources to either confront or moderate extremist groups. In Cyprus, intercommunal fighting in the 1960s would have been much more costly for the two communities if it had meant the loss of millions of tourists (and tourist income). In a similar case that came close to separation, with the 1995 Quebec referendum (a result of a failure of the Charlottetown Accord in a popular referendum three years earlier), the economy and economic interests played a key role in saving Canada's future in Quebec.[22]

Moreover, it is unlikely that any force in the island will challenge the settlement through violent means. Despite the polarizing effects of the referendum there were no major examples of physical violence. For the most part, the 'no' camp in both communities reacted in a polemical yet non-violent manner. As mentioned earlier, the social, political and economic characteristics of Cyprus and Europe today are fundamentally different from those of the 1960s.

Workability of Annan V

Opponents of Annan V argue that the plan is unfair and therefore dysfunctional. Former Dean of Indiana University and Rector of Intercollege in Nicosia Van Coufoudakis points out that 'the proposed system is dysfunctional, given the apparent veto powers granted to the Turkish Cypriots and the fact that disputes will be resolved by non-Cypriots, as in the case of the Supreme Court and the Central Bank'[23]. Criticism also focuses on the disparity between decisions of the European Court of Human Rights (ECHR) and provisions on the Annan Plan on property and the right of return.[24] In many respects, the Annan Plan prioritizes the rights and security of Turkish Cypriots and the rights of post-1974 Turkish settlers, thus limiting rights and options for Greek Cypriots willing to resettle in the future Turkish Cypriot constituent state. It is important to identify some of these problematic provisions in the Plan in order to suggest potential improvements and realistic alternatives.

To begin with, the Turkish Cypriot veto is an essential characteristic of a consociational agreement in Cyprus. In theory, it is possible to have a federal arrangement which allows the two communities to run domestic affairs in their respective constituent states with decisions at the federal level being made by a simple majority irrespective of ethnic origin. Informally, an effort could be made to include Turkish Cypriots in this majority but this will fall short of endorsing a formal veto right for the Turkish Cypriot community. Canada, India and South Africa (for a short period after the end of the apartheid) have established such systems to varying degrees with relative success. Given the percentage of the Turkish Cypriots (in 1960 just above 18 per cent), removing the veto might initially seem a fair adjustment to the plan.

Yet there are several important concerns with the logic of this argument. Firstly, the consociational veto arrangement is not a product of the Annan Plan, but a central feature of the 1959 Agreements, recently reiterated in the statement of political equality included in the July 8th Agreement of 2006. It will be difficult to convince any of the sides at the negotiating table to give up what their respective communities consider inalienable and established rights. Certainly, critics are correct in pointing out that there is hardly any other minority of similar size that has gained such an arrangement elsewhere among democratic federations (the EU being a notable exception, if it is considered a federation).

Nonetheless, these considerations could not be the only criterion in judging a fair arrangement between groups. According to Will Kymlicka, an argument 'in defence of group-differentiated rights for national minorities is that they are the result of historical agreements, such as the treaty rights of indigenous peoples, or the agreements by which two or more peoples agreed to federate'.[25] Kymlicka emphasizes the importance of historic arrangements but recognizes that previous agreements can be made under duress, an argument that both communities in Cyprus can allude to if they wish to withdraw their support from previous agreements. He also addresses the equality argument which assumes that the state must treat its citizens with equal respect. Kymlicka emphatically states that there is a 'prior question of determining which citizens should be governed by which states'.[26] Finally, he argues that 'historical agreements signed in good faith give rise to legitimate expectations on the part of citizens, who come to rely on the agreements made by governments, and it is a serious breach of trust to renege on them'.[27]

Moreover, contrary to conventional wisdom, minority vetoes could potentially add to the functionality of a peace settlement. On the one hand, in a majoritarian federation, there is a temptation not to take minority views seriously into consideration or to rely primarily on non-representative views of the minority. Moreover, if veto rights are informal the question of who to listen to, to what extent and under what circumstances remains undefined and vulnerable to cycles of moderation and escalation. On the other hand, properly crafted consociational arrangements could add a measure of certainty. To this end, the UN plan watered down the 1960s Turkish Cypriot veto significantly. Depending on the issue, a coalition which included 20 to 40 per cent Turkish Cypriots was proposed as a compromise in governing the federal structures.[28]

During the Cyprus referendum, critics of Annan V argued that it was unfair for Cyprus to federalize, if countries such as Israel and Turkey remained majoritarian[29]. While in theory debatable, this argument does not serve any real purpose in Cyprus, since neither Turkey nor Israel is a model of successful ethnic conflict management. State repression, sub-state group terrorism and extensive human rights violations do not provide an attractive alternative to power-sharing. In fact, these two examples clearly demonstrate that majorities often abuse their position and that majoritarianism fails to resolve complex ethnic and national issues.

Still, critics of consociationalism make a fair point when they argue that minority vetoes can lead to 'minority tyranny' and deadlocks. This happens if the minority has extreme demands or tries to sabotage the system, even on the limited number of issues that need to be decided at the federal level. This was not possible in the Annan Plan, however, in either theory or practice. The proposed settlement allowed for an arbitration mechanism through the intervention of a Supreme Court, comprising an equal number of Cypriot judges from the two communities and foreign judges appointed by the UN. The foreign judges were expected to be established international legal experts. Apart from making judicial decisions, the Supreme Court was to settle disagreements over the interpretation of the Annan Plan and resolve deadlocks at the executive level.

Critics of the proposed Supreme Court system argue that the introduction of a foreign arbitration element constitutes an unacceptable and undemocratic violation of Cypriot sovereignty.[30] Yet, divided societies must be creative on the sovereignty question if they are to survive the bigger challenges they face; for example, China demonstrated this kind of creativity when negotiating reunification with Hong Kong by accepting the appointment of foreign judges in Hong Kong's Supreme Court.[31]

Moreover, countries like Cyprus have already granted part of their sovereignty to the EU (at both executive and legislative levels) and to the ECHR (at the judicial level), in the expectation that the benefits achieved by participation in these institutions will outweigh the potential loss of sovereignty. On this point, the arbitration system proposed in Annan V prevents hardliners from sabotaging the system and, in principle, it moderates the views of the two communities during the power-sharing process. Going through the court can be lengthy and risky, often necessitating that sides reconsider their positions, especially since the court will reject unfair and unconstitutional demands, causing local and international shame. Further, decisions of international legal experts have a normative appeal and trigger interest beyond national boundaries. Like China on Hong Kong, parties in Bosnia have accepted limitations to the country's sovereignty and included provisions in the Bosnian constitution concerning foreign judges working with local institutions.[32]

Consociational theorists recommend arbitration systems despite their often undemocratic character. Contrary to public expectations, arbitration systems are not meant to be ideal alternatives to power-sharing; they are not intended to stand in for the elected leaderships for very long. The Anglo-Irish Agreement signed in 1985 introduced an alternative arbitration system in the event that power-sharing between Unionists (Protestants) and Nationalists (Catholics) failed to produce a joint cabinet.[33] This provision was maintained after the signing of the Good Friday Agreement in 1998, allowing London, with the consultation of Dublin, to resume direct rule in the province. As in Annan V, this was criticised as undemocratic.

Yet Northern Ireland also offers a good case of arbitration mechanisms because soon after the signing of the Good Friday Agreements, there was a deadlock, exacerbated when the public voted for hardliners. This was particularly obvious after the victory of Unionist Ian Paisley in the 2003 elections. Paisley who 'spent most of his career deriding reform-minded unionists as traitors'[34] refused to share power with the Nationalists. Nevertheless, direct rule had a moderating effect, leading to the landmark St. Andrew agreement of 2007. There were no major sanctions against the voters in the province (except new water taxes that caused some reactions), but quite simply, local politicians could not survive without making important decisions themselves. Hence, by 2007, the two sides had reconsidered their views and reached a compromise to share power. Indeed, a former opponent of the Unionists said he 'was convinced Paisley was a changed man and his party had been transformed' while Paisley described Sinn Fein's support of the police agreement as miraculous.[35]

As this example suggests, arbitration mechanisms are essential features of a consociational agreement. Peace agreements often fail, but if arbitration mechanisms are in place, arbitrators can maintain stability if a deadlock occurs but more importantly their presence discourages sides from reaching a costly deadlock in the first place. The Northern Ireland example suggests that even with the collapse of a peace process due to the emergence of anti-deal forces, consociational/arbitration arrangements can maintain stability - even transforming erstwhile uncompromising leaders into peacemakers. To cite other examples, Yugoslavia remained united until it lost its arbitrator, Marshall Tito[36] suggesting the need for institutional rather than personal arbitration mechanisms. Belgium does not have a formal arbitration system, but King Albert II can appoint the previous government as a caretaker government when parties fail to form a coalition government.

Finally, Bosnia is an arbitration system *par excellence*, where in addition to ECHR's appointed judges there is an Office of the High Representative, entrusted with overseeing the implementation of the Dayton Accord which ended the war. Despite the bitter experience of a devastating war and the subsequent emergence of nationalist parties, the consociational/arbitration system worked fairly well in stabilizing the country, even to the extent of reversing ethnic cleansing. Currently no Greek Cypriot refugees have been allowed to repatriate while in Bosnia, among the estimated 2.2 million people driven from their homes during the 1992-95 war, an estimated 1.015,394 had returned by 2006. More interestingly, an impressive 457,194 has repatriated under minority status in areas administered by another ethnic group.[37] The success in reversing ethnic cleansing can partly be explained by the authority exercised by the arbitrator, particularly the capacity to readjust policies and incentives in favour of voluntary repatriation.[38] The Office of the High Commissioner even had authority to sack elected officials when they prevented implementation of the accords.

In summary, a consociational system with elements of outside arbitration, while not without its flaws, is the least 'evil option' for divided societies. Majoritarianism can be problematic particularly when hardliners come to power and impose the 'tyranny of the majority'. Turkish Cypriots resent this option, and, in fact, cases such as Turkey and Israel show that it frequently leads to minority secession and political violence. Meanwhile, consociationalism without mechanisms to resolve deadlocks can be vulnerable to abuse when hardliners come to power and fail to reach mutually agreeable compromises. Only consociationalism with elements of arbitration, as in Annan V, can enhance power-sharing and moderation.

Nonetheless, the examples given above suggest that consociational and arbitration arrangements can take multiple forms beyond the Annan Plan. For example, foreign Judges could be appointed by the ECHR (as in Bosnia) if the two sides fail to agree on the appointment of bicommunally-approved Cypriot judges. Another possibility is cross-voting, a system that could allow all Cypriots a double vote, one in their ethnic community and another (with a standardized influence weight of 10-20 percent) in the other community.[39] This system would turn Turkish Cypriots into an electoral minority in the Greek Cypriot community, while the Greek Cypriots would represent an electoral minority in the Turkish Cypriot community. Nominees could be appointed in the supreme court from the poll of the 'most cross-voted' politicians. Additionally, the electoral integration of the two communities would make elites accountable across ethnic lines and add a modicum of moderation to the political system. Admittedly, however, it might unfairly alienate hardliners if cross-ethnic electoral influence exceeds reasonable levels. Finally, politicians on both sides, as well as academics in Cyprus and elsewhere, have suggested a wide range of options that one should consider in moving beyond the 2004 plan.[40]

Fairness and Viability

The question of fairness is central in endorsing the Annan Plan and is highly relevant, not only because it affects functionality, but also because it raises important ethical and practical considerations. Citing international human rights law, the principles of EU *acquis communautaire*, and the need for the settlement to be perceived as just (if it were to be durable), the Greek Cypriot side in the negotiations spoke for the right of refugees to return to their homes.[41] There is an established literature in human rights studies advocating the applicability of universal norms and high standards of retributive justice across similar lines. Others emphasize political expediency, the rights of new owners and the primacy of security concerns.[42] Based on this reasoning, the Turkish Cypriot leadership argued that realities on the ground, distrust, security issues and the principle of 'bizonality' dictated that residence should be strictly controlled.[43]

The UN suggested a compromise where more than half of the Greek Cypriot refugees were to return under Greek Cypriot administration though a new territorial adjustment. For the remaining refugees, it delinked the unrestricted second-house residency right from full property reinstitution and voting as a permanent resident. Aiming to satisfy both human rights and security concerns, the UN suggested that Greek Cypriots could reside in the north but under a number of temporary and permanent restrictions in their voting rights. As for properties it roughly allowed reinstitution of one third of the former properties and compensations for the rest. The idea of delinking refugee resettlement from political and electoral competition could be justified by political expediency but contested on normative grounds since it prioritizes the rights of a new group of owners/citizens over the rights of a formerly indigenous group.

The formula of 'post-settlement readjustment'[44] provides an alternative to the Annan V arrangement. Refugees will be able to have more choice on what they could do at a personal level and no restrictions in settling, voting or even enjoying cultural autonomy in an area administered by another community. If final arrangements deviate significantly from pre-agreed benchmarks, then post-settlement readjustment will be introduced in order to preserve the original balance of the plan. The role of arbitration mechanisms could be crucial in this process since the formula requires a mechanism of renegotiation. This arrangement could maximize the functionality of settlement, by introducing a quantifiable system of monitoring the contribution of each side to 'human rights issues and needs of the other side'. More importantly, post-settlement adjustments could serve as incentives (financial, political and demographic) to each side thus facilitating a smoother refugee repatriation while preserving the original balance of the agreement against unexpected demographic scenarios. For instance, instead of naturalizing Turkish settlers immediately as suggested in Annan V, phases of naturalization could be delayed for the post-settlement period taking into consideration a number of factors including the contribution of settler communities in facilitating refugee repatriation. Post-settlement adjustments could reward local communities, actively assisting, refugees in their resettlement efforts, and they can help rebalance the resettlement if demographic realities shift disproportionately against the interests of any of the two communities[45].

The viability of a settlement depends largely on resolving the refugee issue. Opponents of the plan in the Turkish Cypriot community should be criticised for ignoring the rights of Greek Cypriot refugees and for advocating more restrictions on their rights of resettlement, property reinstitution and voting rights. Kymlicka's work, cited above to defend the historic rights of the Turkish Cypriots, also makes a clear argument for the rights of indigenous people and suggests directions on how the Turkish Cypriot state could resolve the issue. Both constituent states should be multicultural and welcoming to members of the other community. In Bosnia, it was decided that the federal entities cannot be considered exclusively Serbian, Croat or Bosnian Muslim; rather, they must assume a multiethnic character. Ironically, for Greek Cypriot critics of Annan Plan V, this decision was made with the votes of foreign judges—against the wishes of some local judges aiming for ethnic purity.

Would Turkey Implement the Plan?

Critics of the Annan Plan make two opposing arguments concerning Turkey and the European Union. Optimistic critics on the Greek Cypriot side have argued that 'after 1 May 2004 Cyprus would have been in the strongest negotiating position since 1974' and that 'the application of EU laws and regulations will protect more effectively the rights of all Cypriots'[46]. Pessimistic critics maintain that Turkey would not implement the agreement, especially if it were to be denied EU membership[47]. Even though more than half of the Greek Cypriot refugees would have returned under Greek Cypriot administration (probably the most significant concession to the Greek Cypriot side in the settlement), critics argued that Turkey would not give up the territory in northern Cyprus.

The first argument has been proved wrong so far, judging from the failure of the Papadopoulos government to gain any tangible concessions in the post-Annan period. Proponents of the first thesis would argue that it is too early to judge since they expect concessions along Turkey's EU accession path particularly shortly before its accession to the EU. While plausible, structurally it will be difficult to coordinate Turkish accession with simultaneous implementation of a last-minute settlement in Cyprus. The second argument pointing to the possibility of Turkey being denied membership has some merit but adds little to the debate. For one thing, it is generally agreed that failure to integrate Turkey into the EU will affect Cyprus. Turkey is a country with many unknowns, because of the internal struggle between the military and the reformists. Certain risks are generic to all settlements, however, even outside the EU, Turkey will have to honour an agreement because of its political and economic linkages to world financial markets and important decision-making centers.

Moreover, the Annan Plan V provides a fairly good strategy for minimizing the risk to Cyprus. Turkey's obligations would only start when the Turkish Grand National Assembly (TBBM) ratifies the settlement (in another words, the Plan gave a veto right to the Turkish Parliament before the unification process starts). Arguably, any domestic challenges to the settlement, including reactions from the military, would take place before the ratification and before Cyprus becomes a federal republic.

For another, the basic provision of the Annan Plan is to link a number of self-enforceable concessions from Turkey with the country's accession to the European Union.[48] The logic of this linkage was to minimize the 'ambiguity and hope factor' entrenched in the negotiations. Not surprisingly, critics in Turkey feared that concessions in Cyprus would not 'pay off' if Turkey was to deny EU membership. By linking settlement provisions to Turkey's final status in the EU, the UN effectively produced two types of plans, one for each scenario: a more favourable one for Turkey with no accession, and one more favourable to the Greek Cypriots accompanied by Turkey's EU membership. By linking these two issues, the UN aimed for self-enforceable incentives for everyone to work towards the best scenario of including Turkey in the EU. On the negative side, critics are right in pointing out that this linkage or the original starting point of the arrangement is far from ideal, as it makes the basic human rights of Greek Cypriot refugees subject to a larger geopolitical puzzle, in which Cypriots have little say. In a final analysis, though, the content of the linkage can change in the future, and its general logic carries fewer risks for all sides than the 'wait and see' options of the anti-deal camp.

Conclusion

This chapter has focussed on evaluating the main arguments of the Annan Plan's opponents. To this end, it looks at the analogy drawn between the Annan Plan and the Zurich-London Agreements of 1959, determining that such an analogy is inappropriate and suggesting a number of reasons why federalism and consociationalism are applicable in Cyprus today. Moreover, it reassesses the argument that the institutional arrangements in the Plan are dysfunctional in Cyprus and suggests that the logic of the proposed settlement is superior to majoritarianism. Finally, the chapter deals with the fears and expectations regarding Turkey's role. It concludes that the option of negotiating the settlement before Turkey joins the EU through a linkage between accession and self-enforcement improvements for the Greek Cypriot community, as suggested in the Annan Plan, is superior to the risky and prolonged 'wait and see' strategy. The chapter also recognizes several merits in the empirical and normative critiques against the Plan, suggesting the need for a new dialogue 'beyond the Annan Plan'. In considering possible future improvements, the chapter suggests the need for a reformulated arbitration system and an alternative electoral system based on cross-voting, which could enhance moderation across ethnic lines. Finally, it identifies a mechanism for international monitoring and incentives in the implementation process concerning key issues such as refugee rights and repatriation.

Endnotes

The author would like to thank Adrian Guelke, Alpay Durduran, Emine Erk, Erhun Shahali, Erol Kaymak, Kamil Kayral, George Vassiliou, Hasan Tacoy, Joseph Joseph, Kudret Özersay, Maria Hadjipavlou, Nikos Trimikliniotis, Oncel Polili, Osman Ertug, Phedon Phedonos, Roberto Belloni, Sevgül Uludag, Tomazos Tselepis, Yücel Vural and the editors of this volume for sharing their thoughts with me or for providing additional information for this chapter. Naturally, they carry no responsibility for its final content.

1. Roy Licklider, 'The Consequences of Negotiated Settlements in Civil Wars, 1945-1993' *The American Political Science Review*, LXXXIX, 3, 1995, 681-690; Barbara Walter, 'Designing Transitions from Civil War: Demobilization, Democratization, and Commitments to Peace', *International Security*, XXIV, 1, 1999, 127; Angeliki Kanavou 'How Peace Agreements Are Derailed: The Evolution of Values in Cyprus, 1959–74,' *Journal of Peace Research*, XLIII, 3, 2006, 279.
2. Christophoros Christophorou & Craig Webster 'Greek Cypriots, Turkish Cypriots and the Future: The Day after the Referendum', A Development Associates Occasional Paper in Democracy and Governance, No. 16th, 2004, http://www.devassoc.com/msword/occpap16.doc (accessed 2007-08-02)
3. Van Coufoudakis & Klearchos Kyriakides, *The Case Against the Annan Plan,* London, 2004 http://www.lobbyforcyprus.org/materials/caseagainstannanplan.htm (accessed 2007-10-08). American Hellenic Institute, Statement on the UN Annan Proposal for Settlement of the Cyprus Problem, February, 2004, http://unannanplan.agrino.org/AHI.htm (accessed 2007-10-08).
4. James Crawford, *The Creation of States in International Law,* Oxford, Oxford University Press, 491. Crawford, an authority on state recognition, believes Annan V was a federal settlement.
5. Alexander George, *Presidential Decisionmaking in Foreign Policy: The Effective use of Information and Advice,* Boulder, 1980. Robert Jervis, 'Hypotheses on Misperception,' *World Politics*, XXX, 3, 1968, 454-479.
6. Alexander George, 'Adapting to Constraints in Rational Decisionmaking', Robert Art & Robert Jervis, eds., *International Politics: Enduring Concepts and Contemporary Issues,* 3rd edn, New York, 1992, 464.
7. Arend Lijphart, 'Consociation and Federation: Conceptual and Empirical Link', *Canadian Journal of Political Science / Revue Canadienne de Science Politique*, XII, 3, 1979, 499-515.

8. See Nikos Trimikliniotis in this volume.
9. Arend Lijphart, *Democracy in Plural Societies: A Comparative Exploration,* New Haven, 1977. John McGarry and Brendan O'Leary eds., *The Politics of Ethnic Conflict Regulation,* London, 1993.
10. Brendan O'Leary, 'The Elements of Right-Sizing and Right-Peopling the State', Brendan O' Leary, Ian Lustick, and Thomas Callaghy, eds,, *Right-sizing the State: The Politics of Moving Borders,* Oxford, 2001, 15-73.
11. Lijphart, *Democracy in Plural Societies: A Comparative Exploration,* 513.
12. O'Leary, 'The Elements of Right-Sizing and Right-Peopling the State', 44.
13. Jan Erk, 'From Vlaams Blok to Vlaams Belang: The Belgian Far-Right Renames Itself', *West European Politics,* XXVIII, 3, 2005, 493-502.
14. Daniele Conversi, *The Basques, the Catalans, and Spain: Alternative Routes to Nationalist Mobilization,* London, 1997.
15. Michael Keating, *The Government of Scotland: Public Policy Making after Devolution,* Edinburgh, 2005.
16. UNSG. *Report of the Secretary-General on his Mission of Good Offices in Cyprus* ,S/2003/398. April 1, 2003 <http://www.un.dk/doc/S.2003.398.pdf> [Accessed 19 January 2005]. UNSG. The Comprehensive Settlement of the Cyprus Problem, 31 March, 2004.
17. Jan Beyers & Peter Bursens, 'The European Rescue of the Federal State: How Europeanization Shapes the Belgian State', *West European Politics,* XXIX, 5, 2006, 1057-1078.
18. Robert Holland, B*ritain and the Revolt in Cyprus, 1954-1959,* Oxford, 1998; Richard A. Patrick, *Political Geography and the Cyprus Conflict,* 1963-1971, Waterloo, 1976; William Mallinson, *Cyprus: A Modern History,* London, 2005.
19. Harry Anastasiou, 'Nationalism as a Deterrent to Peace and Interethnic Democracy: The Failure of Nationalist Leadership from The Hague Talks to the Cyprus Referendum,' *International Studies Perspectives,* VIII, 2, 2007, 190-205.
20. O'Leary, 'The Elements of Right-Sizing and Right-Peopling the State', 44.
21. Brendan O'Leary, 'An Iron Law of Nationalism and Federation?: A (neo-Diceyian) Theory of the Necessity of a Federal Staatsvolk, and of Consociational Rescue', *Nations and Nationalism,* VII, 3, 284.
22. Richard Johnston et al., *The Challenge of Direct Democracy: The 1992 Canadian Referendum,* Montreal, 1996; Robert Young, *The Secession of Quebec and the Future of Canada,* Montreal, 1995.
23. Coufoudakis & Kyriakides, *The Case Against the Annan Plan,* 10.
24. Claire Palley, *An International Relations Debacle,* Oxford, 2005; Tassos Papadopoulos, 'Address to Cypriots by President Papadopoulos, April 8.' Cyprus News Agency. http://www.hri.org/news/cyprus/cna/2004/04-04-08.cna.html#01 (accessed 2007-08-02), 2004.
25. Will Kymlicka, *Multicultural Citizenship: A Liberal Theory of Minority Rights,* Oxford, 1995, 116.
26. Ibid.
27. Ibid, 119.
28. UNSG, *Report of the Secretary-General on his Mission of Good Offices in Cyprus,* 2003, 18.
29. American Hellenic Institute, Statement on the UN Annan Proposal for Cyprus, February, 2004 http://unannanplan.agrino.org/AHI.htm (accessed 2007 10-08).
30. Coufoudakis & Kyriakides, *The Case Against the Annan Plan*; Papadopoulos, 'Address to Cypriots by President Papadopoulos'.

31. James McCall Smith, 'One Sovereign, Two Legal Systems: China and the Problem of Commitment in Hong Kong' in Stephen Krasner ed. *Problematic Sovereignty*, NY, 2001, 101.
32. Florian Bieber, *Post-war Bosnia*, NY, 2006, 123-9.
33. O'Leary, 'The Elements of Right-Sizing and Right-Peopling the State', 46.
34. Henry McDonald, 'Paisley Hails "Miracle" of Sinn Fein's Police Talks', *Observer*, 30 September, 2007.
35. Ibid.
36. George Schöpflin, 'The Rise and Fall of Yugoslavia', in John McGarry and Brendan O'Leary, eds. *The Politics of Ethnic Conflict Regulation*, 1993.
37. Updated numbers can be found at the UNHCR Bosnia website http://www.unhcr.ba/. Richard Black, 'Return and Reconstruction in Bosnia-Herzegovina: Missing Link, or Mistaken Priority?' *SAIS Review*, XXI, 2, 2001, 177-199.
38. Marcus Cox & Madeline Garlick, 'Musical Chairs: Property Repossession and Return Strategies in Bosnia and Herzegovina', Scott Leckie, *Returning Home: Housing and Property Restitution Rights of Refugees and Displaced Persons*, NY, Transnational Publishers, 2003, 65-83.
39. Neophytos G. Loizides & Eser Keskiner, 'Cross-Voting Moderation for Cyprus,' *Southeast European Politics*, II, 3, 2004, 158-171.
40. See for instance Eckart Kuhlwein, 'Cyprus Three Years after EU Accession: A Member State with a Divided Legal System' Report on the Expert Round of the German-Cypriot Forum (DZF) and the Cyprus Academic Forum (CAF) on the occasion of Germany's EU council presidency, 25-6 May 2007, European Academy Berlin; SEESOX, 'Cyprus after Accession: Getting past 'No'? Workshop Report, Oxford, University of Oxford, May 2006.
41. UNSG, *Report of the Secretary-General on his Mission of Good Offices in Cyprus*, 2003, par. 22.
42. Chaim Kaufmann, 'An Assessment of the Partition of Cyprus,' *International Studies Perspectives*, VIII, 2, 2007, 206-223.
43. UNSG, *Report of the Secretary-General on his Mission of Good Offices in Cyprus*, 2003, par. 22.
44. Neophytos G. Loizides and Marcos A. Antoniades, 'Settlers, Refugees, and Immigrants: Alternative Futures for Post-Settlement Cyprus,' *ISP Discussion Paper,* Discussion Paper 2004-03, (Belfer Center for Science and International Affairs, March).
45. Neophytos G. Loizides, 'Refugee and Settler Issues in Negotiating the Cyprus Problem: What is Dead and what is Living in the Annan Plan', *The Association for Cypriot, Greek and Turkish Affairs*, London School of Economics, May, 2007.
46. Coufoudakis & Kyriakides, *The Case Against the Annan Plan,* 12.
47. Papadopoulos, 'Address to Cypriots by President Papadopoulos'.
48. These provisions included, for instance, the withdrawal of most troops with the exception of small symbolic Greek and Turkish contingents in Annan V (S/2004/43:12).

CHAPTER 7

CONTRA: CONSTITUTIONAL STRUCTURE OF THE ANNAN PLAN

Achilles C. Emilianides

Introduction

This chapter aims to analyse some of the main constitutional issues regarding the fifth version of the plan of the former Secretary-General of the UN, Kofi Annan, for the solution of the Cyprus problem. The first part addresses the question of establishing a new state of affairs, both as regards procedural problems, as well as with respect to the issue of state succession. It will be argued that the method of establishing the new state of affairs was deeply undemocratic and it satisfied Turkey's aim for the partition of the island. The second part of this chapter considers the two main principles of the constitutional structure of the new state of affairs, namely the principles of increased bi-zonality and political equality, and examines the issue of the Turkish settlers. It is suggested that the constitutional structure was based upon division and discrimination and not upon democracy or the protection of fundamental rights. The third part of this chapter focuses on the constitutional character of the new state of affairs, including the executive, the legislative and the judiciary, as well as the position of the United Cyprus Republic (UCR) as a member of the EU. It will be argued that the intended UCR would be unviable and it would not have sufficient constitutional guarantees in order to function properly. The fourth and final part of this chapter will argue that the UCR envisaged in the Annan Plan would have resulted in Cyprus becoming a servant state – a protectorate.

Establishing a New State of Affairs
Procedural Problems

The Annan Plan was submitted for approval in separate and simultaneous referenda on 24 April 2004 with an intended aim to establish a new state of affairs. The UN procedure was highly problematic for several reasons. Firstly, no collective body representing the people of Cyprus had participated in the formation of the plan submitted for approval in the referenda. Nor had the Plan been subject to public deliberation within such a collective body, as is the standard practice.[1] Moreover, the elected president of the Republic of Cyprus, who represented the Greek Cypriots in the negotiations had not approved the Annan Plan. The submitted Plan was the result of the exercise of Annan's unfettered discretion, who, in an unprecedented act, had finalised the Plan himself, even where Federal Laws were concerned.[2]

Essentially the people of Cyprus were called upon to approve three constitutions, namely the federal constitution and the constitutions of the two constituent states, 122 federal laws and 1134 international treaties, namely a total of approximately 10,000 pages out of which only 178 had been translated into Greek and Turkish. While it is understandable that the people need not express an opinion on the complicated provisions of the federal laws, the fact remains that there were several provisions of the federal laws that the Government of the Republic of Cyprus had not approved and which Annan had finalised. What would be the criteria according to which the people of Cyprus would decide whether they should approve legal provisions that the Secretary-General had inserted unilaterally and which their appointed officials had not approved? And while it is true that the Republic of Cyprus had ratified most of the international treaties, the Plan also consisted of 57 treaties which had been signed between the 'Turkish Republic of Northern Cyprus' and Turkey and which had not been published.[3] How were the people of Cyprus supposed to ratify in a referendum internationally unrecognised treaties between a subordinate administration of Turkey[4] and Turkey itself, the content of which was unknown?

Even if the people of Cyprus were to focus only upon the 178 pages, which consisted the core of the Plan, one would still have to reach the conclusion that the people were called upon to confirm complex legal and political terminology, which either community could interpret differently.[5] In addition, Greek Cypriot voters had to decide whether to adopt a Plan, which violated fundamental individual rights of the Cypriot displaced persons, including the right of property and the right to return. Moreover, a subordinate administration of Turkey, namely the 'Turkish Republic of Northern Cyprus' held a referendum, while under the military control of Turkey and with the participation of more than 60,000 illegal Turkish settlers.[6] At the same time approximately 3,000 Turkish Cypriot citizens living in the area not controlled by Turkey's military forces, did not have the right to vote in the referendum.[7]

It should be observed that a member of the drafting team of the Annan Plan has attempted to support the legality of the referenda, by arguing that the settler's participation did not question the international legality of the referenda as an act of self-determination and that the UN had not assumed a formal role of organising the referenda.[8] May a referendum conducted in the method described above, be considered as one aiming at the will of well-informed citizens of a state wishing to establish a viable constitutional life? The answer is no. A plan whose main characteristic was vagueness and which had not been approved by the elected officials of the Republic of Cyprus was submitted to two separate referenda, one of which was held under military control and with the participation of illegal settlers. This is hardly the manner in which one achieves a viable solution of an international problem.[9] Democracy is not about coercion of people who have suffered, *inter alia*, loss of their properties and homes, nor about legalisation of international crimes, no matter what any ambitious UN bureaucrat might suggest.

State Succession and its Problems

The Greek Cypriot side has always considered that the UCR should be a successor of the existing Republic of Cyprus – the only internationally recognised state entity, comprising all Cypriot territory and all Cypriot citizens, both Greek and Turkish Cypriots. On the other hand, the Turkish Cypriot side always stressed that the new state of affairs should consist of the union of two pre-existing states, namely the Republic of Cyprus and the 'TRNC'. This is hardly a matter of theoretical interest only. It is associated with well justified fears that the new state of affairs would fall apart, similarly as in 1963. In a case of breakdown, an answer suggesting that there had been a union of two pre-existing states, might well lead to the permanent partition of the island. This is due to the fact that in such an event there would be two internationally recognised states of equal status, one with Greek Cypriots as citizens and the other with Turkish Cypriots, thus fulfilling a long – term aim of Turkish military.

The most important argument in favour of the view that the new state would be a successor of the existing Republic of Cyprus is the fact that the UCR would exercise the membership rights and obligation of the Republic of Cyprus in the United Nations. The aforementioned arrangements provide a solid presumption that the new state would succeed the Republic of Cyprus.[10] However, there are also several provisions in the Plan leading towards a different conclusion, the most important of which is article 12 of the Foundation Agreement which provides that any act, whether of a legislative, executive or judicial nature, by any authority in Cyprus whatsoever, prior to entry in force of the Agreement, is recognised as valid. Similarly, as already mentioned, several treaties between Turkey and "TRNC" were included in the list of treaties of the new state. Further, while the Annan Plan refers to the 'people of each constituent state',[11] there is no reference in the Plan to the 'people of Cyprus' as a whole. The aforementioned provision satisfied a main aim of Turkey, namely that the citizens of the constituent states would become citizens of the federal state through their respective constituent states and not *vice versa*.

While the ambit of this article does not suffice for a detailed analysis of the issue of state succession, it could be concluded that the Annan Plan does not provide a definite answer to the question of state succession and thus, if the new state of affairs broke down, each side would refer to conflicting legal provisions in order to support its views about the future of the UCR.[12] Essentially the Plan considers as equals the Republic of Cyprus, which is a member of the UN, the Council of Europe and now the EU, and the 'TRNC', which Turkey only recognises and which is admittedly a puppet-state. Thus, the Plan indirectly legalizes the 'TRNC' and implies that the new state of affairs would be the result of the union of two pre-existing legal entities, namely the 'TRNC' and the Republic of Cyprus.[13] Bearing in mind the modern constitutional history of the Cyprus problem, the aim of Turkey for partition of the island might well be considered as a potential – yet as the most likely – outcome.

The Principles of Increased Bi-Zonality and Political Equality
The Principle of Increased Bi-Zonality

The two main principles of the proposed constitutional structure were the principle of increased bi-zonality and the principle of political equality.[14] Although the Greek-Cypriot side had accepted the principle of bi-zonality, the above principle solely referred to the establishment of two territorial zones (the constituent states[15]) in addition to the federal state. The principle of bi-zonality as adopted in the Plan went far beyond this initial arrangement, restricting fundamental human rights.[16]

In so far as freedom of establishment is concerned, article 3 § 7 of the Foundation Agreement provides that a constituent state may limit the establishment of residence of persons hailing from the other constituent state by establishing a moratorium for the first five years after entry into force of the Foundation Agreement and then, by limiting the number of residents hailing from the other constituent state to 6 per cent of the population of a village or municipality between the 6th and 9th years, to 12 per cent between the 10th and 14th years and to 18 per cent until the 19th year or Turkey's accession to the EU, whichever happens earlier. Thereafter, either constituent state may, with a view to protecting its identity, take safeguard measures to ensure that no less than two – thirds of its Cypriot permanent residents speak its official language as their mother tongue.[17]

Although the Plan provides for the possibility of freedom of establishment after the second year of former inhabitants over the age of 65 accompanied by spouses and siblings,[18] this is hypothetical, since no order of the Property Board shall require reinstatement of affected property to a dispossessed owner before a date which is three years after the Foundation Agreement enters into force for property which is vacant, or five years in all other cases.[19] Thus, it becomes obvious that the moratorium of five years is the rule for all but for some extraordinary cases. Following the end of the five-year moratorium, a permanent restriction of the freedom of establishment principles is introduced. Bearing in mind that dispossessed owners have the right to reinstatement of one-third of the value and one-third of the area of their total property ownership, and only so long as a number of requisites is fulfilled, the aim of the Plan seems to be that the two constituent states shall remain separated on the basis of the racial and ethnic origin of their respective citizens, either Greek or Turkish. This constitutional demand for apartheid[20] can hardly be reconciled with EU legal principles, nor with basic democratic rules.[21] Thus, the principle of increased bi-zonality functions as a means for legalising the results of a military foreign invasion in the island.

A second aspect of increased bi-zonality, which is complementary to the aforementioned permanent restriction, refers to the restriction of the right to acquire property in the Turkish Cypriot constituent state. The Turkish Cypriot constituent state may prohibit the acquisition of property by natural persons who have not been permanent residents for at least three years in the Turkish Cypriot constituent state, as well as by legal persons, for fifteen years, or for as long as the gross domestic product per capita in that constituent state does not reach the level of 85 per cent of the gross domestic product per capita in the Greek Cypriot state, whichever is the earlier.[22]

A third and highly important restriction refers to the right to exercise political rights. Political rights at the federal level shall be exercised on the basis of internal constituent state citizenship status, while political rights at the constituent state and local level shall be exercised at the place of permanent residency.[23] The conditions under which a citizen may acquire internal constituent state citizenship status were not provided for in the Plan, but it would seem that permanent residency did not constitute a sufficient condition. However, the most important factor is that an equal number of Greek Cypriot and Turkish Cypriot senators would be elected by people hailing from each constituent state. This exception from the general rule according to which political rights at the federal level shall be exercised on the basis of internal constituent citizenship status, is of particular importance, since the election of the Presidential Council presupposes the consent of at least 2/5 of Greek Cypriot and Turkish Cypriot senators respectively.[24] Bearing in mind that the Presidential Council appoints the members of the Supreme Court of Cyprus, it becomes apparent that the executive, the legislative, as well as the judiciary branch of the federal government, are elected, or appointed, on the basis of the principle of racial discrimination, as a direct result of the principle of increased bi-zonality.

The Principle of Political Equality and the Establishment of the Turkish Settlers

A second principle, which complements the principle of bi-zonality, is the principle of political equality. In practice the principle of political equality leads either to exact numerical equality of each constituent state, or to increased participation of the representatives of the constituent state with the less population, namely the Turkish Cypriot state, simultaneously with provisions which might lead to constitutional deadlocks. While it is true that most states in a federation vary in numerical size, yet having equal rights and representation, the logic behind a multi – state federation is that no single state could hinder the application of majority rule.[25] The principle of political equality would allow the Turkish Cypriot constituent state, with the support of the Turkish Government, to impose all important decisions taken in the island.

As a result the Plan provided for numerical equality of Greek Cypriot and Turkish Cypriot in the Senate,[26] as well as in the Supreme Court,[27] the Public Service Commission,[28] the Federal Police,[29] the Relocation Board,[30] the Alien Board,[31] the Central Bank and the Monetary Policy Committee,[32] as well as the Property Board.[33] In addition several of the aforementioned institutions, such as the Supreme Court, the Relocation Board, the Central Bank, the Monetary Policy Committee and the Property Board would also include a number of non-Cypriot members. While the Presidential Council forms an exception from the principle of exact numerical equality, it is provided that there should exist a *sui generis* veto right of the two members hailing from the Turkish Cypriot constituent state.[34] Another exception from the principle of exact numerical equality is the Chamber of Deputies, which would be composed of deputies from both constituent states with seats attributed on the basis of the number of persons holding internal constituent state citizenship status of each constituent state and provided that each constituent state would be attributed a minimum of one quarter of the seats.[35]

While this would mean on the basis of the existing population that there would be 33 deputies hailing from the Greek Cypriot constituent state, 12 deputies hailing from the Turkish Cypriot constituent state, as well as one deputy from each minority of the island (Maronites, Armenians, Roman Catholics), it is stipulated that the Senate, where there is numerical equality, must eventually approve all decisions of the Chamber of Deputies.[36] A further exception concerns the composition of the public service of the Republic, where the suggested analogy of 7 public servants hailing from the Greek Cypriot constituent state and 3 public servants hailing from the Turkish Cypriot constituent state, is the direct result of the fact that it would be impossible to fill more vacant positions by the relatively few citizens hailing from the Turkish Cypriot constituent state.

In order to completely appreciate the implications of the principle of political equality, as envisaged by the drafters of the Annan Plan, it is necessary that the case of the Turkish settlers is also analysed. The indigenous population of the island (Greek and Turkish Cypriots) has always insisted that the possible legalisation of the Turkish settlers would not only illegally modify the demographic structure of the island and constitute a constant source of tension, but it would further threaten the stability and security of the Republic.[37]

The provisions of the Annan Plan regarding the Turkish settlers are a cause of great concern. At first, it should be observed that the word 'settler' is not used anywhere in the Plan. Any conclusions regarding the legalisation of the Turkish settlers are reached indirectly through the interpretation of the provisions of the Federal Law to Provide for the Citizenship of the UCR.[38] According to article 3 of the said law, any person who held Cypriot citizenship on 31st December 1963, as well as their descendants and spouses, shall be considered citizens of the UCR. In addition to the above, each side may hand over to the Secretary-General of the United Nations a list of people who will also be considered as Cypriot citizens. Such list may number up to 45,000 persons. Such massive legalisation of settlers constitutes a major disrespect to the Resolutions of the General Assembly of the UN[39] and the findings of the Council of Europe.[40]

In addition to the above, upon entry into force of the Foundation Agreement, the Aliens Board would authorize the Turkish Cypriot State to grant permanent residence permits to Turkish nationals up to a level of 10 per cent of the number of resident Cypriot citizens who hold the internal constituent state citizenship of the Turkish Cypriot State.[41] Therefore, approximately 15,000-20,000 additional Turkish settlers would legally remain in the island and would acquire the Cypriot citizenship in four years after the entry into force of the Foundation Agreement.

Out of the remaining settlers, it would appear that approximately 15-20,000 would be allowed to stay as Turkish university staff or students. Any remaining settlers are essentially treated as illegal immigrants and may be expelled as such with financial assistance paid by the Federal Government of the UCR. Bearing in mind the difficulties that modern states have to face with regard to the expulsion of illegal immigrants, it could be accurately argued that the Annan Plan provides no satisfactory solutions with respect to Turkish settlers. It is indeed very likely that nearly all settlers shall remain in the island.[42] In view of the above, the principle of political equality might prove a principle for political equality between the Greek Cypriots on the one hand and the Turkish settlers on the other hand, with the indigenous Turkish Cypriot population constituting a minority in the island.

The Constitutional Character of the New State of Affairs
Executive and Legislative in Deadlock

The Plan provides that the Office of Head of State is vested in a Presidential Council, which shall have six voting members and shall exercise the executive power. At least two of the six voting members must hail from the Turkish Cypriot constituent state.[43] The six voting members of the Presidential Council shall strive to reach their decisions by consensus. Where consensus cannot be reached, the Presidential Council may take decisions by simple majority of members present and voting, so long as such majority always comprises at least one member of each constituent state.[44] Consequently, the Presidential Council will not be able to make any decisions, so long as the four voting members holding the internal constituent state citizenship status of the Greek Cypriot state disagree with the two voting members holding the internal constituent state citizenship status of the Turkish Cypriot state. Moreover, the Presidential Council will not be able to make any decisions in the case of a 3-3 tie of its voting members.

In view of the above, it becomes obvious that there will be no functional decision-maker in the executive of the UCR. The President and the Vice-President of the Council shall rotate every twenty months,[45] as heads of a Presidential Council which had not been selected by them and without the possibility of the President actually controlling whether his ministers perform their duties adequately. The system provided for in the Plan is not only novel, but also unenforceable, especially in a country with the constitutional history of Cyprus. Thus, constitutional deadlocks in the executive level are likely to become normal[46].

As far as the legislative branch is concerned, it is stipulated that an equal number of Greek Cypriot and Turkish Cypriot senators, elected by citizens voting separately as Greek Cypriots and Turkish Cypriots will compose the Senate.[47] Decisions of Parliament need the approval of both the Chamber of Deputies and the Senate, with simple majority, including one quarter of senators present and voting from each constituent state. For a number of important issues a special majority comprising at least two fifths of sitting senators from each constituent state, in addition to a simple majority of deputies present and voting shall be required.[48] In case of disagreement between senators hailing from the two constituent states, constitutional deadlocks in the legislative level shall frequently occur.[49]

A Political Supreme Court of Foreign Judges

In case of a constitutional deadlock, the federal government does not have any practical mechanisms in order to impose its decisions upon the constituent states.

It would seem that the practical solution envisaged by the Plan is for the Supreme Court to reach decisions in order to overcome constitutional paralysis. It is provided that if a deadlock arises in one of the federal institutions which would prevent the taking of a decision without which the federal government or its institutions could not properly function, or the absence of which would result in a substantial default of the obligations of the UCR as a member of the EU, the Supreme Court of Cyprus may take an interim decision on the matter.[50]

An equal number of judges hailing from each constituent state, as well as three foreign judges who would take decisions if a majority cannot be found compose the Supreme Court. Even considering that the judges could reach the decision by consensus, how is any Court supposed to make decisions concerning the exercise of the executive and legislative powers of a member of the EU, including such functions as the election of the members of the Presidential Council or the approval of the federal budget? What legal tools is the Court supposed to utilise under such circumstances in order to reach a decision? The Plan substitutes the will of the people for the will of the judges and in particular for the will of the three foreign judges of the Supreme Court, who are called upon to exercise the executive and legislative competences of the federal organs in cases that a deadlock arises. Such a solution is not only inconsistent with basic democratic principles concerning the separation of powers and representative democracy, but it also leads to a foreign judge-ruled republic, unlike any ever encountered.[51] Even supposing, however, that the Supreme Court would reach a decision through political, rather than legal, criteria, there is still no practical method to implement it, so long as the constituent states are unwilling to co-operate.[52]

Cyprus as a Member of the EU

The governments of the constituent states shall participate in the formation of Cyprus' policy in the EU.[53] The federal government represents Cyprus in the EU in its areas of competence, or where a matter predominantly concerns an area of its competence. Where a matter falls predominantly or exclusively into an area of competence of the constituent states Cyprus may be represented either by the federal government, or the constituent state.[54] The obligations of the UCR arising out of European Union membership shall be implemented by the federal or constituent state authority, which enjoys legislative competence for the subject matter to which an obligation pertains.

It would seem that the drafters of the Annan Plan assume that the two constituent states shall co-operate without tension and that the UCR shall be able to function as a competent member of the EU. This is highly unlikely. Cyprus shall have 'one voice' in the EU; in essence, however, such 'one voice' presupposes that the opinions of the two constituent states coincide.[55] The drafters of the Annan Plan never actually considered it important whether the new state of affairs would be viable, or whether a state entity composed of two politically equal partners could function properly. They were more interested in finding a mathematical equation that would connect legal provisions, in order to satisfy some of the claims of each actor, and principally the claims of a foreign power, namely Turkey. However, living constitutions in European countries cannot be built on the premises of compromise between foreign powers, but rather upon the principles of rule of law, state sovereignty, human rights and democracy.[56]

The UCR as a Servant State

The two constituent states shall therefore be constitutionally opposed; an approach which may lead to division, democratic deficit and manipulation by the mother countries.[57] For instance Turkey might easily impose a constitutional deadlock in Cyprus as a counter against negative developments with respect to its road to EU accession. As a result the UCR would not be able to function, so long as the representatives of any constituent state, induced by a mother country promoting its own political agenda, are unwilling to co-operate in perfect – and never before recorded – harmony.

The Annan Plan expressly provides that Cyprus shall be demilitarized.[58] However, this so-called demilitarization refers only to the existence of Cypriot military forces. On the contrary, non – Cypriot military forces shall remain in the island according to the provisions of the 1960 Treaty of Alliance, which would apply and operate *mutatis mutandis* in accordance with the new state of affairs. Further the 1960 Treaty of Guarantee would also apply *mutatis mutandis* to the new state of affairs; therefore, Greece, Turkey and the United Kingdom would again be the guarantor powers of Cyprus. Not only that, but an additional Protocol to the Treaty of Guarantee provides for the expansion of the Treaty, so that the three Guarantor Powers would now also guarantee the constituent states.[59]

In essence the UCR would be the first state in the world to voluntarily give up its right to self-protection and become completely dependent upon the three Guarantor powers by offering services in exchange for their protection. Thus, Cyprus would be a servant state,[60] a protectorate of Greece, Turkey and the UK, who shall have the only military forces in the island, as well as the right to intervene in case they feel that Cyprus does not comply with its obligations. While it is unlikely that Greece or the United Kingdom would ever interpret the Treaty of Guarantee in such an illegitimate manner, it is well-known that this is the view of Turkey. As a result, the presence of the Turkish army and settlers in conjunction with the alleged right of intervention would constitute a continuous threat and may well dictate political decisions in the island.[61] How would Cypriots feel safe knowing that their protector is the same state which invaded their country, contrary to the 1960 Treaties, international law and the Resolutions of the UN Security Council and General Assembly?[62]

Conclusion

It is therefore submitted that the viability of the UCR shall be explicitly interwoven with the process of Greco-Turkish relations and the EU accession process of Turkey. The Annan Plan is fundamentally flawed, since its drafters did not aim in solving problems in a permanent and stable manner, but rather in finding short term solutions which would facilitate the EU accession process of Turkey. A plan, based upon vagueness and restriction of fundamental human rights and which would potentially lead to insecurity, constitutional deadlocks and tension, was supported by the UN, despite it being inconsistent to the principles of sovereignty and democracy upon which the UN were founded.[63] It is submitted that the Annan Plan failed because its aim was not to serve the interests of either community of the island, or of the people of Cyprus as a whole, but rather the interests of foreign powers, thus turning Cyprus into a servant state, instead of a sovereign republic.

Endnotes

1. Costas Chrysogonos, 'UNSG's Proposal for a New Cypriot Constitution' *Geostratigiki*, 2003, 45, at 14 - 15 (in Greek), rightly observes that the procedure adopted resembled that of a dictatorship attempting to legalise its brute force. Also see Achilles C. Emilianides, et al *The Annan Plan: Five Critical Essays*, Athens, Ypsilon/Egean, 2003 (in Greek), 55-57.
2. And regrettably taking into account the demands of Turkey, during such finalisation of the Plan, rather than the demand for functionality, or viability of the new state, or the needs of either community. See Claire Palley, *An International Relations Debacle*, Oxford, 2005, 131.
3. Annex V of the Foundation Agreement.
4. Terminology adopted by the European Court of Human Rights in *Loizidou* v. *Turkey*, Judgments of 23/3/1995 and 18/12/1996 and *Cyprus* v. *Turkey*, Judgment of 10/5/2001.
5. Indeed that was the aim of the UN as legal advisor to the Secretary – General, Didier Pfirter, affirmed in an interview to *Kibris* TV, 20 March 2003.
6. Palley, *An International Relations Debacle*, 74. See also **Alfred-Maurice** De Zayas, 'The Annan Plan and the Implantation of Turkish Settlers in Northern Cyprus', *The Cyprus Yearbook of International Relations*, 2006, 163.
7. See Ibrahim Aziz, 'Where Do I Live' *Simerini*, 24/4/2004 (in Greek). The insistence of the Secretary-General is even more disturbing, if one considers that Alvaro De Soto, the Special Advisor of the Secretary-General, later suggested that the settlers should not vote if a referendum was to be held in Western Sahara.
8. Frank Hoffmeister, *Legal Aspects of the Cyprus Problem: Annan Plan and EU Accession*, Leiden, 2006, 182.
9. Achilles Emilianides, *Beyond the Constitution of Cyprus*, Thessaloniki, 2006 (in Greek), 181-183.
10. Malcolm Shaw, *International Law*, 5th Ed., Cambridge, 2003, 866.
11. Article 37 § 3 of the draft Constitution
12. For a detailed analysis see Achilles C. Emilianides, *Beyond the Cyprus Constitution*, 183-193. Andreas Syrigos, *The Annan Plan*, Athens, 2005, 210 - 227 (in Greek).
13. See also Auer, A., Bossuyt, M., Burns, P., De Zayas, A., Helmuns, S., Kasimatis, G., Oberndoerfer, D., Shaw, M., 'A Principled Basis for a Just and Lasting Cyprus Settlement in the Light of International and European Law', *Cyprus Yearbook of International*

Relations, 2006, 11 and 14. The drafters of the Plan have admitted that they wanted vague solutions, so each side would be satisfied. See David Hannay, *Cyprus: The Search for a Solution*, London, 2005.
14. See for further analysis Emilianides, *Beyond the Cyprus Constitution*, 199.
15. The term was initially 'component states'. It was changed to satisfy the Turkish Cypriot sides view that the states should be loosely connected. See Savvas Papasavvas, *The Annan Plan: A Constructively Vague Constitutional Future for Cyprus*, Athens, 2003, 46-7 (in Greek).
16. This is why it is referred in this paper as the principle of increased bi-zonality.
17. Article 2 § 2 of the Draft Act of Adaptation of Part D of the Plan in conjunction with article 3 § 6 of the Foundation Agreement.
18. Article 3 § 7 of the Foundation Agreement.
19. Article 17 of Annex VII.
20. To coin a phrase used by Stanley A. De Smith, *The New Commonwealth and its Constitutions*, London, Stevens & Sons, 1964, 280 with respect to the 1960 Cyprus constitution.
21. See also Auer et al, 'A Principled Basis for a Just and Lasting Cyprus Settlement…'; Palley, *An International Relations Debacle*, 163.
22. Article 1 § 1 of the Draft Act of Adaptation, Part D of the Plan.
23. Article 3 § 3 of the Foundation Agreement.
24. Article 26 § 2 of the Draft Constitution.
25. See Andreas Auer, 'Lessons from the Swiss Experience in Federalism and Democracy for the Solution of the Cyprus Problem', paper delivered in the conference *Constitutional and Legal Principles for a European Solution of the Cyprus Problem*, Athens, 1 December 2004.
26. Article 22 §3 of the Draft Constitution.
27. Article 6 § 2 of the Foundation Agreement.
28. Article 30 §1 of the Draft Constitution.
29. Article 31 of the Draft Constitution.
30. Article 7 of Annex VI.
31. Article 135 of the Federal Law providing for Aliens.
32. Article 32 of the Draft Constitution in conjunction with article 14 of the Federal Law providing for the Central Bank.
33. Article 2 of Attachment 2 of Annex VII.
34. Article 26 § 7 of the Draft Constitution.
35. Article 22 § 4 of the Draft Constitution.
36. Article 25 of the Draft Constitution.
37. See Greek and Turkish Cypriot views in Council of Europe, 2 May 2003, Doc. 9799, *Colonisation by Turkish Settlers of the Occupied Part of Cyprus*; Also Loukis Loucaides, 'Expulsion of Settlers from Occupied Territories', *Essays on the Developing Law of Human Rights*, Dordrecht, 1995, 108-38.
38. Annex III, Attachment 4.
39. E.g. 33/15, 9 November 1978; 34/30, 20 November 1979 and 37/253, 13 May 1983.
40. See n. 19; De Zayas, 'The Annan Plan and the Implantation of Turkish Settlers'.
41. Article 10 of the Federal Law on Aliens and Immigration, Annex III, Attachment 5.
42. See also the statement of Didier Pfirter according to which no settler shall be forced to leave according to the Plan, quoted in para. 41 of the Reply of Tassos Papadopoulos to the Secretary-General of the United Nations.

43. Article 26 § 6 of the Draft Constitution.
44. Article 26 § 7 of the Draft Constitution.
45. Article 27 of the Draft Constitution.
46. See Emilianides et al, *The Annan Plan*, 84-90.
47. These provisions are not compatible with Article 3 of the Framework Convention for the Protection of National Minorities, according to which any person belonging to a national minority shall have the right to freely choose to be treated, or not to be treated as such. See Opinion of the Advisory Committee on the Framework Convention, adopted on 6 April 2001, para. 18.
48. Article 25 of the Draft Constitution.
49. See Emilianides et al., *The Annan Plan*, 90-96.
50. Article 36 § 6 of the Draft Constitution.
51. Chrysogonos, 'UNSG's Proposal for a New Cypriot Constitution', 28; Emilianides et al, *The Annan Plan*, 96-101; Syrigos, *The Annan Plan*, 228-241.
52. Hoffmeister, *Legal Aspects of the Cyprus Problem*, 191, misleadingly claims that there is no possibility of deadlock in federal matters where the federal government decides alone on the Cypriot position, ignoring that it is in practice subject to the will of the constituent states.
53. Article 19 § 2 of the Draft Constitution.
54. Article 19 § 3 of the Draft Constitution.
55. See also Palley, *An International Relations Debacle*, 113.
56. Auer, 'Lessons from the Swiss Experience in Federalism and Democracy for the Solution of the Cyprus Problem', 7 correctly observes that: 'a federal state that limits freedom of residence of its own citizens within the constituent states neglects not only one of the basic conditions for peaceful coexistence of the people living in these constituent states, but denies an essential element of federalism'.
57. See also Sunil Bastian and Robin Luckham (ed.), *Can Democracy be Designed? The Politics of Institutional Choice in Conflict – Torn Societies*, London, 2003, 310.
58. Article 8 § 1 of the Foundation Agreement.
59. Article 1 of Annex III of Part C of the Plan.
60. See for further analysis Achilles C. Emilianides, 'Beyond the Servant State Paradigm: The Cyprus Problem Revisited', *Institute of International Relations Yearbook*, 2003-2004, 107-126.
61. See also Giorgos I. Kentas, 'A Realist Evaluation of Cyprus' Survival Dilemma as a Result of the Annan Plan', *The Cyprus Review*, XV, 2, 2003, 13-64.
62. See among others Kypros Chrysostomides, *The Republic of Cyprus*, The Hague, 2000, 117.
63. See the critique of Loukis Loucaides, 'The Legal Support of an Illegal UN Plan by a UN Lawyer', *Cyprus Yearbook of International Relations*, 2007, 19 – 64.

Chapter 8

PRO: RETHINKING THE UN-VIABILITY OF THE CONSTITUTIONAL ARRANGEMENT

Nicos Trimikliniotis

Abstract

This chapter argues that despite the post-colonial Zurich-London legacy and the flaws contained in the final version of the Annan Plan its central pillars provided the basis for a viable, workable and, under the circumstances of *de facto* partition, fair constitutional arrangement for both Greek Cypriots and Turkish Cypriots. The plan's philosophy is in line with human rights conventions, UN resolutions, the EU *Acquis* and the High Level agreements of 1977 and 1979. It defines 'a bizonal bicommunal federation with a single sovereignty, international personality and citizenship'. The alternative – the indefinite continuation of *de facto* partition, or a *de jure* partition, or a 'return' to a majoritarian unitary non-geographical consociation – is unfeasible, dangerous, painful and costly for one side or the other. The chapter offers a reasoned defence of the spirit, but not necessarily the letter of the text, and mechanics: the Plan's constitutional logic is based on a set of sound constitutional and political criteria. It proposes that the interested parties must go *beyond* the Annan Plan to reunify Cyprus as there is scope for significant improvement to meet the post-Annan and post-EU accession era: this would retain the basic constitutional *logic* of a bizonal bicommunal federation and what the two sides have agreed upon without having to start over again from point zero.

1. Introduction: A Historical Rupture - Before and After Annan

Following the publication of Annan I in late 2002, many Greek and Greek Cypriot, and a smaller number of English publications appeared. With few exceptions, the Greek and Greek Cypriot publications opposed the Plan, mostly with opinion and distorted pictures of its content and context. The Plan transformed the terms of the debate by taking a very specific approach towards the notion of the solution, bringing about rupture within political forces like no other Plan or event has since 1974. The Plan appeared when Cypriot society, both Greek Cypriot and Turkish Cypriot, were transforming and coincided with the final stages of Cyprus' accession to the EU and the beginning of Turkey's accession process. It was the culmination of thirty years of interrupted UN negotiations, which eventually resulted in an accelerated process moments before Cyprus' EU accession. It was a process designed to coincide with the beginning of Turkey's own European accession and contradictory internal transformation, which is a by-product of the collapse of the bi-polar world and the expansion of the EU.[1] Yet, the process came to an abrupt end with the Greek Cypriot rejection at the 2004 referendum. It is unrealistic, counterproductive and undemocratic to ignore such strong opposition to the specific plan, despite 65 per cent of Turkish Cypriots voting in favour.

Most Greek Cypriot opponents of the Plan did not only oppose it for 'constitutional reasons', but for its 'totality'. Yet today the dominant Greek Cypriot discourse that appears 'politically correct' is that the Plan was 'dysfunctional'. There are several contentious points, which have been 'constitutionalised' without them being constitutional issues.[2] Many commentators, legal scholars included, conflate everything contained in the Plan as if it were essentially constitutional. In the Greek Cypriot public debate, instead of locating its most important and apparent weakness, there was a 'demonisation' of almost everything contained in the Plan.[3] Even legal scholars depicted the Plan as a 'monstrous legal nightmare', citing 'reasons that swayed a large majority of Greek Cypriots to reject the Plan' as if they were facts or legitimate and well-founded legal arguments, cantering on the argument that the Republic of Cyprus would be destroyed.[4] Tassos Papadopoulos, then President of the Republic of Cyprus, reinforced such views when insisting that the Plan would 'entrench partition'.[5] This particular question was amongst the most crucial political differences between Papadopoulos and AKEL, despite the fact that the party eventually said 'No'. AKEL openly disagreed with the President[6] that the Annan Plan 'does not dissolve the de facto partition, but on the contrary it legitimizes and deepens it'.[7] To this day Papadopoulos remains adamant on this point, repeating to the UN Secretary-General that the final proposals were 'inspired by the Turkish side' and 'deliberately and unjustifiably limit the sovereignty exercised by one of its members'.[8]

This chapter disputes such negative viewpoints and presents the Plan neither as 'hell', nor 'heaven'. It firstly suggests that it was a functional, viable and to a large extent a 'fair' constitutional arrangement that failed to be realised not because of any intrinsic constitutional weaknesses about its alleged 'non-functionality', but primarily because of political reasons that were essentially external to the constitutional logic of the Plan.[9] Secondly, the terms of the debate were such that they reproduced the old power-centred nationalist dialectic that internalised the language of international relations and law, in an 'imperial logic' and 'nationalist logic', which fed into each other.

The 'solution' to the Cyprus 'problem' is often seen in terms of a constitutional formula that would be 'just', 'functional' and 'lasting'. However, these formulaic approaches, which can be interpreted in different and often conflicting ways across the political-ideological spectrum and across the ethnic/communal divide, must be surpassed in order to avoid one-sided and 'ethnicised' approaches based on particular communal or national(istic) vantage points. Was the Annan Plan a 'just', 'functional', 'viable' and 'lasting' solution to reunifying the country and people? What criteria should be used to make such an evaluation? Was the constitutional 'balance', philosophy and rationale 'fair' and 'just' towards each community and what are the 'next best solutions'?

2. Did the Annan Plan Provide for One or Two States? What is a 'Bizonal, Bicommunal Federation'?

2.1. The Cypriot Constitutional Question and the Greek Cypriot Politics of 'Federation'

Whether the UN Plan provided for a federation or confederation is not a semantic question: it is a question of constitutional and international law, which has caused considerable debate and confusion as to the meaning of the terms. More importantly, the answer is likely to affect the interpretation of any future 'solution'. This is a fundamental *constitutional* question because of its highly political and, to a large extent, ideological significance, as it is related to the political settlement of the Cyprus problem. Hence, this analysis is 'politico-legal' and must be neither purely 'legal' (i.e. 'legalistic'), nor purely 'political'.[10] The point of a federal compromise is precisely for reconciling the communities, which transcends *both* 'majority-minority relationship' as well as the current partition. Constitutional devices should guarantee the will for unity at one level and that of diversity on another.[11]

Greek Cypriot critics of the Plan are strongly divided over this matter depending on whether they accept in principle the notion of a 'bizonal bicommunal federation' or whether they consider this to 'entrench partition' amounting to recognition of the territorial results of the invasion and occupation by Turkey, as Tassos Papadopoulos suggested in his speech. This is apparent from the public discourses over the years[12] and more so from the 'spontaneous' pre-election debate,[13] where anti-Annan politicians and lawyers positioned themselves on the question of the desirability of acceptance of a bizonal bicommunal federation.[14] Contrary to some interpretations, the official Greek Cypriot position is that the Greek Cypriot 'No' did not mean 'No to federation'. However, there is certainly a significant percentage amongst the 76 per cent who may oppose a federation. The unambiguous 'mandate' to reject the Plan was contested and remained a highly ambiguous as to the meaning and legacy of the principle of federation until the Presidential elections in February 2008. Whilst Papadopoulos repeated his commitment to the high level agreements, he placed demands on the solution that negate the concept of federation of two politically equal ethnic communities: in a televised message a few months after signing the Gambari agreement (CyBC 11.09.2007) he insisted that 'bizonality is a constitutionally inexistent concept',[15] provoking a strong reaction from AKEL leader, then presidential rival and current President, Demetris Christofias that politicians cannot be 'selective' in accepting agreements.[16] Yet, Papadopoulos seemed 'consistent' with his address to the Greek Cypriots on 7 April 2004, which was seen as an attack on the very core of a bizonal bicommunal federation.[17]

2.2 The Proposed Structure of Governance Under the UN Plan

The Plan provides for the creation of a 'new state of affairs' where the 'United Cyprus Republic' would consist of two politically 'constituent states', the Greek Cypriot and the Turkish Cypriot, which would exercise jurisdiction over the maps agreed with a system of guaranteed majorities based on linguistic grounds in both. Hence, the Plan ensures the 'bizonality' of the federation. The constitution, the supreme law of the land, allocates the functions, powers and competences and guarantees human rights of citizens. Centrally a 'federal government' would exercise jurisdiction throughout the territory of the United Cyprus Republic on a list of competences provided by the constitution, whilst a number of competences would go to the constituent states. A federal court adjudicates over disputes. The legislature consists of a bicameral parliament, the Senate and the Chamber of Deputies, each of which have 48 members, elected for five years, elected on the basis of proportional representation (art. 22, Foundational Agreement). The Senate would be composed of an equal number of Greek Cypriot and Turkish Cypriot senators, whilst the Chamber of Deputies from both constituent states has seats attributed based on the number of persons holding internal citizenship status of each constituent state. Also it provided that each constituent state shall be attributed a minimum of one quarter of the seats. The Presidential Council carries out the executive functions and consists of six voting members (four Greek Cypriots and two Turkish Cypriots) and another three non-voting members, elected by a special majority in a single list by Parliament. There would be a rotating Presidency between the President and the Vice President every twenty calendar months in a 2:1 ratio in favour of the Greek Cypriots.

2.3 The 'New State of Affairs': Constructive Ambiguity, Virgin Birth and the Emergence of the 'United Cyprus Republic'

The Plan explicitly stipulates that sovereignty belongs to the 'United Cyprus Republic' and the neutrality of the terms such as 'the new state of affairs' are diplomatic manoeuvres in the spirit of 'constructive ambiguity' that cannot hide the fact that there is no 'virgin birth'[18] as the Greek Cypriot opponents of the Plan allege. Also, like the Zurich accord, the Annan Plan prohibits both annexation and partition. The 'new state of affairs' was put to two separate referendums on the foundation agreement. The fact that the referenda were separate has led some critics to argue that it will amount to recognition of two sovereignties that legitimates the unrecognised TRNC.[19] But this argument does not hold as it fails to take into account that even under the Zurich constitution the two communities vote in separate lists as the Republic is a country with a single sovereignty which consists of two distinct but politically equal communities. As for the transitional arrangement the provisions contained are the result of tough negotiations from Annan III to V. The interim period of 'cohabiting' between the Greek Cypriot President of the recognised Republic and the Turkish Cypriot leader of the unrecognised TRNC was significantly reduced from one and a half years to 40 days (until 13th June 2004) and the system was fully operational with all laws in place.[20]

2.4 Did the Annan Plan Provide for a Federation or a Confederation?

This issue has attracted considerable controversy. The main anti-Annan legal opinion considers that the UN Plan was not a federation, but something ambiguously 'in between' a federation and a confederation as the majority of Greek Cypriot anti-Annan commentators who supported the 'hard No'[21] opposed the Plan primarily on the grounds that it was 'not a federation'. Papadopoulos repeated this on numerous occasions and was more recently reiterated by the Cyprus Government spokesperson, Vassilis Palmas.[22] Interestingly, some Turkish Cypriot scholars supporting the Plan argued similarly that the Annan Plan was 'a hybrid between federation and confederation without a specific name'.[23]

But what is 'federalism'? As a political principle it combines unity with diversity, self-rule and shared power. It refers to a two level government, a central and a provincial, with a central/federal constitution regulating the powers and functions of each level. By looking at the establishment, development and modus operandi of federal constitutional arrangements, Wheare[24] sets out four basic characteristics of federalism: (a) supremacy of the federal constitution; (b) allocation of powers/competences between 'general' (i.e. federal) and regional (constituent state) governments by the constitution; (c) the general and regional governments 'coordinate between them' and are not subordinate as both operative *directly* on citizens; (d) the role of adjudication in cases of contest between general and regional government and general interpretation of the Constitution is vested ultimately with the Federal judiciary. As the successor of the Ghali 'Set of Ideas',[25] the Annan Plan was a federal system of governance, which contained all of the above elements.[26] A confederation is merely an agreement between two sovereign and independent states; this was not the case with the Annan Plan.

2.5 Independence, Sovereignty, International Personality: State Continuity or State Succession?

Whether the United Cyprus Republic (UCR) would have been a successor state or a continuity of the Republic of Cyprus has legal and political significance, but also a practical importance on the moral legitimacy of both Cypriot communities. One of the main reasons Papadopoulos rejected the Plan in his 7 April 2004 broadcast was that it would 'do away with our internationally recognized state exactly at the very moment it strengthens its political weight, with its accession to the European Union', a view that surprised the UN Secretary-General.[27] But the Plan explicitly provided under Article 2(a) of the Main Articles of the Foundation Agreement (MAFA) that:

> The United Cyprus Republic is an independent state in the form of an indissoluble partnership, with a federal government and two equal constituent states, the Greek Cypriot State and the Turkish Cypriot State. Cyprus is a member of the United Nations and has a single international legal personality and sovereignty. The United Cyprus Republic is organised under its Constitution in accordance with the basic principles of rule of law, democracy, representative republican government, political equality, bi-zonality, and the equal status of the constituent states.

Moreover, Art. 2(a) of MAFA provided that 'the status and relationship of the United Cyprus Republic, its federal government, and its constituent states, is modelled on the status and relationship of Switzerland, its federal government, and its cantons'. Worldwide, the Swiss model is widely used as an example as accommodating conflicts in multi-ethnic societies;[28] whilst the Belgian system is useful in dealing with EU relations.[29] Not only is the explicit wording of the text powerful, but all the primary characteristics set out in international law[30] weigh in favour of the continuity of statehood in international law of the Republic of Cyprus. The Republic will be internally transformed into a federal state rather than two new states as membership in international organisations (UN, EU etc), state property, state archives, state debt, nationality/citizenship continue. Many non-Cypriot[31] and Cypriot authoritative legal scholars[32] consider the federation emerging as 'state continuity'. In his second edition on the creation of states in international law, James Crawford cites the Annan Plan as a prime example of a 'remedial federation'. In his legal opinion, Crawford[33] notes that 'post-Settlement Cyprus will not be a new state but will be the same international legal person as that which emerged to independence and was admitted to the United Nations in 1960', citing the relevant provisions: although not explicitly stated in the Annan Plan, the definitive characteristics mentioned above strongly indicate continuity rather than succession, whilst allowing for 'constructive ambiguity' in naming the animal, hence the neutral references to the 'new state of affairs' and the naming of the baby as the 'United Cyprus Republic' (UCR) which can be equally construed in either way.

Some confusion may derive from Article 2(b), which, however, cannot take away from the validity of the explicit references of Art. 2(a) MAFA:

> The federal government sovereignly exercises the powers specified in the Constitution, which shall ensure that Cyprus can speak and act with one voice internationally and in the European Union, fulfil its obligations as a European Union member state, and protect its integrity, borders, resources and ancient heritage.

The disputed word is 'sovereignty'. Some argued that it lays with the constituent states and not with the United Cyprus Republic and so this will be a segmentation of sovereignty. This is connected with the idea that sovereignty emanates from the constituent state and is legitimated by the separate votes that are required for the agreement to enter into force.[34] But as K. C. Wheare shows in the case of the US, an undisputed federation, 'the states are co-equally supreme in their sphere' in support of his overall conclusion that it is 'necessary for the federal principle' that 'each government [i.e. general and regional] should be limited to its own sphere and, within that sphere, should be independent of the other'. In the case of the Annan Plan, one scholar suggests that 'external sovereignty lies with the federation', but 'internal sovereignty is distributed equally between the central state and the respective federated states'.[35] Clearly, the powers are exercised within the competences of each as provided by the federal constitution which is supreme.

The supporters of the view that the Plan provided for confederation and 'state succession' ignore the evidence supporting the opposite view: they base their opinion on what one legal scholar called 'symbolic' and 'secondary' elements within the Plan and ignore the primary and most cogent provisions that show that it was a federation.[36] A few centuries earlier Walter Bagehot had made similar kind of distinctions between the 'dignified' and 'efficient' elements of the English constitution.[37] The function of these 'symbolisms' is in essence to act as a diplomatic device[38] and as such, as a matter of law they cannot take away the fundamental elements of state continuity, which make the likes of Crawford conclude that the Annan Plan corresponds more to internal evolution of the same state. The international treaties that set up the Republic of Cyprus continue to exist and are affirmed. Cyprus has a single international legal personality and is a member of the UN. EU membership refers to continuity of the accession process of the Republic of Cyprus. Crawford refers to article 17 of the proposed constitution which deals with EU accession:

> Even if the accession of the Cyprus to the EU were to occur simultaneously with the entry into force of the Agreement or shortly thereafter, Article 17 would not imply any emergence of a new State. On the contrary, since it would be intolerable for the EU to negotiate on the accession with a State which would disappear before acceding and be replaced by a different entity.

Secondly, UN membership is consistent with the continuity thesis:

> If Cyprus was a new State, it would need to apply for membership and be admitted to the United Nations, as the Federal Republic of Yugoslavia did in 2000, its claim to continuity not having been accepted by existing membership of Cyprus will continue, the United Nations being invited to take note of 'the new state of affairs in Cyprus.

Finally, the issue of citizenship is also consistent with continuity 'the reference to persons who held Cypriot citizenship in 1960 as the critical date for the primary category of citizens, strongly points the other way'. In fact, as other scholars also illustrate the so-called 'virgin birth did not imply ex post recognition of the TRNC'.[39]

2.6 Allocation of Powers, Competences and the Functions of Governance

The question of allocation of powers and competences between the federal government and the constituent states has a long history in Cyprus. The Greek Cypriots favour a 'strong federation' to remain as close as possible to their goal of a 'unitary state' and the Turkish Cypriots want a 'loose federation', which is closer to a two-state solution or a confederation.[40] The allocation of competences was exactly the same as in the Ghali 'Set of Ideas,'[41] with some additional powers granted to the federal government in the Annan Plan emanating from EU accession and developments.[42] Residual powers (i.e. for matters not explicitly provided for in the constitution) remain with the constituent states, a usual federal practice.[43] The wording of the provision copies article 3 of the Swiss constitution.[44]

At another level the doctrine of 'separation of powers' between the three branches of government, the executive, the legislature and the judiciary requires that these functions be kept distinct without interfering with each other, whilst there is a 'balance and an effective system of checks and balances'. The consociational Republic of Cyprus collapsed only three years after independence and has ever since operated under the so-called 'doctrine of necessity' as a *de facto* mono-ethnically Greek Cypriot controlled state.[45]

The UN Plan provides for a radical change away from the bi-communal American-based presidential system towards a parliamentary form of government modelled on the Swiss model. In fact the system is an improvement from Zurich because it provides what Sartori referred to as 'incentives' for trans-ethnic and trans-communal collaboration by the watering down of the veto powers[46] and provides for common elections rather than separatist electoral processes. Moreover, the system proposed is *more* democratic as it does away with what may be referred to as 'authoritarian presidentialism' or Hailsham's famous term 'elective dictatorship'.[47] The executive pivots a single personality, who is communally elected and appoints the executive with little checks and balances by parliament.

As for the judiciary, particularly at the federal level, it is the last resort in cases of deadlock. The presence of the non-Cypriot judges, which anti-Annan critics targeted, was very much in line with Zurich and was the best solution both sides could find as a deadlock resolution system, which respects political equality.

2.7 Citizenship, Human Rights and the EU Acquis

Art. 3 of MAFA refers to 'a single Cypriot citizenship' regulated under federal law as well as the 'internal constituent state citizenship status' which 'all Cypriot citizens' will enjoy. The Plan lays out a set of complicated rules about preserving 'identity'. An agreed constitutional law dealing with the issue of settlers from Turkey regulates the acquisition of citizenship. Moreover the Plan envisages a federal law on 'aliens and immigration'[48] as well as a federal law for international protection and the implementation of the Geneva Convention on the status of refugees and the 1967 Protocol on the Status of Refugees,[49] which, in the event of a settlement, would replace the current laws on immigration and refugees.

There were four contentious issues over citizenship: (a) the rights of displaced persons (mostly Greek Cypriots) to settle/return to their original homes against the rights of Turkish Cypriots who are currently residing there; (b) the timetables and phases of implementation of the provisions for return; (c) the specific provisions contained about the number of settlers who would be granted nationality; and (d) the exercise of civic duties and political rights within the constituent states.

As far as the exercise of political rights is concerned, the objections raised[50] are not significant, especially in the way differences were resolved with Annan V: basically all residents of the constituent states irrespective of ethnic origin would vote for their respective lower house, whilst the senate would be voted in on a communal basis[51]. Also the extensive transitional timetable over the right to settle is problematic; in fact it would have been impossible to adhere with as it was too long and too elaborate (some extended up to 18 years), although it recognised that the implementation of (re)settlement should be done orderly and taking into account the practicalities of Turkish Cypriot re-housing.

The main objections are related to the provisions on rights of displaced Greek Cypriots to resettle or settle in the Turkish Cypriot constituent state and the numbers of Turkish settlers. The latter issue proved particularly sore for Greek Cypriots: it is widely believed that one of the reasons for the Greek Cypriots 'No' was fear over the 'large numbers' of settlers remaining.[52] Greek Cypriots saw these provisions as problematic in that they were alleged to allow for a 'perpetual inflow of settlers', despite the five per cent cap that was put for any future migration from Turkey and Greece. The property question is a complex issue that should be dealt with on its own right,[53] rather than be considered as part of the 'constitutional question'. As far as the human rights dimension, the formula for compensation and/or restitution was based on the negotiations which may be renegotiated, but it was not a 'gross violation' of human rights as the anti-Annan critics suggest;[54] nor is it a breach of the EU Acquis as Hoffmeister's study illustrated.[55] As for the attack that the Plan was a 'property developers' charter',[56] the resounding 'no' to it resulted in the greatest boost to the selling and developing of Greek Cypriot properties in the occupied territories.[57] Moreover, with the ECHR case of Xenides Arestis,[58] the court seems to regard the 'Property Compensation Commission', a 'court supervised by Turkey', as an 'effective domestic remedy' which may well mean that the Greek Cypriot cases before the ECHR on the question of property in the occupied north will be 'resolved' *without* Cyprus' reunification.[59]

Derogation from the EU Acquis was expected because the negotiated settlement is a compromise based on the transformation of the Zurich consociational antecedent into a 'bizonal bicommunal federation'. The key question is that these derogations do not infringe on basic constitutional and human rights as contained in the Acquis and other international human rights standards. By the time Annan V was finalised the Treaty of Accession had already been signed and these derogations, although unusual, in all the versions of the Plan apparently 'respected the outer limits' of the international and EU framework: in fact, the 'EU favoured a flexible approach to the Act of Adaptation under Article 4 of Protocol 10'.[60] In terms of principles of democracy, the rule of law and human rights, the Plan is in line.[61] Moreover, the Plan met the requirements that the UCR 'speaks with one voice in the EU' and upheld the supremacy of the EU law. Hoffmeister concluded that:

> Any Greek Cypriot legal contention that Annan V does not comply with the principles of EU law or were inconsistent with the relevant UN Security Council resolutions is not convincing.

On the subject of citizenship and rights, the Plan marked a significant improvement from the current constitutional status of citizenship in the Republic of Cyprus which has been subordinated to communal citizenship. For the first time the Cypriot citizen would emerge, transcending the communal divide,[62] albeit within the confines of a federal post-Zurich accord. It would not completely break away from the 'communal' citizenship, but it would move away: (a) at the level of constituent state and municipality there was scope for trans-ethnic/trans-communal political cooperation in the same constituencies; (b) at a federal level the political actors must cooperate to elect a 'presidential council'; (c) at the same time it ensures 'minimum participation' somehow 'melting' or 'watering' down the divisive veto. Overall this significantly improves the 1959 accords.[63]

3. From a Failed Consociational Republic to a Failed Bizonal Bicommunal Federation: Fairness, Functionality and Viability of a 'Remedial' Federation

No constitutional arrangement can be perfect; more so if the system is a product of constitutional engineering. Overall, the UN system proposed, despite its imperfections, was good for immediate functioning and viable governance. It required good will to work, but it also provided for 'state of the art' means for deadlock resolution mechanisms to cope with potential friction. The question of fairness and justice remains open, as this depends on perceptions. A solution will necessarily be a compromise but must be legitimised by the people; they must own the 'solution'.

The Annan Plan is in many ways *more* 'democratic' than the 1960 Constitution. It is not a 'racist' nor an 'apartheid' system as some of its opponents alleged.[64] Democracy cannot be reduced to mere *majoritarian* rule, as the Greek Cypriot ethno-national perspective wants, nor can it be reduced to *a rigid ethnic-communal based system* as the Turkish Cypriot ethno-national perspective desires. The Republic of Cyprus was designed from the outset as a 'consociational democracy' and *not* a 'unitary centralised state' with some 'distortions' (as Greek Cypriot commentators allege).[65]

The political system under the Zurich-London accords centres on an all powerful executive, appointed by the President *and* Vice-President, with separate veto powers and enormous power of patronage. To function it requires collusion by the two communal political elites. Greek Cypriot legal perspectives on the Cyprus question, including Annan Plan critics, ignore the reasons for the duality and consociational nature of the Republic of Cyprus, which was to ensure effective community participation in decision-making. To treat consociationalism and federation as an undemocratic 'distortion' or 'deviation' from the *majoritarian* principle of 'the will of the people' is to deny any accommodation to the problem. On the other side, the hegemonic Turkish Cypriot perspectives stress the *communal* elements and the adherence to the letter of the constitution rather than foster potential commonalities.[66] Within the constitution of the Cyprus Republic there are certain 'distortions', such especially the ethno-communal divide. It is well established that the system failed partly due to its rigidity, but mostly due to the absence of political will to make it work.[67] Any attempt to blame one side or the other on their own is historically inaccurate.[68]

This must be taken into account when examining the various versions of the Annan Plan, including version V, so the mistakes of the past are not repeated. According to Lijphart[69] for the success of a consociation, and to a large extent the same applies in the case of a federation, four key elements are essential: (a) a grand coalition, (b) mutual veto or concurrent majority, (c) proportionality as the principal standard of political representation, civil service appointment and allocation of public funds and (d) high degree of autonomy for each segment to run its own affairs. Elements of consociationalism were necessarily reproduced in the Annan Plan, yet some institutional devices were 'watered down' (e.g. the veto was removed in favour of the 'softer' minimum percentage participation). A geographical-territorial element was introduced to transform the state from a dualist consociational state into a bicommunal bizonal federal polity. If Santori is correct that, constitutions are predictable because 'they are pathways' and that 'constitutions as 'forms' that structure and discipline the states decision-making processes',[70] we may conclude that the Plan was both 'functional' and 'viable', even if it proved eventually undesirable to one side.

4. In Search of the Constitutional Angelus Novus

Federations and consociations in ethically divided societies are costly and time-consuming systems because they need to build alliances and consensus across an ethnic divide. This however is the cost of reunification: it is absurd to reject democracy in favour of dictatorship on the grounds of 'functionality' and 'effectiveness', it is thus equally absurd to reject a reunited federal Cyprus on the grounds that it is not 'functional'. Moreover, often 'functionality' is the code word for the ideology of majoritarianism.[71] This chapter has argued that the Annan Plan was constitutionally workable, fair and viable for the future. But it was nonetheless rejected; therefore we have to move *beyond* the Annan Plan.

Although this chapter gave an overall positive constitutional assessment of the Plan, its failure should lead to a post–Annan and post-accession constitutional framework that draws on the foundational logic of the Annan Plan in a way that both Greek Cypriots and Turkish Cypriots agree on the form of a common bizonal bicommunal federation.

There is scope for improving the Annan Plan. It can be made more viable and more legitimate in the eyes of *both* communities, which means moving beyond the strictly constitutional issues to address the security and military issues; international law and political issues as regards the 'guarantees' and presence of foreign troops; the transitional arrangements, such as reducing the timetables and ensuring implementation; the elements that contain incentives for cooperation and encourage inter-communal action and political representation must be enhanced; and the right of displaced persons to settle and the issue of Turkish settlers should be addressed in a more acceptable way to Greek Cypriots. Finally, in order to address the question of 'legitimacy', the Plan must reconsider the procedure of constitution-making and approval of plan.

Interestingly, time has resolved some matters such as the question of 'virgin birth' because there is no return to the pre-accession era. Other issues however are becoming more difficult, such as derogation from the Acquis. Above all developments on the ground, such as the property question, right of return and other human rights issues remain unresolved.[72] A solution that takes into account this reality must be urgently sought. No matter what the legacy of the UN Plan and the meaning of the popular mandate that was given on the 24th April 2004, there remains a bitterly contested political issue within intra-communal and inter-communal Cypriot politics to be resolved in the political arena. As the two community leaders engage in negotiations, the prospect of a solution in the short-term. In this sense it is crucial that lessons are learnt from the experience of the last failed attempt: the Annan Plan, albeit dead, remains an active force as a constitutional document that will inevitably illuminate any future settlement.

ENDNOTES

1. Nicos Trimikliniotis, 'A Communist's Post-modern Power Dilemma: One Step Back, Two Steps Forward, 'Soft No' and Hard Choices', *The Cyprus Review*, XVIII, 1, 2006, 37-86.
2. As Ahmet Sözen and Kudret Özersay, 'The Annan Plan: State Succession or Continuity', *Middle Eastern Studies*, XLIII, 1, 2007, 125-126, point out that several fundamental issues divided the two communities: (1) the future political system; (2) guarantorship; (3) three freedoms; (4) military status; (5) displaced persons; (6) Turkish settlers; (7) territorial adjustment; and (8) EU membership.
3. Trimikliniotis, 'A Communist's Post-modern Power Dilemma'; Takis Hadjidemetriou, *Το Δημοψήφισμα της 24ης Απριλίου και η Λύση του Κυπριακού*, Athens, 2006, 37-86; Chrysostomos Pericleous, *Το Δημοψήφισμα του 2004, το Περιφερειακό και Διεθνές Περιβάλλον, η Πρόσληψη της Λύσης και η Συγκυρία*, Athens, 2007.
4. See Claire Palley, *An International Relations Debacle*, Oxford, 2005, 221-238. Palley alleged that it was 'a plan of foreign interests' and 'foreign imposed' (Palley 221) and 'serves the interests of Turkey and not the Turkish Cypriots'; Others claim that 'it was too ambiguous endangering the existence of the republic'. Savvas Papasavvas, *Το Σχέδιο Ανάν*, Athens, 2003; Another view is that the state would not be sovereign but a mere 'protectorate' (see Costas Chrysogonos, 'Η πρόταση του ΓΓ του ΟΗΕ για Νέο Σύνταγμα', (in Greek), 'UNSG's Proposal for a New Cypriot Constitution', *Geostratigiki*, I, 2003, 45-48; also Achilles Emilianides, *Οι Συνταγματικές Πτυχές του Σχεδίου Ανάν*, Athens, 2003, 55-69.
5. Papadopoulos address to the (Greek) Cypriot people on all TV channels, 7 April 2004.
6. This is the basis around which the contest between the 'hard No' and the 'soft No' against the Annan Plan remains an unfinished business and will determine the eventual 'legacy' of the Annan Plan in a future settlement of the problem.
7. See AKEL www.akel.org.cy/archive_anakoinoseis_2004.html#_100404.
8. Quoted by Palley, *An International Relations Debacle*, 159.
9. I have analysed this thesis in a number of papers such as Nicos Trimikliniotis, 'A Communist's Post-modern Power Dilemma...'; 'Nationality and Citizenship in Cyprus since 1945: Communal Citizenship, Gendered Nationality and the Adventures of a Post-Colonial Subject in a Divided Country', Rainer Bauböck, Bernhard Perchinig, Wiebke Sievers (eds.), *Citizenship in the New Europe*, 2007; 'Reconciliation and Social Action in Cyprus: Citizens' Inertia and the Protracted State of Limbo', *Cyprus Review*, Volume XIX, 1, 2007; *Η Διαλεκτική του Έθνους-Κράτους, Κοινωνιολογικές και Συνταγματικές Μελέτες για την Ευρω-Κυπριακή Συγκυρία και το Εθνικό Ζήτημα*, Athens, 2008 (forthcoming).
10. Toumazos Tsielepis, 'Η Αλήθεια για το Σχέδιο Ανάν', *Alitheia*, 10 April 2004 outlines how the Annan Plan should be approached; Dimitris Dimoulis, *Το Δίκαιο της Πολιτικής*, Athens, makes a similar argument on a more theoretical level.
11. See Daniel J. Elazar, *Exploring Federalism*, London, 1987.
12. Nicos Trimikliniotis, *The Role of State Processes in the Production Solution of 'Ethnic' and 'National' Conflict: The Case of Cyprus*, unpublished PhD Dissertation, Uni. of Greenwich, London, 2000.
13. From June to September 2007 in *Phileleftheros, Politis, Simerini, Haravgi, Machi* and the TV and radio channels.
14. DIKO Parliamentary spokesperson, Andreas Angelides, a specialist in administrative and constitutional law, revealed that although the party officially supports a bizonal bicommu-

nal federation, in post-accession Cyprus the party need not stick to this idea, claiming that Makarios never supported a 'bizonal federation'. EDEK officials made similar statements. Their veteran leader and honorary chair Vassos Lyssarides, claimed that 'bizonality has 'Nazi terminological origins', while EDEK leader Yiannakis Omirou considers the term 'extremely dangerous' (*Phileleftheros*, 5 August 2007). Similar views are held by the far right EVROKO and Archbishop Chrysostomos II.

15. Papadopoulos expressed his opposition to the idea of 'two ethnically pure constituent state in a federal republic', so he rejects that each constituent states should have an ethnic/communal majority and thus the High Level and the Gampari Agreements.
16. *Phileleftheros*, 16 September 2007.
17. See David Hannay, *Cyprus: The Search for a Solution*. London, 2005; Hadjidemetriou, Το Δημοψήφισμα της 24ης Απριλίου, 2006; Trimikliniotis, 'A Communist's Post-modern Power Dilemma', 2006; Pericleous, Το Δημοψήφισμα του 2004.
18. These are terms used by Hannay, *Cyprus*, 180-185.
19. See Papasavvas, Το Σχέδιο Ανάν; Emilianides, Οι Συνταγματικές Πτυχές του Σχεδίου Ανάν; Palley, *An International Relations Debacle*.
20. Tsielepis, 'Η Αλήθεια για το Σχέδιο Ανάν', notes that the system was operational from the minute of approval of the Plan.
21. See Trimikliniotis, 'A Communist's Post-modern Power Dilemma' for an analysis of the various critics.
22. *Phileleftheros*, 3 September 2007.
23. Ahmet Sözen, 'A Model of Power-Sharing in Cyprus: From the 1959 London-Zurich Agreements to the Annan Plan', *Turkish Studies*, V, 1, 2004, 61-77; Ahmet Sözen and Kudret Özersay, 'The Annan Plan: State Succession or Continuity', *Middle Eastern Studies*, XLIII, 1, 2007, 125-141.
24. Kenneth C. Wheare, *Federal Government*, London, 4th ed., 1963.
25. I have elaborated on this point in *A Federal System of Government: A Constitutional Settlement for Cyprus*, Dissertation, BA Honours, Law and Economics, 1992, Oxford Brooks University.
26. Tsielepis, 'Η Αλήθεια για το Σχέδιο Ανάν'; Alecos Markides, 'Το Σχέδιο Ανάν', *NAI-OXI, Τα Υπερ και τα Κατά*, έκτακτη έκδοση, *Phileleftheros*, 22 April 2004; Petros Liakouras, Το Κυπριακό, Από την Ζυρίχη στη Λουκέρνη σε Αναζήτηση Ομοσπονδιακής Επίλυσης, Athens, I. Σιδέρης, 2007, 407-410.
27. Papadopoulos quoted in the Report of the Secretary General on his mission of Good Offices to the UN Secretary Council, 2004.
28. Linder Wolf, *Swiss Democracy, Possible Solutions to Conflict in Multicultural Societies*, London, 1994.
29. See Michael Emerson and Nathalie Tocci, *Cyprus as Lighthouse of the East Mediterranean, Shaping EU Accession and Re-unification Together*, Brussels, 2004, internet: http://www.ceps.be.
30. See the Vienna Conventions (1978 and 1983), as analysed by James Crawford, *The Creation of States in International Law*, 2nd ed., Oxford, 2006; Malcolm N. Shaw, *International Law*, 5th ed., Cambridge, 2003; and Ian Brownlie, *Principles in International Law*, 5th ed., Oxford, 1998.
31. Such as James Crawford, *Legal Position under the 'Basis for Agreement on a Comprehensive Settlement of the Cyprus Problem, legal opinion*, Prof. James Crawford SC, 21 November 2002; Nicos Alivizatos, 'Τα Συνταγματικά του Σχεδίου Ανάν', *Geostratigiki*, I, January-April 2003, 25-36; Giannis Drosos, 'Η Συνταγματική Διάσταση του Σχεδίου Ανάν' ('The

Constitutional Dimension of the Annan Plan'), *Geostratigiki*, I, January-April 2003, 37-44, Liakouras, Τ*ο Κυπριακό, Από την Ζυρίχη στη Λουκέρνη σε Αναζήτηση Ομοσπονδιακής Επίλυσης*.

32. Tsielepis, 'Η Αλήθεια για το Σχέδιο Ανάν'; Markides, 'Το Σχέδιο Ανάν'.
33. Crawford's opinion referred to Annan I, but these aspects continued in later versions.
34. Loukis Loukaides, who has served as an ECtHR judge, argued this (*Phileleftheros*, 8 September 2002 and recently *Simerini* 12 August 2007, *Phileleftheros*, 20 January 2008). Papasavvas extensively quotes him in *Το Σχέδιο Ανάν*, 48-49. Similar comments are made by Chrysogonos, 'Η πρόταση του ΓΓ του ΟΗΕ για Νέο Σύνταγμα', Emilianides, *Οι Συνταγματικές Πτυχές του Σχεδίου Ανάν*, Palley, *An International Relations Debacle* and Andreas Theophanous, *Το Σχέδιο Ανάν και η Ευρωπαϊκή Επιλογή*, Athens, 2003.
35. Liakouras, Τ*ο Κυπριακό*, 407.
36. Tsielepis, 'Η Αλήθεια για το Σχέδιο Ανάν', 8.
37. The *Dignified* (that part which is symbolic) and the *Efficient* (the way things actually work and get done). Walter Bagehot, *The English Constitution*, 1867 ftp://opensource.nchc.org.tw/gutenberg/etext03/thngl10.zip.
38. See Tsielepis, 'Η Αλήθεια για το Σχέδιο Ανάν'.
39. Frank Hoffmeister, *Legal Aspects of the Cyprus Problem, Annan Plan and EU Accession*, Laiden–Boston, 2006, 60.
40. See Zaim M. Necatigil, *The Cyprus Question and the Turkish Position in International Law*, 1989; Kypros Chrysostomides, *The Republic of Cyprus*, The Hague, 2000; Sözen and Özersay 'The Annan Plan: State Succession or Continuity'; Liakouras, Τ*ο Κυπριακό, Από την Ζυρίχη στη Λουκέρνη σε Αναζήτηση Ομοσπονδιακής Επίλυσης*.
41. Tsielepis, 'Η Αλήθεια για το Σχέδιο Ανάν', compares these in some detail.
42. These include relations with the EU; continental shelf and seabed wealth; crime; ancient monuments and so forth. The fact that the continental shelf and seabed wealth is under federal control supports continuity rather than succession (see Antonio Cassesse, *International Law in a Divided World*, Oxford, 1986, 377-378).
43. See Wheare, *Federal Government*; Elazar, *Exploring Federalism*; Liakouras, Τ*ο Κυπριακό*.
44. Tsielepis, 'Η Αλήθεια για το Σχέδιο Ανάν'; Linder, *Swiss Democracy, Possible Solutions to Conflict in Multicultural Societies*.
45. Little critical literature has been produced that scrutines the 'doctrine of necessity'. See Trimiklinotis, 'Το Κυπριακό «Δόγμα της Ανάγκης»: Μια Δημοκρατία σε Κατάσταση Εξαίρεσης;', *Περιπέτειες Ιδεών*, 15, *Politis*, 1 September 2007; Trimikliniotis (2008 forthcoming). An exception is Costas Constantinou, 'On the Cypriot States of Exception', *International Political Sociology* (2008) 2, 145–164. Most Greek Cypriot accounts are uncritical of the 'doctrine' referred also as 'law of necessity'. See Criton Tornaritis, *Cyprus and Its Legal and Constitutional and Other Problems*, Nicosia, 1982; Chrysostomides, *The Republic of Cyprus*; G.M. Pikis, *Constitutionalism – Human Rights- Separation of Powers, The Cyprus Precedent*, 2006.
46. Giovanni Santori, *Comparative Constitutional Engineering*, 2nd ed., London, 1997.
47. Richard Dimbleby Lecture at the BBC, 21 October 1976.
48. Foundation Agreement, Attachment 5, Law 1.
49. Ibid., Law 2
50. See Palley, *An International Relations Debacle*; Papasavvas, *Το Σχέδιο Ανάν*; Emilianides, *Οι Συνταγματικές Πτυχές του Σχεδίου Ανάν*.
51. Hoffmeister, *Legal Aspects of the Cyprus Problem, Annan Plan and EU Accession*; Liakouras, Τ*ο Κυπριακό, Από την Ζυρίχη στη Λουκέρνη σε Αναζήτηση Ομοσπονδιακής Επίλυσης*.

52. There was much scare mongering by the Greek Cypriot 'no' campaign on this issue. See Palley, *An International Relations Debacle*.
53. See Ayla Gurel and Kudret Ozensay, *The Politics of Property in Cyprus*, Oslo, 2006; Stelios Platis, Stelios Orfanides & Fiona Mullen, *The Property Regime in a Cyprus Settlement*, Oslo, 2006.
54. See Palley, *An International Relations Debacle*; Papasavvas, *Το Σχέδιο Ανάν*; Emilianides, *Οι Συνταγματικές Πτυχές του Σχεδίου Ανάν*; Loukaides, *Phileleftheros*, 8 September 2002.
55. Hoffmeister, *Legal Aspects of the Cyprus Problem*, 230-238.
56. Palley, *An International Relations Debacle*, 187.
57. See Pericleous, *Το Δημοψήφισμα του 2004*.
58. See www.internal-displacement.org/.../(httpDocuments)/6E8DDCA70869EBF3C125723 D0055FA1F/$file/E8C95FAD.pdf
59. *Zaman* newspaper (8 December 2006), which is close to Erdogan's party, welcomed the decision as 'a serious diplomatic success'.
60. Hoffmeister, *Legal Aspects of the Cyprus Problem, Annan Plan and EU Accession*, 238.
61. Ibid, 133-135; 135-137; 137-139.
62. Nicos Trimikliniotis, 'Προς Μια Υπέρ-Εθνοτική Έννοια του Πολίτη: Η Κύπρος Πέραν του Έθνους – Κράτους', 167-244 and (ed.) *Το Πορτοκαλί της Κύπρου*, Athens, 2005, 218-221
63. See Nicos Trimikliniotis (2000; 2005; 2003) 'Το Ελβετικό Σύστημα, το Σχέδιο Ανάν και η Ομοσπονδοποίηση της Κύπρου: Για Ένα Αριστερό Συνταγματισμό', *Theseis* 83, March - April 2003, 43-66 [see website: http://www.theseis.com/76-/theseis/t83/t83.htm].
64. Loukaides, *Phileleftheros*, 8 September 2002; *Simerini* 12 August 2007; *Phileleftheros*, 20 January 2008; Palley, *An International Relations Debacle*; Emilianides, *Οι Συνταγματικές Πτυχές του Σχεδίου Ανάν*.
65. See Tornaritis, *Cyprus and Its Legal and Constitutional and Other Problems*; Chrysostomides, *The Republic of Cyprus*; Pikis, *Constitutionalism – Human Rights – Separation of Powers*.
66. See Necatigil, *The Cyprus Question*; Metin Tamkoç, The *Turkish Cypriot State, the Embodiment of the Right to Self-determination*, London, 1988.
67. See Stanley Kyriakides, C*yprus: Constitutionalism and Crisis Government*, Philadelphia, 1969; Thomas Ehrlich, *Cyprus: 1958-1967*, London, 1974; Kyriakos C. Markides, *The Rise and Fall of the Cyprus Republic*, London, 1977; Ibrahim H. Salih, *Cyprus, the Impact of Diverse Nationalism on a State*, Philadelphia, 1977; Michael Attalides, *Cyprus, Nationalism and International Politics*, Edinburgh, 1979.
68. Papasavvas, *Το Σχέδιο Ανάν* and Emilianides, *Οι Συνταγματικές Πτυχές του Σχεδίου Ανάν*, present such a distorted picture. Necatigil, *The Cyprus Question and the Turkish Position in International Law*, represents Turkish Cypriot propaganda. Arend Lijphart, *Democracy in Plural Societies*, New Haven, 1977, 160, notes: 'The main reason why consociationalism failed in Cyprus is that it cannot be imposed against the wishes of one or more segments in a plural society and, in particular, against the resistance of a majority segment. In this respect, the Cypriot case parallels that of Northern Ireland. The dual imbalance of power constituted the crucially unfavourable factor.'
69. Lijphart, *Democracy in Plural Societies*, 25.
70. Sartori, *Comparative Constitutional Engineering*, 199-200.
71. See Trimikliniotis, 'A Communist's Post-modern Power Dilemma...'; 'Nationality and Citizenship in Cyprus since 1945' and *Η Διαλεκτική του Έθνους-Κράτους*.
72. Ibid.

CHAPTER 9

CONTRA: THE ECONOMIC ASPECTS OF ANNAN V – RECIPE FOR GROWTH OR DESTABILISATION?

Dinos Lordos

Introduction

The Annan Plan, in its five successive incarnations, represented the most complete and thorough effort for the final resolution of the conflict in Cyprus. It was the product of long, hard negotiations between the two sides. In the process of the negotiations significant progress was made on thorny constitutional issues, governance and power sharing at the federal level, as well as the all-important issue of the economy, which is the topic that will be dealt with in this essay.

The observations that follow put a strong emphasis on the need for functionality and economic viability, under a free and equitable economic and social environment within the EU structures and rules. I believe these elements to be essential for the long-term economic and social success and harmony and, ultimately, political stability of the envisaged 'United Cyprus Republic'. The opening of the crossing points on 23 April 2003, which posed no risks to peace then or since has shown that Cypriots can integrate the two relatively small economies, gradually and cautiously in a shorter period of time than previously thought possible.

The Economic Provisions of the Annan Plan

While the Annan Plan appears to strike a tolerable balance in its constitutional provisions, its economic provisions could be improved substantially. Since political equality will be guaranteed by the constitutional structure, the administrative boundaries and the residual sovereignty accruing to each constituent state, economic activity need not be chained or segregated: The market place has its own democracy; people vote there daily with their wallets; if the rules are constricted they will find ways to bypass or disobey them. Any attempt to box-in the economy would create distortions restricting its prospects, increasing the costs, encouraging unlawfulness. Boxing-in the economy, beyond minimum temporary measures, fully endorsed by the EU, would also misalign us from the ongoing transformation of Europe into a true single market of 450 million people. Cyprus cannot afford this. Below are some examples to illustrate:

The Annan Plan envisages adequate protection from frictions over the Federal Budget by providing, in case of deadlock, for repetition of the previous year's budget plus inflation. This ensures the continued smooth functioning of the Federal Government. It would be equally wise if it is agreed that the important activities of independent regulatory agencies such as the Securities and Exchange Commission, the Commission for the Protection of Competition, the Commission for Regulation of Utilities (as well as future similar regulatory activities) would be exercised at the federal level in order to ensure a uniform application in a common economy.

Again, whilst the Annan Plan provides for co-operation between the federated states on such activities as tourism, fisheries, agriculture, social security, labour and other areas[1], it would have been more efficient had there been provided a clearer co-ordination role for the federal government in these important island-wide economic activities.

The Annan Plan proposed that Cyprus would join the Economic Monetary Union (EMU) four years later, (which in fact did take place on 1st January 2008) a condition that would apply to the whole of the island once re-unification was achieved. In order to ensure that Cyprus does not violate its ongoing obligations as a member of the Eurozone, there must be adequate provisions concerning the level of the deficits of the budgets of the Federal and Constituent states and provisions for regulating and coordinating borrowing, both domestic and external by the Federal and Constituent states. The levels of borrowing could be agreed to reflect the development needs of each constituent state over a limited period and until complete economic alignment between them and with the EU as a whole is achieved.

The issues of revenue distribution (Attachment 7, Federal Laws on Taxation and Finances) and public debt (Art. 47) need more detailed clarification before the adoption of any future plan[2]. These are areas which, after application, may be hotly disputed and therefore should be clearly defined. The 'solution' must safeguard from the start economic viability in all levels of government and their continuous ability to service their debts from revenues.

It would also be wise to enshrine all external financial lending, contributions and donations in International Treaties from the beginning and simultaneously with the signature of the agreement for solution.

In line with the previous thought, it would also have been preferable if there had been some careful, analytical, economic models of various scenarios before discussing proposed donations and loans with international bodies.

The provisions about the Central Bank should assert unequivocally that control shall be exercised only at federal level. With the Euro as the island's currency and close monitoring by the European Central Bank, which would also be the primary policy maker, it is hard to see why the Central (federal) Bank should need branches in each Constituent State[3].

Furthermore, the Plan should consider how it will bring a fairly large number of banks in the north[4] up to EU banking standards. This daunting task would be greatly helped if measures were taken to adopt EU banking standards in the north before an agreement to reunify Cyprus was signed.

It is not quite clear in the Plan who regulates other financial institutions (insurance companies, finance companies, cooperatives, depositories and similar). This matter should be looked into more carefully in order to close any loopholes and the competence for this should again be at federal level.

Finally, the notion that donors will undertake to secure the funds needed to finance the cost of the solution is naïve at best. The providers of international aid face far more urgent issues, especially in Africa, Asia and the Middle East, to be in a position to devote significant funds for a solution in Cyprus[5]. What would, instead, be a more pragmatic approach in financing the solution is for the United Republic of Cyprus to issue international bonds on its own security and counter-guaranteed by Greece and Turkey, and establish a fund to ensure that on maturity of the bonds the government would be in a position to discharge its obligations. While donors would be welcome to contribute to this fund, it should by no means rely on them alone, or primarily. More realistically it could be endowed with government-owned properties by both Constituent States and with federal assets (e.g. Semi Governmental Organizations which will eventually be privatized) plus contributions through a temporary special levy on the 'peace dividend' of additional business that Cyprus can reasonably expect after a settlement[6]. Turkey, which will also enjoy a substantial peace dividend, could be asked to continue for some more years with its current $250 million annual contribution to the T/C Constituent State to help align its economy with the EU (or contribute a similar amount to the fund).

The Annan Plan's Property Provisions

The Annan Plan proposes to return about 7 per cent of the 1960 area of the Republic to the G/C Constituent State and estimates that this area was home to around 86,000 G/C in 1974. Their return would lead to the relocation of about 47,000 T/C currently living in this area, of which approximately 23,000 were themselves displaced from other areas in 1974. About 29 per cent of the total area of Cyprus would be retained for the T/C Constituent state[7]. Further, the Annan Plan proposes that approximately[8] one third of the G/C properties remaining in the T/C Constituent state be gradually returned to their rightful owners, after about 5 years, though the actual right to establish primary residence in the T/C constituent state will be more severely limited, to not exceed 18 per cent of the population of the T/C Constituent state after the 15th year. However, houses returned into possession can be used as a second home and the owners can stay there as long as they wish beyond the proposed population-based quotas.

The same rules would apply for the G/C constituent state but these are, in practice, irrelevant because of its much larger size and population.

G/C property owners, who would not be eligible for reinstatement of their property, were to be offered the option to use their 33.3 per cent restitution entitlement to acquire other property in the same municipality, plus compensation in the form of Long Term Property Bonds and Property Appreciation Certificates, at the ratio of 1 bond for every 2 certificates, with 'a yield equal or greater than federal government bonds of similar maturation'. These instruments, which would be issued 5 years after the Agreement was signed, were to be backed only by the property holdings of the Property Board and would be 'legal tender' for the purchase of property from the holdings of the Property Board in the other Constituent State. They would also be tradable on the open market at their freely determined market values, theoretically allowing their holders the choice of instant liquidity or, in the case of the certificates, to await for property appreciation. Bonds would be redeemable on the

25th year after their issue, with a call option granted to the Property Board after the 5th year.

Various authorities, including the Planning Bureau and the Land Registry Office (LRO) have calculated that the value of these Property Bonds plus Property Appreciation Certificates would cap at about C£10-12 billion (€17.1 – 20.4 billion). Detailed calculations in a model[9] which also take account of the effect of cancellations of bonds and certificates due to north-south exchanges, produce significantly lower figures of the order of C£4.2 – 6.8 billion (€7.2 – 11.6 billion) for the net value of the Property Board holdings against which bonds and certificates shall remain outstanding over the medium term, plus about C£500 million (€850 million) for the short to medium term cash shortfall financing requirement as cash outflows for bond redemptions, interest and dividends, overheads and assistance (promised in the Plan) might outpace property sales. Other independent studies[10] also came in at a similar range of C£4 billion to C£6 billion, thus disputing the official numbers and fairly confirming the model used. For the purposes of this text these more conservative figures of this model will be used.

The servicing of the bonds, the cash shortfall and the certificates, with a median 'liability plus equity' value of, say, C£5.5 billion, (€9.4 billion) at an average rate of between 4 per cent-5 per cent per annum, plus the cost of managing the Property Board and Fund would create a 'cash and book' requirement for approximately C£250 million (€430 million) in the first 5 years[11] and thereafter C£280 million (€480 million) each year after year 5. This would create the need to liquidate substantial volumes of property without prime reference to market demand thereby pushing property values down, or alternatively, finance the annual shortfalls by adding these sums to the national debt every year. Even the mere knowledge of the existence of this large supply of property for sale by the Property Board would be enough to drive the property market down! If the shortfalls were booked to the national debt, it is hard to see how Cyprus could afford this additional burden on top of the cost of servicing (let alone paying down) its current debt, amounting to €600 million p.a. for the G/C and about €30-50 million p.a. for the T/C; in addition to the costs of reconstruction and relocations conservatively estimated[12] at €6,2 billion over 5-10 years (with the bulk of expenditure in the first 3-5 years); plus the 'compensations for loss of use' estimated[13] at €2,5 – 3,5 billion to be paid by the Constituent States. To these amounts should be added the normal Development Budget currently at €600 million p.a. for the Republic of Cyprus - i.e. the future G/C Constituent state - with a need for at least €350 million p.a. for the T/C Constituent state to achieve early alignment; from these figures one should deduct Defence savings of approximately €250 million p.a. and the (undefined) government revenues from the hoped-for 'peace dividend' which would greatly depend on the economic arrangements agreed in the Plan. (There would also be the cost of Cyprus' annual contribution to the EU but this would likely balance out with the contribution for the regional development of the north from the EU)[14].

A number of model-based forecasts[15] have been attempted, similar to PBFM 2004, which assume that not all bonds will be issued or be outstanding at the same time and that the Property Board will have adequate revenues from property sales and rentals to finance the interest, dividends and bond redemptions. Even by extending property liquidations over 30 years to minimize the distortionary impact on the property market, the annual property liquidations by the property board would result in a 20 per cent+ increase on the 2002 annual property transactions volume (south-plus-north) of C£ 800 million (€ 1.37 billion), a margin critical[16] enough to sink the island's property market.

More ambitious calculations that aim for a faster liquidation of the property portfolio to eliminate the medium term cash shortfall financing requirement and to speed up the redemption of the bonds have two serious flaws: a) They assume that this small market will be able to absorb any additional amount of property that may be put up for sale, and, b) that such absorption can be achieved without dire consequences for the economy. These two assumptions run against both market realities and economic common sense.

If in fact, so much immovable property does end up vested with the Property Board for resale under the conditions proposed by the Annan Plan, any fears of an impending property glut that will push land values down would become a self-fulfilling prophecy while putting the economy under inflationary pressure. The money supply will expand from the proceeds from the compensation bonds but this expansion will not stem from any increase in the wealth produced. Moreover, this would throw the banking system into a Japan-like[17] tailspin, considering that Property Mortgages (and therefore property values) are the primary security for nearly all lending in Cyprus. Reduced property values would leave the banks exposed and lead to lowered bank credit ratings. This weakening of the banks would seriously affect their ability to attract deposits or raise loans or capital at competitive rates to finance the economy. Bank failures are also quite common in such situations.

The Property Board, by the conditions allowed in Annan V[18], may choose to dispose of its approximately C£5.5 billion land bank over a period of ten years, redeem its issued Bonds, pay the resulting cash balance as dividend to the certificate holders and 'disband' without leaving any unfinished business behind to be managed by others[19] – the 'others' being the directors and certificate-holders of the Compensation Trust. Even though the Plan does not force the Property Board to dispose of everything within ten years, it also does not place limits on how much property can be disposed every year as, indeed, it should not. A 'rapid liquidation' scenario could translate into an annual average rate of property sales of C£420 - 680 million (€720 - 1,160 million) (at 2004 prices), or a near 70 per cent increase relative to 2002 supply! Clearly, under the terms of Annan V, the Property Board is given too much leverage to seriously impact macroeconomic and financial stability, with little apparent control over its decisions and courses of action by the policy-making authorities responsible for macroeconomic and financial stability[20]. The plain truth is that creating a land bank of the same order of magnitude as the country's GDP will cause unavoidable distortions to the economy and to society, including an unnecessary and potentially extremely dangerous increase of systemic risk.

Let us test a number of other more optimistic hypotheses: Let us assume that cheaper land may in fact spur growth, or that foreign demand will underpin and sustain property values:

1. Will Cheaper Land Spur Growth and Sustain Land Values?

(a) Cyprus is third in the world in numbers of residential units per inhabitant (0.6 units: 1 inhabitant)[21]. There is no significant need for more residential housing except for upgrades and holiday homes in a buoyant economy. There will be a real need for the relocation of T/C moving out of G/C properties. Although it makes better economic sense to provide these relocations (which must be provided by the state) on government land at no cost, this potential need could be leveraged into land purchases from the Property Board that would counteract the oversupply effect[22].

(b) However, it should be remembered that the territorial adjustments of the Annan Plan will create a further supply of about 35,000 homes which would be reinstated to their dispossessed G/C owners who are already adequately housed in the South, plus an additional number of reinstated 'second homes' of the same order of magnitude minus the (far smaller) number of homes reinstated to T/C's who are also adequately housed. One can conclude that these reinstatements will add to supply of residential property for sale and thus, relative to demand, depress prices further.

(c) Will Cypriots invest more of their savings in land? Already most of the savings are locked up in land, the trusted asset. Most likely there is not much more that can be invested in the short-to-medium term by an economy of C£6.6 billion (€11.3 billion) (GDP: 2003) with a current savings rate of 4-6 per cent.

2. Will Foreign Demand Take Up the Slack?

Selling homes to foreigners in such numbers as to maintain property values to at least their current levels is unrealistic because it would need average annual sales of about C£1.6 billion (€2.7 billion), (at 2002 prices), when the infrastructure and development costs, overheads and developer's profit for the indicated C£420 –C£680 million (say, average €950 million) annual Property Board Sales are included. Extending the Property Board sales over 20 years gives an equally untenable figure of C£800 million. Moreover, neither the Greek Cypriot nor (particularly) the Turkish Cypriot economy can meet the demand for such a level of construction year-on-year. Building costs would soar and the whole economy would overheat with a high risk of collapse. It should also be considered whether excessive sales to foreigners could also become socially and politically undesirable.

3. Will Property Appreciation Take Up the Slack?

In the period 1974-2002, starting from a very low post-war base in 1974 and through an intense reconstruction period between 1974 and late 1980's property values in Cyprus appreciated by an average 4.8 per cent p.a. in real terms (i.e. after inflation) and in pace with the growth of the economy. The proposed servicing and overhead cost of the Property Board's 'liability plus equity' matches this rate of appreciation, though in nominal terms; therefore any property appreciation will likely reflect the inflation of the period.

However, it should also be remembered that if overall property appreciation stagnates due to the Property Board's liquidations, this will eliminate or diminish the Property Board's ability to meet its annual debt and equity servicing obligations and this would, of course, be instantly reflected in the market value of its property certificates (i.e. its 'shares').

Conclusions

The Economic and Property provisions of Annan V need far deeper analysis and scrutiny than has been given them. Suddenly activating property values which have been lying fallow for over 30 years and which have become, over this long period, a prime element of the market equilibrium will throw the property market into a long disarray and instability with far-reaching consequences to the banking sector, inflation and economic growth. Analytical economic models must be produced and therefore high-calibre, experienced economists must be included in the negotiation and drafting of the economic and property provisions of any new proposal for a solution.

Certainly, the wishful response that these fears are exaggerated and that the solution will alone, bring its own compensating fruits fairly automatically, cannot be considered seriously unless and until such benefits, and the mechanisms that will bring them about, are quantified and identified in sophisticated economic models. These issues are vitally important with far-reaching consequences and must be resolved with the utmost thoroughness from the beginning.

Economic history has repeated itself every time market conditions have been pushed into imbalance: stock prices artificially rising (and then falling sharply) as in the recent past of Cyprus, the infamous 'property boom-bust' of Japan 15 years ago, the US crash of '29, the German economic slowdown following reunification and, more recently the US property boom-then-bust which has thrown the world economic system into turmoil.

The whole economy would go through extensive, hard to predict and drastic readjustments to restore equilibrium. Unless issues are carefully thought through in advance, the economy will not get there fast, nor without the extreme pain and socio-economic upheaval that could threaten domestic stability and thus, the solution Cyprus is seeking.

There must be bolder, more market-oriented, imaginative and realistic solutions for the next attempt.

Some Other Options

Create schemes inducing 'dispossessed owners' and interested buyers to look to the market for solutions: This would cap the 'land bank' to a more manageable size and reduce its destabilizing effect on the macro-economy. The problem of activating fallow land values remains, but that is an unavoidable element of any solution and could be left to the market to correct. History has shown that heavy-handed interference from above delays market corrections. A small nudge or two, is fine, but not a push…

Protect genuine 'current users who are themselves dispossessed owners' and 'owners of significant improvements' (as defined in AP5) who are not illegal usurpers with arrangements respecting their positions and predicaments. A solution should not create more hardship than what it is attempting to cure.

Offer tax incentives, free services and low-interest long-term financing[23] to encourage exchanges, sales, leases and joint-ventures between 'dispossessed owners' and involved (e.g 'current users', 'owners of significant improvements', etc) or interested parties in the Constituent State where a property lies. Such measures could reduce the cost of such deals by nearly 30 per cent between the parties (compared to a normal deal) and make such transactions very attractive for both sides.[24]

Offer, where feasible, favourable Town Planning conditions e.g. higher Floor Area Ratio (FAR) and/or Municipal Services at reduced charges for 'affected properties' to be sold to residents of the Constituent State where the property lies.

Offer similar Town Planning incentives to sellers of such properties with the right to sell these benefits in their own Constituent State.

Make the Property Board **only** a 'Buyer of Last Resort' standing ready to purchase 'affected property' at market prices from 'dispossessed owners' wishing to sell and resell those to interested buyers hailing from the Constituent State in which the property lies on extended terms.

Finance the Property Board by the issue of International Bonds on the security of the Federal and Constituent States with the counter-guarantees of Greece and Turkey, with property assets of the two states and with donations, especially from the guarantor-countries if they will offer to help.

Create Property Courts under the aegis of the Supreme Court and of the ECHR and give them judicial powers for 'affected property' (as defined in AP5) to relieve the ECHR and the Cyprus Courts; in parallel, establish an Arbitration Authority to assist, at no charge, on interstate/intercommunal exchanges, sales, leases or joint ventures.

Create a professional Independent Valuation Authority to provide valuations to affected parties (also free of charge) as well as to the Property Courts, the Arbitration Authority and the 3 governments at low cost.

Going the Extra Mile:

Consider canton/s within each of the two states to increase the number of returning refugees and reduce relocation upheavals as well as costs substantially. The blossoming peace, the mutual tolerance and cooperation and, especially, the total absence of any incidents after the opening of the crossing points on April 23rd 2003 suggest this as a realistic option. One of the alternative versions of the Annan Plan suggested that the Karpas peninsula, at the north-east of the island, could be a G/C canton. The T/C state could consider a canton in the Louroudjina triangle, Lefka region, etc.

Reduce the costs even more substantially and greatly enhance bizonality by reducing the T/C constituent state area to a more realistic 23-26 per cent which corresponds more closely to the actual land ownership and population ratio of the T/C community[25] thereby equalising as closely as possible the volume of affected properties between the two sides.

Deploy imaginative voting systems to safeguard and enhance bizonality[26] without reference to property rights and residence entitlements.

A healthy economy is an essential prerequisite for sustaining a viable solution that will in turn enable all Cypriots, as well as Turkey and Greece to benefit from a substantial and much needed peace dividend. Peace in Cyprus is the next logical and crucial step towards a lasting strategic alliance and fruitful economic cooperation between Turkey, Greece and Cyprus.

Economic harmonization is part of the Annan Plan. Notwithstanding the limited revenue transfers envisaged in the Annan Plan, it must be remembered that obstacles to the creation of the common market for goods, property, capital and labour will also be obstacles to equalization.

The property provisions of the Annan V Plan are not only costly beyond what Cyprus can afford; they are also unrealistic in concept and execution. They were obviously formulated to bridge the totally divergent demands of each negotiating side, without reference to how the property market will react and how the total economy will be affected. However, a failure on this vital issue would bring with it the collapse of the otherwise 'not- unacceptable', but quite fragile solution.

Creating, virtually overnight, a land owner (the Property Board) with a land bank of anywhere from €7 to €11 billion, aiming to dispose of such property within 10 years –even 20 years! - paying in the meantime substantial interest on the bonds and reasonable dividend on the property certificates to at least maintain a reasonable market value for them, plus compensation for loss of use anywhere up to another €4-10 billion (compensation on those land values at 2-3 per cent p.a. over 30 + years, does add up to roughly 60-90 per cent of the actual land values) plus cover its own sizable operational costs, quite stretches the realm of the possible.

To put such figures in perspective, at the time they were proposed they added up to more than the GDP of the country. Far more lenient distortions of their property markets have already thrown into disarray, even turmoil, countries like Japan and the US. There are more viable examples to follow as, for instance, the cases of the former Eastern Bloc countries of Europe, where reinstatements produced less shock on the economy: property values in those countries remained low in the beginning – this was due also to their transition from a communist to a free market economy – and then took off to align, nearly, with the rest of Europe.

The concepts of bizonality and federalism which the various sides are seeking to apply in Cyprus can be better achieved with political measures, not with massive, unbearably costly land redistribution. These concepts also go hand in hand with a unified economy; it is often forgotten that a unified economy will be our 'unavoidable' – and happy – destiny under the rules of the EU, of which Cyprus is already an integral part. It will not be possible to bend those rules, without the tolerance of the EU and beyond a limited period and for genuinely good reasons.

Will the Annan property rules apply to other Europeans buying or investing in the north or south? Shall business be done, between Cypriots, through other European countries? Would the market tolerate and respect such rules or bend them or ignore them? What is the cost, direct and in lost opportunities, of operating an economic system out of line with the European market rules?

Cyprus, now also in the Eurozone, must be as European as its peers to survive with its limited resources of land, water, energy, materials and manpower. That is where Cypriots must turn their attention in the years to come, years that will be characterised by intense competition for food, water, energy and a huge need for foreign investment, to maintain their hard-won living standard.[27]

Endnotes

1. 'The Annan Plan for Cyprus: The Comprehensive Settlement of the Cyprus Problem' 2004 (hereinafter 'AP5'), Article 16, Cooperation and Coordination, 25.
2. AP5, Article 14, Competences and Functions of the Federal Government, 23.
3. AP5, Section C, Art. 32, par. 7, 35.
4. As of 2004 there were nearly 100 banks in the north.
5. This reality was brought home at the Cyprus Donors Conference (16 April 2004) where the total pledged was less than C£200 million (€340 million).
6. Fiona Mullen, Özlem Oguz and Praxoula Antoniadou Kyriacou, *The day after: Commercial Opportunities following a solution to the Cyprus Problem*, Oslo, 2008, 53.
7. a) 29+ per cent for the T/C Constituent State was discussed as a reference point at the 1984 UN Proximity Talks between Spyros Kyprianou, Rauf Denktash and then Secretary-General Javier Perez de Cuellar. b) The Land Registry Office estimated the total area of the Republic at 97.3 per cent and of the SBA at 2.7 per cent. Of the 97.3 per cent, 28.5 per cent in the Annan Plan goes to the T/C Constituent State (thus 29.5 per cent of the area of the URC) and 68.8 per cent to the G/C (thus 70.7 per cent).
8. AP5 proposes 33.3 per cent; but single-property smallholders could get all 100 per cent of their property back; on the other hand, some could opt out; the rule is murky.
9. George & Constantinos Lordos, 'Property Board Fund Model, 2004' (PBFM 2004). Table 1
10. Symeon Matsis estimated C£5 billion in 'The cost of compensation for properties that shall not be reinstated', written 14/03/2004, published in *Politis*, 06/04/2004 and revised to C£6 billion on 21/03/2004 with unknown publication date. Other studies by AKEL and *Politis* produced results of C£5.5b and C£4b respectively; however, publication references are not available. The disparity between these studies and the Planning Bureau/LRO numbers is largely caused by the latter estimating G/C property appreciation at 10 per cent compounded since 1974 (which is high) and valuing T/C properties as if the events of 1964 - 1974 were 'normal' (which is low). According to LRO, in 1974, the average T/C property in the south (£206/donum) was worth just one-seventh of the average G/C property in the north (£1,346/donum). If true, this was largely due to the 'ghetto' condition of T/C properties during 1964-1974; the definition of 'current value' in AP5 proposed to adjust all property values along current market prices 'as if' the events of 1964-1974 and 1974 – to date had never occurred. The independent studies made efforts to adjust for these.

11. The federal government will pay in the first 5 years (AP5, Annex VII, Attach. 2 Sect. A, Art.7).
12. See also 'Conclusions'.
13. See also note 27.
14. These figures were the latest available in 2004.
15. See, for example, Stelios Platis et al, 'The Economics of the Solution Based on the Annan Plan', CIIM Nicosia, Sept 2003 - Section III.
16. Even a 5 per cent imbalance between supply and demand is enough to create a glut or a shortage in any market and cause a large price movement.
17. In the 1990s a property boom led to a property glut in Japan and pushed the economy into a 15-year recession.
18. Annex VII: Attachment 2, Art. 8: Even though the Compensation Trust 'shall have no pre-determined duration', the Property Board is supposed to wound up ten years after entry into force of the Foundation Agreement.
19. Considering that the Governing Council of the Property Board will enjoy immunity from prosecution for their decisions, (Attachment 2, Article 2, Para 15) their prerogative to set prices for, and dispose of, C£6 billion worth of assets over, say, 10 years may prove too corrupting an influence for many.
20. Annex VII, Attachment 2, Section A, Art.3, 4, 5.
21. This translates into 1.8 housing units per Cypriot family!
22. By the conditions of AP5 these relocations should cause minimum disruption. A reasonable estimate would suggest 6,000 homes (of a total of 16,000 needed) could be built on land purchased from the Board. However, on the basis of the indicated land values in the north this would only translate into sales of C£ 15 million (approx.) by the Board.
23. a) Waive Capital Gains and/or Income Taxes, Transfer and Mortgage Fees, (even Property and Municipal Taxes for an initial period) on such interstate-intercommunal transactions. b) Establish two Mortgage Banks (one in each state); each to raise funds with Constituent State guarantees, to provide low-cost/long term property financing exclusively for purchases/exchanges etc. of 'affected properties' in its Constituent State.
24. CGT=20 per cent, Transfer Fee=4-8 per cent, Mortgage Fee=1 per cent, Valuation Fee=0.25-0.5 per cent plus other L.R.O fees for other sevices, plus bank arrangement fees (0.10-0.25 per cent)
25. In the years 1960- 1974 (L.R.O., Cyprus).
26. See Horowitz, Donald et al, 'Ethnic Groups in Conflict', 2000.
27. This essay is adapted from a speech I gave to TESEV, Istanbul, 29 January 2004.

Chapter 10

PRO: ECONOMIC VIABILITY OF ANNAN V

Zenon Pophaides

In its attempt to provide the basis of a comprehensive settlement of the Cyprus problem, the Annan Plan included a number of provisions on the functioning of the economy and the particular economic issues arising from the political claims and sensitivities of the two communities.

In its provisions the Plan conforms to generally accepted principles of federalism[1] and naturally assigns fiscal tasks to the central government and the two constituent states. It recognizes the need for the smooth functioning of markets within the institutional framework of the EU, which the reunified republic was going to accede, had both communities accepted the Plan. At the same time the Plan made an effort to tackle a number of issues relating to the realities 'on the ground' and the respective political positions of the two communities. It is this aspect of the Plan which the Greek Cypriot community intensely criticized.

The Plan aimed at the reunification of the economy and the eventual convergence of living standards in the two constituent states. Taxation and budgetary arrangements involved in practice fiscal transfers from the rich south to the poorer north. Concern was therefore expressed about an eventual increased tax burden falling on the shoulders of the Greek Cypriot taxpayer. It was also felt that the federal government was not granted adequate tools to impose budgetary discipline in the case of failure on the part of the constituent states to conform to agreed fiscal constraints, which in some cases the EU was to externally determine.

While the Plan recognized the need for the smooth functioning of the market in a unified economy, restrictions were nevertheless envisaged, arising from provisions on the property question and imposed limitations on the free movement and establishment of Greek Cypriot citizens in the Turkish Cypriot constituent state. Furthermore, the Turkish Cypriot constituent state was endowed with the power to impose temporary restrictions on the free movement of goods, labour and capital in certain circumstances, although this privilege would not be exercised without the approval of the European Commission.

The Plan provided for a single currency and one central bank divided initially into two branches, each operating in the respective state. Both the management structure and the division of the central bank were heavily criticized in the press as endangering the stability of the economy. In view of the fact that the Turkish Cypriot banking system was reported to present weaknesses, the proposed arrangements were thought to be unsatisfactory, more so because the country would become a member of the euro zone, a target which dictated strict economic and financial criteria.

The property question is perhaps the most difficult economic aspect of the Cyprus question. Properties left behind by both Greek Cypriots and Turkish Cypriots are occupied by users other than their legal owners; current users have undertaken considerable investments on these properties in the form of housing, hotels and other establishments. In many cases entirely new communities arose and housed themselves on land which legally belongs to dispossessed owners. The attempt made in the Plan to tackle this question involved both the exchange of properties, restitution, and considerable compensation to dispossessed owners. The government, political parties and a number of economists expressed the fear that the cost entailed would be of tremendous proportions, which would place an unbearable burden on the limited federal finances.

In more general terms critics, of whom reference will be made below, presented the federal structures and financial cost of the solution as detrimental to economic development, leading inevitably to the bankruptcy of and/or a serious destabilization of the economy. While it is true that some of the concerns expressed have a valid basis, as regards for instance property settlement and the need for fiscal discipline, it is also true that these concerns are greatly exaggerated; the economic foundation of the provisions of the Plan conform, as stated earlier, to principles of economic federalism employed in one way or another in a number of countries (e.g. Austria, Belgium, Switzerland and others). On the other hand it should be stated that a number of amendments which would improve the efficacy of the proposed settlement would be desirable, in order to reduce the risk of financial failure and economic destabilization.

Federal Structures and Economic Policy

The Annan Plan V allocates limited powers to the federal authorities. It also stipulates that the constituent states have the competences for all matters that are not explicitly assigned to the federal government. However, a number of issues arise relating to the definition of 'economic policy', the co-ordination of macroeconomic policy measures and the implementation of the *acquis communautaire*. These issues pose the question of the effectiveness of the envisioned federal structures (or lack of them).

Whereas the Plan sets as a federal task 'the convergence of the economies of the constituent states within the shortest possible time'[2], it does not clearly define the content of the term 'economic' policy, nor does it specify the functions and competences of a federal Ministry of Finance. It is thus unclear how the goal of convergence would be pursued, if the policy instruments are not defined or the necessary powers are not granted to the federal government, more so when the federal authorities would have to strictly limit themselves to the list of competences specified in the Plan.

Another area of concern is the lack of a federal regulatory framework, which would ensure that policies consistent with EU rules and regulations would be followed by the constituent state authorities. While the EU would hold the federal government responsible for the implementation of the *acquis communautaire*, it is not absolutely certain that it would be able to fulfill such obligations, since it is not furnished with the powers to impose policies on the constituent states.

To some extent, Annan V addresses these issues by introducing the idea of a bi-communal advisory council, which would deal with macroeconomic policy co-ordination between the two levels of government. However, this organ cannot take any legally binding decisions.

The idea of decentralization and delegation of authority is inherent in federalism, and the Annan Plan follows this concept, although no great effort was made to address shortcomings and difficulties that are likely to arise. The proposed institutional framework can most certainly be improved, if certain additions and amendments are made to clarify procedures and ensure the availability of effective policy instruments.

As a first priority, the competences of the federal authorities in the area of economic policy should be clearly defined and the functions of a federal Ministry of Finance unambiguously stated. Secondly, since the federal government is assigned with the ambitious task to attain convergence of the two economies, it should be strengthened accordingly. 'It should have the competence to develop and implement a common framework for state policies'.[3] This framework should take into account economic and financial conditions in the two constituent states, and ensure that a) policies applied at the state level are not mutually inconsistent, b) they do not put at risk the stability of the economy and c) they do not result in undesirable competition between the two economies (e.g. tax competition).

Implementing the *acquis comunautaire* should be considered in the same spirit. The role of the federal government as the authority responsible for the adoption of all EU policies dictates that it should be vested with appropriate powers. The federal authorities should possess the necessary legal instruments to enforce the implementation of common EU policies and existing EU law; in view of its significance this issue will be discussed below in some more detail.

Federal Revenues and Expenditures

The Plan envisages a weak federal government in the sense that its competences are confined to specific areas. Being by design weak, the federal government is granted limited revenues.

Indirect taxation falls within the jurisdiction of the federal authorities, but one third of net revenues would be distributed to the constituent states on the basis of an 80 to 20 per cent ratio. Additionally, the federal government would return to the constituent states forty per cent of its proceeds from value-added tax on the basis of an 85 to 15 per cent ratio.

This formula, which has been the outcome of negotiations, is satisfactory in the sense that it allows the federal government to meet expenditures that arise from its normal tasks (i.e. not taking into account additional obligations allocated to the federal authorities in regard of the cost of relocation of part of the population, contribution to the cost of the United Nations peace keeping force etc).

The question of federal finances and expenditures was debated during the period before the referendum in April 2004. Special reference was made to two issues. The first related to the tax burden involved for the two communities. Given the disparities between the two economies it was estimated that on the basis of the envisaged formula the burden of the cost of the federal administration would fall predominantly on the Greek Cypriot community. This is not surprising, since the per capita GDP in the Turkish Cypriot community was estimated to be in 2003 roughly thirty to forty per cent of the per capita GDP in the Greek Cypriot community. The Plan was criticized by Greek Cypriot politicians as being 'unfair', but this was a political not an economic argument; this political choice by the Plan's authors, is in line with the policy followed internationally, that the most wealthy bear the biggest part of the tax burden. On the other hand, the Plan provided for an earliest possible convergence between the two economies, which would gradually allow a more even distribution of the tax burden between the two communities.

The second issue that arose in the debate had to do with the extraordinary tasks and obligations referred to above, burdening the federal authorities with additional cost. This will be given some additional attention below, because of the nature of the problem and the worries that it spread among large sections of the population.

Certain remarks are in place regarding institutional arrangements on taxation and budgeting. Tax harmonization would be necessary, if the goal of convergence would be seriously pursued as an urgent task. Differences in tax rates would create unnecessary tax competition which would affect investment decisions and public finances at the federal and state levels. It would be in the interest of both communities to create effective instruments in order to harmonize their tax systems.

The Plan requires that at least one third of the federal civil servants at every level must hail from each constituent state. In a very small administration this would perhaps imply an increased cost, which would burden unnecessarily the federal budget. A more flexible formula would reduce the risk of an excessive growth of the federal civil service.

Budgeting procedures envisaged conform to general federalist principles. The Plan requires that the budget is approved by both chambers of Parliament with a special majority requirement from the Senate, which is set at two fifths of senators from each of the two communities. On the other hand, the Plan is silent on the role of the executive. It is not certain, if and how the Presidential Council would design the federal budget, nor is it clear if and how a Ministry of Finance would undertake to implement it. There is certainly a need for defining clearly the competences of the Presidential Council in the budgeting process. Moreover, the special majority requirement would create the risk of lengthy negotiations leading to excessive expenditures and deficits.

The Fiscal Position of the Constituent States

The creation of the federal government and its endowment with the revenues from indirect taxation means loss of revenue for the governments of the constituent states, although a considerable amount of this revenue would be returned to the constituent states in the form of transfers.

The loss of revenue would be greater for the Greek Cypriot constituent state which at the initial stages would be expected to finance almost entirely the federal budget. However, this loss of revenue would be compensated partly by savings on expenditures for tasks to be undertaken by the federal authorities. Although it can be plausibly argued that the new federal setting inevitably involves some duplication of functions and the subsequent growth of the consolidated public sector, it is also true that various departments and services (such as the diplomatic service) would fall under the jurisdiction of the federal government, which would be called to bear the cost.

In addition to these savings, the constituent states will benefit from the reduction and eventual abolition of defense expenditures; this is particularly true of the Greek Cypriot constituent state, because Turkey mostly, if not exclusively, covers the cost of military expenditures in northern Cyprus. Since the Republic of Cyprus is currently supporting persons displaced as a result of the war in 1974, it is reasonable to assume that substantial amounts will be saved following the implementation of the solution. These benefits are expected to compensate to a significant degree the loss of revenue to the federal government.[4]

Concern was voiced by government officials in the Greek Cypriot community over the expected cost of reconstruction and rebuilding of the returned areas including the now fenced town of Famagusta. Estimates of the cost vary, as it is not clear what the involvement of the Greek Cypriot state should be. Evidently, this entails a difficult political choice; the community would have to decide what part of the investments required should be assigned to the state budget and what is to be left to the private sector. The financial position of the Greek Cypriot constituent state will also determine the time span over which such investment outlays should be made.

The fiscal position of the Turkish Cypriot constituent state is less clear. Due to lack of reliable and transparent budgetary data it is difficult to assess adequately the current situation and the effects of the Annan Plan on its financial position. However, on the basis of available information, it is unlikely that fiscal arrangements, as envisaged in the Plan, would result in any significant loss of revenue. Moreover, the Turkish Cypriot constituent state would stand to benefit from savings on federal tasks and services; additionally, some windfall profits are likely to accrue, since expenditures for aiding or supporting displaced persons and other groups of the population would perhaps be terminated.

The picture is complicated by the fact that the Turkish Cypriot budget has been presenting large deficits, which are currently financed through Turkey's aid. The deficits have been the result of poor economic performance and lack of fiscal discipline. A solution to the Cyprus problem which would also imply accession to the EU would help the Turkish Cypriot constituent state to embark on a harmonization process with the EU and adopt sound fiscal rules and practices.

Most studies, as described below, agree that reunification of the island would particularly affect the Turkish Cypriot economy positively, resulting in sustainable economic growth and higher per capita income. Such a development would certainly improve public revenue and the overall financial position of the Turkish Cypriot constituent state. Nevertheless, public finances in northern Cyprus underline further the need for fiscal coordination between the federal government and the constituent states. The practice of some European countries with federal structures is perhaps instructive: in order to apply the fiscal rules dictated by the EU, Belgium, Austria and Spain have concluded an internal stability pact between the various state levels.

Extraordinary Costs and the Federal Finances

It is estimated that the revenues assigned to the federal government would be sufficient to meet expenditures, associated with its normal tasks as listed in the

Constitution in the Annan Plan V.[5] However, the federal budget has been burdened with extraordinary costs arising from additional obligations.

The federal authorities are responsible for re-housing those Turkish Cypriots and settlers from Turkey who would have to be relocated, as a result of the envisaged territorial adjustments. The federal government is also made responsible for part of the cost of the UN peace keeping force, so long as it continues to be present on the island. Additionally, the federal government should have to pay for the running costs of the Property Board during the first five years of its operation.

It is not easy to estimate the financial cost implied by the assignment of these extraordinary tasks, since the exact number of Turkish Cypriots who would be relocated is not known, nor is the standard of the housing units required specified. The contribution to the budget of the UN peace keeping force, the size of which has not been determined, is also unknown. However, it is commonly agreed that the cost is indeed very high and in fact lies beyond the normal financial means of the federal authorities. Based on earlier versions of the Plan, the Planning Bureau of the Republic of Cyprus estimated the housing cost of relocating the Turkish Cypriots who would be affected by the territorial adjustments at Cyprus Pounds 250 million, while another 562.5 million would be needed for relocating the Turkish Cypriots who would be affected by the reinstatement of properties to Greek Cypriot owners in the Turkish Cypriot constituent state.[6] In addition to these needs, expenditures for infrastructure must be factored and here it is unclear to what extent the burden will be on the federal government or the constituent state. This reality is in fact implicitly recognized in the Plan, which makes reference to the need for external aid and for this purpose a donor conference was planned to be convened under the aegis of the EU.

The property question and the proposed solution imply serious financial risks for the federal government. The Plan envisages either property restitution or full compensation to all dispossessed owners whose claims for restitution would not be possible to be satisfied. In the latter case the federal authorities would guarantee the compensation bonds, which would be issued in favour of the dispossessed owners who would not be reinstated to their properties. Since the prices at which the Property Board would sell the properties (not to be returned to their original owners) cannot be known ex ante, the federal government would remain exposed to a risk of large proportions.

The kind of problems referred to above would seem to paint a rather gloomy picture for federal public finances. However, these challenges are surmountable. The benefits from reunification would almost certainly increase federal revenue and improve public finances. Strengthening the federal government, through appropriate amendments of some of the provisions of the Plan, would enable it to secure fiscal discipline and macroeconomic stability, which would enhance prospects for fast economic growth. A stable economic environment would make it possible for the federal government to borrow on the capital markets, provided that it would be able to establish its financial credibility; and foreign aid could contribute to filling the gap created by these extraordinary obligations, although it is not certain that large amounts would have been forthcoming.

The Property Question

The proposed settlement of the property question has been one of the most controversial issues dealt with by the Annan Plan, not only because it is politically emotive, but also because of its perceived economic implications. The Plan followed two principles in the formulation of the offered solution: a) the principle of bizonality, interpreted to mean that the largest part of property in each constituent state should be owned respectively by Greek Cypriots and Turkish Cypriots. This actually implied that only part of the properties left behind by dispossessed Greek Cypriots would be reinstated to their legal owners, creating the need for massive compensation; b) the second principle, deriving from the first, consists in the 'full and effective compensation' to which all dispossessed persons should be entitled, if their property would not be reinstated to them.[7]

Following this approach, the Plan provides that 'the restitution entitlement is one-third of the land area and one-third of the *current value* (whichever first applies) of the aggregated affected property of a dispossessed owner',[8] although institutions such as the Church, public or private trusts, etc, are not granted this entitlement. However, the above arrangement is subject to a number of restrictions and exceptions: a) a current user who is also a dispossessed person could claim a title to the property that he or she had been using for the last ten years in exchange for a property of similar value of which he or she was dispossessed; b) a current user could also claim a title to an affected property, if he or she made a significant improvement to it; c) properties justifying compulsory acquisition could not be reinstated; d) properties required for military purposes could not also be reinstated; etc.

The proposed compensation provides for both compensation bonds and property appreciation certificates drawn on a compensation fund. Interest bearing compensation bonds, which would be guaranteed by the federal government would represent one third of total current value of all properties in the portfolio of the Compensation Trust, which would be dealing with property portfolio management. The concept of 'current value', which would be used for the purpose of determining the claimants' amount of compensation, is defined as 'the value of a property at the time of dispossession, plus an adjustment to reflect appreciation based among other things on increase in average sales prices of properties in Cyprus in comparable locations'.[9]

The administration of this settlement is assigned to an independent institution, the Property Board, which would implement the above provisions. Its main task would be to administer the transfer of properties from current users to legal owners and dispose of the non-reinstated property in order to finance compensation claims, through one of its divisions, the Compensates Bureau, which at a later stage would transform itself into an independent legal entity, the Compensation Trust. The aim of the latter arrangement is an efficient management of property portfolio.

The Plan has foreseen that one of the difficulties of the implementation of these provisions would be the inability of Turkish Cypriot current users and other prospective buyers to purchase properties at prices of the order implied by the concept of current value. To meet this problem the Plan provides for a preferential loan scheme under which interest would be subsidized; the federal government would partly guarantee this scheme.

This brief description of the main provisions of the Plan on the property problem indicates its complexity. The value of the properties involved is indeed enormous; attempts to arrive at an estimate vary, but most studies seem to agree on a figure approaching or exceeding the 2003 GDP of the Republic of Cyprus. Views differ significantly about the magnitude of the required compensation with estimates ranging from 4.5 billion[10] to 12-13 billion Cyprus pounds, although some studies were based on earlier versions of the Plan.[11]

The root of the problem of this settlement lies in the uncertainty of the property market in the Turkish Cypriot constituent state. While all dispossessed persons would be granted compensation in the form of property certificates and compensation bonds on the basis of an imputed 'current value', it is not apparent that the real economic value at which the Property Board would sell these properties would reach the imputed value. The fact that the Turkish Cypriot constituent state would be able to impose restrictions on the right of non permanent residents of this state to purchase property (for fifteen years or for as long as its per capita GDP remains below 85 per cent of the corresponding per capita GDP in the Greek Cypriot constituent state) would create distortions in addition to those that in any case would exist, as a direct consequence of the nature of the proposed settlement.

The risk of this uncertainty would actually be borne by Greek Cypriot dispossessed owners and the federal government, which would have to supply the guarantees under the compensation bond scheme. This would create an additional burden on the shoulders of the federal authorities, whose financial position is by design weak. Having recognized this fact, the Plan makes references to the donor conference which would presumably offer financial assistance.

The question which arises is whether this scheme is financially viable. In general terms the success of the proposed solution rests on the ability of the property market in the Turkish Cypriot state to function smoothly and on the reasonable expectation of convergence of the two economies. A successful process of convergence would gradually push property prices in the northern part to a level similar to that of the south. This can more easily be achieved if the right to impose restrictions on non residents is lifted or at least practiced with the utmost care so as not to depress the property market. In that respect the European Commission could by mutual consent actively involve itself, in order to ensure that economic logic is not sacrificed in the name of political aims of doubtful value.

The Turkish Cypriot area is endowed with privileged holiday resorts and tourist development is bound to accrue. This would exercise an upward pressure on land prices. Following accession to the EU demand from foreign investors will increase, as experience in the south has proved. If the property settlement is administered efficiently and the market is allowed to function smoothly, the scheme would not necessarily result in losses, but on the contrary it could possibly realize some profits.[12]

The federal government should not undertake any obligations arising from the property settlement, because this is not justified by its financial position. An alternative approach would involve foreign aid in the form of an international guarantee scheme of the compensation bonds, which would remove the risk that the federal government would have to bear.

The Central Bank and Monetary Policy

Annan V envisages a single currency, which, as the United Nations had clarified, would be the Pound of the Republic of Cyprus. Following internationally accepted practice, art. 32.2 of the proposed Constitution provides for an independent Central Bank 'in accordance with European Union requirements'. The governing organs of the Central Bank would be the Governor and Deputy Governor – who could not hail from the same constituent state – the Board of Directors and the Monetary Policy Committee. In both the Board of Directors and the Monetary Policy Committee the two constituent states would be equally represented; in both a non-Cypriot member is present to facilitate the decision making process; decisions would be taken by single majority. The Plan provides for the possibility of the Central Bank being divided into two separate branches, performing identical functions in each of the constituent states. When the Plan was drafted Cyprus was not an EU member and much concern was expressed regarding the ability of the Central Bank to perform its duties, such as fulfilling the necessary ERM-II requirements and preparations for adopting the euro. This debate is now only of historical interest, since the Republic of Cyprus adopted the euro on 1 January 2008.

The proposed arrangements should be considered in relation to two questions, which are of capital economic significance: a) whether the proposed structure would enable the Central Bank to perform effectively its main duty, which is the maintenance of price stability; and b) how the weak Turkish Cypriot banking sector could be restructured so as to function smoothly in the new environment.

The proposed structure for the Central Bank is generally in line with modern requirements, since its independence is constitutionally safeguarded and its ability to reach decisions is ensured. On the other hand the possibility of separate branches would not serve any useful purpose. In a unitary monetary zone their existence could only create confusion by sending unclear messages, undermining the credibility of the institution. If this proposal also implies the possibility of different approaches to the regulation and supervision of the banking sectors in the two constituent states, it is clearly flawed, because these are functions which can only belong to the Central Bank itself and not to separate branches. But, the Federal Law on the Central Bank of Cyprus seems to appreciate the problem by envisaging that six months after entry into force of the Foundation Agreement, the Board of Directors will invite experts from the International Monetary Fund and the EU in order to review the performance of the Turkish Cypriot branch; the Board of Directors will then decide whether and for how long the branch shall continue to exist.[13]

The Plan does not deal much with the banking system in the north. Reliable data on the Turkish Cypriot banking sector is lacking, but it appears that many banks are severely undercapitalized,[14] as a result of bad lending and investment practices. Once a new regulatory regime is adopted, in line with EU standards, the financial liabilities of these banks will become apparent to depositors, probably leading to panic and a banking crisis. The Central Bank should anticipate and deal with this possibility if and when it arises. There seems to be a need for re-capitalization of the Turkish Cypriot banks which may necessitate assistance from the Central Bank in the form of loans and guaranteeing deposits.

The EU and the Annan Plan

The Plan took seriously into account the wish of both communities to join the EU. The *acquis communautaire* makes available a common framework of policy which can assist economic convergence. EU membership is particularly significant for the Turkish Cypriot constituent state, where the need for modernization and economic growth is vital. The Plan explicitly provides for close cooperation of the two states and for harmonization of their policies in a number of important fields. This would be done through the conclusion of cooperation agreements having the legal standing of constitutional laws. Areas covered could be tourism, environment protection, fisheries and agriculture, industry and commerce, health, sports and education, social security and so forth.

It has been argued above that the role of the federal government should be strengthened, because it is assigned with the ambitious task of narrowing disparities between the two economies within the shortest possible time. Moreover, it represents Cyprus in EU, being mainly responsible for the implementation of the *acquis communautaire*. Thus it should be furnished with the necessary legal instruments to impose EU policies where the constituent states prove reluctant or unable to do so.

Macroeconomic stability is a prerequisite for economic growth. Fiscal discipline is required not only because of the policy of adopting the euro but also because stability is a condition for the smooth functioning of market and a factor favourable to investment. It increases the ability of the country to borrow on the capital markets at low interest rates, a need which could be vital at the initial stages of the existence of the UCR.

As indicated above the federal government should be able to formulate a common policy framework that it and the constituent states would follow. Coordination of fiscal policy could be more adequately attained through an internal stability pact, which would translate EU criteria into binding fiscal and financial criteria for all state authorities involved.

The Annan Plan and Prospects for Growth

Reunification could create the conditions for fast and sustainable growth in both constituent states, leading also to convergence. The Ministry of Finance of the Republic of Cyprus estimated in 2003 a GDP growth for a transition period of five to ten years to fluctuate between 5.0 - 5.5 per cent for the south and around 7.5 per cent for the north.[15] Another study is in this respect equally optimistic, as it expects growth rates to rise to 6 per cent and 8 per cent respectively.[16] There seems to be a general consensus in a number of studies that reunification would have a positive impact on growth potential for the whole of the island.[17]

Although both economies have developed similar sectors, important synergies can be realized and complementarities exploited.[18] Potential for tourist development in the north is enormous, as its valuable resources in this sector have not been fully developed. The north can benefit from visitors who could pay visits to both parts of the country. Complementarities could also arise in the export of educational services, which is proving to be a dynamic economic sector in both communities. Growth in the north would offer new market opportunities for firms operating in the south. Increased labour mobility across the whole of the island could help create a more efficient labour market; labour shortages in the south could easily be matched by labour availability in the north.

The goal of convergence implies the design of policies that could trigger fast and sustainable growth especially in the Turkish Cypriot constituent state. Convergence can to a large extent be promoted through harmonization in the north with the *acquis communautaire*. The Plan comprises a number of provisions to that end, which can be easily reached if the role of the federal authorities is strengthened.

The development gap between the economies of the two communities is often attributed to the less favourable external conditions in the north, such as non-recognition and economic isolation. While reunification would obviously eliminate these factors, other weaknesses should not be underestimated. Fiscal and monetary stability, as the experience of the Greek Cypriot economy indicates, is a significant contributory factor to sustainable growth. While the adoption of the euro would certainly remove foreign exchange risks, there is still a need for a fiscal framework for the re-unified economy. In this context a key challenge would be the restructuring of the public sector in the north, in ways that would favour investment and create opportunities for private sector expansion.

Harmonization with the *acquis communautaire* would enhance the competitiveness of the markets and help to remove current practices that distort incentives. Restructuring the Turkish Cypriot banking sector, within a framework compatible with EU requirements would also contribute to a development strategy. Clarification of property rights, as attempted in the Plan, would create conditions for boosting private investment.

Developments subsequent to the Annan Plan indicate that growth and convergence are realistic goals. Based on a construction boom the Turkish Cypriot economy in recent years achieved substantial growth rates of the order of ten per cent,[19] while the Greek Cypriot economy continued to grow smoothly.

Conclusion

The Annan Plan conforms to generally accepted principles of fiscal federalism and can provide the basis for sustainable growth for both constituent states. Certain provisions should be amended to avoid distortions and allow a smoother functioning of markets. Reunification will be beneficial for both communities provided that institutional problems are removed and suitable policies are adopted. A prospective accession to the EU of the Turkish Cypriot controlled area would benefit the whole of the island and contribute to the strategy of convergence.

The weakness of the federal government is a deficiency which should be rectified, in ways that would offer it the necessary tools for ensuring macroeconomic stability. A common framework for states policies could be an effective tool in this direction. Strengthening the federal government would enable it to promote effectively the policy of convergence and fulfil adequately its obligations arising from EU membership.

The cost of reconstruction is considerable and is most likely beyond the means of Cyprus'. However, it should be stressed that the magnitude of the perceived cost is influenced by political choices and is not exclusively the direct outcome of the Plan. Substantial foreign aid would certainly be needed for implementing some of the provisions of the Plan within the envisaged time limits. The property problem is perhaps the most difficult aspect of the Plan with significant economic implications. While the envisaged settlement may well prove to be self-financing, it could create additional financial risks for the federal government. The property settlement may need to be given additional consideration.

The economic viability of the Annan Plan does not depend only on the content of its provisions and the dynamics of reunification. To a significant degree it depends on the adoption and implementation of effective economic policies both at the federal and the constituent state level.

Endnotes

1. Barry Eichengreen, Riccardo Faini, Juergen von Hagen and Charles Wyplosz, 'Economic Aspects of the Annan Plan for the Solution of the Cyprus Problem', *Report to the Government of the Republic of Cyprus*, III, February 17, 2004.
2. Annan V: The Comprehensive Settlement of the Cyprus Problem, 31 March 2004, Annex 1, Art. 52.
3. Eichengreen et al, 'Economic Aspects', 13.
4. George Vassiliou, 'The Economics of the Solution Based on the Annan Plan', 2003, 11-12.
5. Annan Plan V, Annex 1, Art. 14.
6. Planning Bureau, 'Preliminary Evaluation of Financial Needs in the Case of a Settlement to the Cyprus problem' (Greek), 2003.
7. Ayla Gurel and Ozersay Kudret, *The Politics of Property in Cyprus*, Oslo, 2006.
8. Annan V, Annex VII, Attachment 1, Art.1.12.
9. Ibid., 1.4.
10. Stelios Platis, Stelios Orphanides and Fiona Mullen, *The Property Regime in a Cyprus Settlement*, Oslo, 2006, 48.
11. Constantinos Lordos, 'Economic Aspects of the Annan Plan and the Plan's Property Proposals', *Discussion Paper, TESEV International Workshop*, Istanbul, 26 January 2004.
12. Platis et al, 'The Property Regime', 53.
13. Annan V, Annex III, Attachment 6, Art. 73, Federal Law on the Central Bank of Cyprus.
14. Eichengreen et al, 'Economic Aspects', 57.
15. Ministry of Finance, Republic of Cyprus, 'Economic and Financial Aspects of a Settlement of the Cyprus Problem on the Basis of the Annan Plan', *Pre-Accession Programme 2002-2006*, Appendix III, 2003, 281, 284.
16. Vassiliou, 'The Economics of the Solution', 16.
17. Willem Noe and Max Watson, 'Convergence and Reunification in Cyprus: Scope for a Virtual Circle', *ECFIN*, II, 3, 14 February 2005.
18. Ibid.
19. State Planning Organisation, TRNC, www.devplan.org

Chapter 11

THE TURKISH CYPRIOT VIEWS ON ANNAN V

Erol Kaymak

Introduction

The Annan Plan represents a significant milestone in Turkish Cypriot history. From its unveiling in November 2002 through the referendum held in April 2004 Turkish Cypriots found themselves debating the Plan and the very basis of their political community.

The goal of this chapter is to summarize the debate or discourses regarding the Annan Plan within the Turkish Cypriot community in the run up to the referendum. In the sections that follow, this chapter first introduces the political context prevalent during the period and the significance of the Annan Plan. Secondly, assessments of the Plan are outlined in some detail, breaking the Plan down into analytical components. Finally, the chapter summarizes the referendum process itself.

The Political Context

Even as the Annan Plan was undergoing revisions, information on it was disseminated steadily throughout the phases of negotiation. Significantly, the Turkish Cypriots held a parliamentary election in December 2003 where the Annan Plan featured as the most important issue. It is fair to say that the elections were practically a de facto preliminary referendum on the Plan.

The political landscape itself was affected, with a significant shift of political support away from community leader and president, Rauf Denktash, toward the Turkish Republican Party (CTP) headed by Mehmet Ali Talat, who subsequently became prime minister and later president. His qualified victory[1] in the 2003 parliamentary elections was crucial in eventually sealing the fate of the Plan in the Turkish North. Talat and others championed the Plan and mobilized support that culminated in a 65 per cent 'yes' in the face of Denktash's staunch opposition.

The Annan Plan was rejected by the Greek Cypriot electorate, thus rendering it null and void. Nevertheless, one merit of the process could be the upshot of unlocking the situation in Cyprus. In producing a comprehensive blueprint the UN has introduced the possibility of negotiation on matters of substance rather than procedure. As of writing this has yet to occur. The widespread unpopularity of the Annan Plan among Greek Cypriots has allowed the Greek Cypriot leadership to distance itself from the blueprint. However, it is highly likely that when substantive negotiations resume, through the 8 July 2006 agreement or otherwise, the Annan Plan will serve as a reference.

Symbolically, the Annan Plan represented a new era and a reversal in political fortunes, with the opposition seizing the moment. Rauf Denktash himself did not negotiate the Plan, and was not the brainchild behind its inception. Rather, it has been suggested that the parameters were established through UN discussions with the Greek

Cypriot leadership, while details were shared with the Turkish Cypriot opposition on an informal basis. Thus, opposition groups were in turn privy to the parameters around which a consensus was built among a host of non-governmental organizations in the north.[2] In this way, Turkish Cypriot civil society played a unique and somewhat autonomous role in mobilizing public opinion and thus the political parties themselves.

With the leaking of the Annan Plan on 13 November 2002 demand for information was high. The Plan had been unveiled to diplomats on the 11th, but its dissemination was rapid. The most widely read daily, the *Kibris* newspaper, worked hard to translate as much of the Plan as possible (given that many Turkish Cypriots could not have read the English language text). Other dailies followed suit and soon there was a deluge of information. The government itself produced an official translation made available to the public. The Plan, content wise, proved to be close to the vision of the NGOs that had been promoting a solution. It is significant that Denktash himself did not weigh in until several days after the Plan was revealed, ostensibly due to the sensitivity of Turkish diplomacy at that early phase. Denktash was in New York at the time, recovering from heart surgery operations he had undergone in October. By the time he declared the Plan to be beset with 'traps' it was 21 November. This, in turn, gave a head start to proponents of the Plan whose evaluations were wholeheartedly favourable and who were demanding that the Annan Plan be accepted as a basis for negotiation without delay.

Public opinions mattered because the Annan Plan called for separate, simultaneous referenda to accept its provisions. Although the UN did not intend it, it became increasingly clear that the fate of the Plan could fall on the shoulders of the people. The reluctance of the political leaders on either side of Cyprus to endorse the Plan meant that even the UN joined in the fray, with UNOPS funding a pamphlet that helped explain the Plan to the public in abbreviated terms.

Assessments of the Annan Plan Among Turkish Cypriots

The Annan Plan was widely debated in society and especially through radio and televised media. Often television debates would run late into the night, and on some occasions, into the early hours of the next day. Given the extensive nature of debate, the pros and cons of the Annan Plan, as conceived through Turkish Cypriot discourses are outlined below.

New State of Affairs

The Annan Plan left open the question as to whether a new state will be established or whether the Republic of Cyprus is to devolve constitutionally into a bizonal federation. Kofi Annan considered this to be constructive ambiguity regarding the origins of the proposed UCR.[3]

Proponents among Turkish Cypriots of the Annan Plan tended to emphasize the view that this 'virgin birth' constructed a new indissoluble partnership based on two pre-existing and inviolable constituent states. Similar to Annan, proponents felt this was a pragmatic way to deal with the status problem that plagued negotiations for decades. Positive assessments contrasted the 'new state of affairs' with the 1960 'state of affairs' and found the latter inferior to what was proposed in the Annan Plan. Positive evaluations found little to fault in Annan's attempt to cut the Gordian Knot by being evasive on the ontological questions.

Opponents of the Plan contradicted this positive evaluation, pointing to aspects of the Plan that suggested more continuity than implied by the proponents. Further, in earlier versions of the Plan the term constituent state had not yet surfaced and the word component state was translated literally as 'part' state, which sounds odd in Turkish and does not convey the sense that the constituent state precedes the 'new state of affairs'. Negative assessments suggested that this was not a 'new state', but actually constituted a devolution of the (Greek Cypriot led) Republic of Cyprus and thus was inimical to Turkish Cypriot interests. In the final version of the Plan the constituent state was officially entitled the 'Turkish State' and the term 'Turkish Cypriot' also made its way into the document, emphasizing communal identity and community based citizenship.

The question of the 'new state of affairs' is among the most subjective if not intangible, considering Kofi Annan's view that interpretations of the past and the coming into being of the UCR be left open to interpretation.[4] For Denktash any Plan that fails to overtly reference the pre-existence of two states as the basis of the settlement is unacceptable, thus he opposed the 'philosophy of the Plan'. Supporters of the Annan Plan were quick to point out that the Plan had the effect of legitimizing what had been illegal internationally. The status, political rights, and legitimacy accorded to the Turkish Cypriots outweighed all other considerations.

Simultaneous Referenda

The positive assessment of separate, simultaneous referenda was straightforward. The wording that drafters inserted into the Plan tended to satisfy the Turkish Cypriot anxiety over status. Through the referenda Turkish Cypriots and Greek Cypriots were invited to adopt the Foundation Agreement through their 'inherent constitutive power'. This was tantamount to an exercise of self-determination on the part of the Turkish Cypriot community. It was also a democratic exercise of ratification that lent legitimacy to the Annan Plan. Reference to the UCR as a renewed 'partnership' was also featured in the Plan.

Negative assessments portrayed the process as problematic. From a legalistic standpoint, Denktash has always favored a settlement akin to an international treaty between two states. In the Annan Plan, however, the leaders were asked to sign a Foundation Agreement. Ultimately, the Plan was put to vote without the signatures of either side. Denktash vehemently opposed this method. Furthermore, the wording of the Plan did not provide that Turkish Cypriots have 'inherent constitutive power' independent of that of the Greek Cypriots, despite the fact that separate referenda were to be held.

Sovereignty

The Annan Plan makes overt references to the Swiss and Belgian models (Main Articles, Article 2). Kofi Annan explained that this was done so as to assuage the fears of either side, should the 'new state of affairs' fail. The Annan Plan was meant to establish a unified Cyprus with a single international personality, thus satisfying a Greek

Cypriot concern. Domestically, however, it entailed a bizonal federal system, with either 'constituent state' exercising certain powers not vested in the federal government 'sovereignly'. As in Belgium, the UCR would not entail a hierarchy between federal and constituent state laws.

Debates that ensued tended to treat sovereignty in binary terms: there either was or was not sovereignty in the Plan, as far as the Turkish Cypriots were concerned. This was, in part, due to the odd wording of the Plan. 'Sovereignly' is not a legal term, nor is it listed in dictionaries. Turkish Cypriots spent much time debating the meaning of the term and why Annan had not simply used the term 'sovereign'.

The positive assessment was that the Plan provided for Turkish Cypriot sovereignty through bizonality, with two equal, sovereign constituent states. The federal government also suggested shared sovereignty and as such was unproblematic. As the TRNC was not an internationally recognized state the Plan afforded the Turkish Cypriots status through a constituent state in the north.[5]

Negative assessments were numerous. Starting from the premise that the TRNC was a legitimate (albeit internationally unrecognized) entity with sovereignty, the Annan Plan is portrayed as a step back from sovereignty and statehood. The provision of sovereignty was also deemed inferior to the status accorded to the Turkish Cypriot community in 1960. In the original 'state of affairs' individual political rights were exercised through one's community, and the Turkish Cypriot leadership enjoyed vestiges of political equality, the most tangible evidence thereof being the veto power vested in either executive, where the Vice President was a Turkish Cypriot. The Annan Plan (until Annan V) did not even mention Turkish Cypriots as a political community (Article 3, Main Articles). The negative assessment was that the Plan actually undermined sovereignty by 'diluting'[6] bizonality, which in turn diluted Turkish Cypriot sovereignty. Here bizonality meant two independent, homogenous states.

The broader contextual debate had to do with the status of the TRNC as a viable and legitimate entity, with proponents emphasizing how a settlement to the Cyprus problem would provide Turkish Cypriots with international standing.[7]

Federal Governance

For Turkish Cypriots 'political equality' has always been a *sine qua non* for a settlement. Evaluations of the Annan Plan were held against this standard.

For the executive branch of government the Annan Plan proposed a Presidential Council consisting of six equal members, four from the Greek Cypriot State and two from the Turkish Cypriot State, respectively. Accordingly, a Turkish Cypriot would be head of state one third of the time.

This feature of federal governance found many proponents as manifesting political equality. Whereas the Turkish Cypriots would remain a numerical minority in the Council, the fact that all members were of equal status was considered satisfactory. Moreover, rotation would ensure that Turkish Cypriots held all portfolios, including President of the Council. Those who considered anything less than full political equality – that is, numerical equality at all levels of governance – expressed their disappointment with the 4 and 2 arrangement.

One benchmark, however, was the veto power vested in the Vice President in the 1960 Constitution. Although the Annan Plan euphemistically hopes that decisions would be made consensually, the Plan allows for majority rule with the proviso that at least one member from each constituent state approves. Positive evaluations suggested that the Presidential Council proposed in the Annan Plan afforded Turkish Cypriots an indirect veto, thus political equality. On the negative side, the new system was portrayed as a step back from communal rights granted in the 1960 framework. Under the Annan Plan a 'veto' would only be possible if there was consensus among the Turkish Cypriot members of the Presidential Council. More troubling, still, was the likelihood that those elected to the Presidential Council would be agreeable to the Greek Cypriots (as each Council member elected on a single list would require at least 2/5ths support from Senators from either constituent state), if not actually Greek Cypriot in origin. As the original version of the Annan Plan left open the question as to whether - through demographic changes in the northern constituent state over time - Greek Cypriots might gain an electoral foothold and hence undo the political equality of the Senate, early debate among Turkish Cypriots obsessed on this factor.

It follows that debate regarding political equality in the Senate revolved around the issue of Greek Cypriot resettlement and speculative scenarios for future decades. These debates and speculations abated when subsequent versions of the Plan made clearer to the Turkish Cypriot community that the political equality in the Senate would not be undone. Special majorities on a number of matters were also greeted warmly by a number of proponents, but overall this question did not feature as prominently as overall numerical equality.

The question of constitutional amendment was also addressed, whereby proponents suggested how difficult it would actually be to achieve changes. Opponents were less sanguine, suggesting the ease with which changes could be made, and pointing to the fact that changes were not possible in the 1960 Constitution, a factor favoring the Turkish Cypriots.

The Chamber of Deputies, where representation would be based on relative populations was less controversial overall than the debate on Senate equality. Nevertheless, opponents of the Plan pointed out that political equality demanded numerical equality in all institutions.

Not surprisingly, the problem of 'workability' did not factor into debate. Few Turkish Cypriots fixated much on the welfare of federal institutions, which were, by and large, taken for granted.

Distribution of Competences

The Annan Plan allows for the federal government and the constituent states to 'sovereignly' exercise respective powers. The powers of the federal government are specified in the Constitution.[8] Generally, the federal government would be responsible for external relations and relations with the EU, monetary policy and finances, natural resources and territorial boundaries, communications, citizenship, combating terrorism and organized crime, provision of amnesty (for crimes from within a constituent state), intellectual property, and antiquities.

The powers of the constituent states are those 'not vested by the Constitution in the federal government'. Further, either constituent state would freely organize itself under its own constitution. Thus the Plan aimed to satisfy the longstanding Turkish Cypriot demand that powers remain residual, although this is only implicit. The primary residual power made explicit, however, is policing.[9]

For proponents the distribution provided autonomy and sufficient safeguards against the federal government from becoming intrusive. Provision of policing vested in the constituent state was deemed positive.

Negative assessments considered the relatively limited list of federal powers either excessive or subject to additions pending constitutional amendment. Similarly, the powers vested in the constituent states were not listed, implying they could be invoked by the federal government, once again raising the specter of constitutional amendment.

Overall the powers granted the 'part state' was akin to that of a 'municipality'. The inability of the northern constituent state to engage in international relations was considered a major limitation.

Limits on the numbers of policing personnel and the fact that the Plan provided such personnel per capita suggested that the Turkish police would be 'outnumbered' by their Greek Cypriot counterparts.

Cooperation and Coordination

As this is a technical aspect of the implementation of the Annan Plan it did not feature as prominently as others. However, as the Belgian model was proposed by the Turkish side, it might be thought that evaluations of the various Constitutional Laws, and in particular the Cooperation Agreements, both included with the Annan Plan as submitted to referenda, and further laws and agreements to be concluded thereafter, might tend toward positive.

Indeed, positive evaluations pointed to the aspects of the Plan borrowed from the Belgian experience. Generally, however, this feature of the Annan Plan that was open-ended entailing agreements not yet realized, did not feature as a salient factor in the public imagination.

Supreme Court

Debate over the Supreme Court focused on the role of foreigners in the judiciary. This is somewhat surprising, considering that the Turkish Cypriot historical experience with foreign justices is relatively benign. Nevertheless, as a matter of political equality the fact that deadlocks are to be broken by foreign justices did not sit well with all.

Therefore, the positive assessment that the Court provided for equal numbers of justices from either constituent state fell on the deaf ears of opponents.

The presence of foreign judges also affected sovereignty, thus negative assessments pointed to the anomaly. Of course, there are other countries where foreign judges preside, and the original Cyprus republic was one of these cases.

EU Membership

Membership in the European Union was among the greatest enticers for the Turkish Cypriot community to embrace the Annan Plan. Very few commentators overtly rejected EU membership. The problem was elsewhere.

One problem with EU membership was the alleged illegality of the Cypriot act of accession prior to that of Turkey. According to an interpretation of the London-Zurich agreements and the 1960 Republic of Cyprus Constitution, Cyprus was forbidden to enter into such a union.[10]

Lesser objections focused on the perceived inequality that would emanate from the Plan, with restrictions on Turkish nationals as opposed to Greek mainlanders, from accessing the island. In response, the Annan Plan provides for equal residency restrictions for people of either origin, irrespective of EU citizenship.

The biggest practical potential problem facing the Annan Plan was the way its various provisions and transitional features may be at odds with the application of the European Union *acquis communautaire*. One way about this would be to insert a protocol into the Treaty of Accession that would allow for such derogations. As the Annan Plan was not agreed to in time for the signing of the accession treaty, a protocol was added to the treaty that stipulates that the acquis remains suspended in the north pending a settlement on the island.

By the time the Annan Plan was put to referendum the debate among Turkish Cypriots focused on whether or not the Plan would or could constitute 'primary law' or not. Technically, given the signing of the Accession Treaty in April 2003, only a new treaty would assure primary law status within the EU. If not, it was argued, the Plan could be challenged in courts and would be rendered null and void. A Draft Act of Adaptation was included in the Annan Plan and was prepared in consultation with the European Commission. The Council of the EU would have taken it up prior to accession. Proponents of the Plan considered the Act of Adaptation sufficient guarantee, although this was less than primary law.

Although technically unrelated, debate among Turkish Cypriots also fixated on whether the property regime envisioned in the Annan Plan could stand the scrutiny of the European Court of Human Rights.[11]

Residency Rights

This was among the most contentious points debated on the Plan. Whereas some Turkish Cypriots find the resettlement of Greek Cypriots in the north unproblematic, many of their compatriots remain very wary, especially in light of the provisions of the Plan that relate residency to the exercise of political rights. Furthermore, a distinct minority remains opposed to any intermingling in principle. For them bizonality implied two homogeneous zones and they opposed the resettlement of any Greeks, and would be prone to say that 'Greeks should not enter among us' (*Rumlar içimize girmesinler*).

The positive assessment[12] of the Plan was that the resettlement of the north would be gradual and sufficiently restricted, including restrictions based on village and town populace.[13] Therefore the Annan Plan would not undermine the principle of bizonality.

The negative assessment was that up to 100,000 Greek Cypriots would eventually return to the north.[14] Naturally this figure conflates the return of displaced persons to both areas of territorial adjustment, from which Turkish Cypriots would generally move from, and persons to be granted the right to settle in the Turkish Cypriot State. In any case, the view was that resettlement would undermine bizonality.

Citizenship and the Exercise of Political Rights

The Annan Plan established internal status (constituent state citizenship), and Cypriot (i.e. UCR) citizenship. Internal constituent state citizenship[15] proved to be a contentious issue.

Citizenship was problematic insofar as it is linked with political rights and representation, hence the balance between the communities on the island. Given the asymmetry in populations, it is conceivable that Greek Cypriots could simultaneously constitute majorities in either constituent state envisioned in the Annan Plan. Thus, restriction of either residence or political rights (or both) of Greek Cypriots in the north emerged as the primary means of maintaining a Turkish Cypriot majority in the north. By contrast, the 1960 Constitution was communal, and representation was not based on place of residence but membership in either the Greek or Turkish community.

In the initial version of the Plan, dual internal component state citizenship was possible, and this was a concern among many Turkish Cypriots. In subsequent versions of the Plan internal citizenship became progressively static. In this way Greek Cypriots could not easily attain internal citizenship in the northern constituent state, and thus would be less likely to affect political equality in the Senate. The trade off was to allow for local representation – including in the constituent state parliament – through permanent residence. This did not feature as a very controversial point in Turkish Cypriot discourse, as the gain in federal level equality was deemed sufficient.

Citizenship was contentious in other ways. The provisions of the Annan Plan affected the status of thousands of post-1974 settlers from Turkey. Technically the Annan Plan took those who had citizenship as of 1963 (the year that Turkish Cypriots withdrew into enclaves) as the baseline.

Such persons and their descendents were automatically considered citizens of the UCR. Further, spouses of Cypriots and offspring of mixed marriages were also to be granted citizenship. The criteria for inclusion were being born in Cyprus and length of stay.[16] Overall, Kofi Annan considered that affected persons would amount to approximately 45,000:

> The third version of my plan therefore provides for a list of 45,000 people from each side, priority to be given to people who grew up in Cyprus and to others on the basis of length of stay, while people married to Cypriots would automatically be considered citizens.[17]

Property

Property was *the* issue, especially in the latter stages of debate on the Annan Plan among Turkish Cypriots. The two biggest issues were whether Turkish Cypriots could hold on to properties they currently used in the north (and at what cost), and what would be the fate of Turkish Cypriots who had to vacate Greek Cypriot homes and properties (not affected by territorial adjustment within the north).

With respect to the first question, the Annan Plan allowed for the right of first refusal to Turkish Cypriot 'current users' who were themselves displaced as a result of the interwarring on the island. In this way, Turkish Cypriots who had built on Greek Cypriot properties, or occupied homes owned by Greek Cypriots, could obtain legal title deeds to the said properties. Yet, not all property users in the north were displaced and many had built on lands originally owned by Greeks. For these persons it was also possible to obtain title to a 'significantly improvement to a property' they owned. Potentially the worst affected would be settlers, who often lived in Greek Cypriot homes without significant improvement and without equity in any case. It is conceivable that some of these persons would be enticed to accept compensation (10,000 euro per family of four) in return for repatriation to Turkey.

Turkish Cypriots who were displaced and owned properties in the south could opt for an exchange based on an elaborate property regime designed to compensate owners who would not, under the provisions of the Plan, be reinstated. However, not all Turkish Cypriots owned equity to compensate for properties used in kind. These persons would be the beneficiaries of loans, but, not surprisingly, this feature of the Plan proved unpopular among some affected Turkish Cypriots. Indeed, the exact amount individuals would owe the Property Board remained a matter of speculation.[18] The Board was to assign value to affected properties (the so-called 'current value') that would probably have been lower than market value, hence beneficial to borrowers. Nevertheless, this was not certain, and the fact that many Turkish Cypriots lacked equity became a focal point of the 'no' campaigners.[19]

Later a more nuanced reading of the Annan Plan, as it pertained to restrictions (or quotas) on reinstatement of Greek Cypriot owners, revealed that Greek Cypriots retained the right to long term leasing of lands they owned, so as to pre-empt transfer of title to Turkish Cypriots. Turkish Cypriot negotiators made very clear to UN drafters their concerns and objections to leasing. In the fifth and final version of the Plan that was submitted to referendum, the property regime was significantly altered. Greek Cypriots were no longer to have the option to lease. This final version of the Plan found many adherents, including individuals who had previously opposed the Plan, especially in regards to the property regime. Whereas Turkish Cypriots may have been likely to approve the Plan before these changes, it is probable that these revisions made it more attractive to the undecided.

As for the second matter, the fate of Turkish Cypriots forced to vacate Greek Cypriot properties, the issue was conflated with the broader question of relocation of Turkish Cypriots affected by territorial adjustment. The actual numbers of people to be affected by Greek Cypriot reinstatement of properties was speculative. The UN predicted the number to be in the range of 15,000 to 18,000 all told for.[20] Turkish Cypriot experts calculated a figure closer to 22,000.[21] In any event, the Turkish Cypriots tended to assume that such persons could be relocated to a new town or settlement, as would be the case for the larger numbers of relocated Turkish Cypriots. In fact, the Property Board would have had primary responsibility for assigning alternative accommodation prior to any current user vacating his/her property.

Territory

Territorial concessions were always going to be among the costs to the Turkish Cypriot side. The Annan Plan initially offered two maps for consideration, neither of which the Turkish and Turkish Cypriot authorities found very attractive. One map, however, was less agreeable, as it entailed the return of the Karpas peninsula to Greek Cypriot administration. Much was made of the 'strategic' importance of the peninsula with its proximity to the Turkish southern coast.[22] Additional concerns revolved around the status of the Morphou acquifer.[23] In response to these concerns the UN drafters included water resources under federal regulation and developed a third map excluding the Karpas.

The third map, which was part of Annan III, was retained and included in Annan V. Objections to the third map was that it did not entail 'straight lines' through the Mesaoria. A small debate ensued as to what the percentiles really meant and why, as of the third map, Turkish Cypriots did not receive territories from the British SBAs in the way the Greek Cypriots had. Naturally, this was compensation for loss of shoreline that resulted from the retention of Karpas, which includes many miles of coast.[24] Objections to the map proved a chimera, as when final negotiations were underway in Burgenstock, Switzerland, the Turkish side refrained from challenging the maps.

Depending on the version of the map,[25] certain villages were affected by the territorial adjustment. Out of a total of up to 47,000 persons identified by census figures, the UN calculated that a total of 24,000 people would have to be relocated to totally different places. The Turkish Cypriots assumed that all 47,000 people would be in need of 'rehabilitation' (with an additional 20,000 relocations stemming from reinstatement of properties to Greek Cypriot owners). As a result, the Turkish Cypriot estimates with respect to the cost of resettlement and relocation of at least $2 billion.[26] Indeed, the tendency was to inflate figures beyond these.

Security[27]

Any settlement to Cyprus would entail the withdrawal of Turkish troops. A big issue for the 'no' campaign was security and the status of the Turkish military in Cyprus. The ultimate version of the Annan Plan put to referendum, Annan V, allowed for a continuation of the Treaty of Guarantee and Treaty of Alliance with additional protocols. Substantively this meant that Turkish troop levels would decrease over a phased withdrawal to take place over many years. The initial version of the Plan allowed for several thousand Greek and Turkish troops, respectively, subject to withdrawal upon Turkey's accession to the EU. This went through several changes. The final version allowed for up to 650 Turkish soldiers to remain indefinitely, although complete withdrawal could be negotiated.

According to the sanguine reading of security provisions, the additional protocols to the treaties, far from watering down the guarantees, bolstered them, with the provision that bizonality and the constitutions of either constituent state would also be secured.

By contrast, opponents to the Annan Plan suggested that guarantees were indeed being watered down. Troops would not be able to leave barracks without prior permission and Turkey would be 'imprisoned' into its own territorial waters. The securitized discourse entailed conspiratorial claims that the entire Annan Plan project was designed to undermine the spirit of the Lausanne Treaty that established a 'balance of power' between the 'motherlands' Greece and Turkey since the end of World War I. In Turkish discourse the Treaty of Guarantee is considered a document on par with the Lausanne Treaty.

Thus, for opponents of the Annan Plan disrupting the status quo in Cyprus meant affecting the security of Turkey itself. Further, discourse about the Treaty of Guarantee tends to cloud the distinction between the intent of text, which was the preservation of the 'state of affairs' that was the Republic of Cyprus, as opposed to the reality on the ground, which is the post-1974 situation.

The fact that the Annan Plan does not actually affect the scope of the Treaty of Guarantee with its additional protocols is beside the point in this discourse, since the problem is that the Treaty of Alliance, hence the number of troops to be stationed on the island and the restrictions on military movements emanating from that treaty, is affected. Therefore, in Turkish discourse the Treaty of Guarantee tends to be conflated with the Treaty of Alliance. Ultimately, security concerns of the Greek Cypriot side is not given due consideration, hence the security dilemma is not presented as such.

Economics

The economic costs weighed heavily on the minds of Cypriots, be they Turkish or Greek Cypriot. Among Turkish Cypriots there was concern that the international funding for relocation of Turkish Cypriots would prove inadequate.

There were concerns expressed that funds for compensation would prove to be inadequate, especially for the relocation of persons and homes. The potential insolvency of the Central Bank, on the other hand, was less of a concern among Turkish Cypriots than Greek Cypriots.

Generally there was consensus that the 'economics' of the Plan were the least developed aspect of the proposed comprehensive settlement. There was division, however, between, on the one hand, economic liberals who favored rapid macroeconomic integration and capital investment, and, on the other hand, those who argued that the transitional period would need to be extensive and entail protectionist policies favoring the Turkish Cypriot economy and businesses.[28]

The 24 April 2004 Referendum: the Law on Referendum With Regard to the Solution of the Cyprus Problem

Crucially, the referendum of 2004 might never have been held among the Turkish Cypriots had it not been for the change in government following the December 2003 election. Rauf Denktash's opposition to the referendum was never in doubt. He had already demonstrated his reluctance to sign the Foundation Agreement at the Copenhagen summit in December 2002, but there was still the potential that his hand could be forced by parliament in the days before the critical Hague summit.

On 7 March 2003 the TRNC parliament failed to make quorum on account of the governing coalition parties, thus a bill that would have authorized the referendum to be held was quashed.[29] This led to a significant degree of resentment among supporters of the Plan. Henceforth, the holding of the referendum took on symbolic significance aside from the substantive matter of solving the Cyprus problem.

The Annan Plan debate and on again and off again negotiations coincided with the holding of scheduled elections in December 2003, which proved to be a virtual referendum on the Plan. The international community took an unprecedented interest in the outcome of those elections, and international observers were also commissioned to determine the degree to which the elections were free and fair. Diplomats also issued verbal warnings, ostensibly toward Ankara and at local Turkish Cypriot officials, not to 'interfere' in the outcome of the elections.[30]

As the outcome of the December 2003 election proved less than conclusive, debate on the substance of and process related to the Annan Plan continued. Opponents to the Annan Plan reiterated their claim that the process and the Plan itself were 'imposed' by the UN and great powers, especially the US. Nonetheless, it can also be argued that the entire process was officially consensual, recalling that the decision to submit the ultimate version of the Plan to referenda was taken at the New York summit in February 2004. At the same summit it was also agreed that the sides would submit the Plan even if they failed to come to a consensus of the final wording of the text, thus allowing the UN Secretary General to 'fill in the blanks' in a form of virtual arbitration.

Among Turkish Cypriots the question of the process proved divisive. Rauf Denktash and other opponents of the Plan and the process pointed to the imposition of deadlines that could not be realistically met, whereas, proponents of the Plan blamed Denktash and his allies for the failure to meet the deadlines that would have ensured a referendum prior to the accession of the Republic of Cyprus.

The specific legislation enacted, the Law on Referendum with Regard to the Solution of the Cyprus Problem,[31] was published in the Official Gazette thus paving the way for the referendum to be held in the north. This method was based on the Election and Referendum Law from which the special law derives. The referendum law stipulates that the goal is to submit the Annan Plan to referendum. The referendum was set for 20 April 2004, but could be reset by the Council of Ministers any date prior to the 1st of May, subject to publication in the Official Gazette. The referendum was held on 24 April 2004. According to special provisions of the Election and Referendum Law, the only significant difference between this and the regulation of any other election is that the electoral authorities must produce a unique ballot customized for the referendum.

With respect to eligibility, all TRNC citizens who were registered voters for the December 2003 parliamentary elections could vote. The only proviso was that names of those whose citizenship was revoked would be removed from the lists and new citizens along with those who are older than 18 since the previous election may register. Voters lists for particular ballot boxes were updated accordingly.

Instead of Article 94, sections 1 and 2 that require the ballot to include the names of all candidates/parties, the special law only requires a place to display 'yes' and 'vote' and a place to mark an 'x' to indicate 'yes' or 'no'.

The Special Referendum Law contained a number of problems. Among the most controversial was who was eligible to participate in the referendum. As a significant percentage of Turkish Cypriots live overseas it was an open question as to whether they would be allowed to partake. A further complicating factor was that many settlers from Turkey were granted TRNC citizenship and thus granted the right to vote in local and parliamentary elections. In the end the government decided to allow only persons who under TRNC law had the right to vote, which meant excluding the expatriates. The implications of this are manifold, since it raises questions as to who or what the self-determining unit is.

Other issues included a technical problem with the wording of the legislation that mentioned the submission of the Turkish Cypriot State Constitution along with the rest of the Annan Plan to referendum. In fact, due to disagreements between the government and Rauf Denktash, the document was omitted.

More problematic, however, was Denktash' legal challenge, where he maintained that the entire referendum exercise violated the TRNC Constitution in calling for its dissolution. The Turkish Cypriot Supreme Court, however, disagreed with this interpretation, hence the referendum proceeded, with the Speaker of Parliament signing the bill into law.

On the day of the referendum nearly 65 per cent of Turkish Cypriot voters supported the Plan. However, the rejection of the Plan by the Greek Cypriot electorate not only rendered the Plan technically 'null and void' but politically unviable, as well. A comprehensive settlement to the Cyprus problem would be put off indefinitely. Debates within the Turkish Cypriot community would henceforth shift toward interim models. The EU and UN suggested that the Turkish Cypriots be brought into the fold and out of 'isolation'.

The Annan Plan allowed Turkish Cypriots the opportunity to discuss substantive elements of their political predicament, an opportunity that they duly seized. However, absent a tangible political project, such as the Annan Plan, the political future of the Turkish Cypriot community appears fraught with uncertainties.

ENDNOTES

1. Talat was forced into a coalition government with Serdar Denktash' party, DP. Thus Talat disregarded a protocol signed with other pro-Annan parties prior to the election pledging not to join in a coalition with any party that opposed the UN Plan as a basis for settlement.
2. Crucial organizations included the Bu Memleket Bizim (This Country is Ours) platform that organized mass rallies in favor of the Annan Plan, as well as the Ortak Vizyon (Common Vision) coalition of trade unions and other NGOs.
3. See paragraph 67 of Annan's report to the Security Council (S/2003/398).
4. Opponents of the Annan Plan insisted that the approach entailed the recognition of the continuation of the Republic of Cyprus. See, Taner Etkin, *Volkan* 19 November 2002.

5. The debate as to state succession led to interpretations not only in Cyprus but in Turkey as well. 'Kibris'ta egemenligi Rumlar devrediyor: Erdogan, Türkiye'nin egemenlik hakkini devretmedigini, tam tersi bir devlet statüsünde olan Rum Kesimi'nin egemenligini devrettigini söyledi' (The Greek Cypriots are Conceding Sovereignty: Erdogan Says that Turkey was not Conceding its Sovereign Rights, to the Contrary the Greek Cypriot Side that Enjoyed State Status was Conceding) *Halkin Sesi*, 17 April 2004. Similarly, proponents in Cyprus also considered the sovereignty debate in favor of the Turkish perspective. 'Planda Egemenlik vardir. Planda Siyasi Eshitlik vardir.' (There is Sovereignty in the Plan. There is Political Equality in the Plan) Turkish Cypriot Chamber of Commerce Website, http://www.ktto.net/turkce/2003270201., 27 February 2003.
6. Denktash claimed the Plan reflected the Greek Cypriot philosophy. 'Bir devlet, bir egemenlik ve çogunluk idaresine büyük agirlik veren bir yaklashim. Türk garantisini zaman içerisinde; henüz Türkiye ile Yunanistan anlashmadan, halkin referandumuna sunarak, Türkiye'nin elini kolunu baglamak gibi bir oyunla karshi karshiyayiz' dedi. (He said 'An approach that heavily provides for one state, one sovereignty and majority rule; we are faced with a game where Turkey's hands are tied through referendum prior to an agreement between Greece and Turkey), Kibris, 12 December 2003. Denktash went on to explain that the 1960 accords were on the basis of two 'nations' but the Annan Plan's philosophy was to merge the two to create one nation, thus there was no 'sovereignty' in the Annan Plan as far as the Turkish Cypriots were concerned. Talat's view was that 'Denktash, egemenlik gibi bir konuya takilip kalmistir, CTP olarakl artik boyle sacma konularla vakit gecirilmesine izin vermeyecegiz'. (Denktash is stuck on sovereignty, but as CTP we will not allow time to be wasted on such nonsensical topics) as reported in Volkan, 27 November 2003. Prime Minister Dervis Eroglu, exhoing Denktash's concerns, maintained that Turkey's right of guarantee was being 'watered down', as reported in Kibris, 18 Febraury 2004.
7. For instance, Mustafa Akinci, a prominent supporter of the Annan Plan, considered that 'true sovereignty' could only be achieved through the Annan Plan, since the Plan brought the Turkish Cypriot state into the international legal system. See, Kibris, 7 December 2003.
8. As Annan explains in paragraphs 87 and 88 of his report to the Security Council, 'The Plan equips the federal government with specified powers, comprising those necessary to ensure that Cyprus can speak and act with one voice internationally and in the European Union, fulfil its obligations as a European Union member State, and protect its integrity, borders, resources and ancient heritage. All remaining powers, which are the bulk of the powers and include most matters affecting the day-to-day life of citizens or requiring major budgetary expenditure, would fall within the sphere of competence of the constituent states, which would thus enjoy residual powers.' (S/2003/398).
9. Basic Articles, Part IV, Article 15.
10. On the question of the legality of accession, Denktash repeatedly expressed the view that the 1960 accords provided for the political equality of the communities, thus accession could only occur within that framework. See for instance, *Volkan*, 17 April 2003.
11. Another interpretation of accession had to do with the status of Turkish Cypriots as Republic of Cyprus citizens. By extension, Turkish Cypriots were EU citizens, as well. This had the potential of affecting Turkey's position in Cyprus as 'occupying EU territory'. See, for instance, 'Hepimiz AB Vatandasi' (We are All EU Citizens), Afrika, 15 December 2002. On the other hand, other commentators lamented the fact that EU conditionality had been imposed on the Turkish side, thus the Greek Cypriots enjoyed the right to veto the Plan. See, for instance, the comments of Enver Ozturk of UBP on BRT, 19 April 2004.

12. Annan Plan supporters were confident that the international community would honor its commitments to the proposed settlement package thus providing sufficient resources for resettlement and compensation mechanisms. See, for instance, *Yeniduzen*, 19 November 2002. Moreover, supporters of the Plan tried to reassure settlers from Turkey that their interests were met in the Annan Plan. Mehmet Ali Talat argued that a list of 45,000 settlers meant to be naturalized through the provisions of the Plan was comprehensive. *Kibris*, 7 April 2004. At this point Talat and CTP took the strategic step of incorporating the 'new Cypriots'. This was expressed at the party's general assembly on the same date.
13. See paragraph 99 of Kofi Annan's report to the UN Security Council for an explanation of how the Plan was to have dealt with residency (S/2003/398).
14. The question of resettlement of the north was resisted by those who claimed that repopulation of the north by Greek Cypriots would lead to conflict. See Sabahattin Ismail, *Volkan*, 19 November 2002.
15. See Annan's report to the UN Secuirty Council (S/2003/398) where in paragraph 105 he outlines his complex proposal that limits 'internal constituent level citizenship' in order to safeguard the political equality of Turkish Cypriots in federal level institutions. In paragraph 106 he outlines the criteria by which certain categories of settlers would be granted Cypriot citizenship, with a quota of up to 45000 persons from each side to be naturalized. Other persons could be granted permanent residency.
16. Annan summarized criteria for citizenship in paragraph 106 of his report to the UN (S/2003/398). The question of the granting of 'illegal citizenships' had already emerged within the Turkish Cypriot community as a contentious matter, given the suspicion that the 'new' settlers would be likely to vote against the Annan Plan. See *Kibris*, 14 March 2003.
17. Annan, 2003, paragraph 106.
18. Skeptics of the UN Plan considered the Property Commission to be problematic. It was seen as impossible for the proposed commission to adjudicate tens of thousands of cases.
19. Opponents of the Annan Plan attempted to exploit the fact that settlers lacked equity with respect to the properties they had been granted by the TRNC authorities. See *Volkan*, 19 November 2002. On the other hand, supporters of the Plan insisted that nobody would be victimized by its provisions and that those who would be affected by resettlement, hence displacement, would be provided alternative housing and work. See *Yeniduzen*, 14 November 2002. That said, there was general awareness that the Plan was in various ways incompatible with the property regime that had been establsihed in the north since 1974. See Ahmet Gazioglu, *Kibris*, 7 April 2004. The concern over long term leasing provisions in the Plan was debated among Turkish Cypriots. See Murat Ozkan, *Kibris*, 3 March 2004. Annan V was altered to take into account this Turkish Cypriot concern. Ultimately, however, Denktash thought that the property regime would lead to conflict. See *Halkin Sesi*, 21 March 2004. Annan V was more widely endorsed given the removal of leasing and other changes. See Gazioglu, *Kibris*, 7 April 2004.
20. For resolving contending property claims see paragraphs 109-111 of his report (S/2003/398).
21. Tahir Celik. 'Annan Plani Temelinde Cözümün Kibris Türküne Maliyeti' (The Cost to the Turkish Cypriots of the Cyprus Settlement Based on the Annan Plan), November 2003.
22. The question of the future of the Karpas peninsula was widely debated, as the UN was prone to consider the establishment of a Greek Cypriot canton there. See *Halkin Sesi*, 27 February 2003 and *Volkan*, 28 November 2003.
23. Organizations concerned with the welfare of people who might be displaced argued that modifications be made to limit displacements and provide for sufficient rehabilitation in cases

that people must move. See Kuntay of GUKAD in *Kibris*, 31 December 2003. Supporters of the Plan were not especially concerned about territorial aspects, since, in the words of Izzet Izcan, 'it is a reality that we hold more land in proportion to our population'. See *Afrika*, 19 November 2002.

24. Even the issue of territorial concessions to the Greek Cypriots on the part of the Sovereign Base Areas led to objections on the grounds of equity. See Sabahattin Ismail in *Volkan*, 26 Febraury 2003.
25. See paragraphs 112 through 119 of the Secretary General's report (S/2003/398) for Kofi Annan's explanation of the treatment of territory under the under plan.
26. Celik. 'Annan Planı Temelinde Çözümün Kibris Türküne Maliyeti'.
27. The question of security and the Treaty of Guarantee was divisive in Turkey in the run up to the referendum in Cyprus. Denktash did all he could to raise the security issue in Turkey to deter Ankara from supporting the Plan. This led to public acrimony between Denktash and Turkish Prime Minister Recep Tayyip Erdogan, as well as other members of the AK government. Foreign Minister Abdullah Gul openly contradicted Denktash' interpretation of the Plan in terms of security. See *Kibris*, 17 April 2004. The position of Erdogan and his government was in opposition to the position long held by Denktash that Cyprus' EU accession independent of Turkey was 'illegal' in terms of the Zurich-London agreements. Thus, if Cyprus was to accede to the EU, it would do so with derogations to its primary law. See Denktash as quoted in *Kibris*, 11 November 2004. Whereas Denktash looked upon the potential dissolution of de facto military gurantees of Turkey with concern, others saw the positive side of demilitarization, especially as it negated compulsary military service. See 'Askerlik Kalkiyor' (No More Military Service), *Kibris*, 4 April 2004. Critically, on 6 April 2004 the Turkish Parliament debated the Annan Plan where Foreign Minister Abdullah Gul rebutted most of Denktash' arguments on Turley's guarantorship. See http://www.belgenet.com/kibris/tbmm_060404-1.html. See Annan's explanation of security provisions in the Plan in paragraphs 120-122 of his report (S/2003/398).
28. One of the biggest Turkish Cypriot concerns related to the period of transition and financing. These debates often took place through media, such as when Mustafa Arabacigolu of the DP debated Ozdil Nami of the CTP. See Aktuel on BRT, 19 April 2004.
29. The failure of parliament to reach quorom led to acrimony. The opposition led protests to support the holding of a referendum on the Annan Plan. See *Kibris*, 10 March 2003. At the same time, Denktash prepared to reject the Annan Plan during last ditch negotiations at the Hague. It was hoped that the referendum could be held before the Accession Treaty was signed in April. But, this was not to be because of Denktash' rejection of the Annan Plan.
30. As the potential for a referendum increasingly hinged on the outcome of an election where the oppsition's primary goal was to deliver the referendum denied by the government, the international community took interest in the outcome. Turkish authorities in Ankara were 'warned' by American authorities not to interfere in the outcome. See *Ortam*, 10 September 2003 and *Halkin Sesi*, 10 September 2003.
31. Kibris Sorununun Çözümüne Ilishkin Halkoylamasi (Özel ve Geçici Kurallar) Yasasi (Law on Referendum With Regard to the Solution of the Cyprus Problem (Special and Transitional Provisions) 31, (22 March 2004, Number 2/2004).

PART III

THE REFERENDUMS

Chapter 12

FROM SECRET DIPLOMACY TO PUBLIC DIPLOMACY: HOW THE ANNAN PLAN REFERENDUM FAILURE EARNED THE CYPRIOT PUBLIC A SEAT AT THE NEGOTIATING TABLE

Alexandros Lordos

Introduction

The reasons for the rejection of the UN Plan among the Greek Cypriots have been the subject of extensive research, both qualitative and empirical.[1] In this paper, an additional layer will be added to the analysis; namely, the actual *process* of UN-sponsored negotiations that led to the drafting of the Plan. Can we perhaps trace a causal link between the negotiating strategy chosen by the UN, and the final result of the referendum? Was the process itself structured in such a way, that one could have logically predicted that the final product would fail to satisfy wide cross-sections of Cypriot society? The hypothesis that will be examined in the following pages is that the process leading up to the UN Plan did not include the Cypriot public as a significant player; that what little representation the public had - through its elected leaders - was biased and inaccurate; and that in striving to satisfy the competing concerns of various local and international actors, it was inevitable that the ultimate result would be unacceptable to wide cross sections of the Cypriot public.

To examine the validity of this hypothesis a short description of this UN-led process, which lasted from 1998 to 2004, is in order.

The Process Behind the Plan

The process leading up to what has become known as the 'Annan Plan', has been extensively chronicled by two distinct key actors; namely Lord David Hannay on the one hand, the UK Special Representative to Cyprus until 2003, and Claire Palley on the other hand, constitutional advisor to successive Greek Cypriot leaders.

Lord Hannay's account[2] is essentially a sympathetic interpretation of a multi-year joint effort between the UN, the US and the UK, to lead 'two stubborn communities' back to the negotiating table, and once there, to dynamically lead the process towards a successful conclusion. For Hannay, the Peace Process was a complex balancing act between the competing concerns and differing mentalities of key leaders in Greece, Turkey and Cyprus; the negotiators and intermediaries did their best to find the needed common ground between all these players, and that this 'balance of opposites' was adequately and fairly reflected in the final Plan; but unfortunately, the timing was never quite right, with the various sides never feeling the same level of political pressure simultaneously, and thus never being all adequately motivated for an agreement at the same time.

Palley's account[3] is in contrast entirely critical of the UN approach. For Palley, the UN diverged from its appropriate mandate as a facilitator by becoming a 'key decision maker' in the negotiations; the presence and role of the US and UK special representatives lent a bias to the whole process in favour of the interests of Turkey; that the two leaders in Cyprus were largely bypassed without being given the opportunity to expound their concerns in depth; and that therefore, the final Plan was a slip-shod affair, unworkable on a technical level and unfair on a human level, designed to let Turkey off the hook rather that to re-unite Cyprus.

The temptation to arbitrate between these two diametrically opposed viewpoints will be avoided at this moment. Instead, the common factual ground on which the two authors are basing their differing evaluations will be highlighted, to serve as a basis for our own further analysis.

One point on which the two authors agree, is that the whole process was essentially UN-led rather than UN-facilitated. The UN was most certainly not just 'listening and taking notes', but it was sifting through, collating and evaluating the material coming in from the various sides – ultimately putting it all together in the form of a comprehensive take-it-or-leave it proposal, which then underwent a number of changes based on the objections of the various sides before being put to referendum.

Secondly, both authors agree that the concerns and objections of the 'motherlands' - and more specifically Turkey - were given very serious weight by the drafters of the Plan. In fact, the whole process was *de facto* three-sided, with the UN receiving 'requests for matters to be included in the Plan' from the Greek Cypriots, from the Turkish Cypriots and from Turkey itself. Though Greece had potentially a similar level of influence as Turkey, she typically chose not to exercise this right.

Finally, both authors implicitly acknowledge - if not through assertion then certainly through omission - that the wider Cypriot public had a very limited influence in the whole process. Other than the technical committees which were examining financial and legal issues, and the two leaders who were purportedly representing their respective communities, the negotiating process was otherwise entirely isolated from the concerns and the scrutiny of the wider public.

The figure below is a pictorial representation of this very rigorously structured negotiating process:

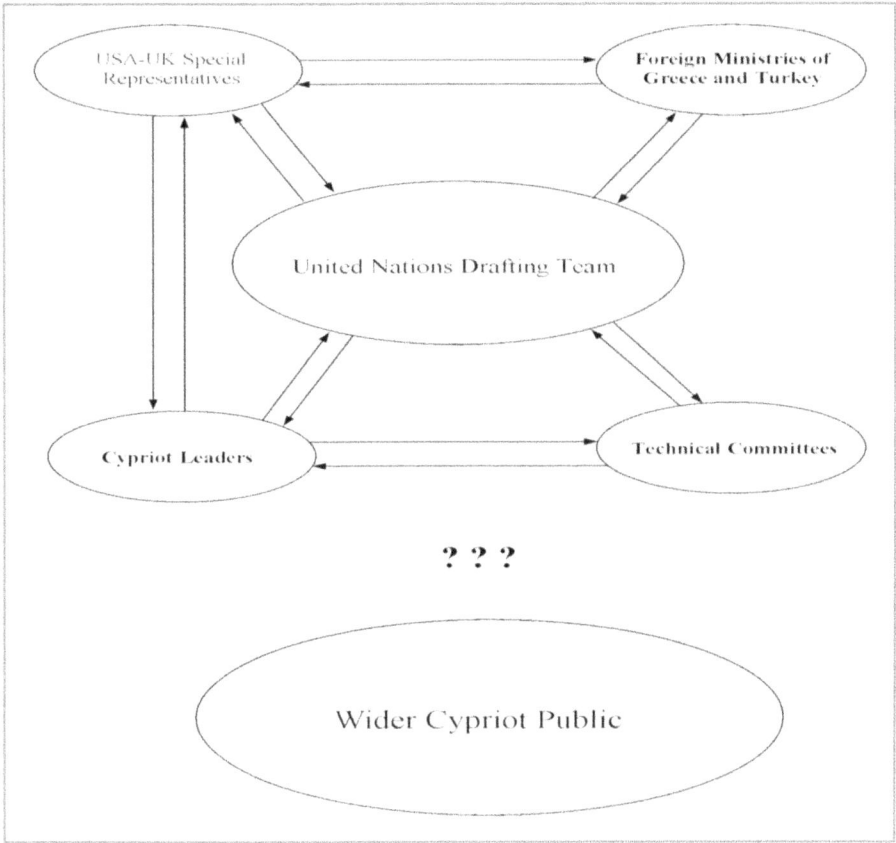

While the power of such a process to push through various potential obstacles is self-evident, at the same time it is also evident that the process twice relegated the sovereignty of Cypriots: Firstly, by demoting the two Cypriot leaders to 'lobbying pressure groups', striving to 'influence' the UN decision makers who had ultimate control of the process, alongside other 'pressure groups' who were also trying to influence the UN 'decision makers', most notably Turkey. Secondly, Cypriot sovereignty was relegated by not providing for a method to hold the leaders themselves accountable to their electorates for their choices at the negotiating table.

Consequent to the first relegation, it could be expected that the Plan would reflect a 'balance' of sorts between Cypriot and non-Cypriot interests, as opposed to primarily dealing with Cypriot concerns. Consequent to the second relegation, we could expect that those provisions in the Plan that were meant to satisfy Cypriots would only achieve their goal in a crude and approximate manner – since the two elderly and UK educated gentlemen that spoke on behalf of the two Cypriot communities, insulated from their public within the context of a highly secretive process of international diplomacy, could only be said to be representative of their electorates in a very crude and very approximate manner. In fact, both leaders were ousted from power before the process was fully over, amidst controversy that they had represented their community poorly at the negotiating table. Rauf Denktash, the Turkish Cypriot leader, was accused of being too uncompromising and thus 'leading the Turkish Cypriot community into isolation', while Glafkos Clerides, the Greek Cypriot leader, was accused of 'going beyond the agreed 'red lines' by giving in to too many of Turkey's unacceptable standing demands'.

Some of the ways in which the two leaders misled the UN intermediaries regarding the true concerns of their communities come across very clearly in Hannay's book.

> The Greek Cypriots would have liked to have had electoral arrangements that involved some cross-voting of Greek Cypriots for Turkish Cypriot candidates and vice-versa, in an attempt to get away from a two-states mentality after a settlement. This idea was anathema to the Turkish Cypriots who feared it could lead to effective domination of Turkish Cypriot elections by Greek Cypriots.[4]

In fact, on a level of public concerns, nothing could be further from the truth. The issue of cross-voting was tested with the Greek Cypriot and Turkish Cypriot public in an extensive inter-communal poll conducted in May 2005,[5] with the results being as follows:

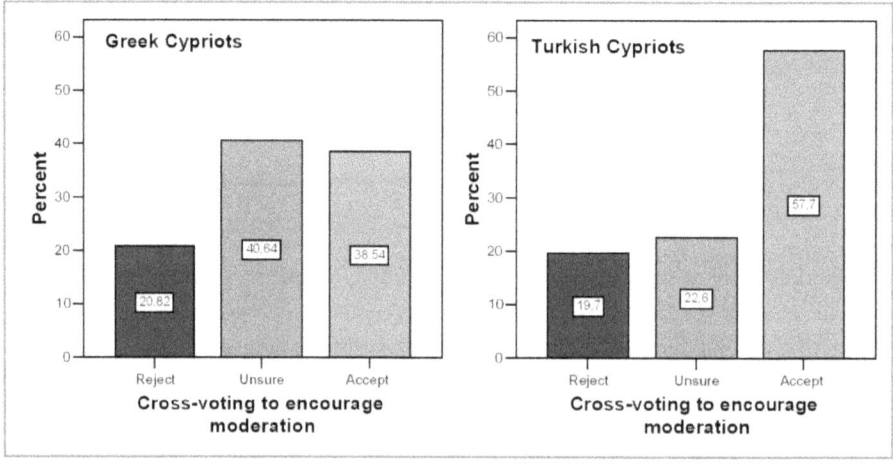

Not only is the Turkish Cypriot public open to the possibility of cross-voting, they are in fact even more enthusiastic over the prospect than the Greek Cypriots themselves! This finding is in fact not surprising, since cross-voting is for the Turkish Cypriots an excellent guarantee that Greek Cypriot politicians will respect their opinions and concerns within the context of the federal legislature. For the Greek Cypriot public, in contrast, while cross-voting is seen as positive in encouraging a co-operative attitude on behalf of Turkish Cypriot politicians, there is also some ambivalence given that Greek Cypriots are generally more suspicious of 'complex' electoral laws, which on an emotional level remind them of the complex administrative provisions of the 1960 constitution.

Hannay's 'evaluation' of Turkish Cypriot views to cross-voting comes of course from Denktash who felt that cross-voting would favour the more moderate Turkish Cypriot parties in Federal elections and render political viewpoints like his own obsolete in the long term. Cross-voting, in other words, was a personal 'anathema' to Denktash, rather than to the Turkish Cypriot community in general. And yet, lacking any access to the wider Turkish Cypriot public, the negotiators concluded that the Turkish Cypriots opposed cross-voting and then went on to shape their Peace Plan accordingly - with all popular voting strictly split along ethnic lines. Another interesting example from Hannay's book, is the following:

> Clerides had made proposals, before and during the period covered by this book, for the complete demilitarization of Cyprus ... these proposals had been rejected both by the Turkish Cypriots and the Turks, who made it clear that any solution must include ... Turkey's right of unilateral intervention ... [and] Turkish troops to remain in Cyprus ... while Clerides continued for public and political reasons to maintain his own proposals, he had, by the time the negotiations began in 1999 ... recognised that they could not provide the basis for a solution.[6]

In this case, Clerides was in touch with the concerns of his electorate to begin with, but as the pressure to conclude a deal mounted, within the context of a secretive process in which he was more accountable on a day-to-day basis to his interlocutors than to his own public, he eventually succumbed and traded away his own community's security concerns - a compromise that his own public did not learn about until the day when it was seen reflected in the UN Plan.

We will examine later in the paper the extent to which security concerns are seen as a critical parameter by Greek Cypriots in any Peace Plan; suffice it to say for now that in exit polls on the day of the referendum 75 per cent of those Greek Cypriots who voted 'no' cited 'Security Concerns' as the main reason driving their choice. By making radical and unauthorised compromises on the security issue, Clerides unwittingly paved the way for the eventual rejection of the UN Plan by the Greek Cypriots in the April 2004 referendum.

It should be acknowledged at this point that Clerides had very few available options at the time he made his decision to accept the Turkish positions on the Security issue; his refusal to do so would almost certainly have caused the whole process to collapse; Cyprus was under political pressure to show a conciliatory attitude in the negotiations as part of its tacit obligations towards the EU which it was striving to join; while the US, the UK and the UN were all pressuring Clerides to make 'a historic compromise for the sake of Peace'. Such was the power, but also the ultimate downfall in the hands of the public, of the rigorous and high-pressure process set up by the UN to achieve a deal in Cyprus.

The Referendum Signals the Death-knell of the 'Secret Diplomacy' Approach in Cyprus

Anecdotal evidence seems to suggest that even up to a few weeks before the April 2004 referendum - and despite the consistently and overwhelmingly negative predictions of the referendum result in various polls - the various intermediaries were optimistic that the Plan would still win the referendum. For instance: One particular sociologist - commissioned by the UN to research in detail attitudes of both communities towards the Annan Plan - sounded the warning bells to the various intermediaries about three months before the referendum. After explaining in detail the specific objections of the public to various provisions of the Plan, and suggesting specific ways in which these concerns could be addressed, he received the following response: 'Do not worry about how the Plan will fare at the referendum. 'Nikos' and 'Demetris' will pull it through to a 'yes''. 'Nikos' is Nikos Anastasiades, chairman of DISY party, while 'Demetris' is Demetris Christofias, chairman of AKEL party. Collectively, these two parties 'controlled' 65 per cent of the Greek Cypriot electorate at the time, and it was felt by the intermediaries that neither of these two parties would have a choice but to support the Plan, that their supporters would follow their lead, and that therefore the Plan would pass.

The refusal of the UN to integrate the various suggestions contained in the research project that they themselves commissioned was no mere oversight: In the very tight negotiating process that the UN had instituted, with very delicate balances being maintained between the Greek Cypriots, the Turkish Cypriots and Turkey, under the intense supervision of the US and the UK, there was really little room to add a new 'unknown variable' at that stage, namely the very extensive concerns of the Cypriot public...

It should be noted at this point that the negotiators did have an opportunity to include Public Opinion analysis in the negotiating process years earlier, when the process leading to a settlement was just beginning, in 1998; specifically, Professor Colin Irwin from Ireland was asked if he could assist with such a programme:

> 'I was invited to attend a meeting of the Greek Turkish Forum in Istanbul in December 1998 ... I made a presentation of my Northern Ireland work to the Greek and Turkish Cypriots present and explained how it was used to help build a consensus around the Belfast Agreement. They subsequently decided they would like to undertake a similar program of research in Cyprus ... although the Greek Cypriot negotiators wanted to go ahead with a poll the Turkish Cypriot government did not ... in the end, no polls were undertaken and without the benefits of an effective program of public diplomacy both the negotiations and subsequent referendum failed in April 2004, and Cyprus remained divided'.[7]

The decision to not include Public Opinion polling in the process at that early stage can be attributed, at least partly, to a desire to not let the process slip out of control. The Turkish side at that time was accepting to come to the negotiating table under very specific conditions, and only within a very specific framework. Arguably, the intermediaries felt that if the public was polled then various concerns would come to the surface which might contravene the pre-agreed negotiating limits of Turkey, and more specifically the negotiating limits of the Turkish military establishment. Thus, the thought to give the Cypriot public a seat at the negotiating table was cast away at that stage, and the intermediaries, as described earlier, placed all their hopes for winning the referendum in the hands of the political parties and in the expectation that the electorate would follow their lead.

As for the hope that the political parties would lead the people to a 'yes', this was frustrated on two different levels. Firstly, AKEL chose in the end not to come out in favour of the Plan, despite its original intention. The major reason for this shift was that AKEL was receiving very strongly negative messages from its electoral base regarding the Plan, messages that it dared not ignore. Thus, AKEL chose to stand on the fence of neutrality, leaning somewhat in the direction of a 'moderate no'. Secondly, even though DISY came out strongly in favour of the Plan, only about 40 per cent of its electoral base heeded its calling, according to exit polls. In fact, the percent 'Yes' vote according to Political Party, as revealed in the exit polls, tells a very interesting story:

Political Party	Position on Annan Plan	Percent who voted 'Yes'
DISY	Strong 'Yes'	40%
AKEL	Neutrality / Mild 'No'	25%
DIKO	Strong 'No'	10%
EDEK	Strong 'No'	10%

In other words, there seems to have been a 'base-line' generic acceptance of the Plan at about 25 per cent, while the influence of one's political party could cause a swing of +/- 15 per cent, up to a maximum of 40 per cent support in a 'pro-yes' party, down to a minimum of 10 per cent support in a 'pro-no' party. Political Party discipline mattered, but nowhere near as much as the intermediaries hoped. The parties were a powerful influence, but not sufficiently powerful to bring about majority support for a Plan over which the Public had such strong negative feelings.

While after the referendum failure there were some muted calls to make some small adjustments to the Plan and bring it back for a new referendum as soon as possible, most players implicitly understood the need to stand back for a while and take stock of the new situation. It is within the context of this intermission that a 'Public Diplomacy' approach has finally began to take root in Cyprus.

The First Stirrings of 'Public Diplomacy' in Cyprus

In the autumn of 2004, an in-depth survey of Greek Cypriot public opinion took place,[8] which examined which possible amendments to the Annan Plan, from the wide range of issues that were being discussed in the daily press at that time, would be considered by respondents to be 'unnecessary', 'nice to have' or 'essential'.

The survey results were published as a booklet in November 2004; in retrospect, the timing could not have been better, since during that period the Greek Cypriot political parties were attempting to encode the changes to the Annan Plan which should be sought by the Greek Cypriot side in case a new round of negotiations was called by the UN. The results of the survey reached their offices just as they themselves were attempting to 'guesstimate' the concerns of their electorate to formulate their position accordingly.

Undoubtedly, the most pertinent aspect of that particular survey was a rank-ordered list of changes to the Annan Plan deemed essential by more than 55 per cent of the Greek Cypriots. The arbitrary cut-off point of 55 per cent was chosen with the reasoning that any Plan which disregards a '55 per cent +' concern will have great difficulty in getting through a referendum. This chart of 'absolutely essential changes' is reprinted below.

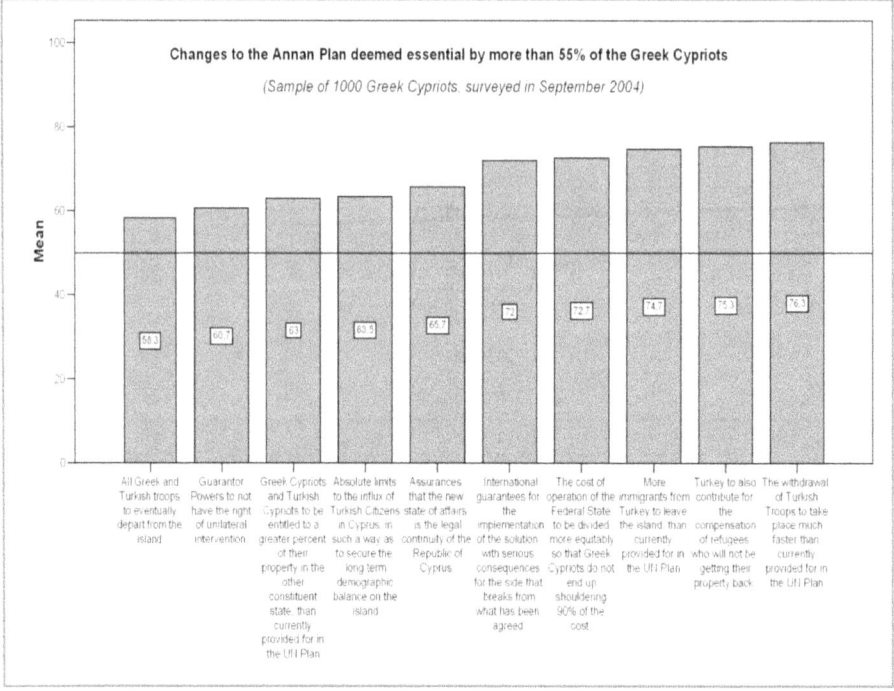

This rank-ordering of Greek Cypriot requirements tells its own story: Security, Settlers, Implementation Guarantees, Property Rights and Financial Equity are some of the major areas of concern that the Greek Cypriot public would like to see addressed in a new round of negotiations.

Returning to the issue of how the survey was received by decision makers: After the Greek Cypriot political parties, the next stop in the presentation was the Turkish Cypriot political leaders and leaders of civil society. While they found the survey results revealing and interesting, they tended to consider the 'proposed changes' as an unacceptable basis of negotiation: According to various Turkish Cypriots who examined the results, 'if these '55 per cent +' changes were made to the Annan Plan then it would be the Turkish Cypriots who would vote 'no' at the next referendum'. At this point, the exhortation was made to conduct similar survey work among the Turkish Cypriots, to examine which changes of those demanded by the Greek Cypriots they would accept and which they would not. This demand was met in an equivalent poll of Turkish Cypriots conducted in January 2005.

The results of this new survey of Public Opinion were made public in February

2005, and formed the basis of a presentation at a conference organised by Wilton Park in Cyprus during that month.⁹ The results - shown in a comparative fashion alongside the equivalent results of the Greek Cypriot poll - were presented in the afternoon of the first day, after a morning panel of Greek Cypriot and Turkish Cypriot politicians which panel, if anything, only served to confirm the current deadlock and the distance separating the official positions of the two sides.

The survey results, in contrast, breathed new optimism into the conference proceedings. Turkish Cypriots were seen in the survey to be quite open to various amendments of the Plan, especially on issues relating to Property Rights, Residence Rights, issues of Financial Equity and Guarantees for the Implementation of the Solution. In contrast, they appeared opposed to any unilateral concessions on Security-related issues and on the issue of Turkish Settlers, but did however appear willing to consider alternative arrangements that were not so much 'a move towards Greek Cypriot positions' but rather 'a totally new way of approaching the problem'. This finding places a definite limit on the usefulness of any process that uses the Annan Plan as its proffered 'basis of negotiations', since some of the contested issues need to be approached with a totally fresh mind if mutually acceptable solutions to these problem-areas are to ensue. Perhaps the Annan Plan could be used in the future as the basis of certain aspects in the negotiations, with changes being made by reference to that particular starting point, but in other areas the only way to achieve a solution is if the two sides start with a blank piece of paper, put down their underlying needs, and then 'brainstorm' together various alternative solutions until they find one on which they can both agree on. As we shall see later in the paper, the next survey to be conducted attempted exactly to emulate such a process of 'inter-communal brainstorming', on the level of public opinion.

The May 2005 Inter-Communal Survey: Defining 'Options for Peace'

Unlike the two earlier projects, the third survey to be conducted was entirely inter-communal: An integrated questionnaire was first prepared in English, which was then translated into Greek and Turkish by the respective polling companies that undertook the responsibility for the actual field-work. The sample was comprised of 1,000 Greek Cypriots and 1,000 Turkish Cypriots, while the data was collected through face to face interviews. The purpose of the survey was two-fold: On the one hand to offer a definitive explanation regarding what factors prompted the Greek Cypriots and Turkish Cypriots to vote the way they did, and on the other hand to discover mutually acceptable solutions to some of the more vexing aspects of the Cyprus Problem - such as Security, Property Rights and the Status of Turkish Settlers.

As to the first issue, what factors drove the Greek and Turkish Cypriot vote, one approach to answering the question is by examining 'segment-by-segment' the perceived acceptability of different aspects in the Annan Plan. In the survey, respondents were reminded in detail of what the Annan Plan provisions were, and were then asked to evaluate the provision as 'Unacceptable', 'Tolerable', 'Satisfactory' or 'Very Positive'. Given that all these proposals represented delicate compromise solutions, most positive responses were clustered around 'Tolerable'. Thus, at the analysis stage the responses were aggregated and recoded in such a way that 'Unacceptable' stood for 'Reject', while 'Tolerable', 'Satisfactory' and 'Very Positive' stood for 'Accept'. The overall percent acceptance of specific aspects in the Plan was as follows:

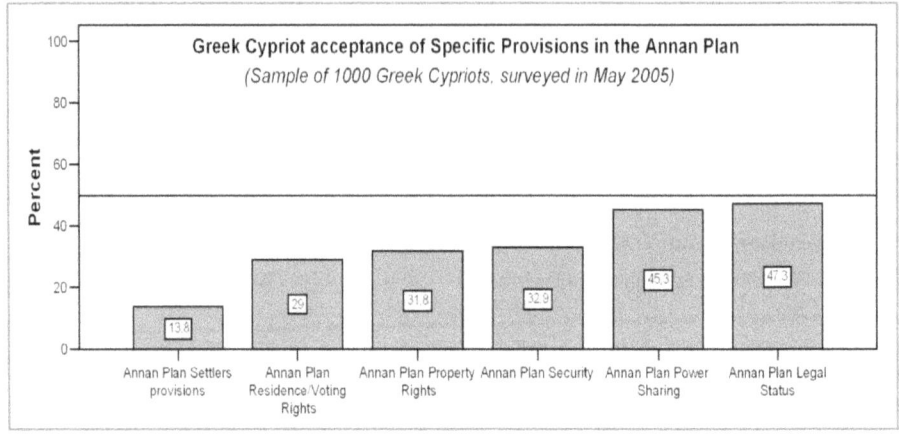

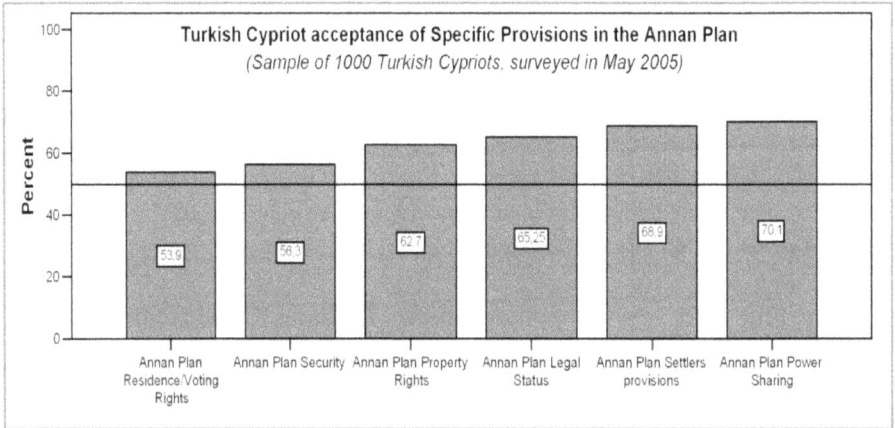

For the Greek Cypriots, the first thing to note about the results is the wide fluctuation in the evaluation of different aspects of the Plan. Far from exhibiting a 'blanket rejection' of the Plan as a whole, the Greek Cypriots exercised a measure of discernment accepting some aspects of the Plan as 'less negative than others'. The hard issues, however, of Security, Property/Residence Rights and Settlers, unfortunately clock in approval ratings that range from 29-32 per cent, for Security and Property/Residence Rights, down to 14 per cent on the issue of Settlers. It should be noted that in all of these three issues, the final shape of the Plan was largely defined by the requirements and demands that Turkey put forward in the final stages of the negotiations. Claire Palley reprints in her book the list of requirements which the Turkish Foreign Ministry put forward to the UN just before the Plan was finalised:

> THE FINAL POINTS CONVEYED TO MR DE SOTO BY AMBASSADOR ZIYAL ON 26 MARCH 2004:
> 1. The percentage of the Greek Cypriots returning to the North should be

reduced from 21 per cent to 18 per cent.
2. The Turkish Cypriot proposal regarding the property issue should be accepted.
…………..
8. Our expectations regarding the security and guarantees should be fully met.
9. Preservation of Greek and Turkish military presence on the island even after the accession of Turkey to the European Union.
…………..
11. Turkish Cypriot citizens originating from Anatolia should not be discriminated against within the framework of a comprehensive settlement…
(reprinted from Palley 2005, 259)

And indeed, in all these points the final conditions placed by Turkey were satisfied, without the concerns of the Greek Cypriot Public - or even the strong objections of the Greek Cypriot negotiators themselves - causing sufficient hesitation to the UN drafting team. It should be noted here that by that stage Cyprus' entry into the EU was a foregone conclusion. In sharp contrast, Turkey's EU aspirations still depended on her appearing to be co-operating for a settlement in Cyprus. Thus, while the best-case scenario for the US-UK intermediaries was of course for the Plan to pass and Cyprus to be re-united, solving Turkey's EU problem at the same time, the absolutely worst-case scenario was for the Plan to fail and for Turkey to be seen as the side responsible for the breakdown. Thus, within this internationalized context, when faced with Turkey's demands for changes to the Annan Plan, it was inevitable that the intermediaries would place those demands at a higher place in their hierarchy of priorities than the 'vague and uncertain' concerns of the Greek Cypriot public - vague and uncertain, of course, from the point of view of the intermediaries, who were not benefiting at the time for a program of Public Opinion Analysis. The danger of Turkey walking out of the negotiations and damaging her EU prospects was a graver threat, more imminent, and more obvious in the minds of the intermediaries than the danger of the Greek Cypriot public rejecting the Plan. Such were the consequences of applying a 'secret diplomacy' model to the case of Cyprus…

As for the responses of the Turkish Cypriots, we see firstly, as expected, that on the whole the provisions of the Annan Plan were acceptable to them. However, in two particular areas their support for the Plan is clearly half-hearted: Security, and Residence Rights. The Security provisions of the Plan only receive a 56 per cent approval rating, while the Residence Rights provisions of the Plan only receive a 54 per cent approval rating. But if these two aspects of the Plan did not satisfy either the Greek Cypriots - as we saw before - or the Turkish Cypriots as we are seeing now, then whom did they satisfy?

In the case of the Security aspect, the relevant provisions of the Plan were primarily acceptable to Turkey herself, who from the very first moment refused to allow the Turkish Cypriots to negotiate the issue independently. For Turkish Cypriots, the final Security provisions of the Plan were perhaps tolerable in that there were Turkish Guarantees in place for their security, but not truly satisfactory, in that the continued military presence of Greece on the island represents for them a potential security threat, given that it was Greece's military presence and its collusion with militant Greek Cypriots in the 1960s and up to 1974, which started the Cyprus Problem for the Turkish Cypriots. With the Annan Plan Security Provisions, Turkish 'strategic concerns' might have been satisfied in terms of maintaining the balance of power between Greece, Turkey and the UK in the Eastern Mediterranean, but neither of the two Cypriot communities had reason to be overjoyed by the particular security arrangements given their dubious and controversial track-record. In this example, we have a case of third-party concerns taking priority over Cypriot concerns.

As for the issue of Residence Rights, the provisions for which only polled a 54 per cent acceptance among the Turkish Cypriots, we have here a case where the leader of the community failed to accurately represent his public's concerns: For Rauf Denktash, the best solution would be if, after a settlement, the two communities lived in total segregation. The Turkish Cypriot public, in contrast, was much more open to co-existence of the two communities on the ground, so long as this co-existence did not imply political domination by the Greek Cypriots. As we would expect, the actual UN Plan reflects more accurately the concerns of the Turkish Cypriot Leader - whom the intermediaries did have access to - than of the Turkish Cypriot Public, whose thinking was quite unknown to the UN drafting team.

Rank-ordering the acceptability of the various provisions in the Annan Plan is not the only way in which the May 2005 survey data can be used to understand the behaviour of the Public at the referendum. More reliable information, in fact, can be provided through a Regression Analysis, wherein the dependent variable is 'Referendum Vote' while the predictor variables are of various types: Underlying attitudes towards the other community, views towards specific aspects of the Plan, political party preferences, and standard demographics. Such an analysis of the data has recently been conducted,[10] and the results are re-printed below:

Predictors of "Yes" vote in April 2004 referendum (Greek Cypriots)	B	S.E.	Wald	Sig.
DISY Supporter	1,96	0,22	83,35	0,00
Annan Plan Security Provisions	1,30	0,24	29,76	0,00
Annan Plan Property Rights	0,64	0,25	6,76	0,01
Annan Plan Settlers Provisions	0,60	0,30	3,93	0,05
Annan Plan Legal Status	0,52	0,26	3,90	0,05
"I would not mind having Turkish Cypriot neighbours"	0,77	0,23	11,37	0,00
"Our side is also to blame for the current situation of the Cyprus Problem"	0,75	0,33	5,12	0,02
"The two communities should go their separate ways from now on"	-0,68	0,30	5,21	0,02
Famagusta District resident	1,58	0,40	15,34	0,00
Refugee Status	0,51	0,21	5,68	0,02
High Education (College+)	-0,60	0,25	5,60	0,02
Low family Income (less than CYP 750)	-0,66	0,25	7,08	0,01
Female Gender	-0,70	0,21	10,85	0,00
Constant	-3,94	0,60	81,23	0,00

Predictors of "Yes" vote in April 2004 referendum *(Turkish Cypriots)*	B	S.E.	Wald	Sig.
UBP Supporter	-2.17	0.29	58.07	0.00
DP Supporter	-1.48	0.31	22.72	0.00
CTP Supporter	1.14	0.29	15.11	0.00
Annan Plan Security Provisions	0.96	0.23	17.09	0.00
Annan Plan Power Sharing Provisions	0.80	0.25	10.24	0.00
Motive: To be able to enjoy the benefits of EU Membership	0.68	0.27	6.42	0.01
"We have much in common with the Greek Cypriots"	0.61	0.21	8.27	0.00
"I would find it natural and acceptable is someone in my family close to marry a Greek Cypriot"	0.51	0.23	4.85	0.03
"The two communities should go their separate ways from now on"	-0.42	0.21	3.87	0.05
"Religion is important in my life"	-0.46	0.22	4.37	0.04
Iskele Region resident	0.84	0.33	6.37	0.01
Low Family Income (up to YTL 1,500)	0.48	0.23	4.58	0.03
Old Age (55+)	-0.87	0.25	11.70	0.00
Constant	-0.47	0.42	3.47	0.06

All the variables have been standardized and thus their coefficients are comparable. A higher 'B' coefficient implies that the particular variable was more strongly influential on the Referendum vote. A negative 'B' coefficient implies that the particular variable was a negatively related to the Referendum vote.

The first point to note is that variables of all four categories - Underlying Attitudes, Views regarding the Annan Plan, Political Party Preference and Standard Demographics all made it into the final model as significant predictors. The process by which the Public decided what to vote was multi-factorial, and cannot be reduced to 'just this' or 'just that'.

The second point to note is the dominating importance of Security concerns in defining referendum vote, both among the Greek Cypriots and among the Turkish Cypriots. Whatever the geo-strategic interests of Turkey or any other third country might be, it would seem very unlikely that any settlement plan would achieve a simultaneous 'yes' vote by both communities in a new referendum unless a way is found for the security concerns of both communities to be simultaneously satisfied.

The third point to note is that underlying attitudinal characteristics (such as nationalist tendencies, desire for separation etc.) did *not* play an important role in the rejection of the Annan Plan by the Greek Cypriots: While a number of attitudinal variables were found to correlate with referendum vote - most notably willingness to coexist with Turkish Cypriots and willingness to take responsibility and ownership of the Cyprus Problem - in all these variables it would appear that Greek Cypriots are positively disposed anyway and their underlying attitudes, if anything, served to mitigate rather than enhance the tendency towards a 'no' vote.

In contrast to attitudinal variables, membership of specific demographic groups was an important predictor of the Greek Cypriot 'no' vote. For instance, those in the lower income categories were more likely than others to reject the Plan, all else being equal. Further qualitative examination has revealed that a concern of this specific demographic group was the possibility that real wages might fall after a settlement due to competition in the labour market from Turkish Cypriot workers. To the extent that this concern was valid - and so far no expert has come out to say that it was not – we have here a case where the Greek Cypriot leadership itself is responsible for not having adequately reflected the concerns of their community during the drafting process: Just like the Turkish Cypriot leadership asked for, and got, safeguards that investment in the north would be regulated in the first few years after a settlement, thus protecting Turkish Cypriot businessmen from a potential inrush of Greek Cypriot capital, so the Greek Cypriot leadership could have asked for equivalent temporary safeguards to protect the Greek Cypriot workforce from an inrush of Turkish Cypriot labourers. They did not however seek such safeguards, since in the absence of reliable public opinion information the specific sectoral concern was overlooked, and in its place the default Greek Cypriot official position that 'anything integrative is good while anything divisive is bad' was the only available policy guideline. Once again, the limitations of a 'secret diplomacy' approach become readily apparent.

From Diagnosis to Cure: Using Public Opinion Research to Discover Mutually Acceptable Alternative Solutions

Beyond providing a basis for the analysis of why and how the Annan Plan was rejected, the May 2005 survey was also utilised in a more forward looking context, to explore potential alternative solutions to different aspects of the Cyprus Problem. An underlying assumption of the approach is that the Cyprus Problem can be divided into segments, or 'sub-problems', and that if each of these 'sub-problems' can be solved to the satisfaction of both communities then the final settlement plan, derived by putting together the solutions to the 'sub-problems', will also be satisfactory to both communities.

The specific segments or 'sub-problems', in which a possible settlement was divided for the purposes of the survey, were six: Security, Property, Residence Rights, Settlers, Power Sharing, and Legal Status. For each of these segments, a number of different alternative solutions were provided, with the hope that for each 'sub-problem' at least one of the solutions would be acceptable to majorities of both the Greek Cypriot and the Turkish Cypriot community. The findings for three of the segments – Security, Property and Settlers – are reprinted below:

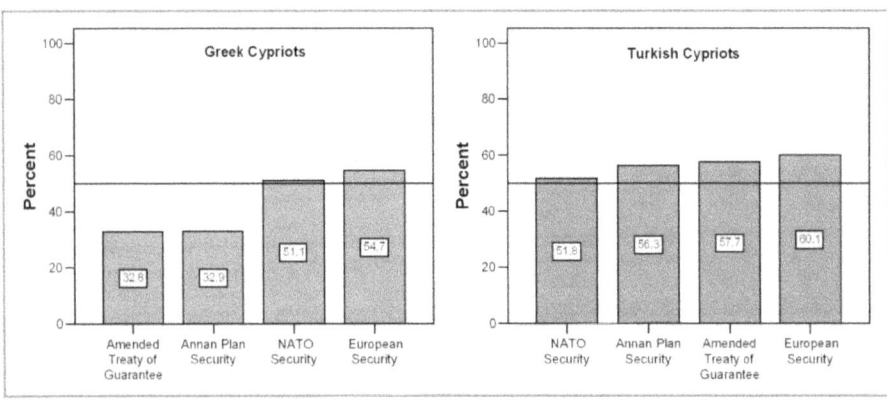

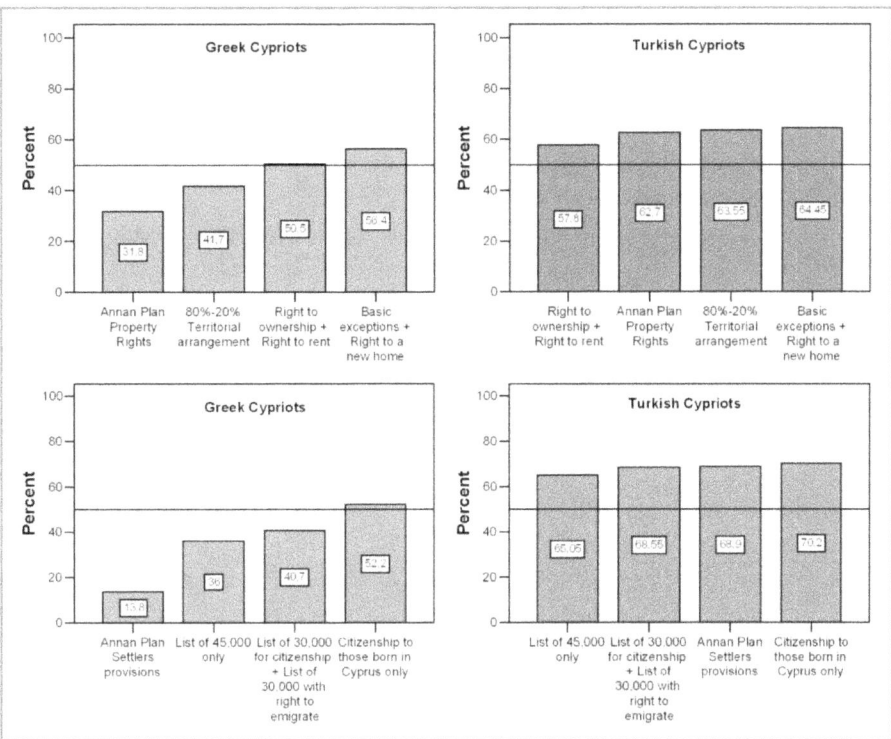

What stands out from the above charts is that, for all three of the presented solution segments, both Greek Cypriots and Turkish Cypriots agree which of the solution options is best – and interestingly, in none of these cases is the relevant Annan Plan provision the most favoured option.[11] While in the case of Turkish Cypriots most options are at least tolerable, leading to the conclusion that various different interpretations of the federal model would be acceptable to them, Greek Cypriots are much more specific in what they will and what they will not accept. The important thing to note from these findings is that if the primary goal of a renewed negotiating process is to achieve *mutually acceptable solutions,* and if all the options are systematically worked through with open-mindedness but also with reference to what the people would accept, then the most likely outcome is that the positions of the two communities will converge and an agreed basis for a settlement will be found.

How Would a 'Public Diplomacy' Approach Actually Work in Cyprus?

While the theoretical value of including the public in deliberations to solve the Cyprus Problem is by now self-evident to most observers, at least insofar as another referendum will ultimately need to be won, the actual means by which such public engagement will be achieved is a different challenge altogether. If the Cypriot public is to 'have a seat at the negotiating table', then the shape of the table must be designed accordingly, in such a way as to make room for the public without crowding out any of the other actors that also legitimately need to be there. To this end, and if it also taken as a given that on the political level the process would be owned by the two Cypriot leaders rather than a UN drafting team, then a renewed peace process in Cyprus would need to satisfy the following criteria:

The UN would be providing facilitation services rather than drafting services, while groups of Cypriots would be responsible for the actual drafting of the peace plan.

The process would be overseen and guided by the leaders of the two communities, but without being limited to them.

Groups of experts would play a role, but an equally important role would be played by groups of society representatives (Women, Youth, Trade Unions, Commerce Boards, Refugees etc.) who would add a human element to the process.

The negotiating teams would have at their disposal reliable public opinion information on a regular basis, providing feedback as to the public acceptability of the various alternative solutions.

External actors, such as Greece and Turkey, would not have direct access to the drafting process – other non-invasive ways should be found for their constructive input.

Putting all these conditions and priorities together, a schematic representation of a peace process based on 'public diplomacy' would be:

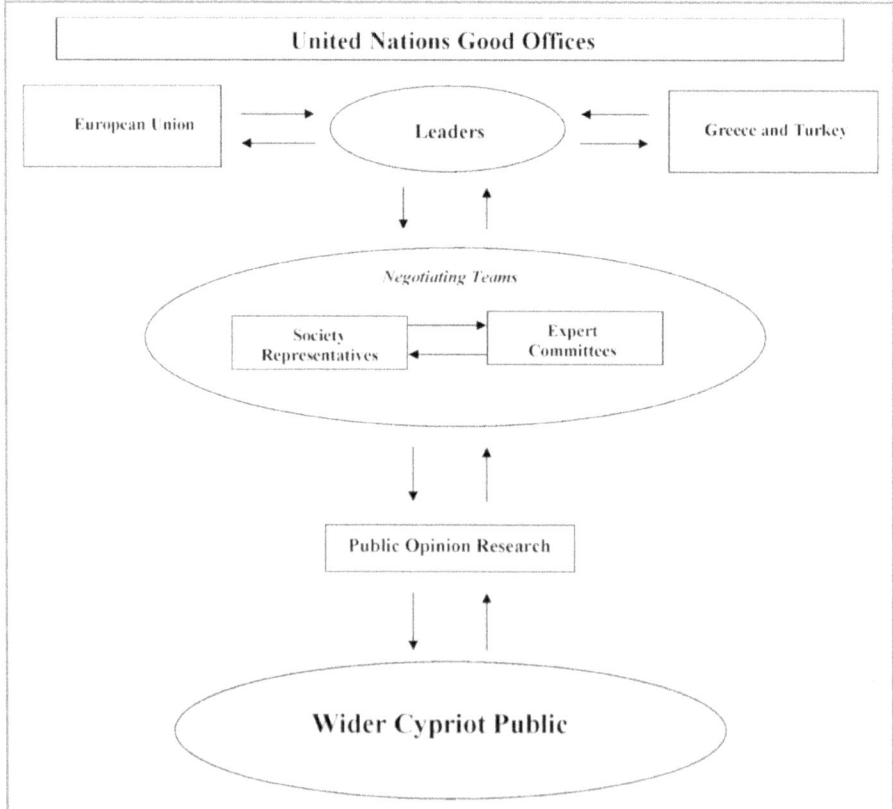

When comparing this schematic representation with the process that has already been formally agreed by the leaders of the two communities on 8 July 2006 (the Gambari Process) there are similarities and differences. Essentially, the 'top half' of the schematic representation, which details the interactions between the UN, the leaders, and the groups of experts, is in essence identical to the Gambari Process, while the bottom half of the schematic representation – society representatives, public opinion research, engagement with the general public – is entirely missing.

A 'glass is half empty' reading of this situation would be that the Gambari process is yet another ill-designed process of secret diplomacy which disregards the Cypriot public, no more likely to produce a Comprehensive Settlement than any of the previous efforts.

Conversely, a 'glass is half full' reading would suggest that the Gambari Process, as already agreed, clarifies adequately the political and technical dimensions of the negotiation, and that all that now remains is to find ways to connect the Gambari Process to the wider Cypriot public. Seen from this second and more constructive perspective, there are no significant practical obstacles to incorporating a societal dimension into the already agreed process; in this way, it can be guaranteed that whatever Comprehensive Settlement is ultimately agreed will faithfully represent the interests of all Cypriots, while eliciting a resounding 'yes' from both communities in a new re-unification referendum.

Endnotes

1. For qualitative approaches, see Michael Attalides, 'The Political Process in Cyprus and the Day after the Referendum', *The Cyprus Review*, XVI, 1, 2004, 137-146; Alexis Heraclides 'The Cyprus Problem and Open Shut Case? Probing the Greek-Cypriot Rejection of the Annan Plan', *The Cyprus Review*, XVI, 2, 2004, 37-54; For empirical approaches see Alexandros Lordos, 'Can the Cyprus Problem be Solved? Understanding the Greek Cypriot response to the UN Peace Plan for Cyprus', *An Evidence-Based Study in Co-operations with CYMAR Market Research Ltd*, November 2004, http://www.CyprusPolls.org, (accessed 15 November 2005); 'Civil Society Diplomacy: A new approach for Cyprus?' 2005, http://www.CyprusPolls.org; 'Options for Peace: Mapping the Possibilities for a Comprehensive Settlement in Cyprus', 2005, http://www.CyprusPolls.org; and 'Rational Agent or Unthinking Follower: A survey-based profile analysis of Greek Cypriot and Turkish Cypriot referendum voters', 2006, http://www.CyprusPolls.org; also Craig Webster, 'Division or Unification in Cyprus? The Role of Demographics, Attitudes and Party Inclination on Greek Cypriot Preferences for a Solution to the Cyprus Problem', *Ethnopolitics*, IV, 3, September 2005, 299-309; Craig Webster, and Alexandros Lordos, 'Who supported the Annan Plan? An exploratory statistical analysis of the Demographic, Political and Attitudinal Correlates' *The Cyprus Review*, XVIII, 1, 2006, 13-35.
2. David Hannay, *Cyprus: The Search for a Solution*, London, 2005.
3. Claire Palley, *An International Relations Debacle*, Oxford, 2005.
4. Hannay, *Cyprus*, 30.
5. Lordos, 'Options for Peace'.
6. Hannay, *Cyprus*, 32.
7. Colin Irwin, 'Public Opinion and the Politics of Peace Research: Northern Ireland, Balkans, Israel, Palestine, Cyprus, Muslim World and the War on Terror', Palestinian Centre for Policy and Survey Research and the Harry S. Truman Research Institute for the Advancement of Peace joint conference: *Public Opinion, Democracy and peace Making*, Jerusalem, 22-3 May 2006, 18-21.
8. Lordos, 'Can the Cyprus Problem be Solved?'.
9. Lordos, 'Civil Society Diplomacy'.
10. Lordos, 'Rational Agent or Unthinking Follower'.
11. For a more detailed account see, Lordos, 'Options for Peace'.

Chapter 13

THE PLAN, PUBLIC DISCOURSE AND THE ROLE OF THE MASS MEDIA IN GETTING TO 'NO'

Yiouli Taki

In April 2004 Cypriots were asked directly to give their consent to the proposed reunification of their island. Whilst many Greek Cypriots assert that the course of their statehood was largely shaped according to the interests of others, this time the final decision would be in their hands. Yet Greek Cypriot society appeared to welcome the opportunity with neither great enthusiasm nor preparedness. There was little significant public debate or critical reflection as to what might be demanded by this novel exercise in direct democracy. It would be apt to describe the Republic and its citizens as having sleepwalked into this process. Symptomatic of this was the fact that legislation governing the conduct of the referendum was ratified by parliament only nine days before the referendum and only a week before the close of the formal campaign period. Further, the regulations put in place related only to the technical implementation of the voting procedure whilst the campaign itself remained unregulated, necessarily diminishing the ability to secure a free and fair environment within which an informed choice could be made.

The relationship between the Annan Plan as such and the voters called to make a choice through the mechanism of a referendum took, in many ways, a highly mediated form. On the one hand, there stood a dense and detailed proposal for a comprehensive solution to the Cyprus problem and on the other, a complex process of decision-making which would finally find expression through the ballot box. The focus of this chapter is on some of the more prominent processes through which that decision was eventually taken, as well as the conditions within which deliberation proceeded. In doing so it explores the nature of this field of mediation with a specific emphasis on the role played by the mass media. Attention is not only directed towards the referendum campaign as such, but takes into account how attitudes to the final version of the Plan were, in the first instance, also conditioned by the process which brought it to fruition. Significance is also given to entrenched dispositions, cemented over time, through which contemporary experience was made sense of, thus providing the basis for a more securely anchored analysis of the outcome. Finally, attention is drawn to the balances struck within the Plan itself and around which contending arguments for acceptance or rejection circulated, influencing significantly the final outcome.

The Negotiations: Reception and Reaction

The career path of the Annan Plan was neither straightforward nor easy. The first version of the Plan, submitted in November 2002, was accompanied by a request that those concerned should clearly indicate whether it constituted a basis for a solution and whether the proposed process and timeframe was acceptable. Assessments of this attached proviso initially dominated much of political discourse in the south since the timeframe proposed was designed to culminate in agreement on principles before the EU's Copenhagen Summit, scheduled the following month. This would then open up a period of negotiation to conclude by February 2003, with the understanding that should disagreement remain, the Secretary General would be empowered to finalise an appropriate outcome. A referendum would then be held at the end of March, a timetable designed by the UN to ensure that the Accession Treaty would be signed by the representatives of a new reunified federal republic in April 2003. Amongst Greek Cypriots, the debate on the substance of the Plan was overshadowed as attention was directed towards ensuring that their response to the UN-imposed conditions would not have a detrimental impact on the Republic's path into the EU.

However, the carefully choreographed process did not unfold as anticipated since, at both Copenhagen and later at The Hague, the Turkish and Turkish Cypriot leaderships simply refused to play ball. As a consequence, the dynamic calculated to drive the UN process had, by this point, already passed its date of expiry.

Despite this, in February 2004, the UN managed to secure an agreement from all parties concerned for an engagement in a process which bore similarity to that proposed by the UN and rejected by the Greek Cypriot political parties in November 2002.[1] From the beginning the coupling of a solution and accession was the incentive offered by the international community to motivate Turkish Cypriots to engage in the process. Greek Cypriots, on the other hand, felt that the process and timeframe proposed by the UN was designed to exert pressure on them, particularly so in a context where Turkey was generally understood to have stalled the preceding negotiations. With the Accession Treaty signed the Plan was, from now on, to be judged exclusively on its own merits. Whilst there was merit to be found it was within a Plan which appeared to many as unfairly shaped by the weight accorded to Turkey's interests. Simultaneously, the compromises involved, including the surrender of a Republic now guaranteed accession, invites the assumption that the eventual referendum result was, even at this stage, a foregone conclusion.

By contrast, Turkish Cypriot calculations involved more profound interests, which they felt were at stake. The Plan offered a route out of political and economic isolation through rehabilitation as a partner in administering the state and the legitimisation of the regionally based aggregation of the two communities arising out of 1974. Consequently, and of considerable importance, the Plan offered to integrate the Turkish Cypriot community as a partner, together with the Greek Cypriots, within the EU. Indicative of this, the referendum question was so designed as to make the relationship between the prospective solution and EU accession of a united Cyprus absolutely explicit. By 2004 this question carried salience for the Turkish Cypriot voter alone.

Henceforth, this asymmetry of recognized incentives, created by the failure of all actors to synchronize their actions, significantly undermined the UN effort. Greek Cypriots became increasingly disposed to perceive the UN, in collaboration with or under the guidance of the US and the UK, as driven by the need to secure Turkey's accession course at the expense of fundamental principles, balance and fairness.[2] When forces external to the island sought to exert a positive influence the actual effect was to ground further these negative perceptions. The resulting climate was hardly conducive to a compromise on a proposed bi-zonal, bi-communal, federal structure. But just how had large swathes of the Greek Cypriot community reached this conclusion and what agencies were at work in sustaining such an environment conducive to this outcome?

The Mass Media: A Just Cause for Complaint?

It is of little surprise that in attempts to disaggregate those factors that influenced the eventual result of the referendum much attention has been focused on the role and conduct of the mass media. After all, the mass media was a strategically important force and the prime conduit through which voters apprehended much of the negotiations process, the nature of the Plan and the ensuing referendum campaign. In playing this role it actively participated in shaping the broader debates about the Plan's merits, or otherwise, as well as providing a platform through which competing 'yes' and 'no' campaigns asserted their respective positions. In short, the mass media was actively engaged in the multi-layered process of opinion formation; how specific events and versions of the Plan were interpreted, shaped and eventually acted upon. The significance of this institution is verified by polling evidence, which indicates that the broadcast media in particular was the primary source of information consulted by citizens during this period.[3]

Both immediately before and swiftly after the referendum vote prominent voices were raised which identified the conduct of the broadcast media in particular as playing a prominent role in cementing the 'no' and, in doing so, failed to conform with acceptable standards guaranteeing free and fair deliberation. From within the EU, the UN, as well as the main opposition party, DISY, these allegations were launched and are touched upon here.[4]

Importantly, whilst there are identifiable patterns of repeated media irresponsibility or even abuse, it is necessary to consider more subtle processes at work which determined the texture and content of the publics deliberations. Beyond immediate appearances there were sometimes quite unconscious conventions, selected formats, styles of reporting or ideological dispositions that, in their combined effect, also played a key role.

Turning to the actual conduct of the broadcast media it is possible to offer some general characterisation of the complex broadcast media environment spanning the period. A notable feature of news reporting was the frequent failure to offer a clear distinction, in practice, between reporting and a tendency to editorialise.[5] Journalists incorporated evaluative comments on events, statements, documents and the negotiations process in general that originated with Greek Cypriot politicians or the President's negotiating team. Simultaneously, the media failed to provide substantiation of such comments beyond generalities.[6]

There was also an observable process of misinformation because of a lack of critical scrutiny of sources consulted. For example, after the fourth version of the Plan was submitted, numerous inaccuracies about the Plan were circulated and remained uncorrected. This form of presentation played a significant role in promoting a sense of injustice among Greek Cypriots, that the outcome would serve the interests of Turkey, while adversely affecting the community's quality of life.[7] Further, in a number of specific cases there appears to have been a deliberate attempt to manufacture news stories and promote a conscious process of disinformation.[8]

Another related feature of news reporting that arose was a consequence of relying on information that was largely, if not exclusively, based upon unnamed 'reliable sources.' These sources were very obviously close to the President and his negotiating team. Claims emanating from such sources were invariably taken at face value rather than being subject to any sustained scrutiny, they were asserted as facts - facts that formed the foundation upon which the rest of the news report was then built.[9] In effect, many journalists became the conduit for what Michael Parenti has identified as 'face value' transmission of perspectives and opinions of those occupying a privileged position through which to control the flow of information rendering the function of the media, in this context, as mere 'stenographers of power'.[10]

One prominent journalist, Costas Venizelos, Chief Editor of *Phileleftheros* newspaper, has written positively of the necessity of the mass media to perform this function in periods of 'national crisis'.[11] He observes approvingly of a tacit agreement negotiated between the media and the government, pursuing 'national aims', to manage the news.[12] This is an arrangement which is governed by rules of confidentiality and not subject to any legal enforcement or laws of censorship. The aim of this practice is two-fold; to protect the pursuit of national aims against foreign interests as well as the transmission of news with the express purpose to influence public opinion. His justificatory description of what is identified as an informal 'channel of communication' between the centre of power and the media in order to determine the news agenda, in conformity with a particular interpretation of the 'national interest', appears to be confirmed by numerous examples of media conduct when seen in their totality. However, by the nature of a tacit arrangement governed by informal rules, and thus unlikely to be exposed within the public domain, it remains a process beyond independent verification.

Complimentary to news reporting were panel discussion programmes, in which the broadcast media aired the views of contending positions. As the vote drew closer the significance of this format was greatly enhanced because they became a nightly feature of the TV schedules and a regular part of daytime scheduling.

In terms of access by those from the 'yes' and 'no' camps, both views were duly represented, yet, the balance in terms of total time allocated tipped decisively in favour of 'no' representatives. The Radio and Television Authority provided an overview of the time allocated, based on ten TV political programmes from 24 March to 20 April. This was presented in terms of time given to 'no' representatives in excess of time given to the 'yes' (as a percentage): RIK (68 per cent); Mega (between the range of 36 per cent and 68 per cent); Antenna (36 per cent); Sigma (32 per cent).[13] However, this information must be approached cautiously. Firstly, it covers a period before as well as after the final version of the Plan was submitted and before the major political parties had finalised their positions. Secondly, the TV channels followed a trend of prioritising party representation rather than types of opinion or apparent inclination towards the Plan.

Turning to their content, the composition of the panels can be seen to be problematic in a number of other ways. With few exceptions those invited to participate were party political representatives, some of whom made repeated appearances. The only other group prominently represented was the legal profession. Consequently, whilst there was the immediate appearance of plurality, in reality public discourse represented through this form of communication was extremely constricted, confined to a stock of established names and with the ensuing debate proceeding within the narrow confines of a template provided by inter-party rivalry with little room for any other dynamic to be set in motion. Frequently, the form of debate which transpired tended towards an adversarial contest marked by mutual disrespect, intemperate engagement and the denigration of the opposition.

Rather than render the disproportionate advantage which accrued to the 'no' position as the unambiguous outcome of a deliberate choice exercised by an individual journalist, editorial team or owner, other factors, of a different order, were at play. Of decisive importance was the way in which broadcasters adopted rules and regulations in relation to balance commonly employed during elections. That is, both the right to and extent of access to media was determined by party political affiliation. With only two parties declaring in favour of the 'yes', this camp was afforded much less media representation. Of course, it need not have proceeded in this manner. In some other liberal democratic states, balance, in the lead up to a referendum, is achieved through according equal time to representatives of campaigns both for and against a proposition, irrespective of the party political support each has.[14] Little if any critical debate was forthcoming about the merits or otherwise of adopting this particular criterion for establishing balance despite alternatives being available. Neither did the legislation, hurriedly pushed through Parliament, entail any obligation on either the state nor the media to provide a balanced or accessible information about the referendum proposal, or provide public funds for the promotion of contending positions; provisions which might have mitigated some of the more blatant effects of media bias. More startlingly, there were no restrictions placed on what was to emerge as the extraordinary disproportionate ability of 'no' campaigners to acquire paid for broadcast time in the form of adverts. So, for example, between 17 and 22 April, 2004, six broadcasting slots were occupied by messages promoting the 'yes' as opposed to 471 for the 'no'.[15]

If a rough balance was achieved according to the prevailing parliamentary party support, it nevertheless should be noted that it was not until both AKEL and DISY had made public their positions in mid-April that the campaign proper was underway. For the previous eighteen months no clear and unambiguous advocacy for provisional acceptance of the Plan had materialised by default, a clear and unambiguous proposal to reject the plan and scepticism about the UN process itself, had not only emerged from November 2002 but it gained in weight, confidence and solidity as time progressed. Importantly this, by necessity, found extensive representation in the mass media as a strong monolithic and familiar position.

Turning to the print media a notable characteristic that distinguished its output from the TV stations was the greater representation afforded to a wide range of opinions and positions across the political/ideological spectrum despite the partisan positions often adopted through newspaper editorialising. This plurality was expressed in a number of different ways and not only did a wider range of views and analysis find expression, but these positions frequently emanated from beyond the political elite or formal party structures. Secondly, the form of delivery through which information, news and opinion were disseminated exhibited significant diversity – articles of varying length, combinations of information and opinion, or news and editorialisation. Finally, the newspapers also generally provided, to varying degrees, a significant provision of information, circulating copies of the Plan in its various forms at key junctures, providing contextualising material and contending interpretations.

Pairing the six daily Greek language newspapers on the island offers a productive way of registering similarities as well as differences across the print media spectrum. So, for example, *Politis* and *Phileleftheros*, the two largest circulating newspapers, shared a common form of presentation that generally kept a clear division between news and editorials. These newspapers tended to reproduce a wider range of views and attitudes towards the Plan than found elsewhere and frequently provided features that attempted to present both the positive and negative aspects of the Plan. Both expended effort on providing contextualisation and supplementary information. So, while all newspapers distributed copies of the Plan in various versions *Politis* and *Phileleftheros,* also provided enabling tools through which the Plan might actually be understood with some degree of fluency.

It is significant that these papers remained formally non-committal in relation to either a 'yes' or 'no' vote from November 2002 until the closing stages of the referendum campaign. The differential attitude of the two newspapers towards the UN process was evident with the submission of the first version of the Plan.[16] It was only in the last days of the campaign that *Politis* openly declared its advocacy of a 'yes' position, and even then, without modifying its policy of presenting a range of diverse opinions. *Phileleftheros*, on the other hand, tended towards a position that reflected the wider conspiracy theories of foreign powers entrapping the Republic of Cyprus. Further, its news reporting over-relied on single and often unnamed sources reproducing a similar practice to that of the broadcast media.[17] In effect *Phileleftheros* subtly reinforced the wider climate sustained in the broader media environment.[18]

Haravgi and *Alithia* are smaller circulation newspapers that are linked to the two largest political parties in the Greek Cypriot community, AKEL and DISY respectively. As such, they tend towards a party orientation that has the effect of generally circumscribing perspectives according to the official party position, though perhaps to a subtler degree in *Alithia*. Whilst *Haravgi* tended to omit direct coverage of statements by its political opponents, *Alithia* did not. Both papers had proportionally a much greater reliance upon staff writers rather than on content solicited from outside the paper. However, while *Alithia* did provide a platform for a range of opinions, which were not congruent with its editorial line, this was not so often the case in *Haravgi* which rarely hosted articles from guest columnists. Finally, whilst *Alithia* published simplified information on the Plan, *Haravgi* did very little by way of providing information.

In the coverage of the period the two papers tended to take diametrically opposite positions. While *Alithia* perceived the role of foreigners in the process as a positive opportunity, which should to be welcomed, *Haravgi* invariably saw the same role as an unwelcome imposition of the strong against the weak. With the completion of the UN process, the former advocated a clear 'yes' position while the latter promoted a 'no' in the referendum, positions that were the predictable outcome of the disposition each of these two newspapers projected prior to the formal position of the respective parties they were aligned to. In his opening speech at the extraordinary Pancyprian Congress of the party on 14 April 2004 the leader of AKEL spoke disapprovingly of the negative position expressed by *Haravgi* in the period prior to the formal adoption of a 'soft no' by the party which was to transpire the same day.

Simerini and *Machi*, two prominent right wing nationalist newspapers, tended to combine news stories with editorialization and promoted a uniform political line from November 2002 to April 2004. Both took a rejectionist stance from the very outset, predicated on a conception of the Plan as fundamentally partitionist. Their positions tended to go beyond a critique of specific provisions of the Plan as such, and encompassed the Plan's underlying philosophy, including the promotion of political equality between the communities.[19] Both papers also indulged in vitriolic anti-Anglo-American and anti-Turkish rhetoric.[20]

In summary, the styles of reporting and editorial positions of the six newspapers reflected a diverse range of dispositions evident amongst the public and the political parties or sections of their deputies. The 'strong no', personified by Papadopoulos and supported by EDEK, DIKO as well as smaller parties was consistent with the bitter attack that *Simerini* and *Machi* sustained against the Plan throughout the life time of the Plan. The 'soft no' of AKEL was formally projected by *Haravgi*. The record of the newspaper prior to the formal decision of AKEL would have presented it with a difficulty should the decision of this party had been for a 'yes' vote. *Alithia* shaped and reflected opinion which was from the start disposed towards a 'yes' vote on the grounds that both the process and the Plan represented a unique and historic opportunity for re-unification and that the failure to act with good will would have had grave consequences for the Republic of Cyprus. Unlike *Alithia*, *Politis* did not carry a party colouration. At the same time, as a relatively young paper, carrying no baggage of reporting on the Cyprus problem during previous phases, it established itself as an alternative conduit of information to *Phileleftheros*. Despite the eventual advocacy of *Politis* for the 'yes' vote, and the conspiracy tinged approach of *Phileleftheros*, their shared policy to extensively reproduce guest articles reflecting a plurality of perspectives and their commitment to providing information on the Plan meant that these papers drew an audience representing both the strong and moderate opinion of the relevant camps.

Gestating the Plan: The Role of Sedimented Dispositions

A characteristic of public dialogue, as well as the content of many media events, was how the reception of the Plan was mediated through dispositions which long predated the Plan itself. An important aspect of this was related to the general form of a solution - a bi-zonal, bi-communal federal structure - which had been on the table since the late 1970's and fleshed out through successive phases of negotiations culminating in proposals submitted by the UN in the 1980s and 90s. The leadership's acceptance of this state of affairs remained abstract and unexplored for large sections of the Cypriot communities.

As a result, an unsettling ambiguity characterized discourse within the Greek Cypriot public sphere; whilst a specific solution was officially accepted and propagated there was very little accompanying effort to give it meaningful substance. Further, the expressed commitment of Greek Cypriot leaderships was almost always heavily qualified; it had to be in conformity with UN resolutions, respect fundamental rights and freedoms, as well as an accompanying disavowal of accepting the consequences of the Turkish invasion.

Potent and unresolved ambiguity, obfuscation or silence occupied the space between the consequences which were more than likely to flow from accepted principles which would materialize in the form, for example, of a Turkish Cypriot north and a Greek Cypriot south, guaranteed by provisions that would secure the respective populations in each of the two regions on the one hand and the declaration that the consequences of invasion would never be countenanced, on the other. Or that this could impact upon the manner in which political rights might be exercised in a future dispensation.

Ambiguous declarations had been habitually and opportunistically sustained in conditions where a carefully drawn debate established clear limits to what was acceptable and unacceptable and truncated deliberation, constricted the range of opinions accorded legitimacy, imposed orthodoxy and minimized risk-taking. Given this, the materialization of a detailed solution, a 'painful compromise' made concrete, it would come as no surprise that particular provisions contained within it were simply written off as the outcome of a pro-Turkish agenda promoted by foreign interests rather than as a consequence of the type of solution that successive leaderships had agreed to pursue.[21] In an important sense, a predisposition to lend support to the informal 'no' campaign was not only making the running before the final version of the Plan was submitted, but well before the negotiations process was underway. This is the backdrop against which the Greek Cypriot community, as well as a large swath of the media, responded to the UN process and the Plan it produced.

Security Fears and the Solidification of the 'No'

Those advocating the rejection of the Plan were not part of a unified nor coordinated, let alone, monolithic camp. The 'no' vote was recommended by a range of media outlets, parties, and individuals. They shared very little ideologically in their evaluation of the Plan and in their rationalisation of their position taken. Some adopted a formal rejectionist stance in November 2002, whilst others, including the President, indicated, to a lesser or greater degree, a negative inclination, but did not formalise this until the referendum loomed. Still others, AKEL being the most significant, combined both positive and negative inclinations promoted through diverse outlets.[22] Thus, at one end of the rejectionist scale stood the President with his call for a 'resounding no', on the other stood AKEL promoting a 'soft no'.

When AKEL's leader addressed the Party's Congress in April 2004 he strongly disapproved of terms such as 'nationalists' and 'chauvinists' who had distorted, misinformed and subsequently took advantage of the public's fears and insecurities which had been stoked up. He added that the necessary conditions for reflection and calm discussion had not been cultivated because divergent opinions were frequently met by the charge of betrayal. But the culpability of the media in amplifying those voices that fuelled an acrimonious and highly charged atmosphere were not identified.

Christofias' address came one week after the President's address to the public on 7 April. In levelling the Plan in strong and direct terms, Papadopoulos assembled a range of the criticisms that had circulated around the Plan and the UN process, and which had become the most vocal, assertive and dominant. In effect, Papadopoulos proved more than adept at exploiting effectively an enabling environment, which anchored the 'commonsense' of the argumentation deployed.

His general approach was reliant on securitising the Plan by insisting that the proposed solution would lead to the surrender of the international status that the Greek Cypriots enjoyed through the Republic of Cyprus. Simultaneously, he asserted, that the viability of the proposed federation was questionable since there were no guarantees that Turkey would implement its part of the bargain and because the Plan contained partitionist provisions.

AKEL's recommendation for a 'soft no' on the other hand rested on two main factors: Firstly, a pragmatic evaluation that not only would a campaign for a 'yes' vote be an uphill struggle, but the time margin left to achieve this was ultimately far too narrow.[23] Secondly, that the Plan had failed to guarantee effectively Turkey's role in implementing relevant provisions of the Plan as well as wider security matters. So, whilst others took advantage of the existing fear and distrust of Turkey in order to flatly reject the Plan, AKEL suggested that the Plan needed to effectively address issues relating to Greek Cypriot fears so that it could be approved. In effect, this was a demand to sooth the basic fears of Greek Cypriots and, in doing so, disable 'nationalists' and 'chauvinists' from exploiting them. The common denominator amongst parties that proposed a 'no' vote was therefore security issues relating to Turkey's role.

The 'fear' factor is deeply embedded within both Greek and Turkish Cypriot societies and, as such, proved a valuable resource in the hands of maximalist camps in both communities displeased with prominent aspects of any compromise solution. The exploitation of these fears has been explored as an aspect of the media processes, leadership positions and long term dispositions evident throughout this period. However, attention also needs to be drawn to the way in which the Plan sought to address these fears since it was the Plan itself which was the prime resource in the hands of those who sought to swim against the current of rejection.

In his exposition on the period David Hanney has written that no settlement could be reached 'unless it also proved possible to banish or at least to diminish the nightmares of the two communities.'[24] He elaborated that for the Greek Cypriots the nightmare was of a 'settlement that somehow enabled the Turkish Cypriots subsequently to secede from the new Cyprus and achieve the international recognition that had hitherto eluded them'. This was an accurate bat incomplete observation because Greek Cypriot fear is not directed at Turkish Cypriots but against Turkey given that when secession actually materialised in 1974 it was the outcome of the Turkish invasion.

Without entering into a debate about the appropriate apportioning of responsibility to the different parties that made, for example, a Turkish invasion possible or whether or not Greek Cypriot negotiators pursued security issues relating to the public's distrust and fear of Turkey the point is to draw attention to the securitization of the Plan in Greek Cypriot discourse, made possible because the Plan did not appear to diminish significantly the Greek Cypriot nightmare.[25]

Viewed from the perspective of the underlying nightmares of both communities the Plan can be characterised as having incorporated a major asymmetry. With each version of the Plan the UN adopted a resourceful approach to issues relating to the Turkish Cypriot nightmare that no matter how 'carefully political equality and balance was nailed down in the settlement itself, the Greek Cypriots would somehow succeed in dominating the institutions of a new Cyprus and would in effect hijack them'.[26] Thus, the Plan provided for political equality grounded on a bi-zonal arrangement and operationalized this through provisions relating to governance, decision making, representation, political rights, internal citizenship and freedom of permanent residence and other issues.

In responding to Greek Cypriot fears, the Plan secured the new dispensation as an independent state with a single international personality and sovereignty and a prohibition on any unilateral change to the state of affairs established by the settlement. However, this same proscription already existed in the 1960 Constitution of the Republic and had not proved sufficient in preventing the imposition of partition in 1974. The Treaty of Guarantee, which was the reference point for Turkey as it sought to legitimize its action, was incorporated into the Plan and modified only to reflect that the new state of affairs established two constituent states. The Treaty of Alliance was similarly also incorporated.

With no change in the status of Turkey vis-à-vis Cyprus, or the concrete imposition of restraints on the guarantor powers, Greek Cypriots were called to make a leap of faith; to take the 'creative risk' of accepting the Plan based on a calm analysis of the potential changes in the Turkish Republic given its growing European orientation as well as on Cyprus' accession. This was in a context where Turkey had singularly failed to engage in any meaningful confidence building measures directed towards Greek Cypriots either then or in the past. Given this unchanging relationship of Turkey to Greek Cypriots, the manner in which the security fears of the two communities were addressed in the Plan posed real limits to the power of persuasion available to those campaigning for a 'yes' vote.

Conclusion

The Annan Plan promised the reunification of Cyprus, yet an overwhelming number of Greek Cypriots voted 'no'. This was a paradoxical outcome given the professed desire, expressed at both leadership and societal level, to see the island reunited once again which has been unpicked in any number of different ways; as the outcome of media manipulation or a failure to countenance power-sharing and so forth.

A more satisfactory approach to this paradox is achieved by refiguring the central presupposition upon which it rests. Rather than perceive the reunificatory intent of the Plan, for which widespread support could be garnered, it was in fact an agreed aim, a return to the status-quo ante and universally accepted within the international community as the right and proper outcome.

Whilst the prospect of reunification failed to translate into an incentive as such, those incentives that were on offer enabled differential opportunities for Greek and Turkish Cypriots to contemplate and eventually act in the spirit of compromise. For Turkish Cypriots the prospect of political equality grounded on a bi-zonal arrangement, directly addressed the ever present fear of domination by the other community and, in establishing this as a golden thread that ran through the Plan, binding together a multitude of provisions. For Greek Cypriots it was difficult to perceive any counterbalancing incentives of a similar weight and with such a deep-seated impact on the structure of the Plan. Consequently, there appeared little ground upon which to cultivate any strong sense of a fair trade-off so necessary to securing a 'painful compromise'. More specifically, the acceptance of bi-zonality – an outcome of the 'realities' imposed by Turkey – was perhaps the bitterest pill to swallow given that the culprit was perceived to be rewarded rather than punished.

In the absence of counterbalancing incentives there was little made available to challenge the criteria, based as it was on already pre-existing dispositions, through which judgement on the Plan tended to be passed. In short, it was difficult for the 'yes' to marshal evidence and related argumentation that Greek Cypriot fears had been addressed with either the same directness or resourcefulness.

Marshalling a persuasive argument against the Plan did not only rest on particular interpretations of the Plan itself. The extent and depth of the rejectionist trajectory was secured with much greater ease by an enabling environment within which it was cultivated. There were distinctive characteristics of the UN process which had an important effect on the conditions within which opinion was shaped – it should be remembered that in an eighteen month period there were five successive versions of the Plan made public. From the outset anti-federalist and other rejectionist forces made the running with those favourably predisposed to the general parameters of the proposed settlement disabled from voicing wholehearted support and constrained by the pressure to express unity with the Papadopoulos leadership during key phases of the negotiations. Further, the gathering 'no' current consistently resonated with the deep-seated and long-term ambiguity entailed in dominant Greek Cypriot discourse.

An assessment of the media's role during this period needs to distinguish between the conduct of the print and broadcast media. Whilst the former clearly editorialised either for or against the Plan a wider range of divergent views found expression in newsprint. The TV stations tended towards the widespread conflation of news transmission and editorialising comment, uncorrected misrepresentation of the Plan's provisions, dangerously distorting reliance on single unnamed sources and so forth. All of which could be judged to overwhelmingly favour those promoting a rejectionist outcome. Yet, seen in the *longue durée*, large swathes of the media also bore a responsibility for reproducing a context within which Greek Cypriot ambiguities in relation to an agreed destination had been sustained, providing the soil within which the rejectionist position was rooted.

Whilst this environment was well beyond any significant modification, let alone transformation, the failure to introduce regulatory procedures to mitigate the worst effects of blatant media bias was within reach. The media environment was not structured according to the particular needs of a referendum which, coupled with the particular nature of the long, drawn out, negotiations process and the very late emergence of a definitive 'yes' created an enabling environment favourable to the 'no'. This was an environment that was further enhanced by a very short campaigning period, itself unregulated according to rules and regulations appropriate to a referendum, which meant the uphill struggle waged by the 'yes' tendency was in fact so steep as to almost defy gravity.

Endnotes

1. In 2002 the majority of political parties rejected both the 'asphyxiating timeframe' and the proposed arbitration to be exercised by the Secretary General.
2. See, Claire Palley, *An International Relations Debacle*, Oxford, 2005.
3. The following is based on a media monitoring exercise that documented the relevant output of the major print and broadcast media organisations. A subsequent content analysis of representative samples provided a verifiable basis upon which to draw conclusions.
4. Gunter Verheugen's comments on 21 April, 2004 addressed to the European Parliament during the closing stages of the referendum campaign. The UN asserted that their efforts to provide explanations and clarifications about the Plan were 'hampered by the media climate on the island.' (See; 'Report of the Secretary General on his mission of good offices in Cyprus' S/2004/437 28 May 2004, para 71). In April 2004 Anastasiades lodged a letter of complaint to the European Parliament regarding the conduct of the media and the government, during the campaign.
5. See, for example, the Mega evening news on 29 March, 2004. Towards the conclusion of the initial outside broadcast the Mega journalist asserted that 'he (Papadopoulos) considered, rightly I would say, that the mediators could have been more fair…as we also said yesterday he is the negotiator for the Greek Cypriot side and all must have trust in him and in any case I think that especially after these last three days any criticisms must abate.'.
6. For example, the lead introduction to Sigma's evening news on 29 March, 2004, began with the declaration that: 'The news from Lucerne is bad. The new revised Plan is much worse than the previous one. The Plan almost satisfies all the illogical positions of the Turks and does not take into consideration the proposals of the Greek Cypriot side.'
7. On the 29 March, 2004, an Antenna reporter conveyed the following inaccurate information: 'The Turkish demand for the enforcement of bi-zonality is fully satisfied. Political rights of the Greek Cypriots who will settle under Turkish Cypriot administration are nullified and the Senate, which will consist of 24 Greek Cypriots and 24 Turkish Cypriots, will be ethnically cleansed.' This was repeated on the other channels.
8. On 26 February, 2004, Sigma reported its own self-generated 'Gallops' (their term) which

were in fact vox pops. The report was characterized by leading statements and questions. It reported that the 'overwhelming majority' of the Greek Cypriots were disappointed in the developments. Questions included: 'After the last unacceptable document submitted by Denktash are you optimistic or pessimistic?' The journalist continued with the following: 'The attitude of the occupying leader has lead the overwhelming majority of Greek Cypriots to the conclusion that while Rauf Denktash represents the Turkish Cypriot community in the negotiations the solution of the Cyprus problem will remain an unrealizable dream.' No information was relayed about numbers interviewed. A similar practice was observed on 16 March, 2004. Another example was broadcast on 3 April, 2004. Sigma reported 'that the security of the Greek Cypriots is at the mercy of Turkey.' This was presented as a news item resting on a study undertaken by a group of 'specialists' yet the report carried neither name nor institution to indicate the authority or authenticity of the claims. The same tactic was employed on 6 April under the banner, 'a revealing document on the property issue produced by experts is in the hands of the President.' A statement followed that property arrangements constitute an 'optical illusion' due to the limitations regarding residency in the other constituent state and other limitations. Again, no source was indicated.
9. For example, on 25 February, 2004, De Soto submitted Denktash' document entailing the Turkish Cypriot positions to Papadopoulos. The reactions on that day responded to this development: On RIK1's main news a journalist reported that in making his submission, Denktash had opened up the issue of sovereignty and demanded permanent and extensive derogations from the EU acquis. With this document, Denktash revealed his 'old, familiar bad self'. The issues he raised are outside the parameters of the Plan, outside its philosophy and outside the agreed process for the talks. According to 'very reliable information' the UN submitted Denktash' position to the Greek Cypriot side without any comments, 'just as the UN treats Denktash with neutrality when he raises unacceptable positions at the negotiations table'. A Mega journalist, on the same day, reported that Denktash drafted a letter which has prompted those who have seen it to comment that he reminds us of 'his old, familiar bad self'. The journalist listed a range of issues included in Denktash' document but none of the channels felt it necessary to elaborate as to how all the points raised, as they maintained, were categorically outside the parameters of the Plan.
10. See Michael Parenti 'Methods of media manipulation' www.media-alliance.org/article.php?story=200405131713495558 (accessed 5/7/2007)
11. What constitutes a crisis and are its boundaries, was not made clear. See Costas Venizelos, 'The press during periods of crisis', *The Mass Media and Foreign Policy*, Nicosia, 2004, 117-119.
12. The author is prone to slippage in naming the institution discharging 'national aims'. He migrates from naming the 'government' to the 'executive power' and to 'the President'.
13. Information released by the Radio and Television Authority.
14. For example in the UK and Australia.
15. This evidence is based on statistics produced by the Radio and Television Authority.
16. The editorial positions of the two newspapers in response to the submission of Annan I utilised different points of reference thus evoking different sentiments. *Phileleftheros* made repeated reference to the catastrophic consequences of Annan I for Cypriot Hellenism, repeatedly calling the government to explain the predicament Greek Cypriots faced. *Politis*, on the other hand, projected a calm tone, recognising both the significance and difficulty of the situation; giving due recognition to both the positive and the negative elements in Annan I and stressing the importance of drawing the EU into the difficult process that lay ahead. See unsigned editorials of the two newspapers between 11 and 18 November 2002.

17. Between 13 February 2004 and 1 April 2004 numerous headline articles of *Phileleftheros* made repeated use of: 'according to diplomatic sources', 'according to information'.
18. Following the submission of Annan IV on 29 March, 2004 *Phileleftheros* published a list of 'the damages and gains for the two sides' on its front page. For Greek Cypriots it listed points of dissatisfaction and for Turkish Cypriots it listed those changes that satisfied their demands. See *Phileleftheros* 30 March 2004. Three days after the submission of Annan V the main editorial of *Phileleftheros* commented that 'the issues pointed out by the President upon his return to Cyprus were measured and accurate…The difficult question that preoccupies us is why did the foreign mediators not help the President of the Republic and Cypriot Hellenism to take a positive position at the referendum? Would a 'No' vote by the Greek Cypriots serve any of their expediencies, would it serve their plans?' *Phileleftheros* 3 April 2004. This at a time when the paper was at pains to call for a calm evaluation of the Plan and before any major political party took a position in relation to the proposed solution.
19. *Simerini*'s headline on 12 November 2002 read: 'Nightmare Solution Plan – A three headed confederation'. Its unsigned editorial on the previous day carried the title 'Frankenstein State'. As early as 10 November *Machi* carried an editorial under the title 'Ready for the Big No'. The newspapers' commentaries on 12 and 13 November clarified that a solution based on three states and four parliaments was unacceptable.
20. On 13 November 2002 the main editorial of *Simerini* stated that 'with the assistance of the Anglo-Americans the UN has stabbed us in the back'. The headlines of *Simerini* on 21 November 2002 and 22 November 2002 read 'Hanney's Blackmail' and 'The British Noose' respectively. On the eve of the submission of Annan I *Machi*'s main editorial referred to American communication strategists and psychologists who utilised various means, including bribes, to recruit local politicians, business persons and journalists to influence public opinion in favour of the Plan, see *Machi*, 30 March 2004. This alleged role played by the US was coupled with the Anglo-American conspiracy at the negotiations level. See for example, 'We Won't Give a Dowry Sir', *Machi* 26 March 2004 and 'Behind our Backs', *Machi* 27 November 2004.
21. On 18 November 2002, one week after the Plan had been submitted, a panel was asked, by a prominent RIK journalist, as to why it was that the political elite failed to prepare the public for a solution. The same question could be asked of the media.
22. AKEL mainly disseminated its position through *Haravgi* newspaper and Astra radio station. Whilst *Haravgi* cultivated a negative atmosphere in relation to the UN process and the Plan, Astra did not exclude those positively inclined towards a solution based on the Plan. Negative, circumspect and positive inclinations in relation to the same issues were also disseminated by different representatives.
23. The recommendation was to seek a postponement of the referendum and, if this was not granted, the Party's position would be to call for a 'soft No'.
24. David Hannay, *Cyprus: The Search for a Solution*, London, I.B. Tauris, 2005, 28.
25. The issues that were raised during the negotiations, as well as during the campaign period, were many and various. The security nightmare described here is highlighted because of its prominent evocation in public discourse combined with the evident asymmetry of approach to this issue embedded in the Plan.
26. Hannay, *Cyprus: The Search for a Solution*, 28.

Chapter 14

CONSTRUCTIONS OF SOLUTION(S) TO THE CYPRUS PROBLEM: EXPLORING FORMAL CURRICULA IN GREEK CYPRIOT STATE SCHOOLS

Stavroula Philippou & Andrekos Varnava

Abstract

This chapter explores the role of Greek Cypriot state education in framing national expectations regarding a solution to the 'Cyprus problem'. It analyses primary and secondary state school formal curricula in the Social Studies subjects of History, Geography and Citizenship Education and discusses how solutions to the Cyprus problem are discursively constructed in text. What follows serves as a case-study of how curriculum operates as a political text in the context of a prolonged and intractable conflict such as the 'Cyprus problem' and how it shapes a particular vision of the future by constructing a national identity which draws upon a particular vision of the past.

Introduction

In the aftermath of the referendum on Annan V, public discussions largely focused on explaining the reasons why people voted 'yes' or 'no' across the divide or factors influencing their vote. In the case of the Greek Cypriot 'no', education featured prominently in these discussions, as some argued that state education did not provide for constructions of solution(s) to the Cyprus problem, which would make plans such as the Annan plan comprehensible and acceptable to Greek Cypriots.[1] This chapter examines this argument by exploring the role of curriculum in framing expectations for solution(s) to the Cyprus problem and examining Greek Cypriot public definitions of the Cyprus problem and its solutions as these are exemplified in school textbooks. It thus builds upon the work of other research on Greek Cypriot curricula in treating them as political texts.[2] It focuses on formal state curricula used in Greek Cypriot primary and secondary schools until the school year 2003-2004 to explore how potential solution(s) to the Cyprus problem were envisioned in the syllabi (*analytika programmata*) and school textbooks (*sholika eghiridia*) in place for key Social Studies subjects (Geography, History and Citizenship Education). The focus of this chapter on formal curricula and Social Studies can be located historically in the mechanisms of state formation since modernity. As the Greek Cypriot educational system is centralised with national curricula (and state controlled textbook production), it could be anticipated that the way the Cyprus problem is addressed would be quite evident in formal curricula and would hold a key place in the social formation of young people's views of the Cyprus problem. Historically the curricular space of Social Studies subjects has held a significant position within national educational systems, helping to develop national identities by drawing upon concepts of time, space and citizenship. Thus it could be anticipated that it is a key curricular space wherein Greek Cypriot education would attempt to address the Cyprus problem. Consequently, formal curricula and Social Studies are explored in this chapter as an important intersection of two key mechanisms in the discursive construction of potential solutions for Cyprus' divided society.

Locating Curriculum Research: Contributions and Challenges

The role of policy, curricula and education in constructing or imposing nation-states has long been documented. Historically nation-states have formed based on an exclusive or ethno-cultural model of community formation, a model which draws a direct, causal link between culture and an ethnos.[3] This model, social constructivists argue, mobilised education, media and other state mechanisms, to construct nation-states and shared national myths, heroes, symbols, ideals and historical narratives.[4] A number of quantitative and qualitative studies of textbooks and curriculum materials have shown the historical role that modernity has ascribed to state education and Social Studies subjects in particular to form national identities since the eighteenth century,[5] for example, in the US,[6] the UK,[7] the Balkans,[8] Western Europe,[9] Greece and Turkey[10]. Such ethnocentrism has been increasingly less salient in textbooks of countries like Germany and France,[11] but strongly persists in South-Eastern European countries where nationhood is still contested[12].

The fact that such a significant volume of research has been conducted on textbooks exemplifies their political importance in national educational systems.[13] Textbooks are very significant because they reflect curriculum developments, specify and interpret the content of the curriculum and structure it so it is suitable for teaching and learning.[14] They thus perform a very important pedagogical role, since they often dominate the entire curriculum to the exclusion of other materials.[15] Even though textbooks are in interplay with the curriculum and teachers, they are extremely important not 'as texts themselves but for what broader social and political debates, struggles, and orientations they represent'.[16] As Schissler and Soysal point out:

> Textbooks do not just convey knowledge; they represent what generations of pupils will learn about their own pasts and futures as well as the histories of others. In textbooks, we find what a society wishes to convey to the next generation […] [T]he analysis of textbooks is an excellent means to capture the social and political parameters of a given society, its social and cultural preoccupations, its anxieties and trepidations. […]. History, geography, and civic textbooks, though simplified, lay out for us the basic temporal, spatial, and discursive organization of regions, nations and the world.[17]

Knowledge of textbooks used in Greek Cypriot schools largely draws upon research conducted on textbooks published in Greece.[18] There is a scarcity of research on Greek Cypriot textbooks. The few studies conducted are quite recent and focus on history textbooks. These explore the ways in which national narratives are unfolded and reproduced in these materials.[19] For example, in a comparative study of 'History of Cyprus' textbooks used in Greek Cypriot and Turkish Cypriot schools Papadakis[20] argues that the official historical accounts of the Greek Cypriot and Turkish Cypriot communities mirror each other in the ways in which they construct blame, silence the pain of others, de-legitimise the historical existence of others, similarly to how each community claims that Cyprus 'belongs' to them on historical grounds in official and popular discourse.[21] This chapter builds upon the research already conducted, as well as broadens the focus to include textbooks used in three Social Studies subjects (rather than in just history textbooks) and at the same time narrows the focus to how 'solutions' to the Cyprus problem are envisioned.

Research Design
Sampling

The data analysed for this paper are documents comprising of Social Studies (History, Geography, Citizenship Education) syllabi, textbooks, workbooks and teachers' books which were used in Greek Cypriot state primary and secondary schools in the Republic of Cyprus until the school year 2003-2004. These documents are listed in Table 1, which maps out their duration in teaching periods, length, year and edition of publication.[22] Next to each teaching material a code (e.g. G3a, C4b etc.) will be used in the presentation of findings to refer to each document; the first capital letter denotes the subject (G, H and C for Geography, History and Citizenship Education respectively), the number indicates the grade level and the small letter the type of document referred to as shown in Table 1. In the presentation of findings, when this code is followed by numbers (e.g. H7a, 56), these will denote page numbers.

Table 1: Documents analysed for Geography, History and Citizenship Education

Grade	Subject and duration	Title of textbook	Textbook Code	Pages	Published
3	Geography 2*40'	*Gnorizo to perivallon mou* [Getting to know my environment]	G3a	112	2001, 15th Edition
4	Geography 2*40'	*Gnorizo to perivallon mou* [Getting to know my environment]	G4a G4b	150 144 269	2002, 6th Edition; 1998, 1st Edition
5	Geography 2*40'	*Gnorizo ton kosmo* (Evropi kai Mesi Anatoli) [Getting to know the world (Europe and the Middle East)]	C5a		2006, 13th Edition; 1993, 1st Edition
	Citizenship Education	*Ginomai kalos politis* [Becoming a good citizen]	G5a	72	2001, 19th Edition 1983, 1st Edition;
6	Geography 2*40'	*Gnorizo ton kosmo* (Afriki, Ameriki, Asia, Okeania) [Getting to know the world) (Africa, America, Asia, Oceania)]	G6a	223	1995, 1st Edition

	Citizenship Education	*Ginomai kalos politis* [Becoming a good citizen]	C6a	76	2004, 22nd Edition 1983, 1st Edition;
3-6	Geography	*Geografia* [Geography]	G3-6a	256	1999, 2nd Edition
3-6	History	*Istoria* [History]	H3-6a	192	1995, 1st Edition
5-6	History	*Istoria tis Kyprou* [History of Cyprus]	H5-6a	144	1995, Edition not shown
7	Geography 1*45′	*Taxidi sti Gi mas* [Journey to our Earth]	G7a	108	1999, 2nd Edition; reprinted 2002
8	Geography 2*45′	*Geografia tis Kyprou* [Geography of Cyprus]	G8a	88	2002, 2nd Edition; reprinted 2005
		Taxidi stin Evropi [Journey to Europe]	G8b	108	2004, 2nd Edition revised; reprinted 2005
9	Citizenship Education 1*45′ (one trimester)	*Politiki Agogi* [Political Education]	C9a	83	2004, 3rd Edition (partly revised) 1996, 1st Edition;
7-9	History 2-3 *45′	*Istoria tis Kyprou gia to Gymnasio* [History of Cyprus for Gymnasium]	H7-9a	118	2004, 7th Edition 1994, 1st Edition;
12	History 2-5 *45′	*Istoria tis Kyprou gia to Lykeio* [History of Cyprus for Lyceum]	H12a	317	2002, 5th Edition 1992, 1st Edition;
	Citizenship Education 1*45′	*Politiki Agogi* [Political Education]	C12a	326	1993, Edition revision; 1995, 5th Edition

The analysis also included the geography (G4b, G3-6a) and history/civics teachers' books (H3-6a) for the last four grades of primary school, both published first in 1995. Another set of documents analysed were the aims and contents prescribed for the three subjects in the official curricula/syllabi documents which are mandatory for all state Greek Cypriot schools and are published by the Ministry of Education and Culture. What follows is a brief description of what pupils are taught at each subject and grade so as the findings presented later in the chapter can be contextualised within each subject area.

For Civics and Citizenship education, teachers can choose topics from textbooks C5a and C6a according to time they have available cross-curricularly, whereas C9a and C12a are taught in a fixed teaching period for the subject (see Table 1). As far as Geography is concerned, the curriculum is based upon the 'expanding environment curriculum' or 'widening horizons' conceptual framework that McMurry first used in 1903;[23] pupils first study their immediate environment (classroom, school, neighbourhood, community, village, town or city), Cyprus and Greece but not Turkey. In the 5th-8th Grades they proceed to distant locations, European and others, including Turkey at the 7th Grade. Cyprus as a focus of study reappears in the 8th Grade. The textbooks used for Geography are all published in Cyprus. In History, most of the textbooks used are published in Greece.[24] However, the textbooks analysed for this study were those entitled 'History of Cyprus' which are published in Cyprus and taught at the 5th-6th, 9th and 12th Grades parallel to the textbooks from Greece, since these textbooks study the Cyprus problem. In Citizenship Education, textbooks from Greece are also used in class; however in this study only the textbooks published in Cyprus were analysed. The Curriculum Development Service of the Ministry of Education and Culture in Cyprus published all the textbooks included in Table 1.

Analysis

To analyse the data outlined above, a constructivist perspective was adopted and qualitative analytical methods were employed, to conduct 'traditional' thematic coding. The theoretical framework guiding the analysis drew upon the literature on largely historical, social and political analyses of how the Cyprus problem and potential solutions to it have been constructed, since it provided analytic tools which were mobilised in the analysis of the documents. At the same time, the themes/coding framework were developed in the process of the data analysis, as certain patterns emerged from the text which refined the coding scheme. The analysis proceeded in two phases: during the first, the analysis involved a coding of the curricula devoted to the Cyprus problem in the three subject-areas and a descriptive account of the way and degree to which the Cyprus problem was portrayed in each subject. Then followed a content analysis of the documents through the thematic coding scheme which was developed from the literature and the data itself and is shown in Table 2. The focus was on three dimensions of the curricular documents: the first dimension referred directly to solutions to the Cyprus problem. Historically, interested parties have proposed various political solutions to the Cyprus problem: these were used as analytic tools in analysing the text in order to map the solutions constructed in the textbooks for the future. In searching for solutions, politically designed to apply in the future, there was a need to analyse content which addressed the past, since the solutions were construed in relation to how the problem more broadly was represented historically; the second dimension was therefore the historical background to the Cyprus problem. As historical narrative was analysed, a third dimension emerged: it addressed constructions of Cypriot identity, which underpinned the construction of the historical past, present and future. As Koulouri argues for the case of history textbooks 'history books, particular, may reflect the image a human society has for its past and, indirectly, the way it imagines its future'.[25] In searching therefore for envisioned solutions in the future, the need arose to address the past and, by extent, Cypriot identity; or in other words any solution in the future was found to be grounded in historical narratives of the past.

Table 2: Thematic Coding Scheme (Phase 2)

Solution (s)
- 1960s
- During 1974
- After 1974

Cyprus Problem
- allocating responsibility/blame
- establishing legitimacy
- the problem as violation of human rights (loss of life and property, displacement, no freedom of movement)

Cypriot Identity
- use of language: Cypriots
- historical narratives
- minority-majority discourse
- Cypriot identity and Greece
- Cypriot identity and Europe

The findings are presented by drawing simultaneously from the three subject-areas (Geography, History, Civics and Citizenship Education) structured under the three themes of Cypriot Identity, the Cyprus Problem and Solution(s) in this order so as to illustrate the framing of each theme by the other: from identity to constructions of the problem and by extent to its potential solutions.

Cypriot Identity

Cypriot identity constructions are important because they legitimise the particular creation of the political problem and certain solutions over others with regards to the identity of a potential future political entity and its citizens.

One of the most salient mechanisms by which identity is denoted is the use of language. In his study of Greek Cypriot history textbooks Koullapis noted that the history of the island is construed as part of the Greek national history in a number of ways, one of which is the interchangeable and synonymous use of the terms 'Greek' and 'Cypriot' to denote identity.[26] This practice is also employed in the civics and geography textbooks: using the term 'Cypriot' or 'nation' to systematically denote Greek Cypriot or Greek nation in Cyprus, implies that all Cypriots are Greeks and that others, including Turkish Cypriots, are not Cypriots.

A second mechanism was located within the historical narratives provided in the textbooks; the quote which follows is quite characteristic and exemplifies the historical construction of Cypriot identity as Greek:

> Achaeans colonised the island right after the Trojan War and contemporary Cypriots are considered their descendants. Archaeological research and findings provide evidence of the incorporation of Cyprus to the

Greek world which continued from those Classical times, to the Byzantine period and today. The Greek element, despite Ottoman occupation and rule for 300 years, comprises 80 per cent of the population. *Only* 11 per cent of the population are Turks and they are the *remnants* of the Ottoman conquerors and a product of Islamisation of part of the inhabitants of the island. Cyprus since 1960 is an independent state. During the last decades, Cyprus has, despite obstacles and the brutal Turkish invasion in 1974, done miracles. [...] Cyprus, based on archaeological heritage, on the Christian and European tradition and culture follows its European orientation and destiny. Conquerors come and go. Nobody succeeded in changing its Greek and European character (G8a, pp. 8-9, emphases added)

In this narrative, as in many other instances in the social studies textbooks, Cyprus is defined as Greek, monocultural and exclusive of other (old and new) communities and minorities of Cyprus. In another geography textbook, a section entitled 'The residents of Cyprus' describes the population in terms of national or religious groups (Greeks, Turks, Maronites, Armenians and Latins); it thus explains to pupils that

Greeks came to the Cyprus for the first time at least 1400 before the birth of Christ. Later, after the Trojan war, more Greeks came and built various cities [...]. In this way they dominated all over Cyprus and the Greek language was spoken by all its inhabitants. Thus, as the time passed, Cyprus became a Greek island.

Turks conquered Cyprus in 1571, that is 3000 years after the Greeks came. They brought here many Turkish soldiers with their families. They inhabited various rich areas of the island. In the years that passed their number increased significantly (G4a, p. 37).

It is perhaps surprising that this linear chronological historical narrative of victimisation which essentialises Greek identity into blood-bonds of brotherhood and into an undifferentiated national group is articulated so clearly in geography textbooks as in the above quotes; however, it is this same narrative which is constructed in the history textbooks.[27] Since Cyprus is constructed as 'historically Greek' and Turks as recent conquerors, then the presence of Turkish Cypriots is de-legitimised because they are construed as remnants of 'conquerors' or products of 'islamisation',[28] or at best, a minority. However, facing Turkish Cypriots as a minority and not a community with equal political rights undermines the political and legal groundings of the 1960 Constitution and a federation. The understanding of 'rights' over Cyprus as analogous to population percentages comes through every time the demography of the island is described. For example, in G8a's chapter on 'Population', the text explains that 'in Cyprus the population is not homogeneous neither from a religious, nor from a national point of view. During the Ottoman and British periods there were religious groups (see Table 9.1.3[29]). These turned into national groups and two of them were recognised as 'communities' since 1960 with the declaration of the independence of the island.

The Greek Cypriots constitute the *majority of the population* with the *largest community*, whereas Turkish Cypriots constitute the *second community* of Cyprus' (p. 73, emphasis added). As this quote illustrates, though in terms of facts and figures, the presence of other communities and minorities is articulated, it is at the same time undermined by the 'majority-minority' discourse, which delegitimises Turkish Cypriot political rights based on numerical grounds. This point is in line with Kizilyurek's argument that Greek Cypriots face Turkish Cypriots as a cultural and not as a political community, as a religious minority with no rights in the exercise of political power in Cyprus, thereby undermining the sense of 'political equity' that various solutions to the Cyprus problem require.[30]

This is closely related to the fourth mechanism we identified, which refers to the content ascribed to the Cypriot identity as compared to the Greek one. In C6a there are sections on the Greeks and Turks of Cyprus, whose identities are defined as national (ethnocultural) and distinct, each attached to a respective motherland, using national symbols and anthems respectively. Cypriot identity on the other hand is ascribed a civic content, which attaches Cypriots to the Republic of Cyprus as a state and as a place of residence with no emotional or psychological appeal; this is also the case in the civics curriculum for primary education.[31] This kind of emotional or psychological appeal is more evident in the textbooks analysed when historical, economic or cultural bonds with Greece are explained; for example, there are many chapters in the geography textbooks on Greece but no clear explanation of why this is so or why Greece is taught in parallel to Cyprus. The answer can be located in the narratives of identity: "Since ancient times the Greeks of Cyprus have close relations with the rest of the Greeks […] This collaboration continued in the modern era. Today Greece is our main support in the struggle for freedom of our particular [idiaiteri] homeland. The Greek people and our Greek immigrants [apodimoi] help in every way for the deliberation of our occupied lands' (pG4a, p.91). Also, diasporas as a theme appears quite prominently, especially in geography textbooks, since at the end of many chapters on various countries of the world and Europe, a section comments upon the Greek and Greek Cypriot immigrants residing there and their economic and political support to the case of Cyprus abroad.

Finally, a fifth mechanism by which Cypriot identity is ascribed its content is through Cyprus' relations with Europe; indeed the European context provides a forum wherein it is clarified. As in the first quote, and in other instances in the text, Cyprus is construed as European because it is firmly associated with the Greek-Roman culture and Christian heritage. This is supported by an understanding of 'Europe' as a concept ascribed with ethno-cultural content which is inherited from the Greeks and the Romans; for example, it is stated that 'The European civilisation is the continuance of the ancient Greek and Roman civilization. An important element of the European cultural heritage are also the teachings of Christianity' (G5a, 100). G8b has also been found to represent Cyprus as homogeneously Greek-speaking and Christian Orthodox in maps depicting languages and religions in Europe (G8b, 15; 107).

Having identified some of the mechanisms by which a Cypriot identity is constructed and the contents ascribed to it, we now investigate how the Cyprus problem is addressed in the textbooks; as we argue below, the understandings of the problem are rooted in the narratives of identity we have located in this section.

The Cyprus Problem
Allocating Responsibility

Three key themes emerged in the analysis of the ways in which the Cyprus problem was referred to in the textbooks analysed. Firstly, it was salient that when the Cyprus problem was in focus, the text attempted to 'explain' facts by allocating responsibility or blame; the narrative was consistent in all textbooks (particularly history textbooks) in allocating responsibility to others: namely, Turkish Cypriots, Turkey, Britain, America and Greece. This was achieved by who was directly 'blamed' in the text, but also by the emphasis on certain historical periods over others. For example, H12a blames three 'divisive elements' in the 1960 Constitution for the subsequent tragedy that befalls Cyprus: the Turkish Cypriots received rights beyond their numerical strength and the Constitution included provisions that prevented the state's smooth running. These provisions are not listed, but instead it is stated that the Turkish Cypriots were made a community alongside the Greek Cypriots. The third point, which is critical about the Treaty of Alliance and Treaty of Guarantee, does not relate to the Constitution, but reflects the Greek Cypriot leadership's opposition to these at the time. It is also stated that the Turkish Cypriots insisted on the full implementation of the agreements, resulting in the state's non-viability (H12a, 276); the majority-minority discourse thus appears in this example again as commented above, as a reason why the 1960 Constitution failed: Cyprus, the pupils are told, was the first state with a Constitution that denied the majority the right to rule (H12a, 272). Examples of other power-sharing Constitutions between religious or linguistic groups, such as in Switzerland and Lebanon, are not provided.

A similar example of the attribution of responsibility to the Turkish Cypriots occurs when the breakdown of the 1960 Constitution in 1963-4 is presented: they are portrayed as having secretly made military preparations and, through the TMT terrorist organisation, silenced progressive Turkish Cypriot voices, in order to push for partition (H12a, 276). No mention is made of the methods the Greek Cypriot political elite used to push for *enosis* during the 1960s. The textbook claims that Makarios proposed thirteen amendments to the Constitution so the state could run smoothly, which Turkey rejected and forced the Turkish Cypriots to attack at various points across Cyprus. All the textbooks reflect this position, referring to the December 1963 events as the 'Turkish Cypriot revolt', thus implying that Greek Cypriots had no responsibility for them. It outlines that the Turkish and Turkish Cypriot leaders forced the Turkish Cypriots, who were living peacefully with Greek Cypriots, to move into enclaves and for members of parliament and ministers to withdraw, as part of a plan found in Dr Kutchuk's office dated 14 September 1963 (281). The British are also blamed for separating the warring communities with the 'Green Line', which played into the hands of the Turkish Cypriot policy of partition (280). Greek Cypriot responsibility for the 1963 clashes is thus not acknowledged in this narrative. Richard Patrick and the memoirs of Glafkos Clerides[32], one of the key players in the events, show that the Greek Cypriot political elite's policy was outlined in the 'Akritas Plan'. This document outlined the strategy to achieve *enosis* by amending the 'negative' provisions of the 1960 Constitution; abrogating the Treaties of Guarantee and Alliance, which forbade *enosis* and allowed the intervention of Greece, Turkey and Britain to restore the 1960 Constitution; gaining international support for the Greek Cypriot right to self-determination; and finally by legitimising *enosis* through a plebiscite on the right to self-determination. In order to enforce the Akritas Plan, the creation of a Greek Cypriot paramilitary group was envisaged and duly a number of them were formed. By not referring to these events, H12a silences the Greek Cypriot leadership's responsibility in the 1963-4 events, a pattern which appears again in the way the Agios-Theodoros and Kofinou crisis of 1967 is treated in the text.

Another example is how the history textbooks treated the coming to power of the Greek Junta as the start of Cyprus' problems, which they held responsible for the coup and the invasion. H7a implied that the Cyprus problem started with the coup and its story begins in 1967 with the Junta's coming to power. There is reference to EOKA B bombing police stations and trying to assassinate Makarios. Members of the National Guard and EOKA B, under orders from the Junta in Athens, overthrew Makarios and thus the lawful government was replaced with an illegal government. H12a continues in this same vane (285). It goes beyond the scope of this study to examine this at length. It suffices to say that the Greek Junta is portrayed as monolithic in its hatred of and desire to remove Makarios, making no distinction between the Papadopoulos regime and that of General Ionnides. Glafkos Clerides and Makarios Droushiotis have shown that not all in the Junta supported the '*enosis* and only *enosis*' line. Indeed it was the Papadopoulos government that had initiated the inter-communal talks, which began in 1968 and which at one point had found a solution acceptable to the two negotiators, Glafkos Clerides and Rauf Denktash, and the Greek and Turkish governments, but Makarios was the stumbling block.[33] Those responsible are hidden behind labels such as Greek Junta, the National Front and EOKA B, while nothing is mentioned about the intra-communal and inter-communal killing for which responsibility burdens all sides. This approach is also evident in the presentation of the 1974 events. Turkey, the textbooks claim, used the coup as an *excuse* to invade. H7a mentions that the National Guard, weakened by the coup, failed to provide an adequate defence, so the blame again falls on the coupists. Turkey is also to blame: Ankara cited the Treaty of Guarantee and the protection of Turkish Cypriots as the reason for the intervention, a claim which is subsequently undermined by the text, when the two phases of the invasion are presented and Turkey's 'real' aim, occupation of more territory, is revealed with the second invasion of 14 August (H12a, 298).

Establishing Legitimacy for the Republic of Cyprus

Apportioning blame to others was closely linked in the text with the second theme, that of the legitimacy of the Republic of Cyprus. This occurs chronologically for the 1963-4 and the 1974 events. H10a establishes the legitimacy of the Greek Cypriot controlled government in the face of the withdrawal of the Turkish Cypriot members in 1963-4 by referring to the UN Resolution 186 in 1964 when the international community recognised the Republic of Cyprus. The textbook then refers to how the Republic formed the National Guard to counter a Turkish invasion and the George Papandreou government sent 8,000-10,000 Greek troops to make Cyprus 'self-defendable'. Nothing is said about the legality of either of these developments, which are justified in the face of Turkish threats to invade (281) the legitimate government controlled areas.

The post-1974 case of Cyprus is clearly construed as a case of violation of statehood of an internationally recognised state by a foreign state; this is particularly salient in C6a, C9a and C12a, wherein concepts such as the 'state', the 'nation', and 'regime' are defined. For example, C6a explains: 'For a state, to come into existence, it needs its own territorial areas, its own people and state power. It also needs international recognition. The whole of Cyprus, from one end to the other – free and occupied – is the territorial area of the Cypriot state [*politeia*], the Cypriot state [*kratos*]. All the citizens of Cyprus, regardless of age, gender, religion, language and nationality constitute the Cypriot people' (p. 9). A bleeding Cyprus, split in two by barbed wire, the top half under a military boot decorated with a Turkish flag, follows this text. The legend to the image reads as follows: 'The territorial integrity and sovereignty of the Cypriot state were blatantly violated by the Turkish invasion of 1974'. The text thus manages to both legitimise the statehood of the Republic (despite the coup) and to allocate responsibility to an entity from 'without' rather than from 'within' (despite the background of inter-communal conflict).

The Problem as a Violation of Human Rights

Understanding the Republic of Cyprus as the only legitimate state on the island during and after 1974 set the background for the third theme which emerged from the analysis and which included the frequent references to humanitarian and human rights issues. The 1974 war emerges as a cutting point when the textbooks shift from the political/military events to humanitarian and human rights issues. This was reflected in all the documents, even when the topics or chapters did not directly relate to the political problem. For example, C5a comprises of three chapters which at a first glance are not about the political problem: 'My life at school', 'My life in my family' and 'My life in the community'. But, there are frequent references to the Cyprus problem in each of these three chapters, when, for example there is reference to the schools in tents soon after 1974; to schools under occupation; to the violation of the family asylum by the Turkish invaders; and to villages under Turkish occupation, which pupils are asked to locate. Other examples in G3a, G4a, G5a, C12a are those of pictures of villages, natural cites, churches and archaeological monuments which are presented with legends referring to them being inaccessible and deserted after 1974.

In C6a, C9a and C12a human rights are taught as special topics, with an emphasis placed on the right to freedom, personal security and decent living, the freedom of movement and living within the territorial area of a country and the right to own property. Pupils are asked to identify those basic rights of the Cypriot state that are violated by Turkey. Elsewhere these rights are clearly articulated:

> [E]very state [politeia], every state [kratos],[34] has the right to be sovereign, independent and territorially integral. In Cyprus these rights and all basic human rights have been violated by Turkey, with the invasion of 1974 and the illegal occupation of 36,3 per cent of Cypriot territory. The Cypriot state is constantly struggling, in various ways, to achieve the restoration of its violated rights. It has appealed many times to the United Nations Organisation and has achieved the approval of many resolutions which support the rights [dikaia] of Cyprus. These resolutions can, if they are respected from Turkey and are implemented, bring peace and freedom to the island' (C6a, 10).

This quote encapsulates how the Cyprus problem is construed as an international problem of violation of statehood by a foreign state, as well as a problem of violation of Greek Cypriots' human rights. The UN and its resolutions are invoked to support this argument; elsewhere the European Union and the Council of Europe are also provided as international actors in the Cyprus problem that could contribute to a solution. Cyprus's EU membership becomes a forum wherein respect for human rights can be addressed, because of EU regulations and the *acquis communautaire*; the EU is therefore ascribed a key role in protecting human rights or as a key factor in the Greek Cypriot leadership's struggle to restore them. For example, in G5a of European geography, in the chapter on the EU, human rights is highlighted in bold typing and in a separate paragraph, amongst other aims such as the environment, health, education and cultural development (p. 112). Later in the text it is stated that 'Cyprus expects from the EU to support the effort of the government for the protection of our cultural treasures which are in the occupied areas and which are in danger of total destruction' (p. 112). The role of the EU in the Cyprus problem is further elaborated upon with the legend on the picture of a demonstration which focuses on the families of Greek Cypriot missing persons: 'Turkey, with its invasion of Cyprus in 1974, violated and is still violating basic human rights of its inhabitants. The Cypriot people are investing many hopes on the EU for the implementation of its statements [*diakirikseis*] in our land [*ston topo mas*]' (p. 112). The monological construction of human rights as those of the Greek Cypriots' and the parallel silencing of Turkish Cypriots' human rights, and the understanding of the problem as a 'clear' issue of violation of an internationally recognised state, also reveals the simplistic ways in which potential solutions to the problem are constructed.

Solution(s)

References to potential solutions to the Cyprus problem in the past or in the future are rare, but when they occur they are largely located in the secondary history and civics textbooks, because of the reference to the various agreements and talks that took place between the leaders of the two communities and the UN both before and after 1974 (e.g. in C9a, 53-56; C12a 159-164). The discussion below is structured around different solutions which have at various points been negotiated.

For the textbooks, the 1960 Constitution was a solution compromising the different aspirations of the two communities, ending the colonial period and marking the beginning of independence. H7a states that the Cypriots would taste freedom for the first time (246) and that they received independence with relief (272); this statement is paradoxical, it implies that the Greek Cypriots felt that independence equalled freedom, when they had fought for the island's *enosis* with another country and not independence. H7a also states that the Greek Cypriots had hopes for a new life of peace, democracy and freedom, which contradicts what is subsequently revealed, that despite its preclusion they continued to desire *enosis* (276), although their leadership knew that the Turkish Cypriot leadership and people opposed it. The textbooks thus legitimise *enosis* as the preferred solution of the Greek Cypriots, a process apparent throughout the presentation of the 1960s. H7a states that in 1965 George Papandreou and Makarios agreed that *enosis* was the right solution to the Cyprus problem and on 27 June 1967 the Cyprus parliament reaffirmed this when it voted that the struggle [*agonas*] would continue until all of Cyprus was united with 'mother Greece' (285). H12a then states that in 1968 Makarios abandoned the solution of *enosis* in favour of independence (289). But in the speech made in January 1968 he did not abandon the solution of *enosis*: 'A solution, by necessity, must be sought within the limits of what is feasible, which does not always coincide with the limits of what is desirable'.[35] Makarios was not abandoning *enosis*, but merely postponing it until it was feasible; meanwhile a solution based on independence – the feasible but not desirable – would be sought. This tension between the feasible and the desirable remains unresolved in the textbooks. As Gregoriou argues *enosis* was officially abandoned in the 1960s, but the 'nostalgia' for *enosis* did not allow the development of a Cypriot identity or the development of trust between the two communities.[36] Similarly, after 1974, although the concepts of the Greek nation, nationalism and *enosis* began to be discredited amongst Greek Cypriots, they were not extinguished.[37]

During 1964, the American Dean Acheson, the Secretary of State who had played a key role in the implementation of the Truman Doctrine, proposed several plans, in his capacity as special envoy of President Lyndon B. Johnson, based on *enosis* and territorial compensation to Turkey. In Acheson I Turkey would get a substantially sized sovereign military base in the Karpas Peninsula; the Turkish Cypriots not moving into it would receive two or three geographical entities (cantons) that they would administer, but ultimately be under Greek authority; with the rest joining Greece in sovereignty. Ankara agreed to this as a basis for a solution. But while the Papandreou government considered Acheson I, the gist of it was published in the Athens newspaper *Vima*, which disparaged the plan and said that the Papandreou government would reject it. Papandreou blamed Makarios for leaking the plan.[38] Acheson then presented Acheson II, which envisaged a 50-year Turkish lease to the base in Cyprus and the cession of Kastelorizo to Turkey. At first Papandreou accepted the proposal, but then changed his mind.[39] H12a refers to the US involvement in 1964 as an 'intervention', stating that the Greek and Cypriot governments flatly rejected Acheson's plans (283).

When 1974 is in focus in the textbooks, nothing is said about the negotiations in Geneva and the Turkish proposals for a solution between the first and second phases of the Turkish invasion. Given Turkey's position of strength the proposals were an ultimatum, which if not accepted would result in a second military operation. This Clerides, who was the acting president, knew, and although he was willing to accept a bi-communal, bi-zonal federation, he knew Makarios was not. At the second Geneva Conference, Clerides pressed for the full implementation of the 1960 Constitution; the British for the temporary reversion to it, subject to negotiations for a new constitution for a bi-zonal bi-communal federation; Denktash demanded a republic based on two federated states; while the Turkish Foreign Minister, Turan Gunes, proposed a bi-communal and independent republic, with the Turkish Cypriot autonomous zone comprising six districts and 34 per cent of the island, and the Greek Cypriot autonomous zone comprising two districts. According to Clerides the Gunes plan was no more acceptable than the Denktash proposal, especially since there was a window of forty-eight hours in which to negotiate and accept it. The British tried to convince Clerides to accept geographic separation and a Turkish Cypriot area of between twenty and thirty per cent. Clerides requested forty-eight hours to consult Makarios, Karamanlis and leaders in Cyprus. The Greek and British delegations agreed; Denktash agreed so long as Turkey did; but it remained silent. Within two hours of the conference breaking up, Turkish forces restarted military operations.[40] By not focusing on these complexities, the textbooks portray Ankara as the culprit and avoid discussing geographic separation, including the solution of a bi-zonal, bi-communal federation before 1974.

After 1974 discussing solutions to the Cyprus problem are limited to the February 1977 Makarios and Denktash agreement outlining the solution to the Cyprus problem based on four articles (including the creation of an independent, bi-communal, bi-zonal federal democracy), which are given in H12a, C9a, C12a. H12a states that since then, two further developments have occurred: the first is the Kyprianou-Denktash agreement of 1979, which affirmed the Makarios-Denktash agreement; and the second is the unilateral declaration of independence of the Turkish Cypriot state in 1983 as an illegal state recognised only by Turkey. C9a and C12a make reference to the 1984 meetings with Perez De Cuellar and the 1988-90 meetings between Vassiliou and Denktash, the failure of which is attributed to the attitude of Denktash and Turkey. H12a concludes that Turkey has not changed from this position, while the Republic of Cyprus remains steadfast behind its just cause with the support of the international community to find a peaceful solution, which will result in the withdrawal of the occupational troops and the settlers, the securing of the unity and independence of the state, and the guaranteeing of all the basic rights and freedoms for all its inhabitants (303). The solution envisioned in this narrative is quite simple: since the Cyprus problem is about Turkey having violated the Cypriot state and human rights (as discussed in the previous section), all that is needed is for Turkey to follow UN resolutions to reverse this violation. This logic is in line with allocating responsibility entirely to Turkey and allows the textbooks to envision the solution as a simple matter of 'return', a re-acquisition of what was 'ours' and is now lost; and the restoration of Greek Cypriots' human rights. For example, C5a ends with photographs of Lapithos and the legend: 'The beautiful Lapithos, today occupied, awaits that the villagers come together again' (71). Thus, the occupied areas are portrayed as currently empty, waiting for their Greek Cypriot owners to return; as if this will happen in an unproblematic manner and without the political changes required for a federal state, the agreed political basis for a solution, to come into existence. References to federal states occur under other contexts: first in the geography textbooks when federal countries such as Switzerland (G5a), US and Australia (G6a) are studied and second in the secondary civics textbooks (C9a, 19-21; C12a, 49-58) when examples of 'simple' and 'complex' states are given; in the latter case these include the federal states of the US, Switzerland, India, the Soviet Union and Yugoslavia. However, this is presented as factual information and is not further explored or paralleled to Cyprus; the textbooks thus do not address the political bases upon which federal states stand such as sharing of power, political equity [politiki isotita], co-existence of central and peripheral governments and others.

Discussion

Solutions to the Cyprus problem, as identified in the Social Science curricula analysed in this study, are largely neglected in the text, at least when compared to the elaboration provided on the other two themes of Cypriot identity and the Cyprus problem. This emphasis allows the Greek Cypriot narrative to focus more on the past rather than on the future; on the causes and who is to 'blame' rather than on solutions and ways forward. The textbooks emphasise the legitimacy of the Republic of Cyprus and its violation by Turkey, thereby approaching the problem as an international dispute, which resulted in human rights violations. The inter- and intra-communal conflicts are superficially addressed, since the Turkish Cypriot perspectives and concerns are not provided, the various solutions historically proposed by various parties are largely silenced and the compromises required by each side are not discussed. When a solution is in focus, it is largely construed with terms of 'return' of all Greek Cypriot refugees to their properties, demilitarisation, restoration of human rights and reunification, as if return to the 1960 Constitution can occur unproblematically. This approach is in stark contrast with the official political rhetoric of all governments of the Republic of Cyprus since 1977, that they pursue a solution of a bi-communal, bi-zonal federation of varying forms at different historical periods. Mavratsas has argued that Cypriot political leadership discusses a federal solution at the level of foreign affairs, but uses a nationalist-dismissive discourse within Cyprus, which does not provide for a federal solution.[41] Irwin also found contradictions between what Greek Cypriots perceive as an ideal solution to the Cyprus problem, and the solution pursued at the political level.[42] Our study provides support for these arguments, since the Social Studies curricula we analysed do not seem to prepare the future Greek Cypriot citizens for the bizonal, bi-communal state aimed at a political level as a solution to the Cyprus problem, or indeed, for any other solution. Another study amongst young pupils on the curricular area of *I know, I don't forget and I struggle* concluded that 'for the younger generations of Greek Cypriots, the national goal of the post-1974 curriculum is discursively empty; it falls short of constructing an imagination of what the future will look like in a reunified Cyprus'.[43] The lack of content for any 'vision' of solution is also indicated by Herodotou and Stogias, who in their study of *Den Ksehno* and *Cypriot Literature* textbooks, found that the pursuit of peace, as a solution to the Cyprus problem, is often construed as a gift from God, as a historical necessity or as fate, which leaves little room for political assertiveness on behalf of future citizens.[44] Similarly, past research on the two primary school civics textbooks has shown that emphasis is on theoretical knowledge of political institutions and the rights and responsibilities of citizens rather than on the practice of citizenship through pupils' democratic participation in decision-making, organisation and management. Consequently, the citizens portrayed in these textbooks have no active role beyond remembering the occupied areas and wishing to return there.[45]

Because of the key role of human rights in the ways in which a solution is constructed in the textbooks, the 'human rights discourse' permeates quite prominently the textbooks analysed; however, they are not 'historicised' as concepts and neither is the UN as an organisation. In consequence, 'human rights' and the UN are employed in the text to reaffirm the violated 'rights' of the Greek Cypriots, thereby silencing the violation of human rights of the rest of the communities and minorities in Cyprus, which historically lie at the heart of the Cyprus problem as well. This is an interesting finding, given that human rights (and their perceived insufficient restoration) was one of the key reasons why some Greek Cypriots rejected Annan V. As Koutselini and Papanastasiou have argued 'the civic education curriculum has focused on issues underlying the roots of the national problem and consciously resists any alteration to the situation and opposes conflict resolution without prior restoration of human rights'.[46]

In conclusion, this chapter indicates how curricula and textbooks need to be revised so that they better meet political changes over the last thirty years, as well as to address disparities between official policy and the solutions provided for in official curricula. The documents analysed in this study have primarily been published in the early 1990s and some of them do not go beyond the 1980s in their scope. Future textbook research needs to broaden its focus to investigate the emergence of the Cyprus problem historically at different periods; to include more subject areas (particularly *Den ksehno* and language curricular areas); and to compare with Turkish Cypriot textbooks, so as to explore the extent to which education supports common visions for the future of Cyprus. It must be noted that despite the importance of curricula as official texts, there are differences in how teachers perceive the curricula, how they are enacted in the classroom in interaction with pupils and how pupils experience them. This argument does not de-emphasise the importance of formal state curricula, but it highlights the importance of future research focusing on the broader social context, on teachers' and pupils' representations of solutions to the Cyprus problem and how these are negotiated in the classroom in interaction with the textbooks analysed in this chapter. This suggestion may be applicable to any textbook research, but is of particular importance in the case of the topic of our study, since the nationalist history textbooks used in Turkish Cypriot education until 2004 when they were subsequently changed (POST-RI, 2007), do not seem to have influenced the Turkish Cypriot majority 'yes' vote in the referendum on Annan V. This exemplifies the non-linear but highly complex relationships between curricula and societies.

ENDNOTES

1. See Kosta Pavlowitch, 'A Great Leap Backwards for Cypriot Democracy', *Cyprus Mail*, 25 April 2004; Simon Bahceli, 'Turkish Cypriots at the Crossroads', *Cyprus Mail*, 9 May 2004.
2. Mary Koutselini-Ioannidou, 'Curriculum as Political Text: The Case of Cyprus', *History of Education*, XXVI, 4, 1997, 395-407.
3. Lars-Erik Cederman, *Constructing Europe's Identity: The External Dimension*, Boulder, 2001.
4. Ernest Gellner, *Nations and Nationalism*, Oxford, 1983; Benedict Anderson, *Imagined Communities*, London, 1983; Anthony Giddens, *The Nation-state and Violence*, Cambridge, 1985; Eric Hobsbawm, 'Introduction: Inventing Traditions', (ed.) E. Hobsbawm & T. Ranger, *The Invention of Tradition*, Cambridge, 1989; Hobsbawm, *Nations and Nationalism since 1780: Programme, Myth, Reality*, (3rd ed.)., Cambridge, 1994; Cederman, *Constructing Europe's Identity*.
5. Hanna Schissler, & Yasemin Nuhoglu Soysal (eds.), *The Nation, Europe and the World: Textbooks and Curricula in Transition*, New York, 2005.
6. Sonia Nieto, *Affirming Diversity: The Sociopolitical Context of Multicultural Education*, NY, 1992.
7. Janet Maw, 'Ethnocentrism, History Textbooks and Teaching Strategies: Presenting the USSR', *Research Papers in Education*, VI, 3, October 1991, 153-69.
8. Achilleas Kapsalis, Kyriakos Bonides, & Athena Sipitanou (eds), *I Eikona tou 'Allou'/Geitona sta Sxolika Vilvia ton Balkanikon Choron* (*The Image of the 'Other'/Neighbour in the School Textbooks of the Balkan Countries*), Athens, 2000; Christina Koulouri, 'The Tyranny of History', C. Koulouri (ed.), *Teaching the History of Southeastern Europe*, Thessaloniki, 2001, 14-25.
9. Martin McLean, *Britain and a Single Market Europe: Prospects for a Common School Curriculum*, Kogan, London, 1990; David Coulby & Crispin Jones, *Postmodernity and European Education Systems*, London, 1995; Yasemin Nuhoglu Soysal, Teresa Bertilotti & Sabine Mannitz, 'Projections of Identity in French and German History and Civics

Textbooks', Schissler & Soysal (eds.), *The Nation, Europe and the World*, 13-34.
10. Georgios S. Flouris & Pella Calogiannaki, 'Ethnokentrismos kai Ekpaideysi: I Periptosi ton Balkanion Laon kai Tourkon sta Ellinika Scholika Vivlia' ('Ethnocentrism and Education: The Case of Balkan Peoples and Turks in Greek Textbooks'), *Paidagogiki Epitheorisi (Pedagogical Review)*, 23, 1996, 207-248; Anna Frangoudaki, & Thaleia Dragona, *Ti ein'i patrida mas? Ethnokentrismos stin ekpaidevsi [What is our homeland? Ethnocentrism in education]*, (2nd ed.), Alexandria Publications, Athens, 1997; Vasilia Lilian Antoniou & Yasemin Nuhoglu Soysal, 'Nation and the Other in Greek and Turkish History Textbooks', Schissler & Soysal (eds.), *The Nation, Europe and the World*, 105-121.
11. Soysal, Bertilotti & Mannitz, 'Projections of Identity in French and German History and Civics Textbooks', 13-34; Jacques E. C. Hymans, 'What Counts as History and How Much Does History Count', Schissler & Soysal (eds.), *The Nation, Europe and the World*, 61-81;
12. Koulouri, 'The Tyranny of History', 14-25.
13. Michael Apple & Linda K. Christian-Smith, 'The Politics of the Textbook', Michael Apple & Linda K. Christian-Smith (eds.), *The Politics of the Textbook*, London, 1991, 1-21.
14. Mary Koutselini-Ioannidou, 'Theoritiko Plaisio gia tin Axiologisi ton Scholikon Egcheiridion' ('Theoretical Framework for the Assessment of Textbooks'), *Nea Paideia (New Pedagogy)*, LXXIX, 1996, 70-77.
15. Nieto, *Affirming Diversity*; Flouris & Calogiannaki, 'Ethnokentrismos kai Ekpaideysi' ('Ethnocentrism and Education'), 207-248.
16. Schissler & Soysal (eds.), *The Nation, Europe and the World*, 280.
17. Ibid., 7-8.
18. In Greek Cypriot education there is a National Curriculum and a single-textbook policy which prescribes the use of official textbooks for all state schools. Some of these books are published in Greece and are used as main or supplementary materials in primary and secondary schools. Also, the Curriculum Development Service of the Ministry of Education and Culture in Cyprus produces several textbooks to replace or augment those from Greece.
19. AKTI, *Ekthesi gia ta vivlia tis Istorias kai Logotehnias tis 6is Dimotiku se shesi me tin proothisi tis vias kai tu ethnikismu [Report on the History and Literature Textbooks of the 6th Grade of Primary Education with regards to the promotion of violence and nationalism]*, Nicosia, 2004; Loris Koullapis, 'The Subject of History in the Greek Cypriot Educational System', Koulouri (ed.), *Clio in the Balkans, The Politics of History Education*, Thessaloniki, 2002, 406-13.
20. Yiannis Papadakis, 'Narrative, Memory and History Education: A Comparison of Schoolbooks on the "History of Cyprus"', *History and Memory*, XX, 2, 2008, 128-148.
21. Yiannis Papadakis, 'Nationalist Imaginings of War in Cyprus', R. Hinde & H. Watson (Eds.), *War a cruel necessity? The bases of institutionalized violence*, London, 1995, 54-67.
22. When possible, both the first year of publication and the year of publication of the document analysed are provided.
23. D. J. Skeel, 'Social Studies in the Primary School', Torsten Husén & Neville T. Postlethwaite (eds.), *The International Encyclopaedia of Education* (2nd ed.), Oxford, 1994, 5572-8.
24. Pupils study ancient history in the 3rd and 4th Grades, medieval (Byzantine) in the 5th Grade and modern history in the 6th Grade; this cycle of Ancient-Byzantine-Modern history is repeated in the 7th, 8th and 9th as well as in the 10th, 11th and 12th Grades respectively.

25. Christina Koulouri, 'Introduction', *Clio in the Balkans*, 15-48, 32.
26. Koullapis, 'The Subject of History in the Greek Cypriot Educational System', Koulouri (ed.), *Clio in the Balkans*, 406-13.
27. Ibid; Papadakis, 'Narrative, Memory and History Education: A Comparison of Schoolbooks on the "History of Cyprus"'.
28. Costas M. Constantinou & Yiannis Papadakis, 'The Cypriot State (s) in Situ: Cross Ethnic Contact and the Discourse of Recognition', *Global Society*, XV, 2, 2001, 125-148.
29. Table 9.1.3 is entitled 'Population by national groups, per cent' and provides the percentages of Greek Cypriots, Turkish Cypriots, Armenians, Latins, Maronites and Others in 1881, 1901, 1946, 1960 and 2002. Similar tables appear in G4a.
30. Niazi Kizilyurek, 'I adinati politiki isotita: I antilipsi tis istorias os paragon gia tin epidioksi askisis tis eksusias stin Kypro' (The Impossible Political Equity: The Perception of History as a Factor to Pursue Power in Cyprus), 2007. Retrieved on 12 December 2007 from http://www.vimaideon.gr. *Vima Ideon, Issue 07/12/2007.*
31. Stavroula Philippou, 'European Citizenship/Identity and Curriculum in Cyprus: Exploring Ways Forward', Proceedings CDRom of the Conference 'Citizenship, Multiculturalism, Cosmopolitanism', POLIS-Citizenship Association, University of Cyprus, Nicosia, 2007.
32. Glafkos Clerides, *Cyprus: My Deposition*, I, Nicosia 1989, 220-1; Richard A. Patrick, *Political Geography and the Cyprus Conflict: 1963-1971*, Ontario 1976, 36.
33. Clerides, *Cyprus*, II, 357-60; Clerides, *Cyprus*, III, 68-82.
34. It is possible in Greek to use the terms *politeia* and *kratos* to denote state, the difference being that *politeia* is a more legal word to denote an organised state, while *kratos* better refers to power and thus the organs of the state that enforce authority.
35. Patrick, *Political Geography and the Cyprus Conflict*, 145.
36. Zeleia Gregoriou, 'De-scribing Hybridity in 'Unspoiled Cyprus': Postcolonial Tasks for the Theory of Education, *Comparative Education*, XL, 2, 2004, 241-266.
37. Koutselini-Ioannidou, 'Curriculum as Political Text'.
38. Claude Nicolet, *United States Policy Towards Cyprus, 1954-1974: Removing the Greek-Turkish Bone of Contention*, Mannheim, 2001, 259-62.
39. Makarios Droushiotis, *Cyprus 1974*, Mannheim, 2006, 29.
40. Polyvios G. Polyviou, *Cyprus: Conflict and Negotiation 1960-1980*, London 1980, 171-185. Polyviou was part of the Greek Cypriot delegation to Geneva.
41. Caesar Mavratsas, *Opsis tu elliniky ethnikismu stin Kypro (Aspects of Greek nationalism in Cyprus)*, Athens, 1998.
42. Colin Irwin, *Public opinion and the politics of peace research: Northern Ireland, Balkans, Israel, Palestine, Cyprus, Muslim World and the 'War on Terror'*, 2005. Retrieved on 30 August, 2007 from http://www.peacepolls.org
43. Miranda Christou, 'A Double Imagination: Memory and Education in Cyprus', *Journal of Modern Greek Studies*, 24, 2006, 285-306.
44. Herodotos Herodotou & George Stogias, *I fysikopoiisi tis Eirinis mesa apo ta Kypriaka anthologia kai ta vivlai tou 'Den kserhno kai Agonizomai' (The naturalisation of Peace in the Cypriot anthologies and the books of 'I don't forget and I struggle')*, Unpublished essay for the Masters in Education Sciences Programme, University of Cyprus, Nicosia, 2007.
45. Mary Koutselini & Constantinos Papanastasiou, 'Civic Education in Cyprus – Issues in Focus', *Children's Social and Economics Education*, II, 3, 1997, 113-129.
46. Ibid., 113.

CHAPTER 15

A PSYCHOLOGICAL ANALYSIS OF THE GREEK CYPRIOT 'NO'

Panicos Stavrinides

Introduction

Why did the Greek Cypriots reject the Annan Plan with such a vast majority? Why was it demonized so much by politicians and citizens? Were the arguments against the plan based solely on reason? I do not argue that the rejection of the settlement plan was not, among other things, a product of the sociopolitical and historical myths and realities that are related to the Cyprus issue. I argue, however, that the rejection of the Annan plan was a psychological expression as well. It was the manifestation of fear (or phobia) against something that was perceived as a threat. This conclusion will be based upon the empirical study that was conducted by my research group at the University of Cyprus which examined the intensity and the quality of fears for coexistence in the two Cypriot communities. The study was conducted in 2006 and the results were first published by the daily Greek Cypriot Newspaper *Politis* in June 18th 2006.

Psychologists agree that fear is an autonomous response towards something we perceive as threatening.[1] It is one of the basic emotions that through evolution, it assisted in survival. As an autonomous response it is not necessarily (or even should not be) accompanied by an effortful cognitive process. Thinking requires the activation of reasoning capacities. Fear does not require that. Therefore, when we feel that something is threatening our integrity we are less likely to adopt it and we are much more likely to avoid it.

Walter Cannon proposed that when people fear something, a process labeled *fight or flight* emerges. Which means that under threatening conditions, people have to decide whether to express aggression towards that condition, or try to get away from it.[2] I will argue that in the case of the Annan Plan, the Greek Cypriot majority had experienced a collective fear and it resulted in both fight and flight responses.

Therefore, the two key questions that emerge from the above are: why did the Greek Cypriots feel that they were threatened by the proposed settlement? And, how did they express both a fight and flight response?

The Empirical Study of Greek Cypriot Fears

A study that my colleagues and I conducted after the referendums aimed at gaining an understanding of the types of fears the Greek Cypriots feel when asked about a future settlement of the Cyprus issue (see Appendix I for statistical details). The findings of this study showed clearly that the Greek Cypriot community is filled with fears that can be either seen as realistic or symbolic. In the literature of social psychology when people feel threatened that an out-group (Turkish Cypriots or Turkey in this case) will damage their economy, their standard of living, their sense of security, they refer to what we call realistic fears. On the contrary, when they feel that the 'others' will cause damage in their values, beliefs systems, and culture, then they refer to symbolic fears.[3] That was the case in the findings of the study. The notion of coexistence threatens Greek Cypriots. They feel that if they agree to live under a common state, the crime rate will increase in the country. For example, more murders, more burglaries, and even more rapes would take place compared to the current state of affairs. Furthermore, they feel that the economy will go downhill. This, according to what people reported, will happen because unemployment will rise, people will be earning less money, and there will be less job opportunities. Moreover, people in the Greek Cypriot community are afraid that community conflict between Greek and Turkish Cypriots will take place once again as it did in the past. Worse, they feel that under this new settlement Turkey will be more likely to invade the island and occupy Cyprus as a whole. These are fears that exist in the Greek Cypriot community and can be labeled as realistic fears.[4] Here, a distinction must be made. Realistic threats are not necessarily real in their nature. They are realistic because they describe perceived consequences in people's pragmatic issues, like jobs, money, and security. This does not mean that such fears or threats are real in the sense that they are justified by reality.

On the other hand, Greek Cypriots report symbolic fears as well. They feel that in the case of a settlement they will lose their Greek heritage. This will happen because they claim that the Greek language, the Greek national identity, the Greek-Orthodox religion and the Greek customs will disappear from the island. This particular fear is of special interest because it is highly related with the internalisation of national identity. How does the process of internalisation of national identity explain why some people develop more symbolic fears?

Fears, National Identity and Ideology

Part of the empirical study was to examine the relationship between fears as a united emotional entity with national identity and ideology. For the purpose of this study ideology was measured in a typical scale left to right. National identity on the other hand, was measured through the scale of the internalisation of national identity.[5] This is a measure that has been widely used over the past few years and it shows how strongly people tend to internalize their national identity. The problem in the case of Cyprus and Greek Cypriots more specifically is that they had to decide which national identity they were referring to. Purely Cypriot identity, or Greek identity, or even Greek Cypriot national identity could be examined. Since the aim was to compare differences between Greek Cypriots and Turkish Cypriots as well, Greek national identity for Greek Cypriots and Turkish national identity for Turkish Cypriots was explored. That way, the data is on the basis of a national identity that is completely different in the two communities. The results of that analyses showed that fears are strongly associated with both national identity and ideology. The more people feel afraid that negative consequences will occur as a result of a solution, the more they tend to internalize their national identity. Also, the more fearful people are the more they tend to place themselves in the far right of political ideology. And finally, the internalization of national identity is associated with more right wing ideological stance. What do these associations mean? For one thing, they show that fears may be the product of other social/psychological processes which are manifested indirectly through emotions. The internalization of national identity for instance, may be an expression of nationalism.[6] Nationalists are more likely to identify themselves with the 'mother land'. They are also more likely to feel proud because of their perceived Greek heritage, they are more likely to feel happy because they are Greek and they are more likely to feel offended if someone says something negative about Greece. And of course, nationalist people are more likely to identify themselves with right and extreme right ideological positions. This data must be analysed with caution. The findings of this study refer to tendencies. They do not draw a picture of the Greek Cypriot society as a whole. It is not true to say that Greek Cypriots are nationalists and extremists. The truth is that there is a significant proportion of the population that leans towards these characteristics and creates a tendency within the society. It appears that through the years of division on the island, many of the Greek Cypriots adopted a fearful emotional disposition towards Turkish Cypriots and with an increase in what others may call as 'patriotism'[7], both nationalism and more extreme ideologies were cultivated. Actually, the associations discussed here can be related with similar findings in the relevant literature. It has been documented that from the early years children who internalize strongly their national identity also tend to express more out-group bias.[8] That means that the internalization of national identity is related to more negative expressions about a group they consider for some reason as an out-group. The similarity with the study lies in the fact that fears are associated with the internalization of national identity. Could fears be related with out-group bias? This can be assumed to be a strong hypothesis. The more fears people feel about an out-group the more negatively biased they should be.

Fears and Dominated Groups

Another interesting finding of this study is that there are differences in the intensity of fears between several subgroups of the Greek Cypriot community. Women are significantly more fearful than men and this finding is consistent across all types of fears. Furthermore, people with low education are also significantly more fearful than people with a university degree. Moreover, and perhaps the most worrying finding, young people between 18 and 25 are significantly more fearful than older people. Also, people who were displaced and or lost a member of their family during the war of 1974 are more fearful than people who were neither displaced nor had experienced a loss in their family. The last two findings were strongly expected because it shows how traumatic a direct experience with war can be. On the other hand however, one should wonder why should younger people feel more fearful than older people? After all, they had never even had direct contact with Turkish Cypriots. Contact is one of the most frequently applied approaches to conflict resolution.[9] According to Allport (1954)[10], under certain conditions, bringing together individuals from opposing groups could reduce intergroup prejudice.

Also, why should women feel more fearful than men? And finally, why do people with low education show more fears?

Women, the young and those low educated people are what are labelled as dominated groups. Typically speaking, women are not in key positions in Cypriot society, at least not to the extent to which men are. A man in Greek Cypriot society is more likely to become a president, a member of the parliament, a minister, a government official of any kind and hold a significant position in the social, political, and financial area. The same can be said about people with low education and younger people, even though for the latter group other aspects must be taken into account as well. Generally speaking however, this finding shows that the more fearful groups are those that have never felt the confidence of creating their own future but they have always relied on other and more powerful groups. As for the younger generations two more issues may explain their intensity of fears: fear for the unknown and "paying the price" of the social representations created by the political, educational, and religious elite after 1974. Younger people have never had the opportunity to relate with Turkish Cypriots. It is always more likely to become afraid of something you do not know anything about instead of something you actually know and are related with.[11] Furthermore, it can be argued that the social representations that were developed after 1974 in the Greek Cypriot society are not representations of reconciliation, but the contrary it could be argued.

Comparing the Two Communities

How similar or different are the two communities in this study? The findings show that they are quite different. The most important difference is that Turkish Cypriots are significantly less fearful than Greek Cypriots. Furthermore, they place themselves much more to the centre of the ideological scale. But, contrary to what was expected by our research group, they have shown higher scores on the internalization of their Turkish national identity. For this result we hold great reservations because it may not represent an objective dimension of Turkish Cypriot collective psychological process and it may be an artefact instead that may represent the way questions on national identity were translated into Turkish. If however, that is an objective finding it may represent the Turkish Cypriots tendency to attach themselves to the only entity that is left for their collective self image. After the Greek Cypriot rejection of the Annan Plan, Turkish Cypriots felt that their compatriots rejected them as well. Only Turkey is left to identify with when it is realised that it is Greek Cypriots that govern and represent the Republic of Cyprus, while the so-called TRNC is isolated and unrecognized and, the European Union does not see them as an integral part of European society. Contrary to that, Greek Cypriots may no longer feel that strong need to identify with Greece. That is because, even though they have rejected the settlement plan of the UN, they can still identify themselves with the Republic of Cyprus and moreover they can also identify themselves as European citizens.

Turkish Cypriot fears cannot be predicted as easily by the processes of the internalization of national identity and ideology, compared to Greek Cypriots. This provides a more optimistic view for the future because they still appear to be ready for reconciliation. Or, more correctly, they are more ready than the Greek Cypriots.

Will this always be the case? Emotions do change through experience. And as it appears, the majority of the Turkish Cypriots perceived the Greek Cypriot rejection of the Annan Plan as a traumatic experience. The social uprising of the Turkish Cypriots in 2003 with the demonstrations for peace and reconciliation has created a psychological atmosphere that was loaded with positive tendencies towards the unification of the island. That is after all why the vast majority of the Turkish Cypriots accepted the Annan Plan. Even after the rejection of the Plan by the Greek Cypriots there still is a critical mass that has not yet rejected the idea of a solution to be found in the near future. But, as time passes without reaching a solution it is possible to expect a shift in people's attitudes and emotions. Who can say that if the same study was conducted today similar results would be obtained? I am afraid not. An interesting process has taken place in Turkish Cypriot society that needs further analysis. As already mentioned, the Turkish Cypriots felt that by rejecting the Annan Plan the Greek Cypriots had rejected them. That means that they have transformed a political action by the Greek Cypriot community as a hostile personal act that is directed towards them. Therefore, if Turkish Cypriots interpret the rejection of the Annan Plan as a personal attack towards their own future, it is expected that negative emotions are more likely to increase and positive emotions more likely to decrease. How can such a scenario be avoided? The answer is to avoid all wrong examples the Greek Cypriots have set after 1974 events. That means they must avoid following leaders that will create a sense of fear and threat among the Turkish Cypriot people. They must also avoid developing a media establishment that promotes negative images for the Greek Cypriots. And definitely, they must not allow nationalism through a so called patriotism to enter the educational system. I would also mention the impact of the religious leaders as well, but Turkish society is much more cosmic than Greek Cypriots and therefore the impact of religious figures is much less.

What conclusions can be drawn from the above findings? First, the Greek Cypriot community has not been prepared to accept the idea of coexistence in a federal state as a possible future solution to the Cyprus problem In contrast, the educational system, politicians, religious figures, and other well established institutions, have contributed to the development of a collective fear response. Those fears are well structured in peoples minds, they are crystallized, and worse, they are intense. They are well structured because each fear is constructed by dimensions that are strongly associated with each other. They are crystallized because they are separated from other fears as individual and independent threats. Finally, they are intense because despite the fact that fears are expressed at different levels between people, the average score of the Greek Cypriot population is significantly high.

It may be argued that the Turkish Cypriots may feel the same way as the Greek Cypriots bat this has no basis. The study examined the Turkish Cypriot fears as well. They are less structured, not as crystallized, and more importantly less intense. It is justified to argue that the psychological 'wall' the Greek Cypriots have built over the divide is by far higher.

What makes the Greek Cypriot study even more concerning is the fact that younger people express significantly more intense fears. People who have not experienced real contact with Turkish Cypriots and they have grown up with a sense that Turkey and the Turkish Cypriots are the enemies that have caused so much harm to the Greek Cypriots feel much more reluctant to accept the idea of sharing a common state.

The Fight and Flight response

People in the Greek Cypriot community were emotionally primed to respond in a negative manner towards anything that would arouse the threats described above. Once the Annan Plan was presented in its final form the Greek Cypriot establishment failed to see it as an opportunity. Instead for various reasons it was perceived as a threat and as such it was delivered to the people. The people were ready to react in a negative way. When the vast majority of political leaders, the media, and the financial and religious key figures described the proposed settlement as a threat for the Greek Cypriot interests, the job of rejecting the Plan by the people was a very easy task. The people would not be ready to resist to their autonomous fear responses and engage in a rational analysis of the proposed plan. Negative emotions overwhelmed the vast majority of the people and any attempt to present the positive aspects of the United Nations' proposals were doomed to fail. That is where the fight and flight response can be observed. People decided to act in an aggressive way towards everything the Plan resembled and psychological aggression towards those they blamed for delivering such a plan was also observed. Immediately, people and nations from the international community that were previously seen as friends were labeled as enemies, conspirators, and against the Greek Cypriots and their fair cause. In the same lines, people within the community of Greek Cypriots were labeled as traitors. As far as the flight response, it was also easily observed. Anything that represented the Annan Plan, anything that had to do or was related to the Annan Plan had to go away. Even the leader of this community, Tassos Papadopoulos expressed this collective fear (that he had also helped in creating in people's minds) when after a meeting with the Secretary General of the UN he told reporters that he would not even call the man by his name in order to avoid associations with the settlement plan that had his name on it. In general, Greek Cypriots felt that they had to run away from the Annan Plan and they did so at the speed of light.

It is not an exaggeration to argue that the Greek Cypriots reacted with great emotion towards the settlement plan. The Plan was presented as a threat and threats create fears. It is surprising that these days, almost four years after the referenda, leaders in the Greek Cypriot community feel the need to label the Annan Plan as 'dead'. A settlement plan that is understood by people as dead can not be threatening any more. Therefore, a new representation is being developed at the collective level. A representation that has the message that our fight and flight response were effective in the sense that it killed the threat we have faced. Whether the Greek Cypriots have executed the right thing or an innocent victim, I believe it still remains to be proven.

Another hypothesis that I make is that over the past four years a *transformation and diversion process of emotions* has transpired. This hypothesis lies on the premise that the Greek Cypriot fears have been transformed in their nature and have diverted from the initial target as well. Before the Annan Plan, the Greek Cypriots felt threatened by Turkey, Turkish Cypriots, and violent acts against them as a product of their 1974 experience. Now, after four years since the referenda and the accession to the EU the previous fears may have changed in their nature. They also seem to be diverted from Turkey as the initial fear stimulus to the Annan Plan in 2004, to any settlement similar, and I am concerned that this process of diversion may lead to a fear response for any kind of settlement in the near future. If this hypothesis proves to be correct then we may observe an increased number of people in the Greek Cypriot community accepting the idea of permanent division and less people pursuing a settlement that will unify land, people, economy, and culture. As a conclusion to the above analysis cultivating a certain fear response at the societal level does not necessarily mean that it will remain in its initial nature. It may hold strong as an emotional response but it may be transformed and diverted towards unpredictable fears and unpredictable directions. Fear of Turkey in 1974 was an emotion to be expected and rationally explained. Fear of anything that would lead to a settlement in 2007 was not something many people expected to happen and there is uncertainty when the end may be.

The security vs insecurity issue

A strong claim made by the Greek Cypriot community (that is both leaders and the majority of citizens) since the Annan Plan was rejected, has to do with the feelings of insecurity the Greek Cypriots feel over the constant threat of Turkey as an invading and occupying power. Ironically, however, that same claim was also made by the Turkish Cypriots for years, up to the 2003 uprising of the Turkish Cypriot society against the Denktash regime. They felt that Greek Cypriots backed by Greece aimed at either oscillate them from the Republic of Cyprus or even worse extinct them from the island. How rational are the Greek Cypriot claims now and how rational were the Turkish Cypriot claims before? Can they be justified solely by real events or are they at least partly an exaggeration of both sides in order to gain political points in the negotiations for solution? To my understanding, and based on what was found from the empirical study, both communities had reasons why they should feel insecure. At the same time however, the Turkish Cypriot community had played the insecurity card for thirty years, creating myths over how Greek Cypriots would treat them. And when the time allowed for a better understanding of the so called Greek Cypriot threat, the whole Denktash and Ecevit propaganda collapsed. Unfortunately however, the Greek Cypriots exaggerated feelings of insecurity took turn. The Annan Plan, loaded with all those fears mentioned above, acted as a mediating factor between the true danger that appeared in 1974 and the mythical insecurity present today. Does this mean that the Greek Cypriot community will wait for another thirty years to realize the truth behind these insecurities as it happened with the Turkish Cypriots? Not necessarily if analysed within the contemporary versus the 1974 context of local and international politics. At the same time however, if no political will and leadership is shown, the Greek Cypriot community may go through a phase of extended introversion, irrational fears, and exaggerated insecurity.

Concluding remarks

I am concerned that the collective emotional response that I have described is even worse. That is because my analysis concludes that the emotional responses of the Greek Cypriots should not be described as collective fears or collective threats, but they should be labeled as collective phobia instead.

Fear is an autonomous emotional response towards a condition that threatens the individual who experiences the emotion. That means that a prerequisite for fear is the existence of a real stimulus that if not dealt with will potentially create harm. The keyword here is the term real. The fears that Greek Cypriots feel have to be justified by reality. When analyzing the fears that came up in our study, I concluded that none of those fears were justified. How can rapes show an increase just because there will be a common state to share? How could there be fewer jobs when our small and isolated economy will grow almost double in size? Why should the community which is the vast majority of the island lose its culture and language? How could Turkey invade in a country that is a full member of the EU? To all the fears I have mentioned above, I fail to find one that I can rationally justify.

Therefore, what do we observe here? Collective fears or collective phobia? Phobia is defined as an intense fear that is irrational in nature because reality can not justify the threat. In other words, when someone crosses a motorway while a truck heads right towards him, that person's fear is definitely justified. And I suppose that flight response would be a good choice instead of the fight. In the case of phobia however, people develop irrational and unjustified fears over things that do not actually threatened them.

A major issue however, that is the product of the Greek Cypriot settlement phobia, is how a phobic society will react in a future solution that may be proposed. For a phobic individual a good psychotherapist is needed. For phobic societies the answer is strong leadership. If leaders in the Greek Cypriot society do not start cultivating a new collective representation that will allow people to accept a solution, then any solution proposed in the future will fail. Furthermore, another concerning related issue is emerging. Not only as a society we suffer from settlement phobia, but a new collective disorder starts showing its symptoms and that's what I call as social paranoia. Paranoid individuals generally feel threatened by non existing things. More worryingly, they form strong beliefs that other people are conspiring against them to do them harm or to manipulate their actions. Greek Cypriot society is moving in that direction as well. Over the past few years Greek Cypriot have labeled as enemies countries and people that traditionally did not show any animosity towards Cyprus. Governments and NGO's are accused of conspiring against the Greek Cypriot interests. Internationally respected politicians are characterized as enemies when previously were seen as friends. All these, not only help in the process of transformation and diversion of fears that I have discussed, but they also affect peoples minds in adopting such ideas to be true and leading the society towards collective paranoia.

A phobic society is a difficult issue that may lead to wrong decision-making and a collective introversion. I am very concerned however that if apart from a phobic society, we also become a psychotic one, then the prospects for any kind of settlement for unification are not good. That is because we have already experienced the consequences of collective phobia which I believe that they are less severe to those we will experience if we become collectively psychotic.

Therefore, based on the above analysis and the findings of the empirical study, I conclude that the Greek Cypriot community has suffered a collective trauma because of the 1974 events. Leaders that could have helped the healing process over the last three decades have failed to do so. Instead they cultivated the trauma in such a way that when a resolution to the trauma was offered the people were not ready to accept it. Instead, the leaders exploited the collective trauma and have transformed it into a collective phobia. Now it is up to the leaders to choose between treating the collective phobia or to add another disorder as well.

Appendix I: Statistical Tables of the Empirical Study

Table 1: Correlation coefficients between fears, hopes, national identity and ideology of the Greek Cypriot sample

Factors	1	2	3	4	5	6	7	8
1. Economy-Crime	1	.74**	.58**	-.55**	-.53**	-.44**	.45**	.29**
2. Hostility		1	.64**	-.63**	-.53**	-.42**	.33**	.28**
3. Identity Loss			1	-.43**	-.37*	-.36**	.20**	.28**
4. Reconciliation				1	.66**	.54**	-.24**	-.30**
5. State Function					1	.53**	-.20**	-.34**
6. Multiculturalism						1	-.31**	-.35**
7. National Identity							1	.48**
8. Ideology								1

** $p < .01$, * $p < .05$

Table 2: Correlation coefficients between fears, hopes, national identity and ideology in the Turkish Cypriot sample

Factors	1	2	3	4	5
1. Economy – Identity Loss	1	.74**	-.48**	.07	.51**
2. Hostility		1	-.49**	.21**	.56**
3. Hopes			1	-.20*	-.45**
4. National Identity				1	.28**
5. Ideology					1

Table 3: Differences between Greek-Cypriots and Turkish-Cypriots on the fears, hopes, national identity ideology

	Mean	SD	t	p
GC-fears	2.71	.96	7.72	.01
TC-fears	1.81	.95		.01
GC-hopes	2.59	.93	10.76	.01
TC-hopes	3.91	1.15		.01
GC-national identity	1.86	1.18	10.95	.01
TC-national identity	3.42	1.51		.01
GC-ideology	4.33	2.66	2.34	.05
TC-ideology	3.61	2.77		.05

ENDNOTES

1. Marcia Barinaga, 'How many things get that way', *Science,* CCLVIII, 1992, 887-888.
2. Walter B. Cannon, *Bodily Changes in Pain, Hunger, Fear and Rage* (2nd ed.). New York, 1915.
3. Walter, G. Stephan, & Cookie, W. Stephan, 'The role of threat in intergroup relations'. In D. M. Mackie & E. R. Smith (Eds), *From Prejudice to Intergroup Emotions: Differentiated Reactions to Social Groups,* New York, 2000, 191-207.; Michael A. Z rate, Berenice Garcia, & Azenett Garza A. & Robert Hitlan, 'Cultural threat and perceived realistic group conflict as predictors of attitudes towards Mexican immigrants', *Journal of Experimental Social Psychology,* XL, 2004, 99-105.
4. Walter G. Stephan, Oscar Ybarra, Carmen Martinez, Joseph Schwarzwald & Michael Tur-Kaspa, 'Prejudice toward immigrants to Spain and Israel: An integrated threat theory analysis', *Journal of Cross Cultural Psychology,* XXIX, 1998, 559-576.
5. Martyn Barrett, & Evanthia Lyons, *National Pride and the Public Collective Self-esteem Associated with the National Group,* Paper presented at the Fourth INTAS Workshop on the Development of National, Ethnolinguistic and Religious Identity in Children and Adolescents Living in the NIS, Uppsala University, Uppsala, Sweden, August 2001.
6. Katja Meier-Pesti & Erich Kirchler, 'Nationalism and patriotism as determinants of European identity and attitudes towards the euro', *Journal of Socio-Economics,* XXXII, 2003, 685-700.
7. Daniel Bar-Tal, 'Patriotism as fundamental beliefs of group members', *Politics and the Individual* III, 1993, 45–62; Herbert C. Kelman, 'Patterns of personal involvement in the national system: a socio-psychological analysis of political legitimacy', in Roseau, J.N. (Ed.), *International Politics and Foreign Policy.* New York, 1969, 276–288; Amelie Mummendey and Bemd Simon, 'Nationale Identifikation und die Abwertung von Fremdgruppen', in Mummendey, A., Simon, B. (Eds.), *Identität und Verschiedenheit,* Bern, 1997, 175–193.
8. Mark Bennett, Evanthia Lyons, Fabio Sani & Martyn Barrett, 'Children's subjective identification with the group and in group favoritism', *Developmental Psychology,* XXXIV, 1998, 902-909; Rebecca S. Bigler, Lecianna C. Jones & Debra B.Lobliner, 'Social categorization and the formation of intergroup attitudes in children', *Child Development,* LXVI-

II, 1997, 530-543; Rebecca S. Bigler, Cristia Brown Spears, & Marc Markell, 'When groups are not created equal: effects of group status on the formation of intergroup attitudes in children', *Child Development*, LXXII, 2001, 1151-1162; Z. S. Masangkay, F. F. Villorente, R. S. Somcio, E. S. Reyes, & D. M. Taylor, 'The development of ethnic group perception', *The Journal of Genetic Psychology*, CXXI, 1972, 263-270; Drew Nesdale & Debbie Flesser, 'Social identity and the development of children's group attitudes', *Child Development*, LXXII, 2001, 506-517; E. Poppe & H. Linssen, 'In-group favoritism and the reflection of realistic dimensions of difference between national states in Central and Eastern European nationality stereotypes', *British Journal of Social Psychology*, XXXVIII, 1999, 85-102; Adam Rutland, 'The development of national prejudice, in-group favoritism and self-stereotypes in British children', *British Journal of Social Psychology*, XXXVIII, 1999, 55-70; Yona Teichman, 'The development of Israeli children's images of Jews and Arabs and their expression in human figure drawings', *Developmental Psychology*, XXXVII, 2001, 749-761.
9. Miles Hewstone & Rupert Brown, 'Contact is not enough: An Intergroup Perspective on the Contact Hypothesis', in M. Hewstone & R. Brown (eds), *Contact and Conflict in Intergroup Encounters*. Oxford, Basil Blackstaff, 1986, 3-44.
10. Gordon W. Allport, *The Nature of Prejudice*. Cambridge, 1954.
11. Walter G. Stephan & Cookie, W. Stephan, 'Intergroup Anxiety', *Journal of Social Issues*, XLI, 3, 1985, 157-175.

Chapter 16

THE ROLE OF SECURITY: PERCEPTIONS OF ADVANTAGE AND DISADVANTAGE

Hubert Faustmann

This chapter focuses on the role of security issues for Greek and Turkish Cypriots when voting in the referendum on the Annan Plan. Although there were many reasons why Greek Cypriots opposed the agreement, according to a poll conducted on the day of the referendum, three quarters of those who voted against the Plan listed concerns about security as being their primary motivation for voting 'no'.[1] Clearly, the Greek Cypriots felt that their security needs were not adequately addressed in Annan V. In contrast, the overwhelming majority of the Turkish Cypriots voted in favour of the agreement. Given that their security concerns were as grave as those of the Greek Cypriots, it is fair to assume that the Turkish Cypriots considered the security arrangements of Annan V sufficient. This text will argue that while all essential security demands of the Turkish side were met, a number of key Greek Cypriot security concerns were insufficiently addressed. The first requirement is to outline the official positions of the two communities, as well as those of Greece and Turkey on the core security questions.

The Greek Cypriot Position

Given that Turkey and not the Turkish Cypriots is the main threat in Greek Cypriot perceptions, most communal concerns revolve not around identity issues (with the exception of the question of the presence of Turkish settlers, which was also securitised[2]) or governance but on safeguards against Turkish influence and military intervention in Cyprus. The Greek Cypriots allege that the true goal of Turkey and the Turkish Cypriot leadership is still *Taksim* (partition) and that they will secede some time after the conclusion of an agreement and then turn the current *de facto* partition of the island into an internationally recognised one. The Greek Cypriots also fear that Turkey will exercise its military superiority in the region and possibly conquer an additional part or the entire island using the Treaties of Guarantee and Alliance as a justification as it did in 1974. In that context, the approximately 35,000 Turkish soldiers currently on the island are perceived as a massive security threat. Moreover, the Greek side feared that the Turkish side would not stick to its part of the deal, that is, the return of territory as well as property, and the reduction of troops which stretched over a time span of up to eighteen years and just cash in on the Greek Cypriot concessions provided for in Annan V, which would have been implemented without delay once the agreement came into force.[3] Within this framework the official Greek Cypriot security positions on core security issues can be defined as follows:

1. A secession of a federal state should be impossible.
2. The island should be completely demilitarised. The presence of Turkish troops

on the island is accepted for a certain period of time but not indefinitely. Turkish troops should be reduced in numbers as soon as an agreement is reached and then a timetable should be prepared for their complete withdrawal from the island.[4]
3. An UN-led international peacekeeping force with an enhanced mandate will for a limited period of time police the island thereby safeguarding the individual and collective security of all Cypriots.
4. The Treaties of Guarantee and Alliance should be modified. The international peacekeeping force should maintain order and supervise the full implementation of the agreement. Only if the international force were to prove unable to fulfil the task, would the old Guarantor states have the right to intervene jointly or unilaterally. But a trigger mechanism ideally involving the UN Security Council should be incorporated to avoid Turkey's abuse of this right.
5. Any territory to be returned to the Greek Cypriots should be put under UN administration until its handover to the Greek Cypriot constituent state.

The Turkish Cypriot Position

Turkish Cypriot demands have their roots in their numerical minority and aim at communal security revolving around the issues of preservation of a Turkish Cypriot identity within their constituent state. Security concerns are based on their widespread fear that the ultimate goal of Greek Cypriot policy is still *Enosis* (union of Cyprus with Greece) or at least a reduction in the equal political status of the Turkish community to that of a minority. Moreover, they suspect that the Greek Cypriots will try to overcome any agreement by force in the future, as was the case in 1963, and that there will be insufficient protection for the Turkish Cypriots against violations of the agreement or the use of violence if Turkey loses its right to intervene as well as its military presence. Securitised concerns were centred around the fear that the Greek Cypriots, who enjoy economic and numerical superiority, will dominate them and that they will eventually lose majority status within their own constituent state, especially after the implementation of the three freedoms (movement, property and settlement) as well as through the return of property to Greek Cypriot ownership. The ideal core security requirements demanded by the Turkish side[5] for any settlement can be summarised as follows:
1. The security ties with the respective motherlands should be maintained. Therefore, the 1960 Treaties of Guarantee and Alliance should continue to remain in force as a safeguard for the Turkish Cypriots and Turkey.
2. The number of Greek and Turkish troops under the Treaty of Alliance should be increased.
3. Internal security and the administration of justice should only be in the hands of the federal states.[6]
4. There should be permanent restrictions on the freedoms of settlement and property, in order not to jeopardise a Turkish Cypriot dominated federal state.
5. Both founding states should possess separate sovereignty. The Turkish Cypriot side originally demanded that the Turkish Cypriot people enjoy a separate right of

self-determination and that they must be able to cede should they feel dominated economically or politically by the Greek Cypriot side.[7]

6. Territorial concessions should be limited also for security reasons. At a later stage of the negotiations, the Turkish military demanded a straight border line between the two constituent states for military and strategic reasons, an allusion on two deep territorial extensions of the Greek Cypriot constituent state into the Turkish Cypriot constituent state in the last versions of the Annan Plan.[8]

There was only one alteration in the position of the Turkish side concerning the security aspects of a settlement after the change of government in Turkey and the change from Rauf Denktash to Mehmet Ali Talat and Serdar Dentkash as the main Turkish Cypriot negotiators prior to the Burgenstock talks in early 2004.[9] Denktash's demand for a Turkish Cypriot right for self-determination and therefore secession was dropped. The possibility of secession had never been included in any version of the Annan Plan anyway.

Security Concerns of Turkey and Greece

The security requirements of Greece and Turkey are as equally important as those of the two Cypriot communities. Turkey shares Turkish Cypriot fears but has vital interests of its own. In particular, the Turkish military and the diplomatic circles consider strategic control over Cyprus and a military base there a necessity. For Turkey, the continuation of the Treaty of Guarantee and Alliance, which in Ankara's interpretation allows Turkish unilateral military intervention in case of a breach of the Cyprus settlement and the indefinite continuation of its military presence, was a key demand during the negotiations on the Annan Plan. Turkey also wants to avert an escalation in Cyprus that could jeopardise its EU membership aspirations and harm Greco-Turkish reconciliation. Similarly, Greece shares Greek Cypriot fears and knows that its own security would be directly affected by any occurrence of inter-communal violence or a conflict between the Republic of Cyprus and Turkey. Because of its military and geostrategic inferiority, Athens has a greater interest than Turkey in averting an escalation in Cyprus.

Athens has not striven to extend its influence on the island after 1974 although in military terms both countries have remained closely allied: Greece has stationed a regiment[10] on the island and is tied to Cyprus via a defensive military pact. In contrast to Turkey, a gurantor status or a permanent military presence after a solution of the Cyprus problem are not considered vital by Athens.

On a political level, Athens has largely followed a hands-off policy after 'delivering' the island's EU membership. 'Cyprus decides and Greece supports', was the official policy line taken by any Greek government during the last years and Greece has by and large adhered to it prior and after the referendum. Although the newly elected Karamanlis government (and its predecessor) supported Annan V, the Greek Prime Minister kept a low profile about it. Athens did not exert political or public pressure on the Greek Cypriot side to change its stand or influence the electorate in Cyprus and has remained a loyal supporter of official Greek Cypriot positions since.

An Evaluation of the Security Aspects of the Annan Plan

In view of these positions, the central question is how the Annan Plan addressed the core security concerns of the parties.

Turkish Cypriots and Turkey

Overall, the Turkish side should be pleased with the way the Annan Plan addressed their security concerns and this contributed to their support for it. Annan V, like all previous versions, precluded *enosis* (as well as *taksim*) for good and was based on the political equality of both communities at the central level.[11] Unlike the constitution of 1960, Annan V did not provide for a veto right of a Turkish Vice President. But it ensured that on all levels of higher executive and legislative decision making the support of a significant number of the Turkish Cypriot representatives (varying from 25 to 40 per cent) was required. In substance, the Turkish Cypriots – as a community – were provided with an absolute veto right on a legislative and executive level, though not with numerical equality in the Presidential Council and the House of Representatives. Turkish Cypriots enjoyed far reaching autonomy and legislative and executive sovereignty within their constituent state, whose government would be completely in their hands.[12] Internal security within the constituent states was the responsibility of the constituent administrations. Turkish Cypriot fears of a repetition of 1963 were pacified since Turkey kept its status as a guarantor power and its right to maintain troops on the island permanently.[13] In fact, Turkey arguably extended its powers as it remained a guarantor power for the independence, territorial integrity, security and constitutional order of the United Cyprus Republic (UCR), as well as gaining the same rights for *both* constituent states.[14]

Fears of Greek Cypriot numerical domination were also satisfactorily addressed from a Turkish Cypriot point of view, since the maximum percentage of Greek Cypriots within the Turkish Cypriot constituent state was restricted to 18 per cent of the population for a transitional period of 18 years or until Turkey joins the EU. Even after that, permanent restrictions limiting the number of Greek Cypriot permanent residents to 33 per cent would have been possible since the Turkish Cypriot constituent state could act to ensure that 2/3 of its permanent residents have Turkish as their mother tongue.[15]

Another Turkish Cypriot concern was to safeguard their political equality from being undermined in the long run by Greek Cypriots establishing residency in the north and seeking Turkish Cypriot internal constituent state citizenship. Annan V made it impossible for Greek Cypriots to 'pose' politically as Turkish Cypriots and therefore vote for (or even run as) Turkish Cypriot senators by stipulating that voting for the federal senators was based on mother tongue rather than internal constituent state citizenship.[16] Economically, the Annan Plan provided acceptable safeguards for the Turkish Cypriots against Greek Cypriot domination since it would have limited their right to buy property for fifteen years or until the north's GDP had reached 85 per cent of that of the south.[17]

As for the number of Turkish troops on the island, the Turkish record is mixed.

The withdrawal of its estimated 35,000 troops would have stretched over a period of 14 years or until EU membership.[18] In one of the most significant changes between Annan III and V, Turkey gained the right to maintain indefinitely 650 troops as stipulated in the 1960 Treaty of Alliance (which also provides for 950 Greek soldiers), while in Annan III the remaining 6,000 Greek and Turkish troops would have been withdrawn upon Turkey's entry into the EU, 'unless otherwise agreed'.[19] The only negative aspect for the Turkish military was the fact that the presence of Greek and Turkish troops would have been reviewed every three years, 'with the objective of total withdrawal'. This still made removal of the remaining troops impossible without Ankara's consent since the provisions of the Treaty of Alliance, on which their permanent presence is based, would remain untouched. Moreover, the Turkish government was unable to increase its military presence on the island permanently. The 650 Turkish soldiers deter Greek Cypriot hostile activities towards the Turkish Cypriots. Most importantly from a Turkish perspective, they secure a bridgehead for the arrival of Turkish reinforcements in case of a military intervention. Turkey was able to ensure that, until it joins the EU, neither NATO nor the EU can send troops to the island without the approval of Athens and Ankara. Ankara still kept an indirect veto right over the deployment of troops even after its EU accession provided it could maintain its influence within the Turkish Cypriot community and the Turkish Cypriot elites. Any international military operation would always need the consent of both constituent states and therefore a majority within the Turkish Cypriot leadership could veto any military deployment on the part of Turkey. The EU's Common Security and Defence Policy is therefore limited by Turkey's veto right which subjects the use of force on the island to Ankara's approval at least until the EU accession of Turkey. Unsurprisingly, the Greek Cypriot side rejected this provision as another limitation on the sovereignty of the UCR.[20] As with many other Turkish demands, this only makes sense should Turkey wish to intervene again in Cyprus, in case of open hostility between the EU and Turkey or in the event of a Greek-Turkish war.

The demand of the Turkish military for straight border lines is not satisfied in Annan V. However, information from a senior Turkish Cypriot official indicates that this Turkish demand, on a less significant issue anyway, had been put forth for tactical reasons.[21] It was mainly introduced to gain bargaining power on the 'real' issue of the quality of Turkish rights, so the failure to achieve straight border lines cannot be considered a serious flaw from a Turkish perspective.

One of the Turkish Cypriot chief negotiators, Talat, encapsulated the significance of these Turkish successes as well as their negative consequences from a Greek Cypriot perspective as follows:

> […] stationing a permanent Turkish contingent alongside with the ultimate right of unilateral military intervention had been at the heart of the security measures for the Turkish side whereas both were detrimental even fatal for the Greek side. Hence preservation and abolition of those provisions have been the driving efforts of the Turkish and Greek sides respectively; in almost all efforts for a solution of the Cyprus problem. The same happened

this time also. But it came out very clearly that the Greek Cypriot side's efforts were futile and abandoned almost from the beginning.[22]

According to Lord Hannay, the Greek Cypriot side made this concession as well as the offer of complete demilitarisation of the island in early 2002 as a unilateral confidence building gesture in order to allay the security concerns of the Turkish military.[23]

Greek Cypriots

While both Turkey and the Turkish Cypriots achieved their main security aims, things look very different from a Greek Cypriot perspective. Psychologically, the continuation and enhancement of Turkey's guarantor powers was a main motive for the Greek Cypriot 'no', although every settlement proposal since 1974 had envisaged the retention of the Treaties of Guarantee and Alliance. The trauma of the invasion and Turkey's subsequent abuse of its guarantor rights have not been forgotten. The fear that Turkey would invade again if given another opportunity has not lessened either. From an outside perspective, this seems an exaggerated concern, given that it is highly unlikely that a non-EU member state could use force against a member state and inconceivable for two EU member states to use force against each other. Therefore, the Turkish right of guarantee should not have played such an important role, but Greek Cypriots did not sufficiently realise what its place in an EU would mean for the UCR. This makes a repetition of 1974 extremely unlikely, particularly if there is no Greek Cypriot attempt to overcome the agreement through unconstitutional means – the only event in which Turkey could militarily intervene invoking the Treaty of Guarantee. Moreover, during the debate on the Treaty of Guarantee, the Greek side failed to obtain a 'triggering' mechanism to exercise the right of intervention as this was anathema to Turkey. Both sides were fully aware that a triggering mechanism, requiring Security Council approval, would render any 'legal' Turkish military intervention almost impossible: one permanent member of the Security Council would almost certainly veto any such unilateral action.

Complete demilitarisation of the island was not achieved. While the Greek Cypriot and Turkish Cypriot forces would be dissolved, Greek and Turkish troops would remain until Greece and Turkey were willing to withdraw them. The change between Annan III and Annan V from the withdrawal of all Turkish troops upon the entry of Turkey into the EU towards a permanent Turkish military presence was seen by Greek Cypriots as another great success for Ankara. Given that the Greek Cypriots had already achieved the end of a permanent Turkish military presence in Annan III, their strong objection to its reintroduction in Annan V was understandable. Moreover, Greek Cypriots widely believe that the permanent presence of Turkish troops was included in the Plan not for the sake of Turkish Cypriot security but to safeguard Turkey's own interest to control the island. This provision, together with the continuation of a unilateral Turkish right to intervene, played an important role in the Greek Cypriot 'no' vote.[24]

But would the reduction of Turkish troops from the present 35.000 to 650 within a maximum period of 14 years really be unacceptable in the EU context and with provisions creating strong public pressure for their eventual complete withdrawal? The key question here is the likelihood of a military confrontation on the island. Most outside observers no longer consider another Turkish military intervention a realistic option and therefore give a different answer than the directly affected Greek Cypriots who, in their majority, were clearly not willing to take this risk. One can indeed claim that the permanent Turkish military presence combined with the continuation of a Turkish right to intervene almost guaranteed a Greek Cypriot 'no' vote in the referenda – something the Turkish side was very aware of. But further research is necessary before it can be claimed with certainty, as does analyst Gregory R. Copley, that '…the Turkish General Staff pressured the Turkish Government to insert changes in the Annan Plan with the specific goal of creating a document which would have to be rejected by the Greek Cypriots…'.[25]

Implementation was the third main security concern.[26] The above mentioned Greek Cypriot fears are understandable psychologically but seem exaggerated from an outside perspective. This cannot be said of all Greek Cypriot security concerns. The strongest argument used by the 'no' camp was that while the Greek Cypriot side would deliver on all concessions on the day of implementation of the agreement, there were no safeguards that Turkey and the Turkish Cypriot side would stick to their part of the deal. In contrast to the Greek Cypriot concessions, the main benefits for them, the handover of territory, the reduction of the Turkish military presence and the gradual and partial return of refugees, would be implemented over periods of three and a half years (territory), 14 years (Turkish troops) and 18 years (refugees). Even Kofi Annan acknowledged the legitimacy of these concerns and recommended that the Security Council should address the Greek Cypriot fears regarding security and implementation further than the Annan Plan had done by providing for a strengthened UN mission in Cyprus and a Monitoring Committee.[27] However, the Greek side lost a lot of credibility when AKEL and Papadopoulos with the help of Russia torpedoed a UN resolution which would have provided sufficient guarantees, at least as far as the official AKEL view was concerned. The draft resolution provided for a strengthened UN presence entitled 'United Nations Settlement Implementation Mission in Cyprus' and an imposition of an arms embargo on Cyprus in order to support the demilitarisation of the island.[28] The Greek Cypriot side claims that they had nothing to do with the Russian veto and that the reason for it was merely the complete neglect of Russia during the entire negotiation process and in the drafting of the Security Council resolution.[29] However, it seems inconceivable that Russia, using its veto for the first time since 1994, would have acted on such a vital issue without the urging of the Papadopoulos government. Russia maintains traditionally close and friendly relations with the Republic of Cyprus and in particular with the main pillar of the government at that time, the communist party AKEL.

The credibility of Turkey's intention to implement the agreement can be doubted on very good grounds. It rejected the idea of interim UN administration over the territory that would be returned to the Greek Cypriots. It also objected to all Greek Cypriot attempts to broaden the competence of the international force to cover monitoring of the implementation of the agreement. During the negotiations, Turkey tried its best to limit the powers given to UNFICYP under a new mandate after an agreement.[30]

Moreover, Ankara objected to a Security Council resolution under Chapter VII of the UN Charter, which could result in forceful action in case Turkey failed to implement the agreement. Though most governments would not be happy to have a Security Council resolution threatening forceful action hanging over their heads, this objection would not make sense if Turkey did not consider, even remotely, not adhering to the agreement. Ankara's very consistent effort to limit the safeguards for the implementation of the agreement therefore gave strong additional validity to Greek Cypriot concerns. Despite setbacks, the Greek Cypriot side secured some important concessions: the Annan Plan stipulated that during the 'last months' before the transfer of any territory, UN supervision of the activities related to the transfer of the areas would be significantly enhanced and the UN would assume territorial responsibility for the area. Moreover, the Greek Cypriot side kept a low profile over their achievement that the territory to be returned would legally belong to the Greek Cypriot constituent state from the day the foundation agreement would be implemented. The administration of these territories was only 'entrusted to the authorities of the Turkish Cypriot state'.[31] This would enable the Greek Cypriots to claim international support for the return of those territories even in the case of a collapse of the UCR and provided at least some degree of security as far as the return of territory was concerned.

Conclusion

It is beyond the scope of this chapter to give an overall assessment of the Annan Plan. Many of the reasons for the acceptance or rejection of Annan V by individuals in both communities had nothing to do with the core security aspects of the Plan. The Annan Plan is a package deal in which disadvantages for one side in one area might be outweighed by advantages in another. Therefore, any evaluation of the settlement proposal based on the security aspects alone is incomplete and therefore problematic. Nevertheless, since security aspects were of paramount importance to both sides, an evaluation of the Annan Plan from this angle helps to understand the different decisions of both communities and contributes to the wider debate on the document.

In this context, were the Greek Cypriot 'no' and the Turkish Cypriot 'yes' votes rational or reasonable choices from a security point of view? The above analysis seems to provide quite clear answers – at least in the perception of the respective communities. Many Greek Cypriots felt that all Turkish security demands were met while theirs were largely ignored or insufficiently addressed. Interestingly, Greece, whose security would be enhanced by a functioning solution and is harmed by continuation of the conflict, did not share this view. Meanwhile, Turkey and the Turkish Cypriot community were provided with a high degree of security within the framework of the Plan.

There are good grounds for arguing that the Greek Cypriot security concerns related to the Treaty of Guarantee and the presence of Turkish troops were exaggerated and should have not been a reason to reject the Annan Plan. Many Greek Cypriots and their leadership focused so strongly on the Treaty of Guarantee and the danger of another military intervention that they did not realise how difficult it would be for Turkey to intervene on the island again. As long as the Greek Cypriots did not take any drastic and unconstitutional measures to change the state of affairs established by the Annan

Plan, a Turkish military intervention against an EU member state would be an unrealistic scenario. Therefore, the continuation of the Treaty of Guarantee can be considered an acceptable risk. The same unrealistic perception of the Treaty of Guarantee seems to have prevailed within the Turkish military which was obsessed with maintaining rights for intervention which would be far more difficult to implement than in the years prior to 1974.

In this context, it is not to Turkey's credit that it tried to limit the rights of the UN wherever it could to preserve its own and to diminish repercussions in case of its non-adherence to the settlement. This Turkish behaviour increased Greek Cypriot fears concerning implementation of the agreement by the other side. Indeed, Greek Cypriot concerns about implementation were justified given the uncertainty regarding Turkey's prospects of joining the EU, even though the start of accession negotiations was considered very likely at the time of the referendums.

Greek Cypriots were asked to accept a bet on the future and decided in the majority not to risk it: if Turkey was to consolidate into a liberal-democratic country, an EU member state and if the disputes between Athens and Ankara were finally settled, then the core security provisions of the Annan Plan would not have been a problem. However, if Turkey's EU aspirations failed and anti-Western or at least anti-EU forces gained control of the country, then a settlement in Cyprus, whose implementation would be drawn out over 18 years and which would allow Turkey to maintain at least 3,000 troops on the island for 14 years, is an invitation to pay back the Europeans via Cyprus or to exert pressure on the UCR. Since formal membership negotiations have begun, the difficulties recorded in Turkey's accession course, coupled with widespread public opposition to its membership in many EU countries, still justify Greek Cypriot concerns regarding implementation of the long-term provisions of the Annan V Plan.

If an amended Annan Plan or a new settlement is designed in the future, some recommendations based on the above analysis can be made:

1. Greek Cypriot security needs have to be addressed to a higher degree than was the case in Annan V.
2. Implementation: a UN resolution guaranteeing the implementation of any agreement by referring to Chapter VII of the UN Charter should accompany any future agreement.
3. The Treaty of Guarantee: a provision asking for consultations between the government of the United Cyprus Republic and the three guarantor powers every ten years (or upon mutual agreement) could allow the Treaty to die a peaceful death in a situation of political stability in which all sides no longer perceive each other as threats, while maintaining this highly symbolic right for the sake of Turkish/Turkish Cypriot approval of any future deal. It could also expire upon the entry of Turkey into the EU.
4. The agreement should call for a faster withdrawal of the bulk of Turkish troops and quicker implementation.[32]
5. Since a continued military presence of Turkish troops is a core security need of the Turkish Cypriot side, soldiers from both 'mother countries' should be embedded after a fixed transitional period in a multi-national UN, NATO or EU-peacekeeping

force with an enhanced mandate ensuring its ability to act should intercommunal violence reoccur. The end of the mandate of these peacekeeping troops should require the approval of separate legislative majorities of both communities.

1. Individual security:
   a. EU membership as well as the presence of such an international force will provide sufficient safeguards against any violation of basic human rights for both communities.
   b. The international force should have the means to guarantee the security of those Cypriots who live in the federal state controlled by the other community. Therefore its authority must be superior to that of the federal police forces and it must have the right to investigate alleged abuses of power by the security forces of the federal state if the respective federal authorities are accused of misconduct.
7. External threats:
   a. Cyprus' membership in NATO would be the best safeguard against any external threat.
   b. At least one of the British bases should be transformed into a NATO base as a safeguard against any external threat or the 'illegal' involvement of the mother countries. This would also allow the Greek and Turkish contingent to be embedded into a NATO force under the supreme command of the alliance.
8. Threats to Turkey: with the exception of the Greek and Turkish contingents, the British (and NATO) bases and an UN-led international force, the provisions for demilitarisation should be maintained. An exception could be possible to allow Cypriot participation in military (mainly peace keeping) activities of the EU or NATO abroad if voted for by separate legislative majorities. For this purpose the creation of a small, lightly armed, professional army not exceeding several hundred men could be considered. The supreme command should rest with Cypriot generals from both communities. As a result, Cyprus would not pose a military or strategic threat to Turkey.

ENDNOTES

1. The poll was conducted by the Greek Cypriot TV channel 'Mega'. Mega poll figures quoted from the speech of Labour MP, Andrew Dismore, *House of Commons*, 6 July 2004.
2. Coined by the Copenhagen School the term refers to a process by which non-politicised issues become first politicised (i.e. subject of political debate) and then securitised (i.e. political actors convince their audience that an issue poses a security threat). Georg Frerks, 'Promoting Human Security: To Securitise or De-securitise?', paper at the 57th Pugwash Annual Conference, *Prospects for Disarmament, Dialogue and Cooperation: Stability in the Mediterranean Region*, Bari, Italy, 21-6 October 2007. See for the question of Turkish settlers, Hubert Faustmann, 'Cyprus: Security Concerns and the Failure of the Annan Plan', *Suedosteuropa Mitteilungen*, June 2004, 63-64.
3. Tassos Papadopoulos, President of the Republic, to the Foreign Media, 25 April 2004, 3-4.
4. Glafkos Clerides, then President of the Republic of Cyprus, interview by Mehment Ali Birand, broadcast by 'CNN Türk' Television on 3 November 2001.

5. The term Turkish side refers to both Turkish Cypriots and Turkey in this text.
6. 'Security, law and order and the administration of justice in its territory will, among others, be under the jurisdiction of each Partner State.' Statement by the then Turkish Cypriot President Rauf Denktash in his negotiations with Glafkos Clerides, 'Far Reaching Settlement Vision from Denktash', *Turkish Daily News*, 12 April 2002.
7. 'Turkey: Denktash Explains Views, Conditions for Peace on Cyprus', *Istanbul Cumhuriyet* (Internet Version) in Turkish from 29 March 2002 (FBIS Translated Text); address by *Rauf Denktash* to a conference on the issue of water and land on 1 April 2002 in Morphou (Güzelyurt), quoted from Nicosia «Bayrak Radio 1» in Turkish (5.00 GMT) on 2 April 2002 (FBIS Translated Text); Denktash Comments on Possible Recess in Talks, Missing Persons, 3-Region Proposal, Nicosia «Bayrak Radio 1», see above.
8. This was part of the '20 Indispensable Articles' formulated as key demands of the military at the MGK (National Security Council) meeting on 23 January 2004. The 20 'Indispensable' Articles at the MGK meeting, *Istanbul Milliyet* from 24 January 2004 (FBIS Translated Text).
9. Talat replaced Dentkash after his victory in the 2005 presidential elections.
10. Though officially the number of Greek soldiers is around 900 (in line with the Treaty of Alliance), the estimates about the real number of Greek troops currently stationed in Cyprus range from 1,200 to about 2,700. Confidential interviews conducted by the author.
11. *The Comprehensive Settlement of the Cyprus Problem*. 31 March 2004, Main Articles, Article 1, Paragraph 6.
12. The Legislative consists of two chambers: Senate (48 members, 24 from each community) and a House of Representatives: (48 members, proportional representation but at least 25 per cent of the representatives must come from one constituent state). Decisions are taken by simple majority but at least 25 per cent of the votes in the Senate must come from one constituent state (in special cases the percentage is increased to 40 per cent). A Presidential Council heads the executive. It is elected with special majority by the Senate and confirmed by simple majority in the House of Representatives. It consists of six voting members and its composition is proportional to the number of persons with internal constituent citizenship status. But at least two must be from each constituent state (i.e. at least two have to be Turkish Cypriots). Non-voting members can be added but at least one-third of the non-voting members must come from each constituent state. Decisions are made by simple majority but at least one vote from representatives of each constituent state is needed. Two of the members of the Presidential Council become President and Vice President. They have to come from different constituent states and they rotate office every 20 months. The central administration is composed proportionally according to the population ratio with the exception of the police force which would be manned at a 50-50 ratio. *The Comprehensive Settlement of the Cyprus Problem*. Main Articles. 31 March 2004, Articles 2 and 5. See for the administration and the police Annex I, Articles 30 and 31.
13. Ibid., Article 1. Paragraph 3.
14. *The Comprehensive Settlement of the Cyprus Problem*. 31 March 2004, Annex III: Additional Protocol to the Treaty of Guarantee. Article 1.
15. Ibid., Article 3.
16. *Report of the UN Secretary-General on his mission of good offices in Cyprus*, 28 May 2004 (S/2004/437), Paragraph 52.
17. *The Comprehensive Settlement of the Cyprus Problem*. 31 March 2004, Main Articles, Article 3 and Section D.: Draft Act of Adaptation to the Terms of Accession of the United Cyprus Republic to the EU, Article 1 Property, Paragraph 1.
18. Both Greece and Turkey could keep 6,000 soldiers on the island until 2011 and 3,000 until 2018 or until the EU membership of Turkey (whichever is sooner). Ibid., Main Articles. Article

18. Paragraph 1b and Annex IV: Additional Protocol to the Treaty of Alliance.
19. Ibid., 'Annan III and V', Article 8 and Annex/Apendix IV: Additional Protocol to the Treaty of Alliance.
20. *The Comprehensive Settlement of the Cyprus Problem*. Main Articles, 31 March 2004, Article 8, Paragraph 4.
21. Confidential interview of the author.
22. Mehmet Ali Talat, *Prospects for a Settlement to the Cyprus Problem within the Framework of the Annan Plan*, Unpublished MA thesis (Eastern Mediterranean University, 2003), ftnt 2.
23. David Hannay, *The Search for a Solution*, London, 2005, 159. For criticism of this concession, see Costa Carras' contribution to this volume.
24. The security aspect and the unilateral right of Turkey to intervene clearly topped the list of the most negative aspects of the Annan Plan with 33.4 per cent in a survey conducted shortly before the referendum. Second came the continued presence of Turkish settlers with 14.1 per cent. The poll was conducted for the Greek newspaper *Kyrikatiki Eleftherotypia* on 15/16 April 2004. Another poll released in November 2004 showed that 76 per cent of the 1,000 Greek Cypriots interviewed demanded the withdrawal of Turkish troops, 75 per cent demanded that more settlers leave the island, and 73 per cent wanted the cost of the new federal state to be divided more equitably than provided for under Annan V before they would consider voting 'yes' in another referendum. The researchers conclude: 'These three particular demands have such strong and widely based support among the Greek Cypriot population, it is doubtful that any plan which fails to take them into account could possibly be approved in a second referendum.' *Cyprus Mail*, 9 November 2004, 6.
25. Gregory R. Copley, *Options and Outlook in the Eastern Mediterranean*, Paper given at the American Hellenic Institute Seminar 'Cyprus: the Road Ahead and US Interests', Washington, DC, 19 May 2004, 4; See also by Copley, 'Turkish Strategic Imperatives and Western Intelligence Failures Let to the Collapse of Cyprus Resolution Talks', *Defense & Foreign Affairs Daily*, 24 June 2004.
26. See for a more detailed account of Greek Cypriot implementation concerns, Claire Palley, *An International Relations Debacle*, Oxford, 2005, 145-147.
27. The number of UN troops would be doubled under the Annan Plan, to about 2,400, in order to assist the implementation of the plan. Moreover, a Monitoring Committee composed of representatives of the guarantor powers, the federal government, and the constituent states and chaired by the UN would monitor the implementation of the agreement. *The Comprehensive Settlement of the Cyprus Problem*, 31 March 2004, Main Articles, Article 8; «Cyprus Mail», 31 August 2004, 3, and *Report of the UN Secretary-General*, 28 May 2004 (S/2004/437), Paragraph 84.
28. *Report of the UN Secretary-General*, 28 May 2004 (S/2004/437), Paragraph 84.
29. Interview of Ambassador Erato Kozakou-Marcoullis, Director Political Affairs Division (Cyprus Question), in the Ministry of Foreign Affairs, 25 August 2004; For the official reasons of the Russian veto see the speech of the Russian representative in the Security Council, *Gatilov*, Provisional Verbatim Record of the 4947th meeting of the UN Security Council, 21 April 2004 (S/PV.4947).
30. Talat, *Prospects for a Settlement to the Cyprus Problem within the Framework of the Annan Plan*, 62.
31. *The Comprehensive Settlement of the Cyprus Problem*, 31 March 2004, Annex VI: Territorial Arrangements, Article 3. For the UN role, see Article 1 Paragraph 1 of the same Annex.
32. That this would significantly increase the acceptance of any settlement by the Greek Cypriot side was confirmed in a poll in 2004. Alexandros Lordos, '*Civil Society Diplomacy: A new approach for Cyprus?*', Nicosia, February 2005 <http://www.dzforum.de/0501.php>.

Chapter 17

THE RISE OF THE AK PARTY AND ANKARA'S CHANGING ROLE: PAVING THE WAY FOR THE 'YES'

Tozun Bahcheli & Sid Noel

Introduction

Referendums are by design reductionist events: there are no political leaders or parties to be elected, no party platforms to be considered in their entirety, and no possibility of voting for a third option since even the most complex question must ultimately come down to a simple 'yes' or 'no'. Yet referendum outcomes are difficult to explain. Despite the seeming simplicity of the referendum process – 'let the people decide' – the choices made by voters may be (and usually are) influenced by a plethora of factors, of which the most clearly identifiable are campaign-specific. These include the arguments put forward by the opposing sides, the credibility of the leaders making the arguments, the degree and type of engagement by political parties and civil society organizations, the effectiveness of advertising, and the extent and quality of media coverage. One approach, therefore, is to explain the behaviour of voters in terms of stimulus and response – their choices are explained as responses to 'cues' directed at them by leaders, parties and others who play important roles in the campaign.[1] While such an approach can be valuable, it offers only a partial explanation because it takes insufficient account of contextual factors that may be influential. Such factors can be longstanding cultural and ideological outlooks, which may condition how voters respond to given cues, but also external factors, such as changes in the regional and/or international environment, the cumulative impact of decisions made over time by key external actors, and cues emanating from these actors.

An alternative (or supplementary) explanatory approach is to view the outcome of a referendum as being 'path dependent' – that is, as a decision shaped by its historical setting, and by past decisions whether internally or externally made. As Adrian Kay explains: 'A process is path dependent if initial moves in one direction elicit further moves in the same direction; in other words, the order in which things happen affects how they happen; the trajectory of change up to a certain point constrains the trajectory after that point.'[2] This chapter will argue from a path-dependency perspective that the coming to power in Turkey of the Justice and Development Party (AKP) in November 2002 and a series of decisions the AKP government took in connection with Turkey's application for membership in the EU, were key determinants of the trajectory that produced a resounding Turkish Cypriot 'yes' vote in the April 2004 referendum on the Annan Plan.

The Rise of the AKP

The AKP had been in existence for only fifteen months when it was swept to power with a huge majority in the parliamentary elections of 3 November 2002 and formed the first majority government in Turkey in over a decade. The party's relative newness, however, did not mean that it was without antecedents. It had grown directly out of earlier Islamic parties that, over several decades, had built sizeable support and enjoyed some electoral success. In particular, many of the leading members of the AKP had formerly been members of the Islamist Refah (Welfare) Party (RP) and its successor the Fazilet (Virtue) Party, both of which had been banned for allegedly violating Turkey's principle of secularism.

Following the banning of Fazilet in 2001, a group of its younger members led by Recep Tayyip Erdogan, a businessman and Istanbul's popular former mayor, and Abdullah Gul, an economist and member of parliament since 1991, decided to split from it and start another new Islamist party, the AKP, to contest the 2002 parliamentary elections. But this time the new party was clearly differentiated from its predecessors. Adroitly downplaying the AKP's Islamist roots, Erdogan and Gul positioned the party as a moderate, reformist, business-oriented party of the centre-right. As Bulent Arinc, a reformist colleague of Erdogan and Gul, put it: 'we need to steer ourselves from the margins of society and become a party that can be trusted by everyone'.[3] Skillfully capitalizing on the shortcomings of the incumbent three-party governing coalition, which had become deeply unpopular as a result of a series of corruption scandals and its ineptitude in the face of a severe economic recession, the AKP first and foremost held out to voters the promise of clean, competent government – a promise that was lent credibility by Erdogan's widely admired reformist administration of Istanbul – and was duly rewarded by the electorate. So poor was the performance of the outgoing parties that none obtained the required ten percent to be represented in the new parliament.

Although many rank and file members of the AKP felt strongly about traditional Islamist issues, such as removing the ban on wearing headscarves in universities and government offices, the AKP election strategy was not to force such issues, or to defer them, in order to avert a confrontation with the secular establishment. Instead, it pointedly 'pledged the party's support for secularism, democracy and Turkey's traditional pro-Western foreign policy, particularly EU membership'.[4] All of these reassuring goals were important, but it was the last – the pursuit of full membership in the EU – that was swiftly adopted as the dominant, even obsessive focus of AKP policy once the party had achieved office and power.

This was not altogether surprising, except perhaps in the level of the AKP's commitment. In varying degrees all of Turkey's secular parties had declared their support for EU membership and any reneging by the AKP would have proved deeply divisive. EU members had long wavered in their willingness to accept Turkey as a member, prompting many Turks to wonder whether Turkish accession could ever be realized. But in 1999, reversing earlier rebuffs, the Helsinki meeting of the European Council had given Ankara a significant incentive for pursuing accession by declaring Turkey a candidate for full membership. One of the few notable achievements of the coalition government that preceded the AKP was its passage of EU-mandated legislation, including banning the death penalty. The AKP's decision to pursue EU membership was thus consistent with the policy of its predecessors. However, whereas parties that formed governments before the AKP often struggled to achieve a consensus on the merits of EU membership, the AKP, with its solid parliamentary majority, was uniquely in a position to achieve reforms and remove the remaining obstacles on the path to accession.

That a party with Islamist roots became the ardent champion of EU membership is remarkably ironic. The leading members of the AKP had previously held senior positions in the banned Islamist parties that had adamantly opposed Turkey's membership of the EU. Just a few years before the AKP took office, Gul (who was at that time an RP member of parliament) had declared that 'a key aim of the RP was to protect Turkey's values against the EU'.[5] Yet by 2002 there was no more eloquent advocate of the cause of EU membership than Gul.

In reversing their earlier views on the EU membership issue, Gul and other AKP leaders appear to have undergone a genuine conversion, based on their reassessment of where Turkey's best future prospects lay, both politically and economically. But it must also be noted that their sharp turn towards the pursuit of EU membership was a political master-stroke that at once opportunely confounded their critics, averted a clash with the Turkish secular establishment, and even effectively shielded the AKP against a possible future military intervention. As the (self-appointed) guardians of secularism, the military leaders were suspicious of the AKP, but they also strongly favoured EU membership in the belief that it would safeguard Turkey's secular order and help preserve Turkey's territorial integrity. For secularists generally, EU membership was seen as the ultimate realization of the Kemalist mission to make Turkey an integral part of the West. Indeed, except from some marginal groups, practically all segments of Turkish society supported EU membership. Longing for better times and smarting from the effects of the severe economic crisis of 2001, three quarters of the Turkish public expressed support for EU membership at the time that the AKP formed the government.[6] Whatever may have been the mix of motives that propelled the AKP towards the pursuit of EU membership, the decision to do so was a profoundly consequential step. Though it was perhaps not fully realized at the time, the AKP's European agenda would define the available options for many key policy choices, not least those related to the settlement of the Cyprus issue.

The AKP and the Cyprus Issue

For several decades practically all Turkish politicians paid lip service to Cyprus as a national cause and the defense of Turkish Cypriot rights as a national imperative. Governments in Ankara, while formally obliged to respond to periodic UN-led initiatives to broker a settlement, for the most part were content to leave the issue alone and to preserve the post-1974 status quo, which amounted to a policy of maintaining the division of Cyprus indefinitely. By 2002, however, there was a new factor at work that would soon cast the *status quo* into question: namely, the looming prospect of Cyprus's accession to the EU. For several months preceding the Turkish parliamentary elections in November 2002, Greek and Turkish Cypriot leaders had been meeting regularly with a team representing the UN Secretary-General in anticipation of a new and, this time urgent, UN initiative to settle the Cyprus dispute prior to the island's becoming an EU member. But many Turks (and others) had become accustomed to such seemingly desultory meetings that always ended with no real progress towards an agreement.

It was no surprise, therefore, when Cyprus did not feature in the parliamentary election campaign of 2002. Such was the degree of consensus on the Cyprus issue, and hence its general neglect, that there was not even a difference of opinion between the Islamists and the secularists. In fact, the leading Islamists were hard-liners in complete agreement with the military. In the event, it was not the hard-line Islamist parties but the AKP that was put to the test on the Cyprus problem.

Prior to the election of the AKP, the Turkish government had unsuccessfully tried to persuade European governments to defer Cypriot accession, arguing that the island's EU membership should await a political settlement. Ankara had also tried in vain to gain EU acceptance of its position that there be no linkage between Turkey's accession course and the settlement of the Cyprus issue. However, while acknowledging that there was no formal linkage, EU officials regularly advised Ankara that an unresolved Cyprus issue would hamper Turkey's EU prospects. In fact, the EU was in a tight bind of its own making. It had agreed to admit Cyprus without making reunification a pre-condition, and now Greece – whose diplomats had been instrumental in shepherding the Cypriot application to a successful conclusion – was threatening to use its veto power to sink the EU's planned expansion to include ten new states if the Cypriot accession did not proceed as scheduled. Realistically, Brussels had left itself with no real choice except to admit a still-divided Cyprus, thus in effect importing the longstanding Cypriot imbroglio into the EU. At the same time, it hoped that the prospect of membership would somehow serve as a catalyst and that a new UN initiative would secure the island's reunification prior to the planned accession date.

It was against this background that the AKP was confronted with the Cyprus issue when, eight days after its electoral victory, UN Secretary-General Kofi Annan submitted his plan for a settlement. The Annan Plan provided for the reunification of Cyprus as a federation with some consociational power-sharing features similar to those in Belgium and Switzerland.[7] Turkish Cypriots had to forsake their claim to a sovereign state and agree to make substantial territorial concessions to the Greek Cypriots. Also, except for token forces, the plan called for the eventual withdrawal of Turkish and Greek troops. While for the Turkish Cypriots these were losses, perceived or real, the plan also offered them substantial gains: the provision for two equal constituent states, one Greek Cypriot and the other Turkish Cypriot, in a loose federation meant that Turkish Cypriots would exercise a wide measure of self-government and in spite of Greek Cypriot objections, the plan provided that Turkey's role as a guarantor in Cyprus, in accordance with the 1960 Treaty of Guarantee, would remain unchanged.

Given the AKP's EU aspirations, it was only too clear to its leaders that accession to the EU of a still-divided Cyprus would, at a minimum, seriously complicate Turkey's own accession bid and perhaps even derail it completely. There was thus no lack of resolve on the part of the new AKP government to do whatever it could to help bring about a settlement on Cyprus. First, however, it would have to settle upon a way of dealing with the Turkish Cypriot leadership, and particularly with its long-time leader and President of the Turkish Republic of Northern Cyprus (TRNC), Rauf Denktash. No sooner had the UN Secretary-General presented his draft plan than Denktash declared it unacceptable, citing among other reasons the plan's lack of recognition of Turkish Cypriot sovereignty. For decades Denktash has been able to count on virtually automatic support from the Turkish government for his policies and pronouncements. But this time the only response from Ankara was a deafening silence, and when the AKP issued its policy statement on Cyprus it declared at the outset that the UN plan was negotiable. The AKP thus implicitly accepted Brussels's linkage between Turkey's EU aspirations and Turkish support of UN efforts to achieve a settlement. Erdogan boldly declared on 2 January 2003: 'I am not in favour of the continuation of the policy that has been maintained in Cyprus over the past 30-40 years…We will do whatever falls on us. This is not Denktash's private matter.'[8]

Denktash, however, though weakened by the AKP's repudiation, remained a force because of his public standing as a patriot and senior statesman and his deep connections with Turkey's secular establishment. He had many allies whom he could call upon for support. In addition to the Republican Peoples Party (CHP), the main opposition group in parliament, his supporters came primarily from three quarters: the senior ranks of the foreign ministry, senior military officers and President Ahmet Necdet Sezer. All came out against the Annan plan and backed Denktash over the AKP government. Faced with opposition from these key sections of the political and military establishment, the AKP leaders began to vacillate. As veteran Turkish journalist Cengiz Candar put it, 'through inexperience' the government 'wavered and left room for manoeuvre to Denktash and die-hards in Ankara who do not want a settlement'.[9]

The AKP had to hastily improvise a public case for continuing to negotiate – which meant, in effect, making a case for the plan itself, which it did by emphasizing its positive aspects, such as the wide measure of autonomy that Turkish Cypriots would continue to enjoy in the proposed federation and the retention of Turkey's rights as a guarantor power, which would ensure Turkish Cypriot security. Opponents of the plan countered by attacking what they considered to be its shortcomings, such as the dissolution of the TRNC and the abandonment of the dream of separate statehood for the Turkish Cypriot community, the proposed resettlement of large numbers of Turkish Cypriots, and weaker security arising from the withdrawal of the bulk of Turkish troops from the island. They also invoked the perennial complaint that Turkey was being pressured by European governments to trade major concessions in Cyprus for the uncertain prospect of EU membership. The opposition CHP and various nationalist groups sensed that the AKP had made itself vulnerable by endorsing concessions over Cyprus, yet their barrage of criticism of a sell-out did not dent the new government's high approval rating among the Turkish public. Two factors account for this. First, while Cyprus was a nationalist 'hot button' issue and could prove explosive, the fact that yet another UN plan had been put on the table was not in itself sufficient to stir much excitement. And second, during the course of the prolonged debates on the various revised versions of the Annan Plan, support for the AKP position began to build, with various influential civil society groups, such as the Turkish Industrialists' and Businessmen's Association, as well as many academics and newspaper columnists, actively praising its stance. Some columnists even declared the Annan Plan a victory for Turkey.[10] Ultimately, Turkish public opinion proved receptive to the government's argument that it was possible to secure a fair settlement in Cyprus and that such a settlement was necessary in order to achieve progress toward EU membership.

The AKP leadership, however, had failed to anticipate this development and its early wavering enabled Denktash and his supporters in Turkey's military-bureaucratic establishment, at a critical point in the Cyprus negotiations, to take a hard line that contradicted the AKP's more conciliatory stance. Specifically, Denktash's rejection of the revised version of the Annan Plan presented in March 2003 fatally undermined the AKP's case for securing a negotiated political settlement. The damage had been done, and the result was to remove any resistance that may have existed within the EU to the prospect of admitting a divided new member. The way was thus cleared for the Greek Cypriot government to sign the EU Accession Treaty on 17 April 2003, thereby securing membership for Cyprus.

The significance of missing what was, in effect, the final deadline for a negotiated settlement was subsequently acknowledged by then foreign minister Gul, for it soon became clear that it represented a major foreign policy failure of the new government and exposed its woeful lack of experience in international negotiation. Of the AKP's senior figures – namely Prime Minister Erdogan, Gul, and Bulent Arinc (Speaker of the House) – only Gul had any experience at all. Later, in a candid interview with Fikret Bila of the Turkish daily *Milliyet*, he declared: 'If I had two more months' experience, I would have concluded this matter [Cyprus] at The Hague in 2003.'[11]

It was not until several months after the failed summit at The Hague that Erdogan attempted to recover from the setback by overriding Denktash's Turkish supporters and obliging him to return to the negotiating table, with the blunt warning that, if no agreement were reached, Turkey would support submitting the issue to the arbitration of the UN Secretary-General. 'For me, the Annan plan is a suicide,' Denktash defiantly declared, to which Erdogan icily responded 'we have always said that the plan is negotiable.'[12] But by then – with Cypriot accession a done deal and with President Papadopoulos, a nationalist hard-liner, firmly in control on the Greek Cypriot side – the possibility of a negotiated settlement was remote. Negotiations were restarted in February 2004 and predictably led nowhere. In the absence of a settlement, it was agreed that the Secretary-General's final draft would be put to simultaneous referendums in both parts of the island on 24 April 2004.

The Role of Ethnic Kin Politics

The contest between the AKP government and the Turkish Cypriot leadership brought into sharp relief the complex relationship that had always existed between mainland and Cypriot Turks – and which in the past both had preferred not to examine too closely. For Turkish Cypriots, feelings of solidarity with the motherland and gratitude for its backing were balanced by a sense of dependency, of being the inferior partner in a metropolis-hinterland relationship, and, no matter how much support they have received in the past, by an ever-present fear of betrayal or abandonment. For many Turks, on the other hand, feelings of affinity and support for the Turkish Cypriots were tempered by suspicions that their island kin showed too little gratitude for Turkey's sacrifices, or worse, that that they were prepared to put their selfish interests ahead of the wellbeing of Turks. This latter sentiment surfaced strongly in some circles in Turkey during debates over the Annan Plan and Denktash's opposition to it, with some commentators complaining that 200,000 Turkish Cypriots were being allowed to jeopardize the European aspirations of 69 million Turks.[13]

Few Turkish Cypriots would deny Turkey's indispensable role in defending them against Greek Cypriots during the communal conflicts of the 1960s and '70s and averting *enosis*. Given their almost total dependence on Turkey for more than a decade after the collapse of bicommunal government in 1963, Turkish Cypriot questioning of Turkey's authority to decide policy during this period was virtually unthinkable. However, Turkey's bolstering of the Turkish Cypriots *vis-à-vis* Greek Cypriots in the aftermath of the island's partition in 1974 ushered in a more nuanced and subtly altered relationship between the Turkish community and the mainland. Moreover, after 1974, for the first time in their history, Turkish Cypriots were physically concentrated in one area and hence better positioned to govern themselves than had previously been the case when they were divided up among scattered enclaves. And as their institutions of self-government expanded and developed so too did their confidence, their faith in their own leaders, and their sense of distinctiveness *vis-à-vis* the motherland. Among the signs of the change that was taking place in their political culture was the proliferation of political parties. Prior to 1974, party activity and dissent had been discouraged on the grounds that the Greek-Cypriot threat required a united front. But thereafter, with security no longer a matter of paramount concern, political activity flourished, with parties of the left challenging the nationalist parties of the right and Turkey's role in Turkish-Cypriot society and politics being debated openly, as never before.

However, while the Turkish-Cypriot parties of the left performed well enough to become junior partners in several coalition governments, they also complained of a persistent Turkish bias in favour of the parties of the right. They did so with considerable justification, for there was no doubting Ankara's preference for right-wing nationalist parties that stressed close relations with Turkey and, in particular, for the leadership of Denktash. The latter had served as his community's principal representative in all UN-led inter-communal talks after 1968, and after the founding of the TRNC in 1983 he was elected to successive terms as president. Under his leadership, a coalition of nationalist, centre-right parties had prevailed in every Turkish-Cypriot election (pre-and post-TRNC) for almost three decades. A charismatic politician with a reputation as tough negotiator, he always took care to promote Turkey's strategic interests in Cyprus as much as Turkish-Cypriot political interests. His ties with prominent figures in the Turkish military, political parties, and diplomatic service were close and deeply cultivated. His political longevity, moreover, gave him a significant advantage in dealing with Ankara: Turkish premiers, foreign ministers, and chiefs of the military would come and go, but Denktash remained in office, seemingly the one permanent fixture in a rapidly changing political landscape.

Taking advantage of a series of short-lived Turkish coalition governments throughout the 1990s, the experienced and persuasive Denktash effectively took the lead in setting Turkish policy towards Cyprus, and Ankara followed. In 1998 he declared what had become obvious for some time: that he would accept only a two-state confederation as a solution – which seemingly slammed the door on any future settlement since his proposed solution was one which the Greek Cypriots would never accept. By this time, however, many Turkish Cypriots, particularly the younger generation, had begun to ask whether there might not be other possible solutions, and to resent Ankara's automatic support for Denktash. They were also unhappy about the level of influence and interference that Turkish authorities exercised in the day-today affairs of the TRNC, which was the other side of the coin of what Denktash's critics regarded as his too-close relations with Ankara. A report by the Economist Intelligence Unit described Turkish-Cypriot misgivings in these terms: 'although the administration of President Denktash firmly supports the Turkish presence and accepts Turkish guidance in many aspects of domestic policy affairs, opposition to Turkish involvement in the Turkish Cypriot society at large, as epitomized by the slogan 'This Land is Ours', is considerable'.[14]

By the year 2000, and more evidently by 2002, increasing public sentiment against Turkish influence and for a more assertive articulation of Turkish-Cypriot interests led to increasing questioning of Denktash's leadership. He was seen by his critics as excessively rigid and locked in a time warp, producing in 2003 a significant shift in electoral support away from the nationalist parties of the right that stressed closer ties with Turkey. Rather than still *more* integration with Turkey (which at that time Denktash was promoting as a response to the EU's acceptance of Cypriot membership), Turkish Cypriots increasingly turned to the parties of the center-left that favoured *less* integration, greater Turkish-Cypriot independence, reunification under a federal settlement and, through the latter, the manifold benefits of EU membership. According to public opinion polls cited by the Turkish-Cypriot daily *Yeniduzen*, 11.5 per cent of Turkish Cypriots supported integration with Turkey in 1997; but support for integration dropped to 8.2 per cent in 1999, 7.7 per cent in 2000, and a mere 5.1 per cent in 2002.[15] By contrast, the popularity of the support for EU membership was confirmed in a poll conducted by the EU in September 2002 which showed that '87.4 per cent of Turkish Cypriot citizens would vote in favour of EU membership'.[16]

Getting to 'Yes'

It was thus against a background of growing Turkish-Cypriot disenchantment with Denktash's rejectionist policies and Ankara's omnipresent influence in TRNC affairs that the AKP government inherited the Cyprus issue in November 2002. Unencumbered by past commitments over Cyprus, and uneasily aware of Denktash's close involvement with those who were now their domestic political opponents, the AKP leaders had no reason to defer to his judgment on the Annan plan, or indeed on anything. Moreover, by this time it was becoming clear that the Cyprus issue and Turkey's application for EU membership were linked, despite endlessly repeated Turkish assertions to the contrary. The AKP therefore had ample reason to fear that the admission into the EU of a divided Cyprus would negatively affect Turkey's own application for membership – and the pursuit of EU membership was something that the AKP leaders had made the centerpiece of their agenda, their number one policy priority. If a settlement could be reached, 'a very important problem between Turkey and the EU will be removed,' Erdogan frankly admitted.[17] Not surprisingly, therefore, he favoured a negotiated settlement in Cyprus and was prepared to make concessions to get one.

Previously, there had never been more than a sliver of difference between the official Turkish stance and that of Denktash's governing nationalist coalition. But, in a stunning reversal of fortunes, with the election of the AKP, a new party had taken power in Turkey whose natural allies in the TRNC were the centre-left parties. These parties shared the AKP's pro-settlement, pro-EU goals and, like the Erdogan government, were locked in a struggle against the anti-settlement, anti-EU camp led by Denktash. The AKP's Cyprus policy amounted to political earthquake in Ankara and it did not take long for the shock waves to be felt in the TRNC.

Buoyed by the AKP victory, in the TRNC parliamentary elections in 2003 the centre-left coalition succeeded in cracking Denktash's long political dominance. In what was practically a referendum on the Annan Plan, the main centre-left parties, the Turkish Republican Party (CTP), and Movement for Democracy and Peace (BDH), between them won a narrow majority of votes and tied the centre-right coalition in seats, each winning 25. The CTP leader, Mehmet Ali Talat, was called upon to form a government and was able to do so by bringing the centre-right Democratic Party (DP) into the coalition. The political effect was immediate and dramatic: when Denktash tried to rally his supporters in Turkey Erdogan harshly rebuffed him: 'Whatever you want to say, say it in Cyprus.'[18] With Talat as chief negotiator, the official TRNC position on the Annan Plan turned from no to yes. It was this turnaround that set the stage for the 24 April 2004 referendum.

As the Greek and Turkish Cypriot communities headed towards voting day the political momentum on the two sides went in opposite directions. On the Greek Cypriot side, the 'yes' campaign went badly from the very beginning. It was conspicuously not orchestrated by the government, was late getting started, lacked coherent leadership, and had no effective media and advertising strategy; two major political parties that might have put their organizations behind it were divided and did nothing, supposedly to await instructions from their party conferences which were to take place just before the referendum date. While it did have the strong support of the international community, and particularly the EU, this was of dubious value. By contrast, on the Turkish Cypriot side, the Yes campaign went extremely well. It was ably orchestrated by the same centre-left coalition parties that had formed the government after the 2003 elections and whose activists and local organizers were enthused by the prospect of another challenge. It was supported by the Chamber of Commerce and practically every important business interest and endorsed by a wide range of civil society groups. The media gave it generous air time and generally favourable treatment. Not least – and most unusual for any enterprise in the TRNC, which had never received international recognition – it basked in the approval of the international community, whose supportive envoys and emissaries symbolized the glittering EU future that awaited, needing only a 'yes' vote. The 'no' campaign, by comparison, seemed backward looking and defensive, with even its attempt to appeal to Turkish cultural nationalism undercut by the AKP government in Ankara, which had left no doubt that it strongly supported a 'yes' vote. The AKP leaders did not overtly intervene, and had no need to do so. Under Talat's direction, the pro-Annan coalition mounted a vigorous, well-organized campaign and, as the AKP desired, delivered a solid (65 per cent) 'yes' vote. That the 'no' side nevertheless obtained 35 per cent was less a measure of its effectiveness in the campaign than of the remarkable hold that the idea of a separate national life continued to have for many Turkish Cypriots, especially those of an older generation.

In any referendum the motives of voters are mixed. Perhaps those who voted yes also wanted a separate national life, but as part of a federal state that would be less in Turkey's orbit and in which they would also be citizens of the EU. And that is what might have happened had the Annan plan been jointly endorsed. In the end, however, the even more decisive 'no' vote of the Greek Cypriots (76 per cent) meant that the Turkish Cypriots' support for the 'yes' side was in vain: Cyprus entered the EU still divided and with the Turkish Cypriots excluded.

Conclusion

The decision of the newly elected AKP government in Ankara to pursue accession to the EU as its highest priority illustrates how a policy decision taken externally, for reasons having nothing to do with Cyprus, could fundamentally affect the path of future political events on the island. In effect, it created a trajectory that ended with a decisive Turkish Cypriot 'yes' vote. The AKP's decision was in keeping with the approach followed, with a greater or lesser degree of commitment, by previous Turkish governments, whatever their political colouring. But it must also be noted that the AKP could have chosen a different option – by nominally maintaining the continuity of Turkish policy towards the EU while devoting the bulk of its energy to pursuing a domestic agenda of reform, which was widely expected and would have pleased many in its core constituency. This latter option would not have necessitated a fundamental change in Turkey's approach to Cyprus. The AKP's commitment to EU accession, however, made a fundamental change inevitable.

For decades the Turkish view of the Cyprus issue had been that it was, first, a matter of Turkish national security, given the island's close proximity to the Turkish mainland, and second, one of protecting the rights of their ethnic kin on the island, who were seen as a stranded national minority. Turkish Cypriots broadly shared this view (though they placed more emphasis on the second aspect). From the AKP's perspective the Cyprus issue had two dimensions. First, while not denying other more traditional concerns, it was seen as at worst a roadblock and at best an irritant to Turkey's relations with Europe. Second, Cyprus had been a matter which its predecessors had complacently allowed to stagnate, but which now cried out for a fresh initiative, especially one that the Turkish Cypriots themselves seemed ready to embrace. It was therefore in the AKP government's interest to reframe the Cyprus issue as one affecting Turkey's – and the Turkish Cypriots' – relations with the EU. It was unlikely to succeed in doing so, however, as long as Denktash and his Turkish allies continued to dominate the discourse, framing the issue (as they had successfully done for decades) in narrow national security terms. Within Turkey, the AKP's efforts to frame a new discourse struck a responsive chord with influential sections of the media and among leaders of pro-EU business and other civil society organizations. Also, Erdogan himself intervened to derail Dentash's efforts to rally support for his anti-agreement position in Turkey.

Ultimately, it was in the TRNC that the referendum would be decided and there the AKP adopted an overtly non-interventionist strategy. Hence none of its principal figures played a public role in the yes campaign, correctly perceiving that to do so would leave them open to accusations of using undue influence – not only by the Greek Cypriot no side, but probably also by the Turkish Cypriot 'yes' side whose leaders would have rejected the suggestion that they were mere puppets whose strings were being pulled in Ankara. Moreover, the AKP could stand aside with little risk, since it had already prepared the ground for the referendum by sending a series of well-timed, unambiguous cues to the pro-EU coalition in the

TRNC that they had a new ally in Ankara and the days of automatic Turkish support for Denktash and the nationalist parties was over. Finally, the AKP signaled to Turkish Cypriot voters that if they voted 'yes' they would not be isolating themselves from Turkey but instead joining their ethnic kin in moving together in a new and more hopeful direction. If those voters had faced opposition by Ankara their path to a 'yes' would have been littered with obstacles, making the outcome problematical. Instead, because of the AKP government's EU policy and the resulting positive cues, the path to a 'yes' was straight and smoothly paved.

ENDNOTES

1. See, Lawrence Leduc, 'Opinion Change and Voting Behaviour in Referendums', *European Journal of Political Research*, XLI, 2002, 711-732; For an application of this approach to a Mediterranean case see Michelle Cini, 'Culture, Institutions and Campaign Effects: Explaining the Outcome of Malta's EU Accession Referendum', *West European Politics*, XXVII, 4, 2004, 584-602.
2. 'A Critique of the Use of Path Dependency in Policy Studies', *Public Administration*, LXXXI-II, 3, 2005, 553; See also Gerard Alexander, 'Institutions, Path Dependence, and Democratic Consolidation', *Journal of Theoretical Politics*, XIII, 3, 2001, 249-70.
3. *The Economist*, 13-19 November 1999.
4. Gareth Jenkins, 'Muslim Democrats in Turkey?', *Survival*, XLV, 1, 2003, 54.
5. Abdullah Gul, interview, 23 December 1994 (Ankara), quoted in Philip Robins, 'Confusion at Home, Confusion Abroad: Turkey Between Copenhagen and Iraq', *International Affairs*, LXXIX, 3, 2003, 553.
6. A survey conducted by two researchers at Bogazici University in Istanbul in 2002 indicated that 74 percent of the respondents would vote in favour of Turkey's membership should a vote be conducted on the issue. See Ali Carkoglu and Kemal Kirisci, '*Turkiye Dis Politikasi Arastirmasi*' (Survey of Turkish Foreign Policy), Bogazici University, March 2002.
7. We have elsewhere examined these features in detail. See Tozun Bahcheli and Sid Noel, 'Power-Sharing for Cyprus (again)? EU Accession and the Prospects for Reunification Under a Belgian Model of Multi-level Governance', Sid Noel (ed.), *From Power Sharing to Democracy: Post-Conflict Institutions in Ethnically Divided Societies,* London, 2005, 215-38.
8. *New York Times*, 2 January 2003.
9. *Financial Times*, London, 15 December 2002.
10. Foremost among the pro-Annan columnists was veteran journalist Mehmet Ali Birand. See his 'Turks have won in Cyprus', *Milliyet*, Istanbul, 16 November 2002.
11. Interview with Fikret Bila, *Milliyet*, Istanbul, 20 December 2004.
12. *Agence France-Presse* (English), 19 December 2003.
13. 'Why, mutter some Turkish diplomats, should 200,000 or so people in northern Cyprus scupper the European ambitions of 69 million plus Turks?' *The Economist*, 16 January 2003.
14. Economist Intelligence Unit, *Country Report: Cyprus*, December 2000.
15. *Yeniduzen*, Nicosia, 3 October 2002.
16. Economist Intelligence Unit, *Country Report: Cyprus*, December 2002.
17. *Anatolia News Agency*, Ankara, 19 December 2003.
18. BBC, *Monitoring Europe*, 11 April 2004.

PART IV
THE AFTERMATH

Chapter 18

REUNIFYING CYPRUS: ESSENTIAL CHALLENGES

Robert I. Rotberg

Because the Republic of Cyprus is such a success, there are few real (as distinct from romantic or political) incentives for comprehensive bargaining over reunification with the 38 per cent of the island that it claims as its own, *de jure*, but since the traumatic events of 1974 has been controlled, *de facto*, by Turkey and the unrecognized (but seemingly 'sovereign') Turkish Republic of North Cyprus. The biggest obstacle to a negotiated settlement of outstanding differences – to the acceptance of a reconfigured Annan Plan or something better – is that the *status quo* works and has long worked, especially for south Cyprus. Few shots are fired across the green line; UN soldiers and monitors have little to do except to watch Cypriots and tourists cross the green line in both directions.

Every term of ordinary discourse – sovereign, *de jure, de facto,* controlled rather than occupied – is bitterly contested and controversial. But, in late 2008, any discussions capable of leading to a lasting solution to the Cyprus problem – to removing its continued bifurcation – must accept the facts on the ground. They trump history and injury and must, inevitably, influence the kinds of compromises that could conceivably lead to a successfully negotiated, sustainable, reunification of the two parts of the island.

The facts, at least for concerned and well-acquainted outsiders, start with the reality that southern Cypriots, mostly Greek-speaking, are content, prosperous, and well governed. With annual GDPs per capita at the upper end of the European continuum, with their membership in the European monetary union, and with few inhibitions (except the availability of water) to their continued growth as citizens of a thriving little nation-state, geo-strategically they hardly require the reunification of the island. Admittedly, for historic reasons and for reasons of national pride, the Republic of Cyprus wants 'its' territory back, wants Turkish soldiers off the island, wants its citizens to have their properties returned, and supports a 'right of return' for the dispossessed and their descendants. Those desires are natural and cannot be gainsaid. But they are not sought at any price. In fact, since the rebuff to the Annan Plan by referendum failure in 2004, southern Cypriots have been able to respond lazily and comfortably to the mixed rewards of potential reunification. Southern politicians also well know the political dangers of conceding too much, if anything, to the north in order to clinch a deal.

In the north, on the other hand, Turkish Cypriots are eager for reunification. Their annual per capita GDPs would improve, possibly as much as five-fold (over time) through inclusion in the European Union (EU), greatly expanded trade, freedom of movement and access to employment opportunities within Cyprus and the EU, the considerable benefits of the Euro versus the long inflated Turkish Lira, greater tourism revenues, and becoming part of a globally recognized polity. North Cyprus is well led and well governed, a great change from the long perverse rule of Rauf Denktash, father of the disputed northern republic.[1] Under Denktash, there were many disincentives to union, most of which have now been erased. President Mehmet Ali Talat, Denktash's liberal successor, is eager, unlike Denktash, to lead northern Cypriots into a union with the south. He is well positioned, too, to persuade the Turkish military and the Turkish state to let their people go. Furthermore, Talat presides far less than his predecessor over a corrupt, and corrupted, satrapy of Turkey and of the oligarchical securo-class that then ruled Turkey.

Fortunately, too, the political stars of modern Turkey are aligned in favor of a Cypriot reunion: Turkey wants to smooth its possible entry into the EU. By shedding north Cyprus and regularizing its testy relations with the Republic of Cyprus, Turkey would be able to remove several of the remaining obstacles to entry.

What could conceivably revive and sustain the negotiations that seemed so promising and so close to success when UN Special Representative Alvaro de Soto was shuttling back and forth between President Glafcos Clerides and Denktash from 2002 to 2004? EU and United States pressure on both sides to conclude an agreement was strong then and could be more relentless now, if a serious new plan were on the table, or if Talat and President Demetris Christofias of the Republic of Cyprus sat down and decided (as Clerides and Denktash might have done) their communities' respective futures.[2] The Annan Plan, discredited in south Cyprus as it is, still contains the seeds of solution or, more likely, abundant detail on subsidiary issues that empowered negotiators could deploy to great effect.

Good negotiators seek agreements that respond to the needs of the contending parties. Annan's team tried in early 2004 to gain Turkish and TRNC support. Their final plan permitted numerous Turkish troops to remain in the north and limited the number of Greek-Cypriots who would be allowed to return to their old (pre-1974) homes there. It also curtailed the rights of Greek-speakers to vote in the north.

Annan IV (modified from the 2003 and 2002 versions) also called for a weak federation of two largely autonomous states.[3] But Greek-Cypriots viewed the proposed federal arrangement as too limited, giving Turkish-Cypriots an unwanted veto over federal decisions. They believed that the Annan Plan inserted a Turkish Trojan horse into their midst forever.

In Annan IV, Greek-speaking and Turkish-speaking Cypriots were to share executive and legislative functions according to a complicated formula that gave the numerically fewer Turkish-speakers (18 per cent of the population of the island) an equal say. Greece, Turkey (with its troops), and Britain were to guarantee the contemplated agreement, and a UN force would continue to oversee peace on the island.

Turkey and some of the anti-Denktash TRNC leaders welcomed Annan's last minute concessions. Yet, not unexpectedly, the concessions to the north and Turkey appeared perfidious in the south, and southerners overwhelmingly rejected the Annan Plan, which northerners approved.[4] The task today is to negotiate a settlement that draws on the detailed compromises of the Annan Plan but which explicitly eschews the concessions that led to the Plan's rejection in the south.

The biggest hurdles that must now be overcome mirror the failure of the Annan negotiations. The overriding issues are largely what they were: providing personal security and freedom from discrimination for Turkish-speakers within a reunited island, creating a political formula to distribute power within the island and across both communities, inventing a mechanism that respects that formula and provides a means for non-stalemated effective island-wide government, and – conceivably – innovating a method whereby, over time, Cypriot nationality would trump communal affiliation.[5] That last item is difficult to imagine now, but creating a minimalist confederation – simply linking two polities in a simplistic fashion – bodes less well for success than a grand architectural statement that genuinely tries to unite over time the two communities as communities of Cypriots as well as of both the separate entities and polities.

When the author worked as an American with a small group of powerful Greek-speaking and Turkish-speaking Cypriots (collectively the Cyprus Study Group) between 1999 and 2003, several answers to these key questions suggested themselves. Those answers were never 'agreed upon' in full, particularly since any agreements within the group would have compromised or reflected adversely upon negotiations being carried out episodically but concurrently by de Soto, Clerides, and Denktash. Likewise, the Study Group had only an informal standing. No one within it was empowered to speak for either side. But, once blaming the other side was eschewed and some modicum of trust was established, lessons were learned that bear directly on the central choices remaining if a reunited Cyprus is an objective for which politicians on both sides, and in Turkey, are prepared to bargain about. The long term result would obviously be better for all of Cyprus and for all Cypriots – providing that the comfort of the existing status quo can be superseded in political and constituent minds by the possibility of something much better for everyone.

What follows is an ambitious, non-politically correct, reality-grounded, audacious, intensely controversial proposal covering several of the key issues that conceptually separate south and north Cyprus and bar easy settlement. They carry certain key concepts well beyond the Annan Plan, particularly since the Annan Plan was designed to appeal to a north Cypriot situation that no longer exists. By so doing, the Annan Plan forfeited support in the south, so simply dusting off the Annan Plan and moving forward will not work. The only approach that will work must challenge both north and south to think freshly about Cyprus' future, and about how a rewarding future will best be achieved within the EU.

Each of these bold ideas is heavily contested, and with reason, for any partial or complete acceptance of the suggestions set out below would alter both political landscapes considerably, reconfigure the power valences of the two sides, and conceivably end a stalemate that has benefited two sets of political elites. However, drawing together Cypriots through the rearrangements suggested below could secure the minority its rights and remove its fears, being within the European Community, while simultaneously reinvigorating the majority and, indeed, all of Cyprus. One Cyprus will grow more effectively than its parts. The whole will produce more political goods for the inhabitants of the island than a mere sum of two parts.

Sharing Power

Finding a way to share power is the major, if not the only, serious obstacle to a conclusive agreement capable of bridging the two sides and satisfying the needs and aspirations of each. At present, and effectively since 1974, each of the two polities that comprises Cyprus exercises power within its own domain. That power is fettered only by the Acquis Communitaire in the case of south Cyprus and Turkish law and military preferences in the case of north Cyprus. Denktash never really wanted to give up the considerable power that he wielded in north Cyprus, and so never really wished for a comprehensive settlement. Clerides, on the other hand, was prepared to concede a soupcon of power, or maybe considerably more, to end the 'Cyprus problem' and reunite the island. Talat's approach is rather different from Denktash's, and his motives and sentiments markedly refreshing. The key question is how much will President Demetris Christofias and his south Cyprus associates concede? Will they fully share power over the island?

The Annan Plan never developed an effective formula for sharing power. By 'effective' is meant a scheme capable of providing enduring incentives to both sides and enduring stakes for both sides in the island's future. The sticking point in the Study Group and with the Annan Plan was proportionality. South Cyprus' population is at least five times greater than the population in the north. Moreover, about half of the north's current population is composed of immigrants from Anatolia since 1974. The numbers of Turkish Cypriots now resident full-time in north Cyprus may be fewer than 100,000. Are the northerners, for the sake of a stake in Europe, prepared to share power ceremonially and in terms of certain reserved questions on a 50-50 basis, but legislative and constitutional power only on the basis of population shares, two-thirds to a generous one third? That is the central question.

Conclusive answers to that fundamental question assume a federated state, as in the Annan Plan, with each of the communally based and territorially circumscribed entities being solely responsible (*de jure and de facto*) for a set of enumerated local functions. Those could include entrusting each (subordinate) entity with authority over local law and order, education, health and hospitals, and religious/heritage affairs. Each entity would have a legislature and an executive, as at present. Both would be elected as they now are.

But superimposed above both entities, and responsible to both halves of the island rather than to both communal polities, would be a central government – the United States of Cyprus. The USC would be responsible for multilevel legislative coordination, setting island-wide standards and regulations, and meeting international legal and political obligations. It could not override the powers and responsibilities reserved for the two communal entities, but it would be charged with administering island-wide functions such as customs, fishing policy, open ship-registering and maritime regulation, civil aviation, trade, foreign affairs, granting citizenship and passports, regulating immigration, sanitation, agriculture, tourism, economic development, and so on. There would be a central bank, supervising the banking systems in both entities, but the currency and many regulations would now be European, rather than Cypriot. The USC would control defense and security, subject to international arrangements and the phasing out of all foreign troops, and, possibly, the extraterritorial bases. It would create a border protection force or gendarmerie.

The USC would set standards and safeguard the environment by regulating the island-wide commons and developing energy and water policies. It would supervise an overall heritage policy (coordinating and liaising with the two communities), develop a joint postal system, build and maintain national highways as distinct from communal roads (on the US federal/state and Australian models), and administer policy for telecommunications and the Internet.

The USC could usefully adopt a bill of rights modeled on the US Bill of Rights, or embrace the European Convention on Human Rights as its own bill of rights. A supreme court would be established with jurisdiction over the entire island. It would hear cases brought under the bill of rights, decide inter-entity questions, and serve as an appellate body for cases emerging out of disputes within the entities. Whether the supreme court should have appellate jurisdiction in criminal matters as well as civil disputes should be decided in the final negotiations.

The USC would need its own budget, prepared by the new executive and approved by the new parliament. Central revenues would come from customs fees, shipping registry charges, a value added tax administered island-wide, and a limited income tax. Alternatively, both entities could tax exclusively within their domains and transfer stated proportions of their tax revenues to the central government, but there would be fewer disputes in the future if the central government possessed robust taxing authority.

The central government would occupy federal space and buildings along the green line, with a tiny Canberra or Brasilia carved out of what presently is UN space. The USC would have its own territory, its own police force, and its own bureaucracy. It would function in Turkish, Greek, and English. Those language rights would be entrenched; nothing would destroy bi-communal harmony in the formative years of the USC more than discrimination (as in Sri Lanka's relegating of Tamil to a lesser status during its early years) against Turkish-speakers.

The USC will require an enlightened central executive to organize and administer island-wide responsibilities, and ensure harmony among and between the two communities. Although some of the parliamentary arrangements suggested below might tend to focus power in majority hands, there are a number of artful ways by which power can be shared rather than monopolized.

The Executive

For that reason the USC will want to rotate executive authority for stated terms, either in the institution of a prime minister elected by parliament (see below) or in the institution of an executive president, again elected island-wide (see below) or by parliament. The principle of rotation between persons from each language group would be important in boosting confidence within each community. But (see below) the two prime ministers or executive presidents could (and preferably would) come from the same political party or loosely affiliated political grouping. The leader of the executive could rotate every year, but, given the same party affiliation and a prime minister/deputy prime minister arrangement (with each coming from one of the languages groups) there could be continuity of policy and executive direction even if the titular leader only served for a year and then gave way to his deputy or someone else from the other language.

It is true that the USC could also be organized to enjoy co-presidents, one from each language grouping, with the presidents being the current and future presidents of the bi-communal entities. If that is a preferred outcome, then the co-presidents should preferably be ceremonial, with limited powers. The executive function would in that case best be exercised by a prime minister.

Alternatively, the current and future bi-communal heads could share or, better, rotate, presidential executive responsibilities. For periods of up to a year, the same person would under this scheme lead both the USC and one of its sub-state entities. Such an arrangement might win parochial support, but it would reduce the long-term stature of the USC and the leader of the USC. It would also take away from one critical (and controversial) component of this proposal: that the USC should be an instrument for uniting rather than dividing Cypriots. Anything that emphasizes separation and division would derogate from the underlying goals of the USC.

Given the popularity of parliamentary systems within the EU, given the familiarity of parliamentary systems to Cypriots more generally, and given the innovative manner by which the parliament in the USC could be elected (see below), among the various organizational choices for the new central government an executive prime minister chosen by parliament and two rotating ceremonial presidents chosen alternatively by each community, commends itself. That arrangement is simple to conceive and understand, and would place the new Cyprus on a footing similar to many countries in Europe, and elsewhere.

The prime minister's cabinet would run the USC and organize governmental business. The prime minister would allocate ministerial portfolios to members of his/her team and he/she and members of the team would report to and be questioned by parliament. The rotating ceremonial presidents would receive foreign representatives and other dignitaries, represent the USC in all heads of state functions, appoint judges subject to parliamentary ratification, and receive the election and/or retirement of governments.

The executive, whether ceremonial or not, could be elected by popular vote, with both communities voting together as one island constituency, or separately. If the presidency rotated, voters could choose a Greek-speaker one year and a Turkish-speaker one or two years later. Parliament could also make the choice, again by majority vote, with both chambers (see below) having to agree.

Presidential powers could include all of the usual representational functions, such as receiving foreign and EU leaders; summoning and dismissing parliamentary governments, appointing special commissions, commanding the gendarmerie, and nominating members of the supreme court. Because this last, critical, responsibility is so important in maintaining cross-ethnic trust, the president's nominees would have to be drawn equally from both communities, and from a panel of names approved by a judicial services commission (itself composed of representatives from both communities). Both houses of parliament would have to approve the president's nominees.

Parliament and Parliamentary Powers

Given the nearly half-century of political friction between Greek- and Turkish-speaking Cypriots, there will be an instinctive distrust of power-sharing. A credibly organized parliament rather than an all-powerful presidency could reduce distrust and foster amicable relations between the island's two peoples. A two-house parliament could enhance legitimacy and strengthen the acceptability of a new, power-sharing, central government in the two entities. The lower house, as in most such arrangements, would initiate legislation and be the lawmaker of first instance. But the upper house would be able to modify legislation promulgated in the lower house and exercise a limited, but trust-building, form of veto. It would provide a check on the otherwise all-powerful lower house. The composition of both bodies would obviously be critical to the success of any power-sharing scheme.

One way of alleviating concerns about a majority failing to respect the rights of the minority would be to link the lower house, with its popularly elected representatives and its population-linked Greek-speaking predominance of members, to an upper house with equal representation from the constituent states. An upper house of 50 delegates could either be elected from the two communities or appointed by the heads of the two entities, 25 members from each of the entities. The upper house would be able to delay legislation and, under prescribed circumstances, to veto proposed laws. Those powers, providing that they are reasonable and modest, and prudently exercised, could offer necessary security to the weaker of the two entities composing the USC. They could be designed in such a way as to prevent invidious measures being enacted, especially during the early and anxious years of this constitutional and nation-building experiment.

Those upper house powers would explicitly counter any tendency by the lower house to infringe upon minority rights, alter pre-settlement agreements, or impose injurious laws on the less populous of the two entities (EU rules would also preclude such discrimination.) The lower house would be able to pass legislation by a simple majority, and budgets and spending measures by a 60 per cent majority. But 70 or 60 of 100 seats would be allocated according to population numbers to the south, with 40 or 30 being northern seats. Such numerical arrangements would accord well with the two communal populations, over-weighting – as an incentive for settlement purposes – the number of seats allocated to the north.

Parliament, in the most direct procedure, would elect a prime minister from among its ranks. A ruling party or a ruling coalition would presumably carry the vote, as in most parliamentary systems.

Although entity legislatures would make their own laws, as at present, a central parliament would craft laws for the entire island. However, the entities would have a narrower range than present of the subjects on which they could enact laws – a major difference from the Annan Plan. The island-wide government would also have prescribed jurisdictions. Even so, because the USC would have broader responsibilities than the entities, the configuration and procedures of such a legislative body would be critical to the acceptability and workability of a USC parliament and to the acceptability of power sharing in general. Without a broadly based and broadly legitimate central authority, the USC would be unable to function. Indeed, given the experience of the first Cyprus Republic, where deadlocks quickly led to a sundering of the seemingly strong arrangements brokered by the outgoing colonial authority, the establishment of the USC should include hardly any mechanisms that are subject to later interpretation. Ambiguity is only useful in constitution making when all parties are united on overarching goals.

Any proposed distribution of power between two communities who have learned since the 1960s, if not before, to distrust each other's motives and methods, is bound to be controversial. The two populations are greatly disparate, particularly since so much time has passed since 1974. Their share of the island, 38 per cent in the north and 62 per cent in the south, are much closer in size than their populations, but all of the territory in the north is obviously contested by the south and there are serious southern grievances over usurped villages and towns. Given such considerations, the distribution of seats in the lower house of parliament provides a proxy place for the discussion and possible channeling of the fears and ambitions of both communities. That is where power is normally exercised in democratic states and, if the USC is to come into being, the legislature is the appropriate arena in which Cypriot political differences should be aired and disputes resolved.

Any USC experiment would collapse if parliament became an institution to serve majority interests only, or predominantly. If the USC is to work, it must work for both communities, and most of all must be viewed as a Cypriot institution, not a southern one. That is why separate elections for parliamentary seats from constituencies demarcated within each community, even if a 70-30 or 60-40 split could somehow be agreed, would produce no gains in intercommunal harmony and could lead to intensified enmity.

Although an 80-20 split represents the real approximate population ratio of the two communities, the north has always demanded parity in parliament (or in decision-making overall) as a condition of a negotiated settlement. Since insisting on parity will likely produce a bargaining stalemate rather than concessions or victory, it is important to find an innovative formula for parliamentary elections that gives both communities, not just one, a direct stake in the electoral outcome.

The answer for Cyprus, and an answer that could conceivably persuade the north to accept a 70-30 or 60-40 distribution of parliamentary seats, involves one of several methods of compelling candidates for parliament to canvas for votes from both communities, not just one. As a condition of election, each candidate for parliament would have to seek support from both Turkish- and Greek-speakers; no one could be elected without, say, receiving a minimum number of votes (perhaps 20 per cent of their total) from the other community or more votes from the other language constitutency than her/his competitors. These approaches, used occasionally in national elections in a few countries, are called cross voting. They give bi-communal issues precedence over more narrow communal interests. They further favor candidates who can appeal to both communities over those whose appeals are more secular. This method would help to diminish communalism and, over time, and with the creation of political parties that are island-wide rather than community-based, can and should lead to electoral and parliamentary mind-sets that are more island- than communally-based. The idea is to make it impossible in the USC for Greek Cypriot or Turkish Cypriot legislators to be elected without a measure (however modest) of support from the linguistic community that is not their own.[6]

The same results, and some of the same effects of social engineering, can be achieved by other helpful methods of casting and counting ballots. Instead of individual candidates campaigning in both communities in the first-past-the-post manner, all candidates could be paired, one Turkish Cypriot and one Greek Cypriot. They would seek dual seats, and neither could win without the other winning as well. They would be seated in parliament as paired representatives. If co-presidents, or even rotating presidents were the preferred pattern for the USC executive, this pairing approach could also be employed at the presidential level for elections. In other words, two presidents would be chosen at the same time, by popular vote. By definition, the pairings would have to appeal beyond the confessional group from which they came.

A variant method for parliamentary elections would have voters by proportional representation or by the preferential list method choose from slates containing stipulated numbers of both Greek- and Turkish-speakers. Each party list would, say, have 70-30 or 60-40 candidates from the two communities. They would share an ideology or a set of policies. By definition, those policy frameworks and ideologies would not be confessional and would have, perforce, to appeal across linguistic barriers.

These (and other) innovative methods of electing parliamentarians and presidents and thus appealing beyond or over confessionalism could in time conceivably encourage a renewed sense of Cypriot, rather than Greek Cypriot or Turkish Cypriot nationalism and loyalties. Indeed, the nature of Cyprus – the fact that both communities are Cypriot and share a Cypriot culture, Cypriot cuisine, and a Cypriot approach to the common law despite different languages and religions and the bitter separation since 1974 – argues for a constitutional arrangement that would permit the two communities to grow closer together over time within a united, still communally defined, Cyprus.

Right of Return and Freedom of Movement

As in the Israeli-Palestinian case, one of the unresolved issues in Cyprus concerns rights of return. In principle, both sides now agree that all refugees are entitled to a right of return. But so much time has passed since the pogroms and ethnic cleansing of the 1960s, and since the enforced exodus of the 1970s, that many questions remain regarding who it is that rightfully qualifies as a refugee or an internally displaced person. Is it the actual persons pushed out of their homes only? Or do descendants qualify? And how many generations of descendants should qualify?

No one has a clear picture of the numbers involved. Nor does anyone on either side actually know how many elderly refugees or their heirs would now wish to return 'home,' given the entirely new situations that have been created and the prosperous nature of virtually all of their new livelihoods and living arrangements. Nevertheless, the right of return issue remains politically salient, notably in the south. It cannot be brushed aside.

Thus, any negotiated settlement will have to provide for an absolute right of return in principle. But the politicians on both sides, and the UN negotiating team, long ago accepted that, in practice, any right of return had to be restricted, and regulated by the bi-communal entities.[7] Such a right of return would in practice be limited according to the absorptive capacity of each entity. That means that the availability of schools and public structures, among other considerations, would have to be taken into account before refugees in large numbers could stream back to their old homes. One first step would be to create a register so that property owners could stipulate what they hoped to do with their pre-1974 properties.

A further way of diminishing the potential impact of any right of return, and therefore removing impediments to a settlement, would be to allow the right of return to be exercised for a limited period only – perhaps a short one year from the conclusion of the settlement negotiations. In practice, too, the right of return could be restricted to refugees or returnees who were born before some cut-off date, perhaps 1974.

Those who did not choose to exercise a right of return, but were eligible, could be compensated from EU or US and British funds. Almost everyone assumes that most eligible refugees would prefer compensation to the uncertainties of a return to much altered surroundings.

Now that Cypriots from both sides enjoy freedom of movement on the island, this question, which bedeviled earlier negotiations and was an important feature of the Annan Plan, should be easy to resolve. Any settlement concluded by both sides will presumably include the removal of internal border controls; only the external borders will be patrolled. The USC would be responsible for immigration and customs arrangements. Citizenship, possibly after a transitional period, would be island-wide. Passports and other documentation would be provided by the USC and the EU, thus assisting in the lessening of differences between northern and southern Cypriots. Indeed, more forward looking Cypriots have often envisaged that belonging to the EU, with its protective mantle and expansive human rights purview, provided the best if not the only answer to northern Cypriot anxieties. It would also become an antidote to southern Cypriot chauvinism.

Territorial Adjustments

The resolution of disputes over land – tangible, physical, assets – are always difficult to conclude, even after larger questions of power sharing are decided. The Cyprus case is no different: southern Cypriots, the losers in the 1974 war, seek a major territorial adjustment that aligns more closely (if never perfectly) to the vast population disparities between the two sides. The Annan Plan included imaginative and detailed proposals that would trade territory, return a long-neglected section of Famagusta to the south, and – most important – provide a mechanism outside of the settlement agreement for the enduring resolution of any lasting land questions.

Essentially, three principles should govern the thorny conclusion of questions involving territory:
1. Preference should be given to territory that before 1974 was densely populated by Greek-speaking Cypriots.
2. The dislocation of Turkish-speaking Cypriots should be minimized.
3. The demographical configuration of northern Cyprus should not be altered drastically in order to achieve politically inspired territorial recaptures.

Additionally, by transferring critical segments of Turkish-controlled territory, the pent-up demands of southern refugee groups should be assuaged, or at least balanced. Overall, Greek-Cypriots want far more territory transferred than Turkish-Cypriots are likely to give. Northerners talk about 5 to 8 per cent, southerners 25 to 20 per cent, so there is an expectational gap which needs imaginatively to be bridged.

But the transfer of such a large amount of land, or of any land in any amounts, would depend on where the land was situated, whether urban or rural, and given principles 2 and 3 above, whether the impact on northern Cypriots was bearable. (Southern Cypriots would like to distinguish for all negotiating purposes between pre-1974 northern Cypriots and post-1974 northern Cypriots – the Anatolian immigrant issue – but such distinctions may be difficult to draw given the contemporary composition of the northern electorate.)

Neither the refugee nor the territorial adjustment issue can be resolved fully in the throes of a negotiated settlement. Major approaches and guiding principles can be agreed, but the details – who is to be permitted to exercise a right of return and which lands are transferred and how they are demarcated – must be determined by bi-partisan commissions of experts. Depoliticizing such determinations will be important, especially if the leaders on both sides understand how vital it will be to remove such controversial questions from contentious discourse.

Strengthening Security

No negotiated settlement is possible without the withdrawal of Turkish troops from the north. Whether that repatriation of the Turkish army should take place immediately upon the conclusion of a settlement, or gradually, over several years, could be open to discussion. But once the federated Cyprus contemplated in this chapter is agreed, the troops should go home. They would only serve as an irritant in the new Cyprus, and an impediment to the sustainable reunification of the island.

Although the USC will want a border patrol and a coast guard, as befits an island nation-state, the new Cyprus needs no army. So the island effectively can be demilitarized. Doing so would contribute to long-term harmony on the island, and enable the USC to develop itself without military preparations and expenditures. Each entity would employ a police contingent, and the USC itself would have a police force. Beyond those lightly armed groups, Cyprus would be able to prosper without major arsenals.

Given the experiences under the first republic, however, and given the massive military might of Turkey, Cypriots should have one or more guarantors of the reunification contemplated by the USC. Greece, Turkey, and Britain supposedly safeguarded the first republic, but that combination failed then and in a crisis would fail again. NATO, as a trans-Atlantic institution that includes Turkey and Greece, could substitute for any new combination of guaranteeing nations. NATO is pan-European, and is larger than Europe and includes the United States – all advantages. A radical but helpful idea for the first, say, five years of the USC would be to station small NATO contingents on the island as visible reminders of their guaranteeing presence. They might also be empowered by the terms of the negotiated settlement to intervene under particular, narrow, circumstances, and certainly to prevent any invasions. If they could, it would provide security assurances to anxious members of the minority and the majority.

Historical Clarification

Although opening up old wounds is always problematical when deeply felt and long-standing divides are bridged by a final, unifying peace settlement, the Cyprus Study Group and other leading Cypriots envisaged the potential benefits of some kind of Cyprus truth commission or, more narrowly, a commission charged with the clarification of contested history. Such a commission exercise could strengthen the broad acceptability of a negotiated settlement, and remove from the peace conference itself any need for discussions of "blame" for atrocities. With a commission looking backward, the negotiated settlement itself could peer relentlessly forward.

There have been truth commission type investigations into the troubled pasts of more than thirty post-conflict countries from Argentina to Sri Lanka. The South African Truth and Reconciliation Commission is the best known, but it need not provide the only model for investigations into the events of the 1960s and 1970s in Cyprus.[8]

The new USC and the new Cyprus will need, gradually, a shared history. Indeed, a truly shared history will make the forging of a reunited Cypriot nationality easier and more robust. Such a shared sense of the past is impossible without the stakeholders – the bi-communal citizens – together writing that history, resolving disputes, parceling out blame, and putting the bitter insults and injuries of the past into a shared framework.

Truth commissions seek to provide answers to victims and to offer closure to societies torn by years or decades of conflict. South Africa assumed that it could understand and to some extent expurgate itself of apartheid and apartheid's abuses by hearing the testimony of 22,000 victims and receiving and adjudicating the amnesty petitions of 7,500 South African perpetrators or accomplices. South Africa, thanks to publicly televised hearings and almost continuous press coverage and discussion for five years, believed that it could 'move forward' and put the baleful events of its white-black enmity behind it. South Africa, subsequent to the Truth and Reconciliation hearings, could also begin to write a truthful history acceptable to all contending parties.

The new Cyprus will need a mutually acceptable history that includes a painful unraveling of the events of the 1960s and 1970s.[9] Who did what to whom? – just the facts – and where and when? Such a useful record can best be compiled by a variant on the truth commission process called a historical clarification commission. It would be a bi-communal exercise, with members being appointed by the USC president or co-presidents from among the ranks of sages, historians, and jurists. Such a commission's task would be to sift the tragedies of the past (specific time bounds would have to be set down in the enabling legislation) and apportion appropriate responsibility to governments, vigilantes, guerillas, or others. The Commission's staff would scrutinize the available public evidence and search the non-public records of the Republic of Cyprus and the Turkish Republic of North Cyprus. The Commission would hold public hearings and compel testimony from persons with evidence concerning ethnic cleansing or other past incidents.

Its actions would not be those of a truth commission. The Cyprus commission would not seek 'truth' in such a volatile context. 'Truth' would be difficult to ascertain. Even holding public hearings when so many 'victims' had died would be difficult and contentious, and could reopen the wounds that the negotiated settlement is supposed to close. But the establishment of a historical clarification commission would constitute a trust restoring measure. It would bring healing to the wounds of both communities. It would encourage their members to acknowledge responsibility for attacks and other lapses, to acknowledge personal responsibility, and to apologize. The mere establishment of such a commission would be a confidence building measure and would facilitate broader comity among the communities. In exceptional instances, the Commission might also recommend financial compensation to individuals, villages, or particular sections of either community.

Confidence Building

No matter how carefully and openly the reunification of the island is negotiated, it will be important for the new central government and the subsidiary governments to build confidence throughout the island. A USC ministry of rapprochement could sponsor a host of bi-communal confidence enhancing measures and attempt to broker an atmosphere of mutual respect. Some of those initiatives would include improving what would be the mutual infrastructure of the country. A commitment to spend large sums on, say, the harbors, airfields, and roads of both sides of the island would be an excellent start. Enhancing hospitals, schools, and so on, with EU funds channeled through the USC, would be welcome. So would southern investments in the north, and vice-versa. A promise to teach Greek in the schools in the north and Turkish in the south would be ideal. Creating a cross-communal public television station with programs in three languages would be a positive gesture. Obviously, there would be many projects for young people that would be designed to bring Turkish- and Greek-speaking Cypriots closer together once again.

Selling the Plan

The suggestions for settlement laid out in this chapter will be too radical for many Cypriots. Nevertheless, they commend themselves because nothing less radical and less transformational has a chance of bringing Turkish-speaking and Greek-speaking Cypriots together. Nothing else permits the two sides to risk working together within a common framework for a common goal. Fortunately, many obstacles to a possible settlement have been removed by the ascendance of new leading personalities in the north and south, by the closer fitting of south Cyprus into the European Union, and by the realization in so many quarters that the status quo, peaceful as it is, cannot unleash the potential of an island such as Cyprus. Only reunification, and the end of thirty-plus years of living together tensely, side by side, will give Cyprus and Cypriots an opportunity to grow economically and socially.

ENDNOTES

1. For Denktash, see Robert I. Rotberg, 'Timing is Almost Everything: Obstructionist Leadership, Cypriot Style,' *Fletcher Forum of World Affairs,* XXVIII, 2004, 199-208; Also Michalis S. Michael, 'The Cyprus Peace Talks: A Critical Appraisal,' *Journal of Peace Research,* XLIV, 2007, 592.
2. Serious talks about reunification have occurred throughout 2008. Actual negotiations were beginning in September 2008 as this book went to press.
3. For a sensible analysis of Annan IV, and earlier versions, see Christalla Yakinthou, *Between Scylla and Charybdis: Cyprus and the Problem of Engineering Political Settlements for Divided Socities,* unpublished PhD thesis, U. of Western Australia, 2007, 108-140.
4. For comments on the referendum's failure in the south, see Michael, 'The Cyprus Peace Talks: A Critical Appraisal,' 597-598.
5. For a well-considered treatment of Cypriotism, see Neophytos G. Loizides, 'Ethnic Nationalism and Adaptation in Cyprus,' *International Studies Perspectives,* VIII, 2007, 172-189.
6. For a discussion of cross-voting with specific reference to Cyprus, see Neophytos Loizides and Eser Kerkiner, 'The Aftermath of the Annan Plan Referendums: Cross-Voting Moderation for Cyprus?' *Southeast European Politics,* V, 2004, 158-171.
7. See Michael, 'The Cyprus Peace Talks: A Critical Appraisal,' 591-592.
8. See Robert I. Rotberg and Dennis Thompson (eds.), *Truth v Justice: The Morality of Truth Commissions,* Princeton, 2000.
9. See also Yakinthou, 'Engineering Political Settlements', 78-107.

SELECTED BIBLIOGRAPHY

The Comprehensive Settlement of the Cyprus Problem as finalised on 31 March 2004 [The Annan Plan/AnnanV] http://www.unficyp.org/media/Other%20official%20documents/annanplan.pdf

Alexandrou, Christina, *The Days that Shocked Cyprus: An Evaluation of the Campaigns on the Annan Plan*, Cypriot Students and Young Scientists Organisation, (Nicosia: ISCHYS, 2004).

Alexiou, Alexis, Gurel, Ayla, Hatay, Mete & Taki, Yiouli, *The Annan Plan for Cyprus: A Citizen's Guide* (Oslo: International Peace Research Institute, 2003).

Alexiou, Alexis, Gurel, Ayla, Hatay, Mete & Taki, Yiouli, *The Property Regime in the Annan Plan: A Citizens' Guide* (Oslo: International Peace Research Institute, 2003).

Alivizatos, Nikos, 'Τα Συνταγματικά του Σχεδίου Ανάν' (Constitutional Issues of the Annan Plan), *Geostratigiki*, I (2003).

American Hellenic Institute. Statement on the UN Annan Proposal for Settlement of the Cyprus Problem, http://unannanplan.agrino.org/AHI.htm (2004).

Anastasiou, Harry, 'Nationalism as a Deterrent to Peace and Interethnic Democracy: The Failure of Nationalist Leadership from the Hague Talks to the Cyprus Referendum', *International Studies Perspectives*, VIII (2007).

Argerious III, John Louis, 'The Annan Plan for Cyprus: Why the Neutral Voter Said 'No'', *Florida State University D-Scholarship Repository,* Article 46 (2005).

Attalides, Michael, 'The Political Process in Cyprus and the Day After the Referendum', *The Cyprus Review,* XVI, 1 (2004).

Bahcheli, Tozun & Noel, Sid, 'Power-Sharing for Cyprus (again)? EU Accession and the Prospects for Reunification Under a Belgian Model of Multi-level Governance', Sid Noel (ed.), *From Power Sharing to Democracy: Post-Conflict Institutions in Ethnically Divided Societies* (London: McGill-Queens University Press, 2005).

Bahcheli, Tozun, 'Saying Yes to EU Accession: Explaining the Turkish Cypriot Referendum and its Aftermath', *The Cyprus Review,* XVI, 2 (2004).

Bahcheli, Tozun, 'Searching for a Cyprus Settlement: Considering Options for Creating a Federation, a Confederation, or Two Independent States', *Publius,* XXX, 1-2 (2000).

Baier-Allen, Susanne M., 'So Near and Yet So Far: Elusive Settlement in Cyprus', *Hellenic Studies,* XI, 2 (2003).

Birand, Mehmet Ali, 'Papadopoulos Has Saved Us From Our Complex', *The Cyprus Review,* XVI, 2 (2004).

Bryant, Rebecca, 'A Dangerous Trend in Cyprus' *Middle East Report Online,* vol. 235 (2005).

Bryant, Rebecca, 'An Ironic Result in Cyprus', *Middle East Report Online* (2004).

Bryant, Rebecca, *Imagining the Modern: The Cultures of Nationalism in Cyprus* (London: I. B. Taurus, 2004).

Camp, Glen D., 'Cyprus and East Mediterranean Security Problems: New Developments – Old Problems', *The Cyprus Review,* XVI, 2, (2004).

Carko lu, Ali & Sözen, Ahmet, 'The Turkish Cypriot Elections of December 2003: Setting the Stage for Resolving the Cyprus Conflict,' *South European Society & Politics*, 9/3 (2004).

Carras, Costa, 'Greek-Turkish Forum – First Public Event, March 2002 – Cyprus: Year of Decision', *The Cyprus Review*, XIV, 1 (2002).

Christophorou, Christophoros & Webster, Craig, 'Greek Cypriots, Turkish Cypriots and the Future: The Day after the Referendum', A Development Associates Occasional Paper in Democracy and Governance, No.16th, http://www.devassoc.com/msword/occpap16.doc (2004).

Christophorous, Christophorou, 'An Old Cleavage Causes New Divisions: Parliamentary Elections in the Republic of Cyprus, 21 May 2006', *South European Society and Politics*, XII, 1 (2007).

Christophorous, Christophorou, 'Party Change and Development in Cyprus (1995-2005)', *South European Society and Politics*, XI, 3 (2006).

Christophorous, Christophorou, 'The Vote for a United Cyprus Deepens Divisions: The 24 April 2004 Referenda in Cyprus', *South European Society and Politics*, X, 1 (2005).

Chrysogonos, Costas, 'Η πρόταση του ΓΓ του ΟΗΕ για Νέο Σύνταγμα' (UNSG's Proposal for a New Cypriot Constitution), *Geostratigiki*, I (2003).

Constantinou, Costas M. & Papadakis, Yiannis, 'The Cypriot State(s) *in situ*: Cross-ethnic Contact and the Discourse of Recognition', *Global Society*, XV, 2 (2001).

Constantinou, Costas M. & Richmond, Oliver P., 'The Long Mile of Empire: Power, Legitimation and the UK Bases in Cyprus', *Mediterranean Politics*, X, 1 (2005).

Constantinou, Marios, 'Constitutional Learning for Cypriots in the Light of the Swiss and EU Experience: A Sociological Perspective', *The Cyprus Review*, XIV, 2 (2002) and Part II, XV, 1 (2003).

Coufoudakis, Van & Kyriakides, Klearchos, *The Case Against the Annan Plan* (London: Lobby for Cyprus, 2004).

Coufoudakis, Van, 'Cyprus – the Referendum and its Aftermath', *The Cyprus Review*, XVI, 2 (2004).

Coufoudakis, Van, *Cyprus. A Contemporary Problem in Historical Perspective*. Minnesota Meditteranean and East European Monographs No. 15 (Minneapolis Minnesota: University of Minnesota, 2006).

Demetriou, Olga, 'The EU and the Cyprus Conflict: Review of the Literature', *Working Papers Series in EU Border Conflicts Studies*, 5 (2004).

Demetriou, Olga, 'The EU and the Cyprus Conflict: The View of Political Actors in Cyprus', *Working Papers Series in EU Border Conflicts Studies*, 9 (2004).

Demetriou, Olga, 'The EU and the Cyprus Conflict: The Perceptions of the Border and Europe in the Cyprus Conflict', *Working Papers Series in EU Border Conflicts Studies*, 18 (2005).

Dent, Martin, 'Cyprus: A New and More Hopeful Step in the Struggle to Free the Tempting Morsel from the Net of Entanglement in the Rivals' Aspirations of its

Neighbours to Dominate and Devour', *Journal of Southern Europe and the Balkans,* V, 2 (2003).

Dodd, Clement, 'Constitutional Features of the UN Plan for Cyprus and its Antecedents', *Turkish Studies,* VI, 1 (2005).

Drath, Viola, 'The Cyprus Referendum: An Island Divided by Mutual Mistrust', *American Foreign Policy Interests,* XXVI (2004).

Drosos, Giannis, 'Η Συνταγματική Διάσταση του Σχεδίου Ανάν' (The Constitutional Dimension of the Annan Plan), *Geostratigiki,* I (2003).

Eichengreen, Barry, Faini, Riccardo, von Hagen, Juergen & Wyplosz, Charles, 'Economic Aspects of the Annan Plan for the Solution of the Cyprus Problem', *Report to the Government of the Republic of Cyprus,* III (2004).

Emilianides, Achilles C., Οι Συνταγματικές Πτυχές του Σχεδίου Ανάν, *Το Σχέδιο Ανάν: Πέντε Κείμενα Κριτικής'* (The Constitutional Aspects of the Annan Plan, The Annan Plan: Five Critical Texts) (Athens: Ipsilou, 2003).

Emilianides, Achilles C., 'Beyond the Servant State Paradigm: The Cyprus Problem Revisited', *Institute of International Relations Yearbook* (2003-2004).

Eralp, Doga Ulas & Nimet Beriker, 'Assessing the Conflict Resolution Potential of the EU: The Cyprus Conflict and Accession Negotiations', *Security Dialogue,* XXXVI, 2 (2005).

Faustmann, Hubert, 'In Place of Fear: Security in a Future Cyprus', in: *Report of the Friends of Cyprus,* XLV (2002).

Faustmann, Hubert, 'The Cyprus Question Still Unresolved: Security Concerns and the Failure of the Annan Plan', *Südosteuropa-Mitteilungen* (2004).

Faustmann, Hubert & Nicos Peristianis (eds), *Britain in Cyprus. Colonialism and Post-Colonialism 1878-2006.* (Mannheim/Möhnesee: Bibliopolis, 2006).

Faustmann, Hubert, 'The Role of Security Concerns in the Failure of the Annan Plan and in the Post-Annan Plan Period', *The International Spectator,* XLI, 2 (2006).

Faustmann, Hubert & Kaymak, Erol, 'Cyprus', *European Journal of Political Research. Political Data Yearbook,* XLVI (2007).

Faustmann, Hubert, 'History in the Making? A New Drive for a Solution to the Cyprus Problem', Mediterranean Politics XIV, 3 (2008).

Faustmann, Hubert & Kaymak, Erol, 'Cyprus', *European Journal of Political Research. Political Data Yearbook,* XLVII (2008).

Georgiades, Savvas Daniel, 'Public Attitudes Towards Peace: The Greek-Cypriot Position', *Journal of Peace Research,* XLIV, 5 (2007).

Gorvett, Jon, 'Vote on Annan Plan Results in Reversal of Fortune for Turkish, Greek Cypriots', *The Washington Report on Middle East Affairs,* XXIII, 5 (2004).

Guney, Aylin, 'The USA's Role in Mediating the Cyprus Conflict: A Story of Success or Failure?', *Security Dialogue,* XXXV, 1 (2004).

Gürel, Ayla and Özersay, Kudret, *The Politics of Property in Cyprus: Conflicting Appeals to 'Bizonality' and 'Human Rights' by the Two Cypriot Communities,* PRIO Report 3

(2006).

Hadjidemetriou, Takis, *Το Δημοψήφισμα της 24 Απριλίου 2004 και η Λύση του Κυπριακού* (The Referendum of 24 April 2004 and the Solution of the Cyprus Problem) (Athens: Papazisis, 2006).

Hadjipavlou, Maria, 'Multiple Stories: the 'Crossings' as Part of Citizens' Reconciliation Efforts in Cyprus?', *Innovation*, XX, 1 (2007).

Hadjipavlou, Maria, 'The Cyprus Conflict: Root Causes and Implications for Peacebuilding', *Journal of Peace Research*, XLIV, 3 (2007).

Hakki, Murat (ed), *The Cyprus Issue. A Documentary History, 1878-2007* (London: I.B. Tauris, 2007).

Hannay, David, 'Cyprus: Missed Opportunities and the Way Ahead', *The Wyndham Place Charlemagne Trust 27th Corbishley Memorial Lecture*, September 22 (2003).

Hannay, David, *Cyprus, the Search for a Solution* (London: I.B. Tauris, 2005).

Hatay, Mete, *Beyond Numbers. An Inquiry Into the Political Integration of the Turkish 'Settlers' in Northern Cyprus*, PRIO Report 4 (2005).

Heraclides, Alexis, 'The 55 Year Cyprus Debacle: A Bird's Eye View', *The Cyprus Review*, XV, 2 (2003).

Heraclides, Alexis, 'The Cyprus Problem: An Open and Shut Case? Probing the Greek Cypriot Rejection of the Annan Plan', *The Cyprus Review*, XVI, 2 (2004).

Hitchens, Christopher, 'The Perils of Partition', *The Atlantic Monthly*, March (2003).

Hoffmeister, Frank, *Legal Aspects of the Cyprus Problem*, (Leiden: Martinus Nijhoff Publishers, 2006).

International Crisis Group, 'The Cyprus Stalemate: What Next?', Europe Report No. 171, www.crisisgroup.org/home/index.cfm?id=4003 (2006).

International Crisis Group, 'Reversing the Drift Towards Partition', Europe Report No. 190, www.crisisgroup.org/home/index.cfm?id=5255&l=1 (2008).

Irwin, Colin, 'Public Opinion and the Politics of Peace Research: Northern Ireland, Balkans, Israel, Palestine, Cyprus, Muslim World and the War on Terror', Palestinian Centre for Policy and Survey Research and the Harry S. Truman Research Institute for the Advancement of Peace joint conference: *Public Opinion, Democracy and Peace Making*, Notre Dame of Jerusalem Centre, Jerusalem, May 22-23. http://www.peacepolls.org (2006).

Jarstad, Anna, *Changing the Game: Consociational Theory and Ethnic Quotas in Cyprus and New Zealand*, Department of Peace and Conflict Research, Uppsala University, Report No. 58 (2001).

Kaufmann, Chaim, 'An Assessment of the Partition of Cyprus', *International Studies Perspectives*, VIII (2007).

Kaymak, Erol & Taki, Yiouli, *A Study of the Information Environment & an Outline of International Referendum Standards*, on behalf of Politics, Index (2005).

Kentas, Giorgos I., 'A Realist Evaluation of Cyprus' Survival Dilemma as a Result of the Annan Plan', *The Cyprus Review*, XV, 2 (2003).

Ker-Lindsay, James, *EU Accession and UN Peacemaking in Cyprus* (London: Palgrave Macmillan, 2005).

Ker-Lindsay, James & Faustmann, Hubert, *The Government and Politics of Cyprus* (Oxford et al: Peter Lang, 2008).

Kyle, Keith, 'A British View of the Annan Plan', *The Cyprus Review,* XVI, 1 (2004).

Kyle, Keith, 'Twenty-one Years With Cyprus', *The Cyprus Review,* XVI, 2 (2004).

Kyle, Keith, 'British Policy on Cyprus 1974-2004' in Hubert Faustmann/Nicos Peristianis (eds.): *Britain in Cyprus. Colonialism and Post-Colonialism 1878-2004* (Mannheim/Möhnesee, Bibliopolis, 2006).

Kyriacou, Andreas P., 'An Ethnically Based Federal and Bicameral System: The Case of Cyprus', *International Review of Law and Economics,* XX, 2 (2000).

Lacher, Hannes & Kaymak, Erol, 'Transforming Identities: Beyond the Politics of Non-Settlement in North Cyprus', *Mediterranean Politics,* X, 2 (2005).

Liakouras, Petros, *Το Κυπριακό, Από την Ζυρίχη στη Λουκέρνη σε Αναζήτηση Ομοσπονδιακής Επίλυσης* (The Cyprus Problem from Zurich to Lucerne in Search of a Federal Solution) (Athens, Sideris, 2007).

Loizides, Neophytos & Keskiner, Eser, 'Cross-Voting Moderation for Cyprus,' *Southeast European Politics,* V, 2-3 (2004).

Loizides, Neophytos & Antoniades, Marcos A., 'Settlers, Refugees, and Immigrants: Alternative Futures for Post-Settlement Cyprus,' *ISP Discussion Paper,* Belfer Center for Science and International Affairs, (2004).

Lordos, Alexandros, 'Can the Cyprus Problem be Solved? Understanding the Greek Cypriot Response to the UN Peace Plan for Cyprus', *An Evidence-Based Study in Co-operation with CYMAR Market Research Ltd,* www.cypruspolls.org (2004).

Lordos, Alexandros, 'Rational Agent or Unthinking Follower? A Survey-Based Profile Analysis of Greek Cypriot and Turkish Cypriot Referendum Voters (2006).

Lordos, Dinos, 'No Voter Vindicated?', *Report of the Friends of Cyprus,* XLVII (2004).

Loucaides, Loukis, 'The Legal Support of an Illegal UN Plan by a UN Lawyer', *Cyprus Yearbook of International Relations* (2007).

Mallinson, William, *Cyprus: A Modern History,* (London: I. B. Tauris, 2005).

Mazis, T., *The Mediterranean Geopolitical Structure and the Matter of Resolving the Cyprus Issue in Accordance with the Annan Plan,* (Milan: ISU Università Cattolica, 2005).

Milne, David, 'One State or Two? Political Realism on the Cyprus Question', *The Round Table,* vol. 92, (2003).

Mullen, Fiona (ed), *Economic Perspectives in Cyprus. The Path towards Reunification.* Proceedings of the 2nd Annual Conference of the PRIO Cyprus Centre in Cooperation with MFC S. Platis held on 22 November 2006 in Nicosia, Cyprus. PRIO Cyprus Center (2007).

Mullen, Fiona, Oguz, Özlem & Kyriacou, Praxoula, Antoniadou, *The Day After: Commercial Opportunities following a Solution to the Cyprus Problem* (Nicosia: PRIO Cyprus Centre 2008).

Neophytou, Christos A., 'A Critical Analysis of the Proposed UN Annan Plan for the Settlement of the Cyprus Problem and the Importance of International and European Law in the Shaping of the New Proposed Constitution for Cyprus', *CPE PgDL Dissertation*, (London: Metropolitan University, 2003).

Özersay, Kudret, 'Separate Simultaneous Referenda in Cyprus: Was it a 'Fact' or an 'Illusion'?', *Turkish Studies,* VI, 3 (2005).

Palley, Claire, *An International Relations Debacle – The UN Secretary-General's Mission of Good Offices in Cyprus 1999-2004* (Oxford: Hart Publishing, 2005).

Panayiotou, Andreas, 'Models of Compromise and 'Power Sharing' in the Experience of Cypriot Modernity', *The Cyprus Review,* XVIII, 2 (2006).

Papadakis, Yiannis, 'Discourses of 'the Balkans' in Cyprus: Tactics, Strategies and Constructions of 'Others'', *History and Anthropology,* XV, 1, (2004).

Papadakis, Yiannis, *Echoes from the Dead Zone,* (London: I.B. Tauris, 2005).

Papadakis, Yiannis, 'Narrative, Memory and History Education: A Comparison of Schoolbooks on the 'History of Cyprus'', *History and Memory* (forthcoming 2008).

Papadopoulos, Tassos, 'Address to Cypriots by President Papadopoulos (full text), April 8.' Cyprus News Agency. http://www.hri.org/news/cyprus/cna/2004/04-04-08.cna.html#01 (2004).

Papasavvas, Savvas, *Το Σχέδιο Ανάν: Ένα 'εποικοδομητικά ασαφές' συνταγματικό 'μέλλον' για την Κύπρο* (The Annan Plan: A Constructively Vague Constitutional Future for Cyprus) (Athens: Sakkoulas, 2003).

Pericleous, Chrysostomos, *Το Δημοψήφισμα του 2004, το Περιφερειακό και Διεθνές Περιβάλλον, η Πρόσληψη της Λύσης και η Συγκυρία* (The Referendum of 2004, the Regional and International Context, the Inception of the Solution and the Circumstances) (Athens: Papazisis, 2007).

Peristianis, Nicos, 'A Federal Cyprus in a Federal Europe', in Andreas Theophanous et al. (eds.), *Cyprus and the European Union* (Nicosia, Intercollege Press, 1999).

Pfirter, Didier, 'Cyprus – A UN Peace Effort Under Conditions of ECHR Applicability', in Stephan Breitenmoser et al. (eds.), *Human Rights, Democracy and the Rule of Law, Liber Amicorum Luzius Wildhaber* (Zurich: Nomos, 2007).

Pikis, G. M., *Constitutionalism – Human Rights- Separation of Powers, The Cyprus Precedent,* (Leiden/Boston: Brill Academic Pub, 2006).

Platis, Stelios, Orfanides, Stelios, & Mullen, Fiona, *The Property Regime in a Cyprus Settlement,* PRIO Report 3, (Nicosia: PRIO Cyprus Centre 2006).

Potier, Tim, 'Britain and Cyprus: From Referendum to Reunification?' in Hubert Faustmann/Nicos Peristianis (eds.): *Britain in Cyprus. Colonialism and Post-Colonialism 1878-2006* (Mannheim/Möhnesee: Bibliopolis, 2006).

Potier, Tim, *A Functional Cyprus Settlement: The Constitutional Dimension*, Peleus Vol. 38, (Mainz and Ruhpolding: Franz Philipp Rutzen Verlag, 2007).

Qvortrup, Matt, 'Fair Voting? The Regulation of Referendums in Cyprus in Comparative Perspective', *The Cyprus Review,* XVII, 2 (2005).

Richmond, Oliver, 'Shared Sovereignty and the Politics of Peace: Evaluating the EU's

'Catalytic' Framework in the Eastern Mediterranean', *International Affairs*, LXXXII, 1 (2005).

Robins, Philip, 'Confusion at Home, Confusion Abroad: Turkey Between Copenhagen and Iraq', *International Affairs*, LXXIX, 3 (2003).

Rotberg, Robert I., 'Cyprus After Annan: Next Steps Towards a Solution', *World Peace Foundation Reports,* 37 (2003).

Rotberg, Robert, 'The Cyprus Crucible: the Importance of Good Timing', *Leadership*, XXV, 3 (2003).

Salih, H. Ibrahim, *Cyprus: Ethnic Political Counterpoints* (Maryland: University Press of America, 2004).

Sommer, Jerry, 'Security in Cyprus: Threat Perceptions, Possible Compromises and the Role of the EU', *Bonn International Center for Conversion Paper 44* (Bonn: BICC Bonn, 2005).

Sozen, Ahmet, 'A Model of Power-Sharing in Cyprus: From the 1959 London-Zurich Agreements to the Annan Plan', *Turkish Studies,* V, 1 (2004).

Sözen, Ahmet, 'The Turkish Cypriot Legislative Election of February 2005: The Rise of CTP/BG,' *South European Society & Politics* 10/3 (2005).

Sozen, Ahmet & Özersay, Kudret, 'The Annan Plan: State Succession or Continuity', *Middle Eastern Studies*, XLIII, 1 (2007).

Stavridis, Stelios, 'The European Union's Contribution to Peace and Stability in the Eastern Mediterranean (the So-Called Athens-Nicosia-Ankara Triangle): A Critique', *Fundaci n SIP Zaragoza,* Working Paper (2005).

Syrigos, Andreas, *Το Σχέδιο Ανάν* (The Annan Plan) (Athens: Patakis, 2005).

Theophanous, Andreas, *Το Σχέδιο Ανάν και η Ευρωπαϊκή Επιλογή* (The Annan Plan and the European Option) (Athens: Papazisis, 2003).

Theophanous, Andreas, *The Cyprus Question and the EU: The Challenge and the Promise*, (Nicosia: Intercollege Press, 2004).

Theophanous, Andreas, *The Political Economy of a Cyprus Settlement. The Examination of Four Scenaria.* Prio Report 1 (2008).

Tocci, Natalie, *EU Accession Dynamics and Conflict Resolution: Catalysing Peace or Consolidating Partition In Cyprus?* (London: Ashgate, 2004).

Tocci, Nathalie, 'Reflections on Post-Referendum Cyprus', *The International Spectator,* XXXIX, 3 (2004).

Tocci, Nathalie, 'Towards Peace in Cyprus: Incentives and Disincentives', *Brown Journal of World Affairs*, X, 1 (2003).

Trimikliniotis, Nicos, 'A Communist's Post-Modern Power Dilemma: One Step Back, Two Steps Forward, 'Soft No' and Hard Choices', *The Cyprus Review*, XVIII, 1 (2006).

Trimikliniotis, Nicos, 'Nationality and Citizenship in Cyprus since 1945: Communal Citizenship, Gendered Nationality and the Adventures of a Post-Colonial Subject in a Divided Country', Rainer Bauböck, Bernhard Perchinig, Wiebke Sievers (eds.),

Citizenship in the New Europe (Amsterdam: Amsterdam University Press, 2007).

Trimikliniotis, Nicos, 'Reconciliation and Social Action in Cyprus: Citizens' Inertia and the Protracted State of Limbo', *The Cyprus Review*, Volume XIX, 1 (2007).

Trimikliniotis, Nicos, *Η Διαλεκτική του Έθνους-Κράτους και το Μόνιμο Καθεστώς Έκτακτης Ανάγκης, Συνταγματισμός και οι Περιπέτειες ενός Εθνικού Ζητήματος την Εποχή του Αστάθμητου παράγοντα* (The Dialectical Relationship Between Nation-State and the Permanent Status of Emergency, Constitutionalism and the Adventures of a National Issue in the Era of the Inassessable) (Athens: 2008).

UNSG, *Report of the Secretary-General on his Mission of Good Offices in Cyprus*, S/2003/398,

April 1 <http://www.un.dk/doc/S.2003.398.pdf > (2004).

Varnava, Andrekos, 'Cyprus: A Rendezvous with History?', *Neos Kosmos English Edition*, (Monday 18 August 2003).

Varnava, Andrekos, 'Moving Forward after the Presidential Elections', *Cyprus Mail*, (2 March 2008).

Varnava, Andrekos, 'No Turning Back on Future of Cyprus', *Neos Kosmos English Edition*, (Monday 8 December 2003).

Varnava, Andrekos, 'Still Waiting for a Balanced History of Cyprus', *Cyprus Mail*, 4 September 2005.

Vassiliou, George, 'EU Enlargement: Implications for Europe, Cyprus and the Eastern Mediterranean', *Mediterranean Quarterly*, XIII, 1 (2002).

Vassiliou, George, 'The Cyprus Problem and the European Union', *The Cyprus Review*, XVI, 2 (2004).

Vassiliou, George, *The Economics of the Solution Based on the Annan Plan*, http://www.kema.com.cy/Annan%20Plan%20En.pdf (2003).

Veremis, Thanos & Savvides, Philippos, 'Cyprus After the Referenda of April 24: What Next?', *The Cyprus Review*, XVI, 2 (2004).

Webster, Craig, 'Division or Unification in Cyprus? The Role of Demographics, Attitudes and Party Inclination on Greek Cypriot Preferences for a Solution to the Cyprus Problem', *Ethnopolitics*, IV, 3 (2005).

Webster, Craig & Lordos, Alexandros, 'Who Supported the Annan Plan? An Exploratory Statistical Analysis of the Demographic, Political, and Attitudinal Correlates', *The Cyprus Review*, XVIII, 1 (2006).

Yakinthou, Christalla, *Between Scylla and Charybdis: Cyprus and the Problem of Engineering Solutions for Divided Societies*, unpublished PhD dissertation, University of Western Australia, 2008 (London: Palgrave Macmillan, forthcoming)

Zembylas, Michalinos and Karahasan, Hakan, 'The Politics of Memory and Forgetting in Pedagogical Practices: Towards Pedagogies of Reconciliation and Peace in Divided Cyprus', *The Cyprus Review*, XVIII, 2 (2006).

INDEX

The index is presented in word-by-word order. Notes and tables are marked in italics after the locator, eg: education research coding scheme 196*t2*

1960 Constitution 27–31, 203

Acheson Plans 14, 207
AKEL 82, 108, 168, 188
Anastasiades, Nikos (DISY Leader, Cyprus) 168
Annan I 26
   presented 2002 20
Annan II 26, 47
Annan III 26, 46–7, 48
Annan IV
   European Council 48
   federation 252
   human rights 49–50
   non-voting members of Presidential Council 48
   presidents 49
   public servants 49
   reinstatement 46–7
   submitted March 2004 26
   territorial adjustment 43–4
Annan, Kofi (UN Secretary-General) 20, 29, 58, 78, 146–7
Annan Plan
   Belgian model 83
   civil society 146
   consociationalism 25, 27–8, 116
   constituent states 109
   constitutional principles 68
   demilitarization 103
   demonized 108
   development 28–9, 95–6
   dissemination 145
   dysfunctional 75, 78
   economic provisions 122–4
   fairness 89–90
   federalism 111
   federation 11
   five versions 2, 51
   foreign interests 118*n4*, 182
   Greek Cypriot rejection 5–6
   intercommunal survey results 172–73
   Justice and Development Party (AKP, Turkey) 239–240
   negotiations process 34, 163, 165
   No campaign 187
   partition 66
   philosophy 107
   powers 113
   Presidential Council 101
   property provisions 124–7
   public opinion 168
   security fears 188, 231
   sovereignty 33, 35
   as a threat 218–19
   three treaties 70–1
   timeframe 180–1
   translated into Turkish 146
   treaties 96
   Turkey 91, 181
   Turkish Cypriot status 148
   Turkish settlers 100
   United Nations role 164
   viability 116
   Yes vote 236, 245
   Zurich-London Agreements (1959) 82
Annan V
   arbitration 87
   changed dynamics 26
   demilitarization 228–9
   failed 104
   federal structures 134–5
   financial stability 126
   Foundation Agreement 50
   lack of provision for minorities 50–1
   non-voting members of Presidential Council 48
   political viability 82
   property question 153
   reinstatement 46–7
   security fears 224
   workability 85–9
arbitration 87–8, 90

bi-communality 17, 21, 187
bi-zonality
  Annan Plan 109, 151–52, 187
  constituent states 97–9
  federal settlement 21
  lack of agreement 17
  Presidential Council 99
  property rights 139
  size of Turkish Cypriot Constituent State 130
  sovereignty 148
bicameral parliament 17, 32, 109
bilateral meetings 28
blame allocation 202, 262
Boutros-Ghali, Boutros (UN Secretary-General) 19, 55, 72–3
broadcast media 182, 183–4, 190–1
Broek, Hans van der (EU Commissioner) 57

Candar, Cengiz (journalist, Turkey) 240
Cannon, Walter 213
Central Bank 123, 133, 141–42, 254–55
Chamber of Deputies
  decision making 101
  political equality 149
  proportional representation 109–10
  representation by population ratio 32, 37, 99–100
  United Cyprus Republic (UCR) 49
Christofias, Demetris (AKEL Leader, Cyprus) 6, 109, 168, 188, 254
Ciller, Tansu (Prime Minister, Turkey) 57
citizenship
  education 194–5, 196*t1*
  Foundation Agreement 114
  political rights 152
  textbooks 197, 209
  UCR as a successor state 113
  United Cyprus Republic (UCR) 115, 158*n11*
civil society 146

Clerides, Glafcos (President, Republic of Cyprus, 1993-2003)
  1960 Constitution 207
  agrees to meet Rauf Denktash 60
  Annan Plan 55
  demilitarization 167
  enosis 203
  federal settlement 39*n41*
  moves away from Set of Ideas 19
  negotiations process 166
  offers Turkish Cypriot participation 58
  prepared to negotiate 59
  rejects Set of Ideas 56
compensation 45–6, 124–5, 139, 155
Comprehensive Solution to the Cyprus Problem *see* Annan Plan
confederation 111
confidence building measures 263
conflict management 84
conflict resolution 25, 32, 215
consociational democracy 3
consociationalism
  alliances 117
  Annan Plan 3, 36
  arbitration 87–8
  conflict mediation 33
  defined 25
  democracy 116
  veto arrangement 86
  veto rights 82
constituent states
  autonomy 150
  citizenship 44
  constitutional opposition 103
  fiscal position 136–7
  independence 41
  internal security 227
  multiple options 83
  political equality 111
  residual powers 113
  sovereignty within federation 35–6
  United Cyprus Republic (UCR) 97
constitution 68, 79, 95–6, 149
constitutional amendments 37

constitutional framework 73–6
constitutional issues 4
convergence 134, 136, 143
cross-voting 61, 89, 166, 258–9
cultural autonomy 27
curriculum 194, 209
Cypriot communities 216–18
Cypriot public 164
Cyprus
  accession to EU 59, 62, 241
  consociationalism 84
  defined as Greek 200
  EU Accession 239
  EU membership 205
  history 12–13
  interpretations 210
  open communication 64
  power sharing 254–5
  relations with Europe 201
  single international legal personality 113
  strategic territory 12
Cyprus Problem
  education 198–9, 204–5
  fear of resolutions 219
  Greek Cypriot definitions 194
  legal dimensions 2
  textbooks 202–204
Cyprus Study Group 253–4, 262–3

decision making 76–8, 85, 101, 114, 116
demilitarization
  Annan Plan 68
  incomplete 229–30
  maintained 233
  offered by Glafkos Clerides 60–1
  rejected by TRNC 167
  troop withdrawals 225
  United States of Cyprus (USC) 261
democracy 77–8, 102
Denktash, Rauf (President, TRNC) 2
  agrees telephone links across Cyprus 57
  concessions 16

  continuous leadership 243
  cross-voting 39n28, 66
  demands the freezing of EU application 58
  Justice and Development Party (AKP, Turkey) 240
  loses public support 62, 145
  opposed to cross-voting 167
  opposes Annan Plan 155–6
  refuses to negotiate 59
  rejects all suggestions 21
  rejects Annan Plan 61–62, 147
  rejects Set of Ideas 18, 56
  replaced by Mehmet Ali Talat 26
  terminates negotiations in 2000 26
  two sovereign states 33–5, 207
  uncompromising 166
  writes to Glafkos Clerides 60
displaced persons 114, 117, 160n23, 261
dispossessed properties 128–9, 133–4
dominated groups 216
Draft Framework Agreement 18

earthquakes 58
economic policy 135
economy
  convergence 134
  Cyprus 122
  fears 214
  growth 138
  harmonization 130
  inflationary pressure 126
  reunification 133
  stability 142
education
  analysis 198–9
  blame allocation 202
  community formation 195
  confidence building measures 263
  enosis 202, 206
  federal states 208
  focus on the past 208
  patriotism 217
  portrayal of Cyprus 204

public dialogue 194
reunification 5, 209
solution to Cyprus Problem 206–10
Turkish invasion 207
electoral participation 36, 258
emotions 215, 219
enosis
  abandoned 16
  banned 13
  education 206
  not taught 202
  prohibited 110
  rejected by Turkey 15
  Turkish Cypriot fears 225
  union with Greece 11
EOKA B 15
EOKA campaign (1955) 12
Erdogan, Recep Tayyip (AKP, Turkey) 237, 240, 244, 246
ethnicity 36
ethnocentrism 195
EU membership 237–9, 244
European Commission 140
European Union (EU)
  Annan Plan 142
  Belgian model 111
  financial aid 137
  military operations 41
  representation of Cyprus 48–9
  safeguards 83–4
  sovereignty 87
  Turkish accession 40–1, 64, 91, 237–8
  United Cyprus Republic (UCR) 74, 102–3
Eurozone 123, 131, 133

fear 213–4, 218–21
  differences between communities 222$t3$
federal government
  federal budget 122–3
  financial risks 138
  national jurisdiction 109
  power sharing 254
  powers 149, 158$n8$
  revenues 135–7
  role 142
  United Cyprus Republic (UCR) 74
  weakness 143
federal legislature 76
federal Parliament 49
federal policies 134–5
federal settlement 33–4, 83, 109, 112, 139, 188
federal states 225
federalism 82–3, 110–11, 133
federations 84–5, 117
Foot, Sir Hugh (British Governor, Cyprus) 70
Foundation Agreement
  Article 2 111, 112
  Article 3 98
  Article 12 97
  Article 22 110
  referenda 147
  Turkish settlers 100
  United Cyprus Republic (UCR) 50
Friends of Cyprus 66

Gambari Process 178–9
geography 193$t1$, 197–8, 201
Gobbi, Hugo (UN Secretary-General's Special Representative) 17
Good Offices of UN Secretary-General 15
governance 25–6
Great Britain
  blame allocation 201–04
  declares sovereignty over Cyprus (1925) 12
  Foundation Agreement 50
  guarantor power 13, 68
  influence over EU development 64
  military presence in Cyprus 72
  responsibility for Cyprus problem 2
  Sovereign Base Areas (SBAs) 42–3
Greece
  blame allocation 202
  economic collaboration 64

Foundation Agreement 50
guarantor power 13, 68
military presence in Cyprus 71
reduced influence on negotiations 178
security fears 226–7
weakening influence 41
Greek Cypriot community
Annan Plan debate 180
co-existence 217
collective trauma 221
enemies 218
fears 213–14, 221*t1*
national identities 214
opposes Annan Plan 107
security fears 82, 229–32
subgroups 215–16
troop withdrawals 41
Turkish invasion 224
Greek Cypriot Constituent State (GCCS) 73, 76, 124, 136
Greek Cypriot education 196–8
Gregoriou, Zeleia 206
guarantor powers 65, 71, 78, 103, 189, 229
Gul, Abdullah (AKP, Turkey) 237–8, 241

Hannay, Lord David
appointed 1996 57
cross-voting 166–7
Cyprus: The Search for a Solution 2
demilitarization 229
Denktash, Rauf (President, TRNC) 34
enosis 79*n11*
involuntary actions 69–70
negotiations process 163–4
property rights 61
security fears 188–9
Supreme Court 77
Haravgi 185–6
heritage 214–5
High Level Agreement (1977) 15
High Level Agreement (1979) 17

High Level Agreement (2006) 65
history 196*t1*, 198–200, 203, 262–3
Holbrooke, Richard (Assistant Secretary of State, US) 57
human rights
constituent states 74–6
difficulties 117
discourse in education 209
education 204–5
EU law 115
safeguards 233
UCR Constitution 49–50
United States of Cyprus (USC) 255

ideologies 29, 214–15
independence 13, 189, 206
infrastructure 260
intercommunal fighting
1959 constitution 84
1963 14
1967 15
fears 214
Greece 226
responsibility 203
international aid 123–4
international law 111–12
international military operations 41–2, 74

Juppe, Alain (Foreign Minister, France) 57
Justice and Development Party (AKP, Turkey)
accession to EU 246
Annan Plan 239–40, 244
Cyprus Problem 238–42, 246–7
elected 236–7
national support 241

Karpas Peninsula 129, 154, 159*n22*, 206
Klosson, Michael (US Ambassador to Cyprus) 28–9
Kranidiotis, Yiannos (Secretary-General, Ministry of Foreign Affairs, Greece) 56–7

Kyprianou, Spyros (President, Republic of Cyprus, 1977-88) 18

labour mobility 143
land values 126–7, 140
language 45, 255
legislation 83, 257–8
Levent, Sener 31–2
Lordos, Dinos 57

Machi 186
Macmillan Plan 13
Main Articles of the Foundation Agreement (MAFA) 111–12, 114
majoritarianism 86, 88
Makarios, Archbishop (President, Republic of Cyprus, 1959-1974)
   abandons enosis 20
   constitutional amendments 13–14
   enosis 206
   overthrown 15, 203
   rejected bi-zonal federation 119$n14$
   rejects Turkish Cypriot autonomy 15
   signs Zurich-London Agreements 69
Markides, Alecos 30, 32
mass media 185
media coverage
   Annan Plan 5, 146
   biased 182
   biased presentation 190–1
   No campaign 187–8
   referenda 236
   security fears 188
   Yes vote 245
military bases 226
Miller, Tom (assistant to Richard Holbrooke) 58
minorities 50–1, 100, 201, 253
minority veto 27
misinformation 182–83
moderation 31–2, 88

national debt 125–6
national identities 198, 199–202, 214–15

nationalism 215, 259
non-Cypriot judges 33, 77, 88–9, 102
Northern Ireland 87–8

O'Leary, Brendan 84
opinion polls 170–76

Palmas, Vassilis 110
Pangalos, Theodore (Alternate Minister for Foreign (European) Affairs, Greece) 56
Papadopoulos, Tassos (President, Republic of Cyprus, 2003-8)
   administration 84
   bi-zonality 109
   collective fear 218
   elected 26, 62
   intercommunal talks 203
   No campaign 188
   no vote 66–7
   rejects Annan Plan 108
   reunification 2
   Turkish settlers 79$n7$
   United Cyprus Republic (UCR) 111
parliamentary system 256–9
partition
   abandoned 16
   Annan Plan 188
   legality 66
   prohibited 35, 110
   Turkish aim 224
   United Cyprus Republic (UCR) 97
patriotism 215
Pérez de Cuéllar, Javier (UN Secretary-General) 18
Pfirter, Didier 32
Phileleftheros 185–6, 192$n16$, 193$n18$
Plaza Lasso, Galo (UN Mediator) 11, 14
political co-operation 29–30
political equality
   Annan Plan 148–9
   bicameral parliament 32
   deadlocks 99–101
   non-Cypriot judges 150

representation by population ratio 257
Republic of Cyprus 110
right of participation 49
Turkish Cypriot community 190
Turkish Cypriot fears 189, 225
United Cyprus Republic (UCR) 29, 31, 73–4
political independence 70
political rights 98–9, 114, 117, 151–2, 201
Politis 185–6, 192*n16*
population 200–1
power sharing 254, 257–8
presidency 31–33, 50, 110, 255–7
Presidential Council
  budgeting process 136
  decision making 76
  executive functions 110
  executive organ 48
  Head of State 101
  political equality 149
  representation by population ratio 37, 99
presidential system 13
print media 185, 190
property 45–7, 98, 140, 153
Property Board
  buyer of last resort 129
  compensation 45–6, 124–8, 139
  equal composition 99
  reinstatement 98
  running costs 138
property bonds 125–7, 139
property question 139–41, 144
property rights
  Annan Plan 66
  compensation 115
  difficulties 117
  opinion polls 171, 176–7
  property register 260
  reinstatement 124
  restrictions 225
  right to return 85
  territorial adjustment 152–4

voting rights 89–90
property values 126–8
proportional representation 27–8, 37, 259
public diplomacy 169–71, 177–9
public opinion 146, 168, 176–7, 182

Radcliffe Plan 12–13
reconciliation 216–17
reconstruction 5, 137, 144
referenda
  contextual factors 236
  exit polls 169
  legality 96, 155–7
  legislation 180, 184
  political viability 82
  regression analysis 174–5
  security fears 167
  separate 110, 147
  Set of Ideas 56
  social groups 175–6
regional balance of power 4
reinstatement 45–6, 134
repatriation 88, 154
Report of Kofi Annan on God Offices in Cyprus 32
Republic of Cyprus
  applies to join EU 18–19
  consociationalism 113, 116
  constitutional principles 68
  EU Accession 2, 151, 181
  international recognition 34
  legitimacy 204, 208
  reunification 251
  sovereignty 70
  Treaty of Guarantee 69
resettlement 159*n14*
residence rights
  co-existence 174
  Cypriots 44–5
  equal restrictions 151–2
  limited 98
  opinion polls 171, 173
  restricted 227

reunification
  beyond Annan Plan 107
  detailed plans 30
  economic growth 264
  economic plans 128
  economy 137, 142
  EU membership 181
  functionality 117
  gradual 27
  guarantors 261–2
  No campaign 190
  revenue distribution 123
  security fears 253
  social phobia 221
right to return 45, 89–90, 117, 259–60
Russia 63–4, 230

Sampson, Nicos 15
secret negotiations 176
security fears
  Annan Plan 193$n25$
  implementation of Annan Plan 230
  No campaign 187–9
  opinion polls 173–7
  post-Annan Plan 117
  rejection of Annan Plan 224
  troop withdrawals 154–5
  Turkish invasion 219–20
security issues 60–1, 225
self-determination 226
Senate 32, 49, 99, 101, 109–10, 149
Set of Ideas 18–19, 56, 113
Sezer, Ahmet Necdet (President, Turkey) 240
Simerini 186, 193$n13$
society representatives 178
Soto, Alvaro de (UN Special Representative on Cyprus) 26, 30, 49, 55, 61
Sovereign Base Areas (SBAs) 42–3, 69–70, 72, 154, 233
sovereignty
  Annan Plan 33–4, 158$n7$
  diminished 65
  divided societies 87

  interpretations 29
  lack of agreement 17
  limited 108
  negotiations process 165
  Set of Ideas 73
  two sovereign states 224–5
  United Cyprus Republic (UCR) 110, 112, 147–9, 228
Special Referendum Law (TRNC) 156–7, 160$n29$
Supreme Constitutional Court 32–3
Supreme Court
  deadlocks 37, 77, 86–7, 101–2
  decision making 76–7
  equal composition 99
  negates democracy 69
  non-Cypriot judges 85, 114, 150
  Property Courts 129
  United Cyprus Republic (UCR) 33

Talat, Mehmet Ali (President, TRNC)
  Annan Plan 38$n5$
  Annan V 228–9
  coalition government 157$n1$
  elected 26, 244–5
  naturalization 159$n12$
  negotiates with Republic of Cyprus 6
  reunification 251
  supports Annan Plan 145
taxation 133, 135–6
territorial adjustment 43–4, 89–90, 116, 153–4, 226, 260–1
territorial seas 42, 72, 120$n42$
textbooks 195, 208–10
Thant, Maha Thray Sithu U (UN Secretary-General) 15
Tornaritis, Criton G. (Attorney General, Republic of Cyprus) 70–1
Track 2 diplomacy
  Holbrooke, Richard (Assistant Secretary of State, US) 57
Treaty of Accession 115
Treaty of Alliance
  Annan Plan 189
  continuation 154

modification 225
Republic of Cyprus 69
troop withdrawals 228
troops 40–1, 103
Turkish invasion 224
Treaty of Establishment 69, 72
Treaty of Guarantee
Annan Plan 189
continuation 154
guarantor powers 103
modification 225, 232
Republic of Cyprus 69, 78–9
revised 65
right to intervene 70
security fears 160$n27$
Turkish invasion 224
Treaty of Lausanne (1923) 12
Tricondominium Plan 13
troops
phased withdrawal 154–5, 228–9, 232
withdrawal 40–1, 43–4, 70–71, 117, 261
Tuomioja, Sakari (UN Mediator) 14
Turkey
application for EU membership 63, 104, 226, 236
blame allocation 202
change in government 2002 19–20
concerns with Annan Plan 164
confidence building measures 189
customs union with EU 57
Cypriot EU accession 239
deadlocks in UCR 103
economic collaboration 64
eligible to apply for EU membership 58
EU Accession 182
EU membership 232, 252
Foundation Agreement 50
future invasion 214
guarantor power 13, 68
implementation of Annan Plan 90
international law 71
invades Cyprus 1974 15–16, 55, 70, 203, 205, 207
invasion legitimized 74
military control in Cyprus 65
military presence in Cyprus 71, 103
negotiations process 173, 181
reduced influence on negotiations 178
security fears 173–4, 226–7
territorial compensation 206
threat of invasion 231–2
threatens invasion 15
Treaty of Guarantee 229
Turkish Cypriot community 242–44
UCR as a successor state 158$n5$
weakening influence 41
Turkish Cypriot community
accept Annan Plan 224
autonomy 22
blame allocation 202
calls for partition 13
delegitimized 200
demonstrations for peace 217
favoured in Annan Plan 85
fears 219, 221$t2$, *225*, *231*
feel rejected after referenda 215–16
national identities 213
political equality 227
resettlement 124
reunification 251–2
troops 232
Turkey 242–44
Turkish Cypriot Constituent State (TCCS) 73–5, 137, 142
Turkish invasion 11
Turkish Republic of Northern Cyprus (TRNC)
banking sector 141–43
declared 1983 33
elections 2003 156, 244
lack of international recognition 34–5
legalized 97
legitimacy 110
political parties 242–43

unilateral independence (1983) 17, 207
yes vote 245
Turkish settlers
  citizenship 114, 152
  naturalization 90
  opinion polls 176–7
  property rights 159n19
  resettlement 138
  source of tension 100, 117
twelve point proposal 16–17

UN document
  Preliminary Thoughts 26
UN Security Council 17–18, 56, 58, 205, 231
United Cyprus Republic (UCR)
  Annan Plan 25
  Articles of the Constitution 47–8
  Belgian model 35, 66
  budgetary requirements 136
  Central Bank 123
  citizenship 100
  constituent states 69
  constitution 26–7, 71
  decision making 101
  demilitarization 71, 103
  draft laws 30–1
  EU membership 28, 83, 151
  independence 4
  as a new state 146–7
  parliamentary system 113–4
  possible solutions 263–4
  Presidential Council 30–1
  as servant state 103
  sovereignty 110
  as successor to Republic of Cyprus 96–7, 111
  Swiss model 66, 111
  union of two separate states 95–6
  viability 103–4
United Kingdom *see* Great Britain
United Nations
  confidence building measures 1992 56

Cyprus reunification 1–2
as facilitator 178
implementation of Cyprus Resolution 232
influence in Cyprus 64
mediation 63
membership 113
negotiations 145
peacekeeping force 225
Preliminary Thoughts 59
territorial adjustment 43–4
territorial responsibility 231
Turkish settlers 100
United Nations Force in Cyprus (UNFICYP) 14
United States of Cyprus (USC) 252–54, 260–3
US 64, 202

Vassiliou, George (President, Republic of Cyprus, 1988-93) 18, 55–6
Venizelos, Costas (journalist, Republic of Cyprus) 183
veto arrangement 85–6, 114, 149
voting rights 256–7

Waldheim, Kurt (UN Secretary-General) 16–7
Weston, Thomas (US Special Coordinator) 55, 59–61
Winster Proposals 12

Ziyal, Ugur (Undersecretary, Foreign Ministry, Turkey) 61, 63
Zurich-London Agreements (1959) 69, 72

www.ingramcontent.com/pod-product-compliance
Lightning Source LLC
Chambersburg PA
CBHW050339230426
43663CB00010B/1916